High School Prodigies Have It Easy Even in Another World!

13

STORY BY
Riku Misora

ART BY
Kotaro Yamada

CHARACTER DESIGN BY
Sacraneco

contents
HIGH SCHOOL PRODIGIES HAVE IT EASY EVEN IN ANOTHER WORLD!

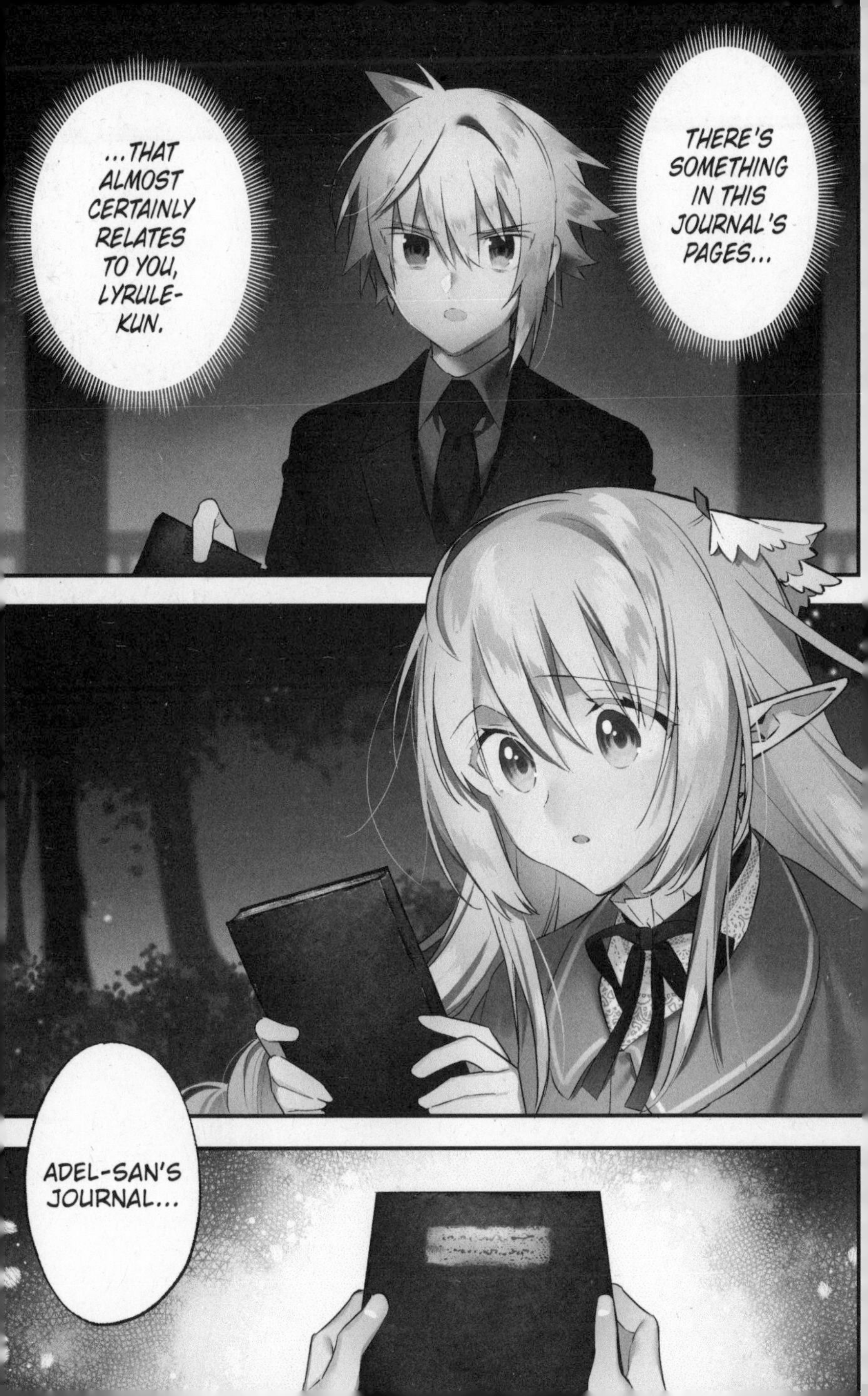
THERE'S SOMETHING IN THIS JOURNAL'S PAGES...
...THAT ALMOST CERTAINLY RELATES TO YOU, LYRULE-KUN.
ADEL-SAN'S JOURNAL...

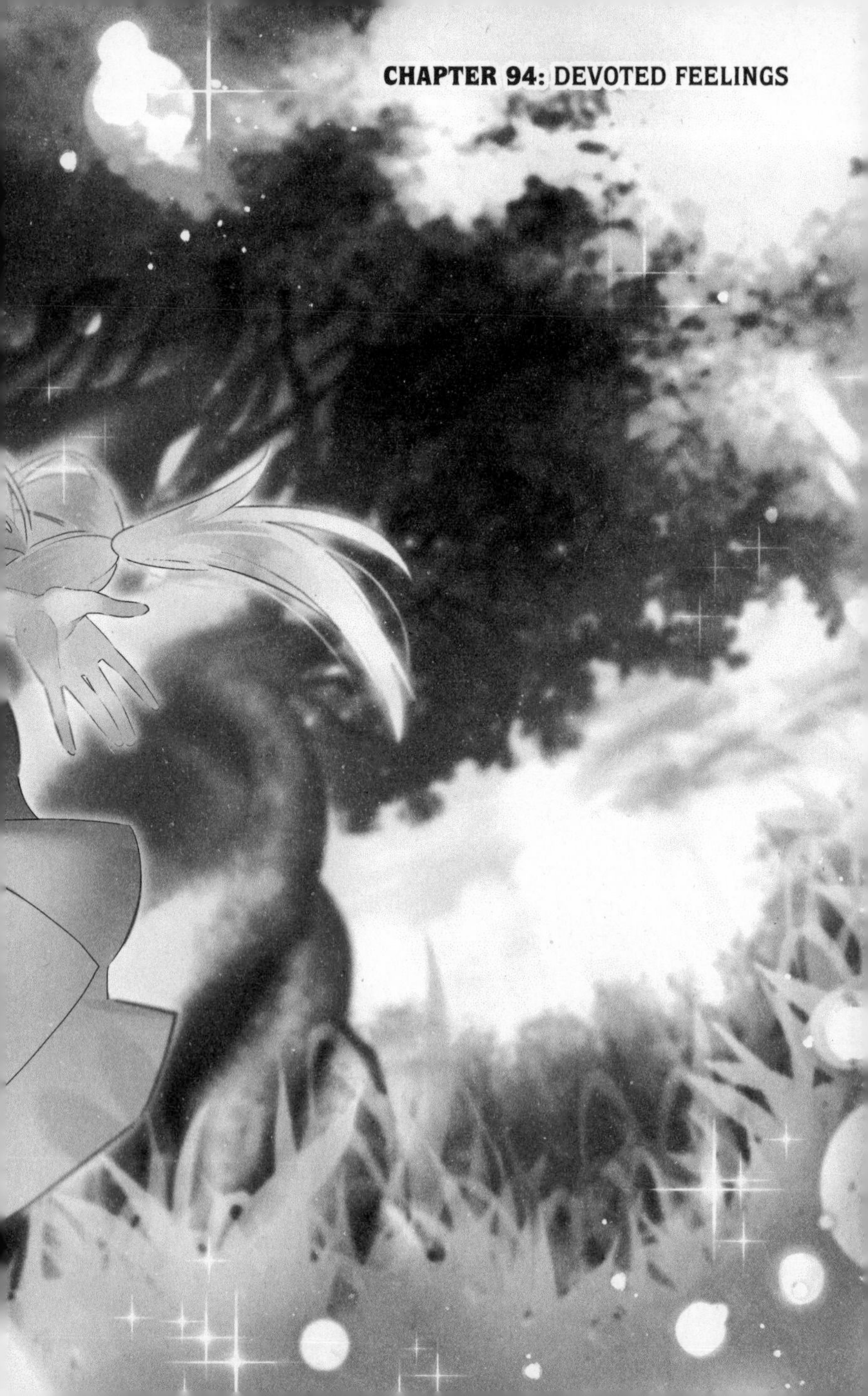
CHAPTER 94: DEVOTED FEELINGS

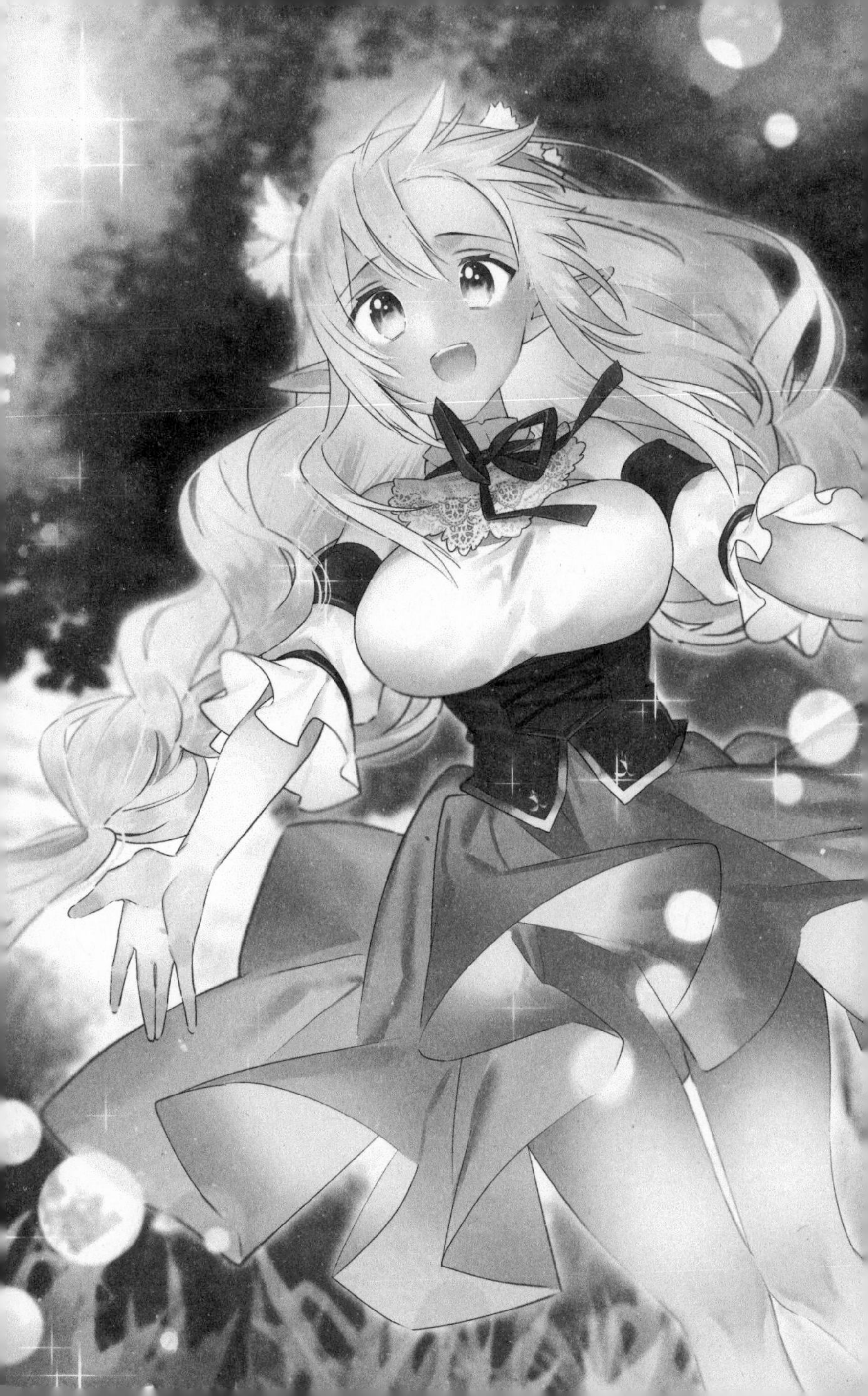

HIGH SCHOOL
PRODIGIES HAVE
IT EASY EVEN IN
ANOTHER
WORLD!

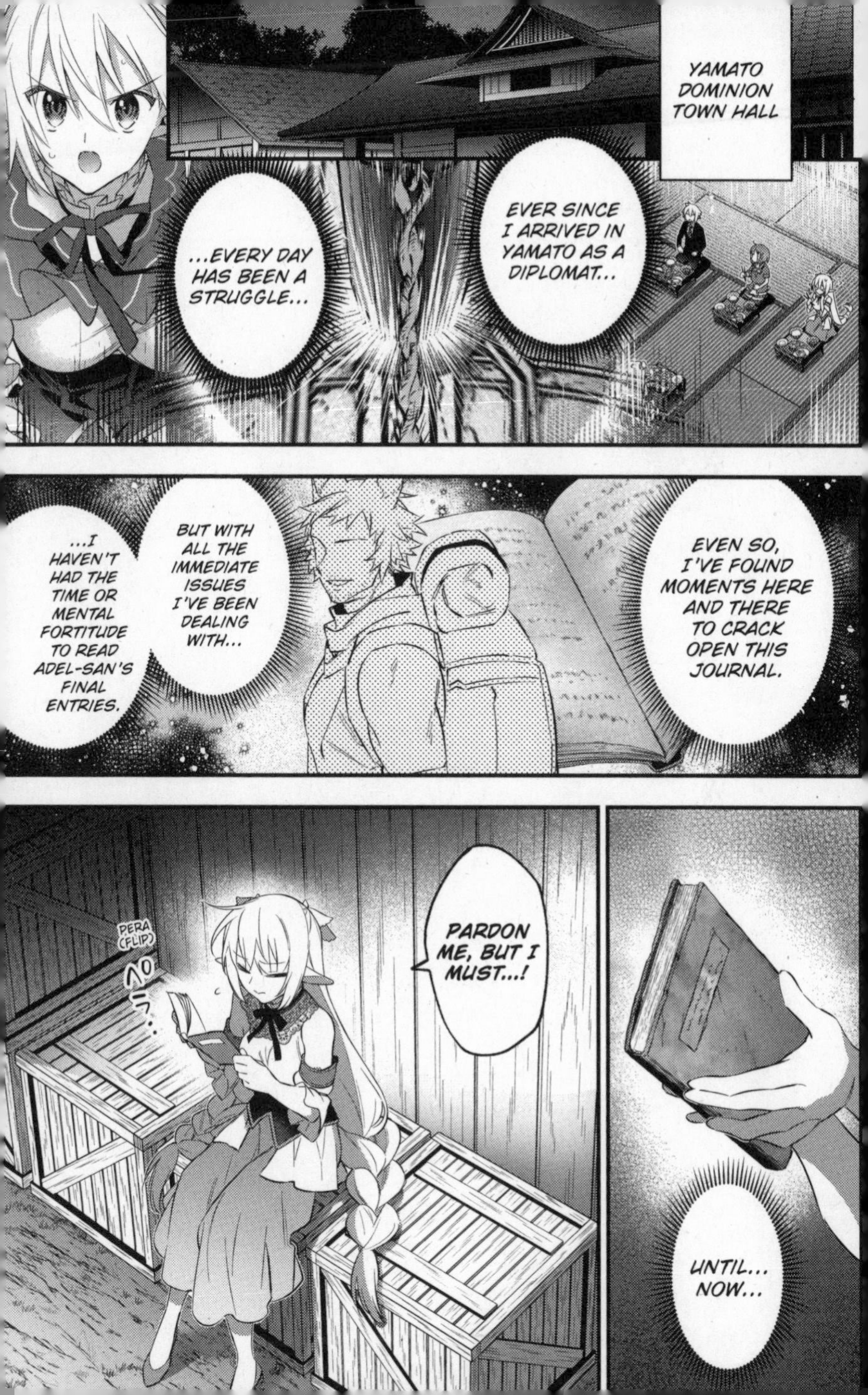
YAMATO DOMINION TOWN HALL
EVER SINCE I ARRIVED IN YAMATO AS A DIPLOMAT...
...EVERY DAY HAS BEEN A STRUGGLE...
EVEN SO, I'VE FOUND MOMENTS HERE AND THERE TO CRACK OPEN THIS JOURNAL.
BUT WITH ALL THE IMMEDIATE ISSUES I'VE BEEN DEALING WITH...
...I HAVEN'T HAD THE TIME OR MENTAL FORTITUDE TO READ ADEL-SAN'S FINAL ENTRIES.
UNTIL... NOW...
PARDON ME, BUT I MUST...!
PERA (FLIP)

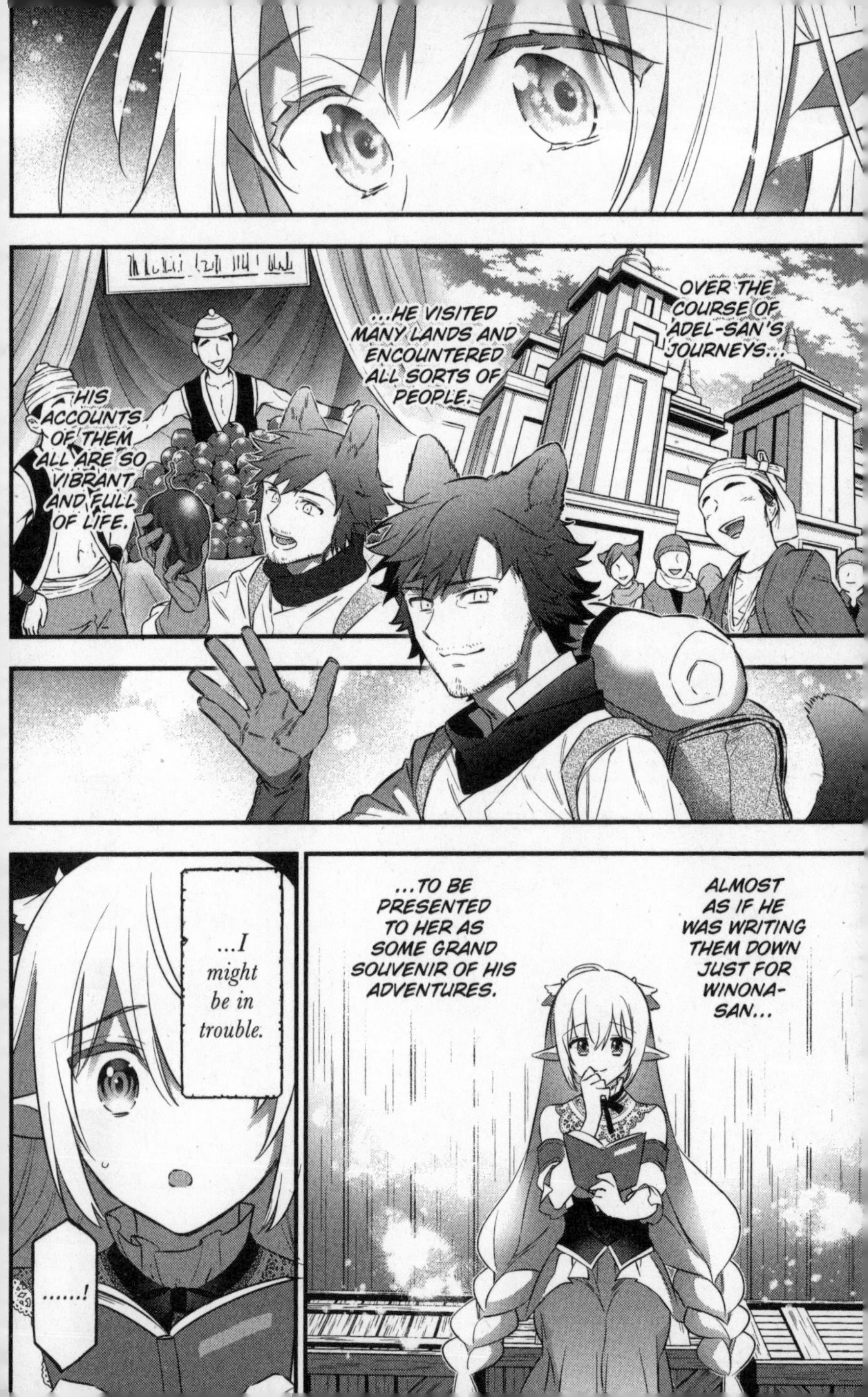
OVER THE COURSE OF ADEL-SAN'S JOURNEYS...
...HE VISITED MANY LANDS AND ENCOUNTERED ALL SORTS OF PEOPLE.
HIS ACCOUNTS OF THEM ALL ARE SO VIBRANT AND FULL OF LIFE.
ALMOST AS IF HE WAS WRITING THEM DOWN JUST FOR WINONA-SAN...
...TO BE PRESENTED TO HER AS SOME GRAND SOUVENIR OF HIS ADVENTURES.
...I might be in trouble.
......!

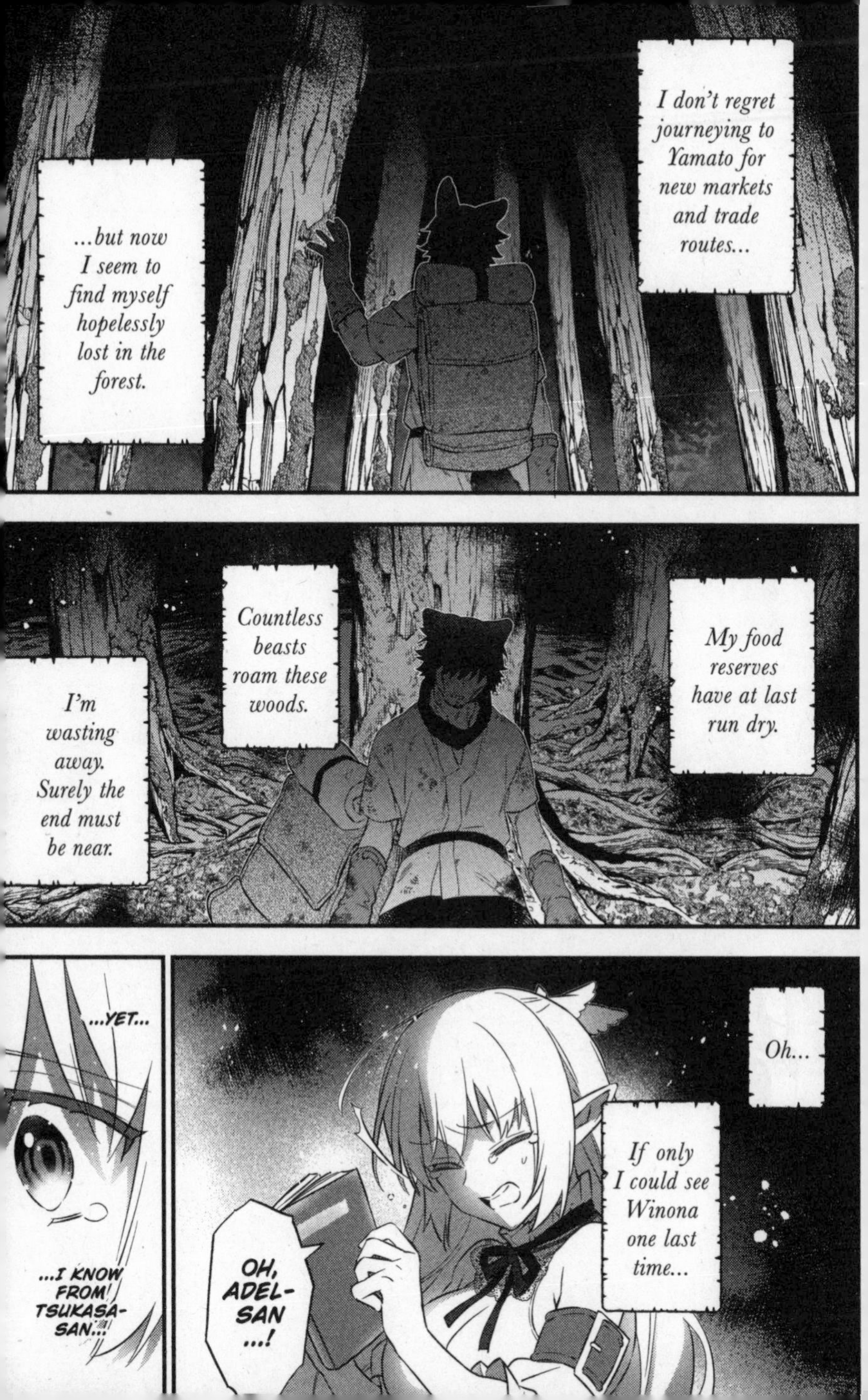
I don't regret journeying to Yamato for new markets and trade routes...
...but now I seem to find myself hopelessly lost in the forest.
My food reserves have at last run dry.
Countless beasts roam these woods.
I'm wasting away. Surely the end must be near.
Oh...
If only I could see Winona one last time...
OH, ADEL-SAN ...!
...YET...
...I KNOW FROM TSUKASA-SAN...!

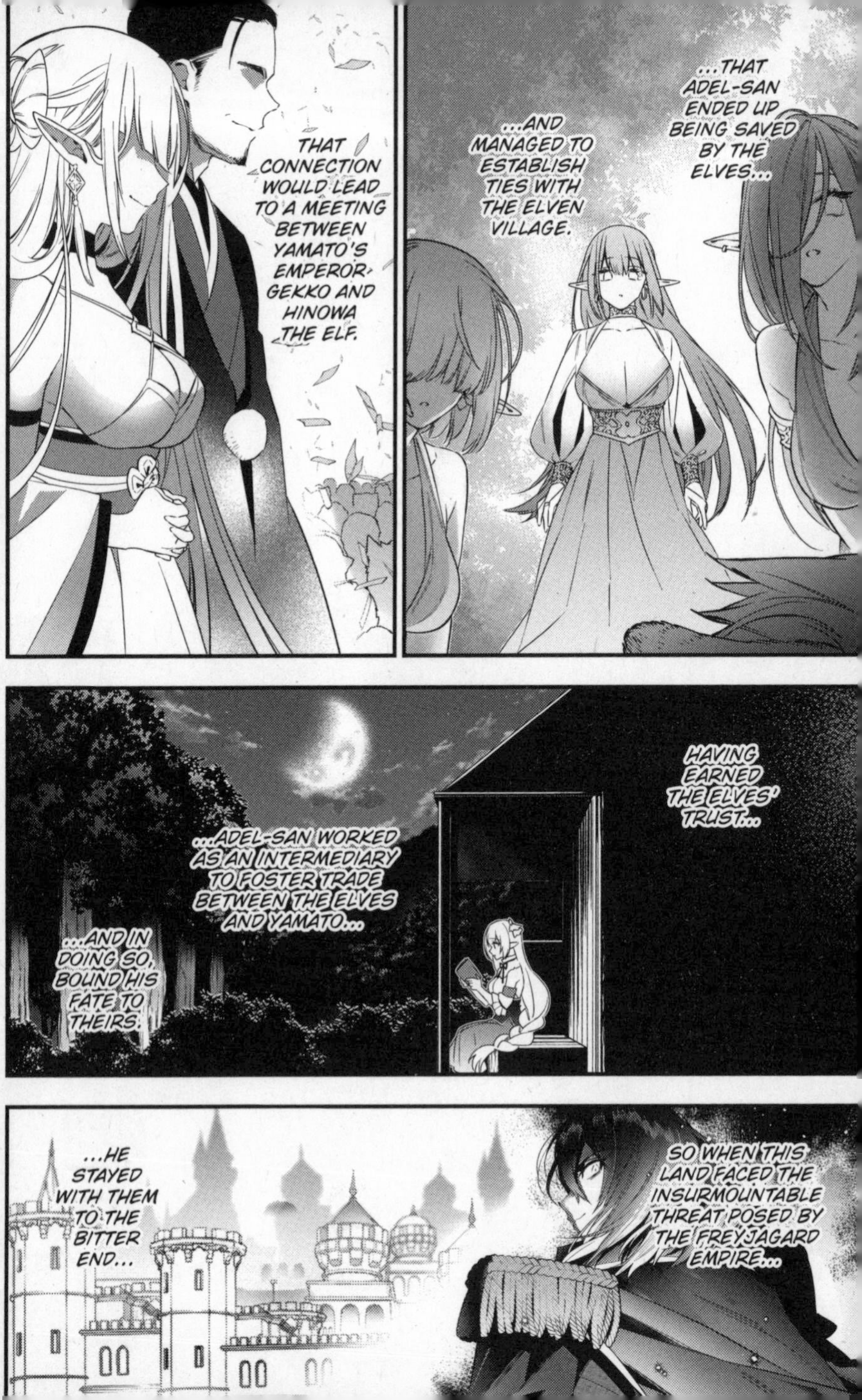
...THAT ADEL-SAN ENDED UP BEING SAVED BY THE ELVES...
...AND MANAGED TO ESTABLISH TIES WITH THE ELVEN VILLAGE.
THAT CONNECTION WOULD LEAD TO A MEETING BETWEEN YAMATO'S EMPEROR GEKKO AND HINOWA THE ELF.
HAVING EARNED THE ELVES' TRUST...
...ADEL-SAN WORKED AS AN INTERMEDIARY TO FOSTER TRADE BETWEEN THE ELVES AND YAMATO...
...AND IN DOING SO, BOUND HIS FATE TO THEIRS.
SO WHEN THIS LAND FACED THE INSURMOUNTABLE THREAT POSED BY THE FREYJAGARD EMPIRE...
...HE STAYED WITH THEM TO THE BITTER END...

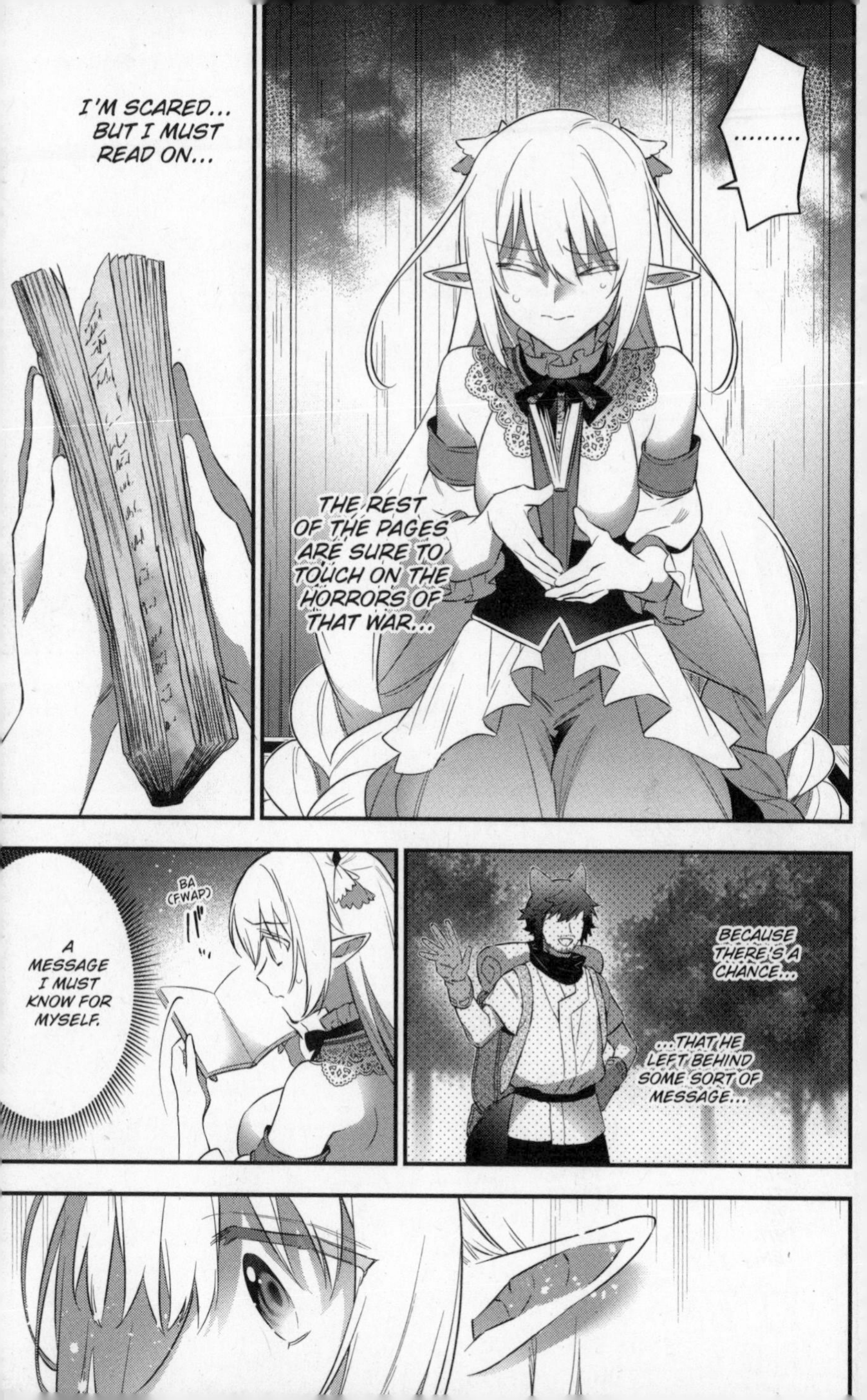
....
THE REST OF THE PAGES ARE SURE TO TOUCH ON THE HORRORS OF THAT WAR...
I'M SCARED... BUT I MUST READ ON...
BECAUSE THERE'S A CHANCE...
...THAT HE LEFT BEHIND SOME SORT OF MESSAGE...
BA (FWAP)
A MESSAGE I MUST KNOW FOR MYSELF.

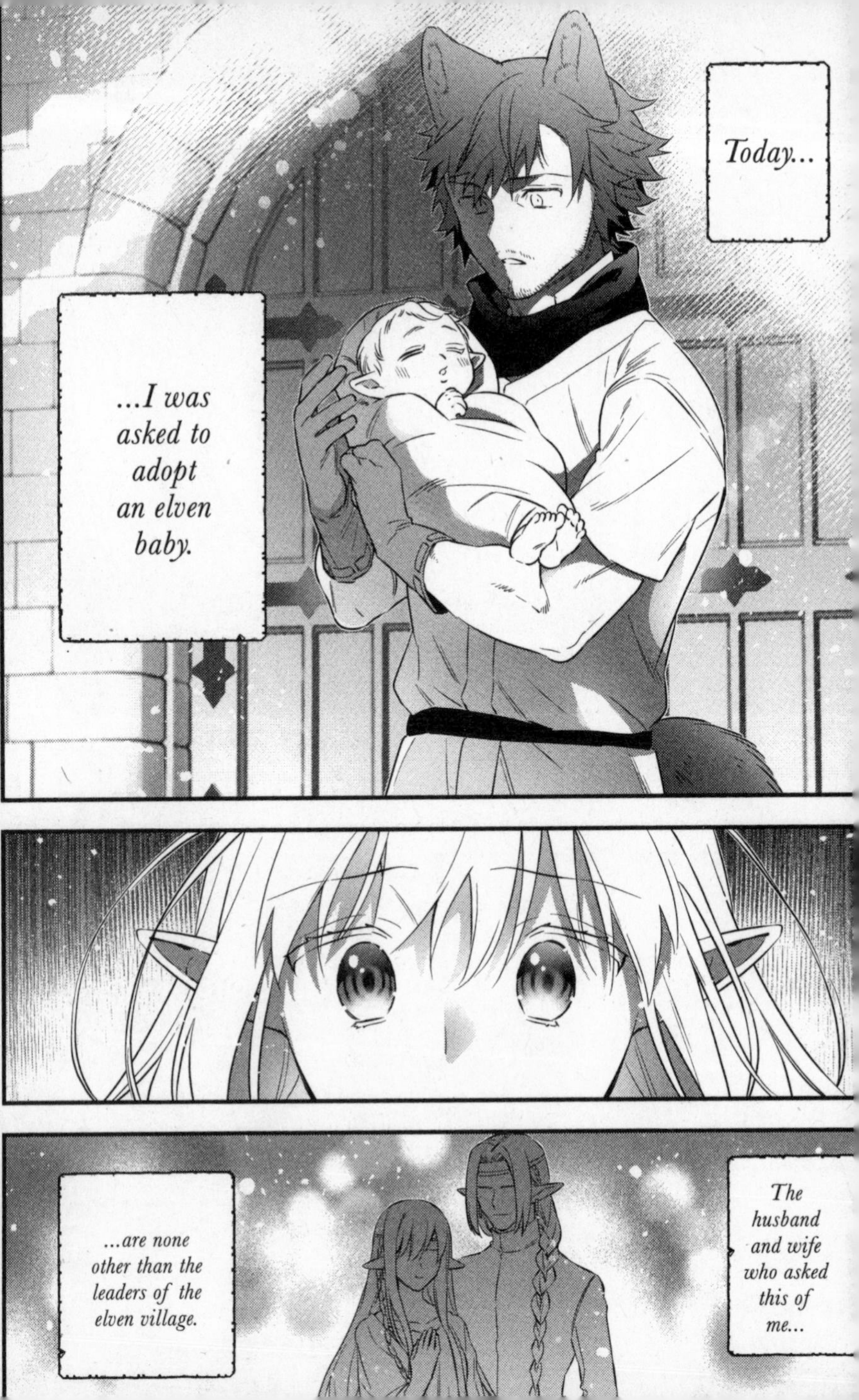
Today...
...I was asked to adopt an elven baby.
The husband and wife who asked this of me...
...are none other than the leaders of the elven village.

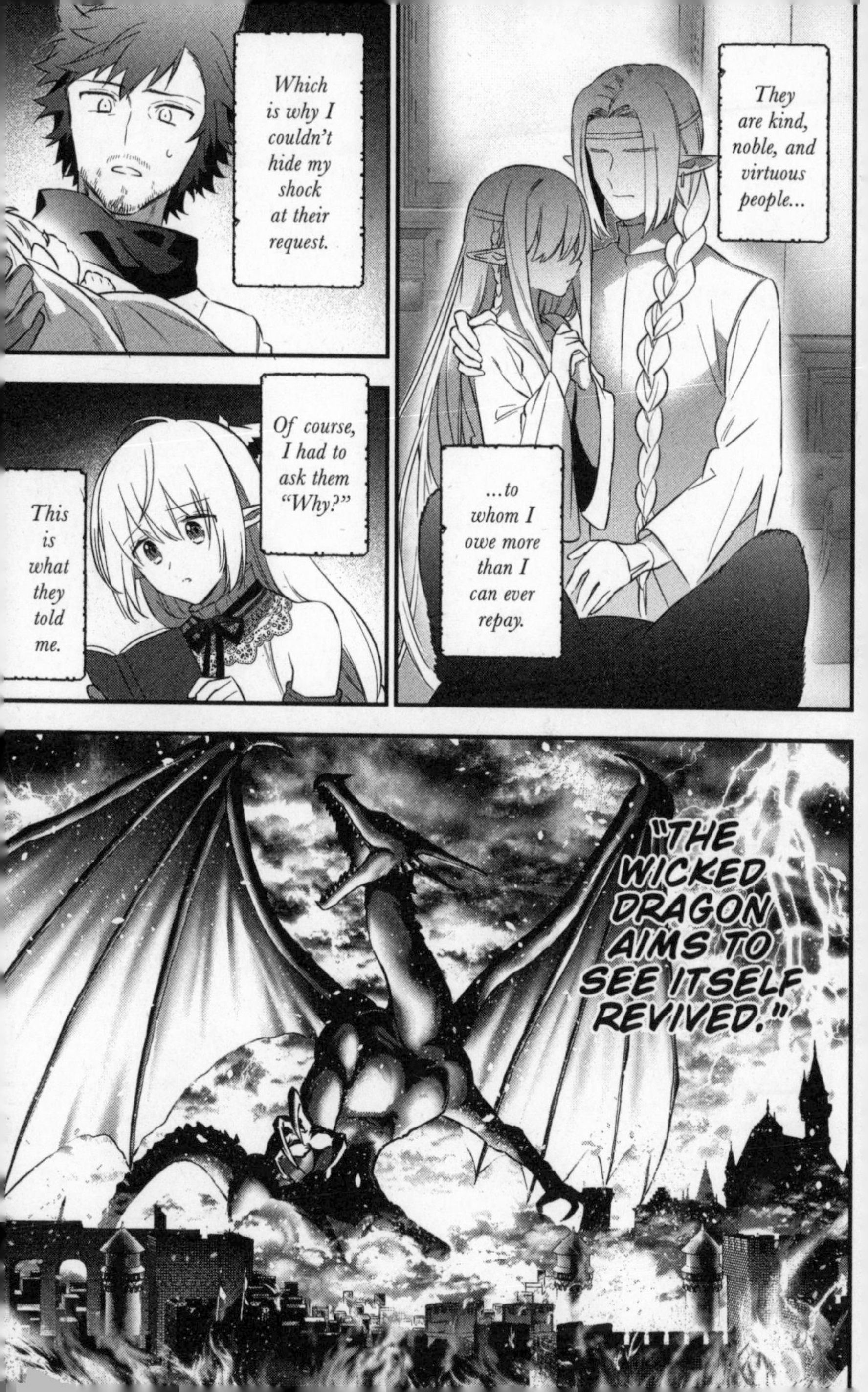
They are kind, noble, and virtuous people...
...to whom I owe more than I can ever repay.
Which is why I couldn't hide my shock at their request.
Of course, I had to ask them "Why?"
This is what they told me.
"THE WICKED DRAGON AIMS TO SEE ITSELF REVIVED."

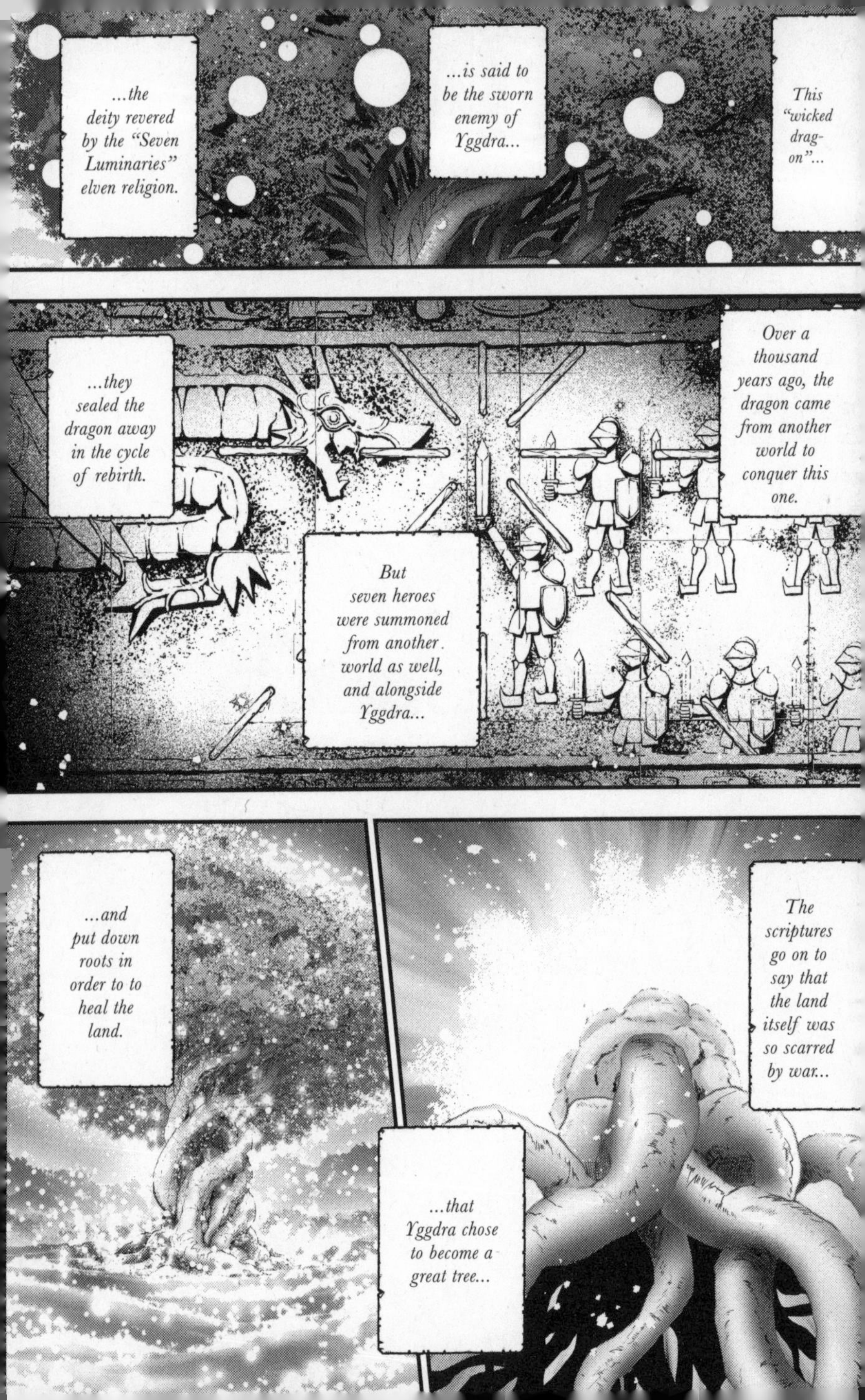
This "wicked dragon"...
...is said to be the sworn enemy of Yggdra...
...the deity revered by the "Seven Luminaries" elven religion.
Over a thousand years ago, the dragon came from another world to conquer this one.
But seven heroes were summoned from another world as well, and alongside Yggdra...
...they sealed the dragon away in the cycle of rebirth.
The scriptures go on to say that the land itself was so scarred by war...
...that Yggdra chose to become a great tree...
...and put down roots in order to to heal the land.

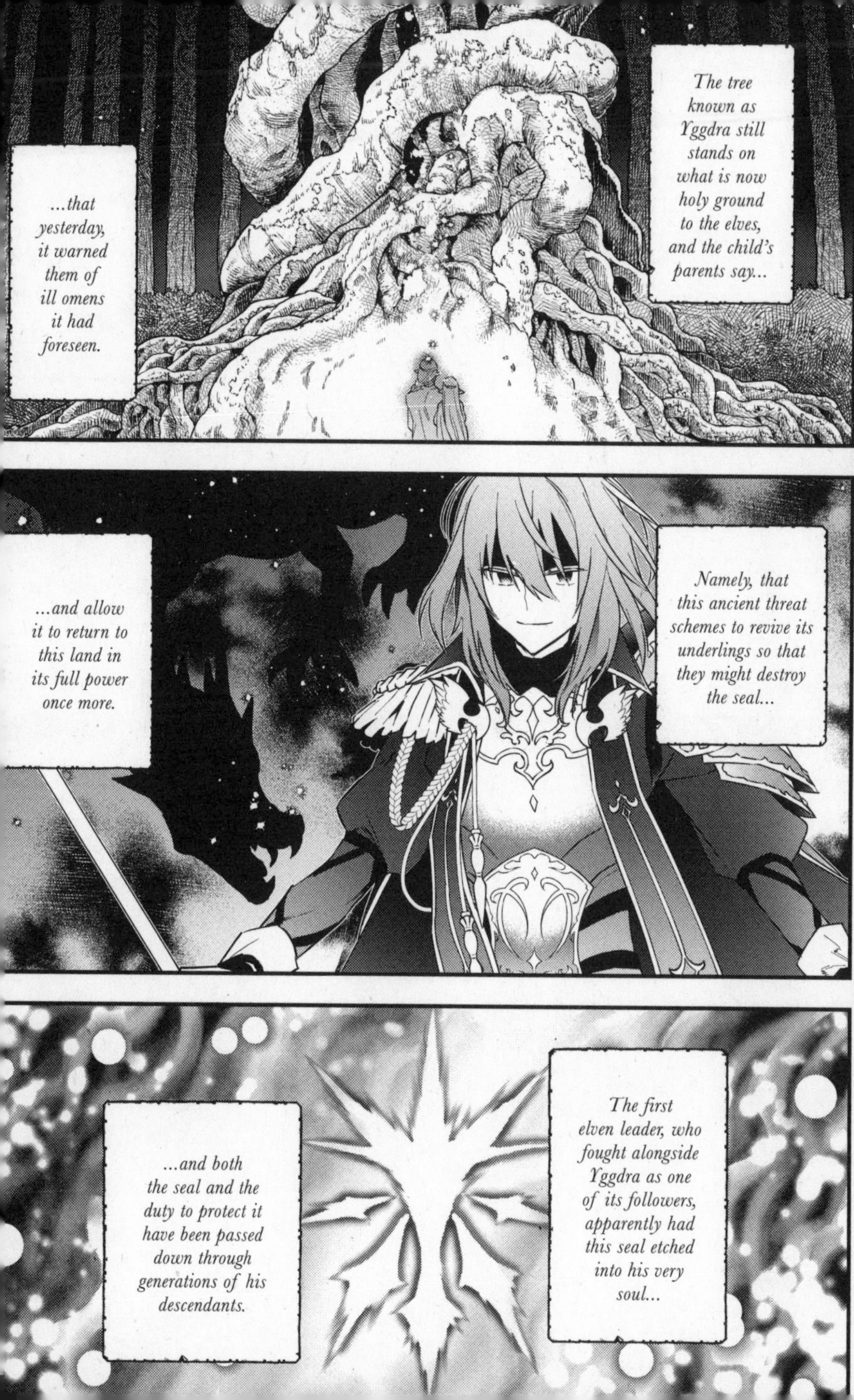
The tree known as Yggdra still stands on what is now holy ground to the elves, and the child's parents say...
...that yesterday, it warned them of ill omens it had foreseen.
Namely, that this ancient threat schemes to revive its underlings so that they might destroy the seal...
...and allow it to return to this land in its full power once more.
The first elven leader, who fought alongside Yggdra as one of its followers, apparently had this seal etched into his very soul...
...and both the seal and the duty to protect it have been passed down through generations of his descendants.

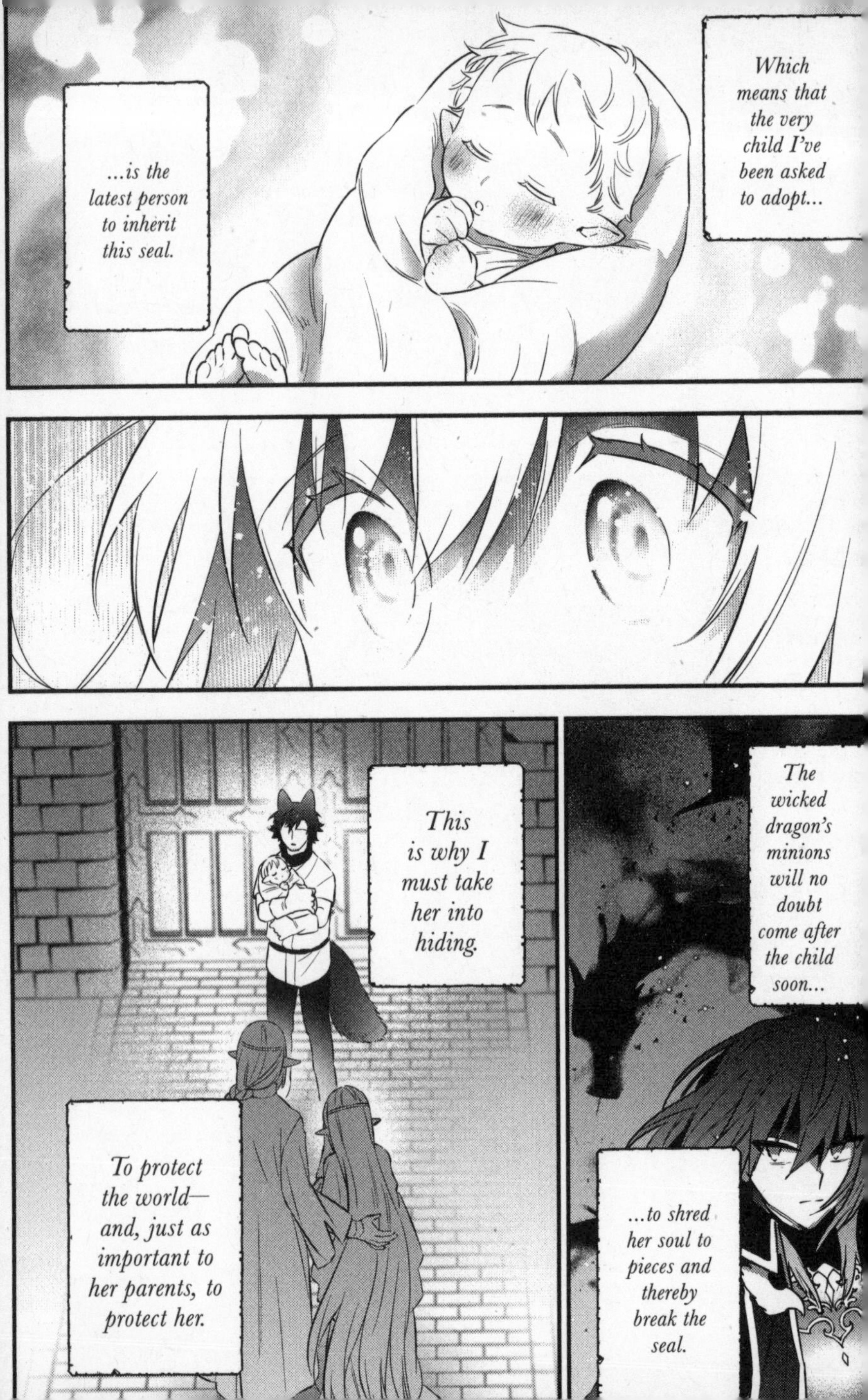
Which means that the very child I've been asked to adopt...
...is the latest person to inherit this seal.
The wicked dragon's minions will no doubt come after the child soon...
...to shred her soul to pieces and thereby break the seal.
This is why I must take her into hiding.
To protect the world—and, just as important to her parents, to protect her.

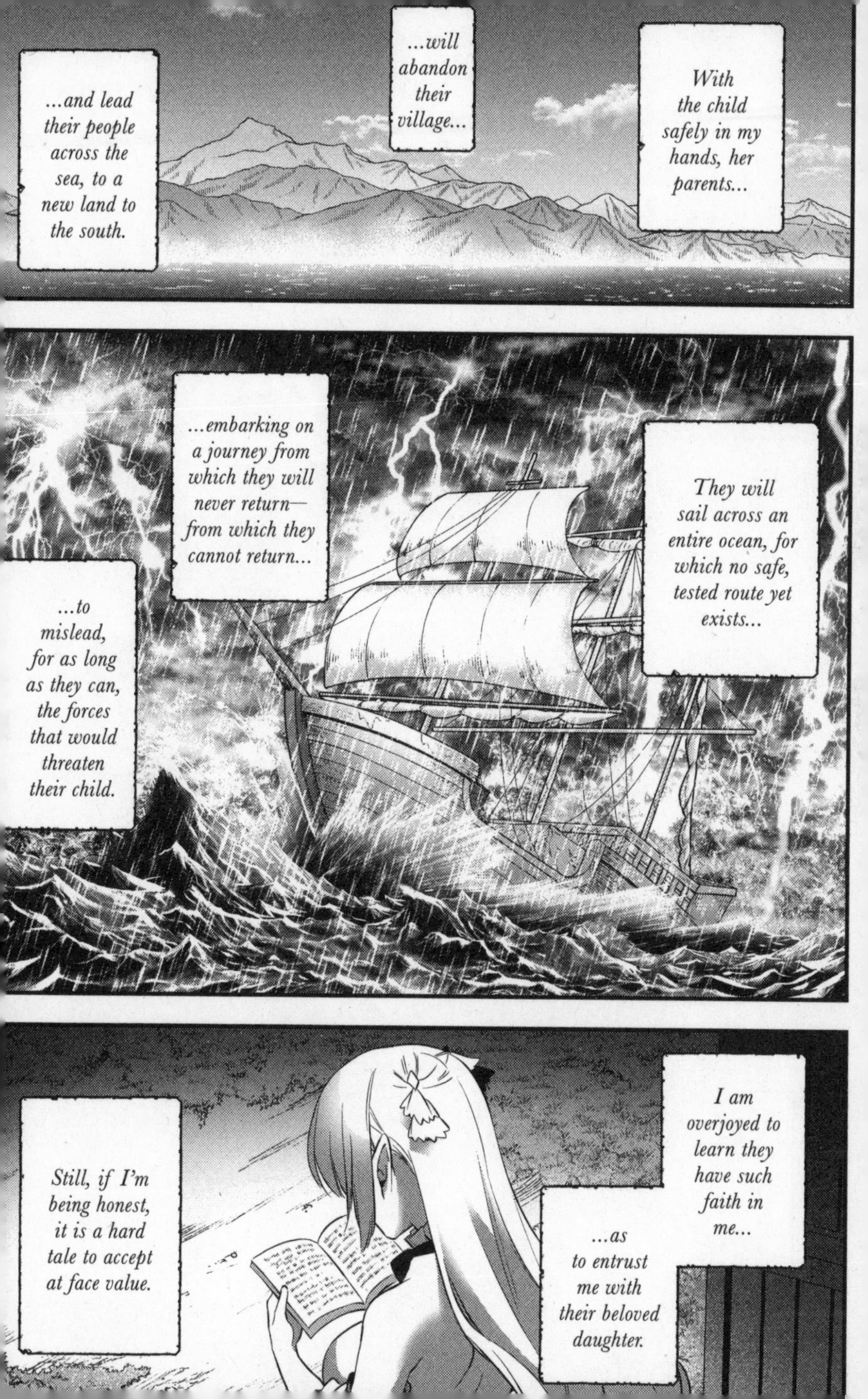
With the child safely in my hands, her parents...
...will abandon their village...
...and lead their people across the sea, to a new land to the south.
They will sail across an entire ocean, for which no safe, tested route yet exists...
...embarking on a journey from which they will never return—from which they cannot return...
...to mislead, for as long as they can, the forces that would threaten their child.
I am overjoyed to learn they have such faith in me...
...as to entrust me with their beloved daughter.
Still, if I'm being honest, it is a hard tale to accept at face value.

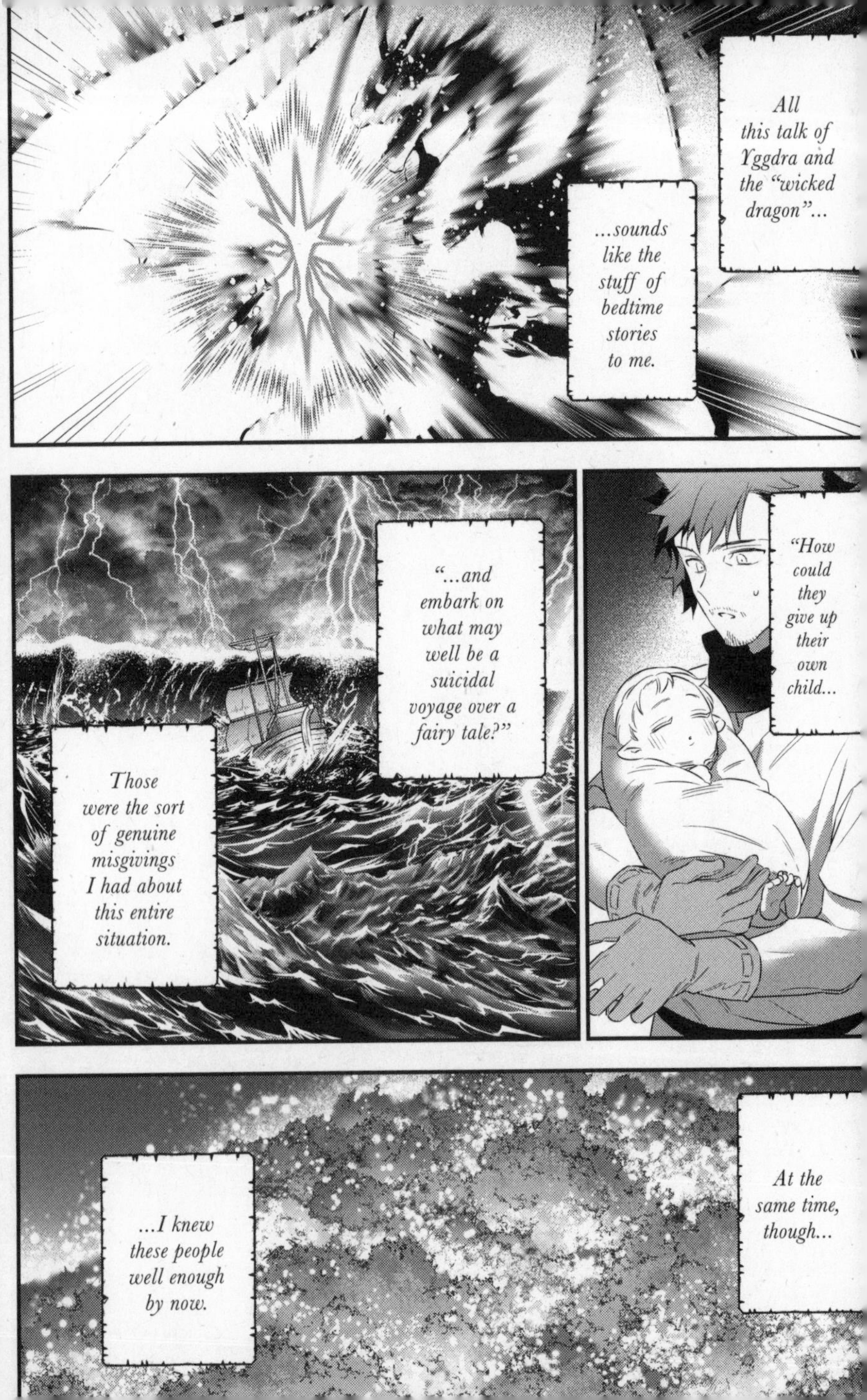
All this talk of Yggdra and the "wicked dragon"...
...sounds like the stuff of bedtime stories to me.
"How could they give up their own child...
"...and embark on what may well be a suicidal voyage over a fairy tale?"
Those were the sort of genuine misgivings I had about this entire situation.
At the same time, though...
...I knew these people well enough by now.

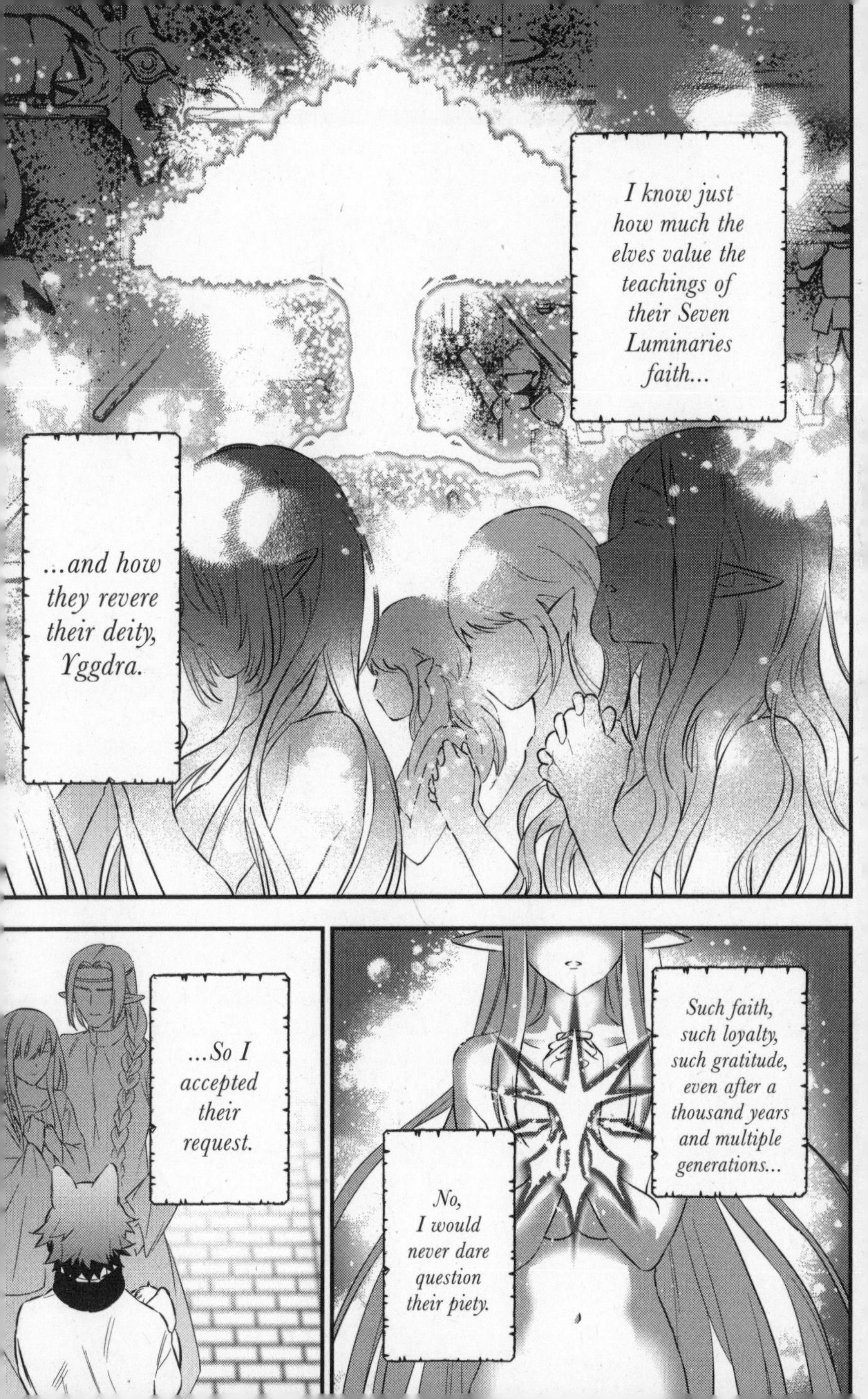
I know just how much the elves value the teachings of their Seven Luminaries faith...
...and how they revere their deity, Yggdra.
Such faith, such loyalty, such gratitude, even after a thousand years and multiple generations...
No, I would never dare question their piety.
...So I accepted their request.

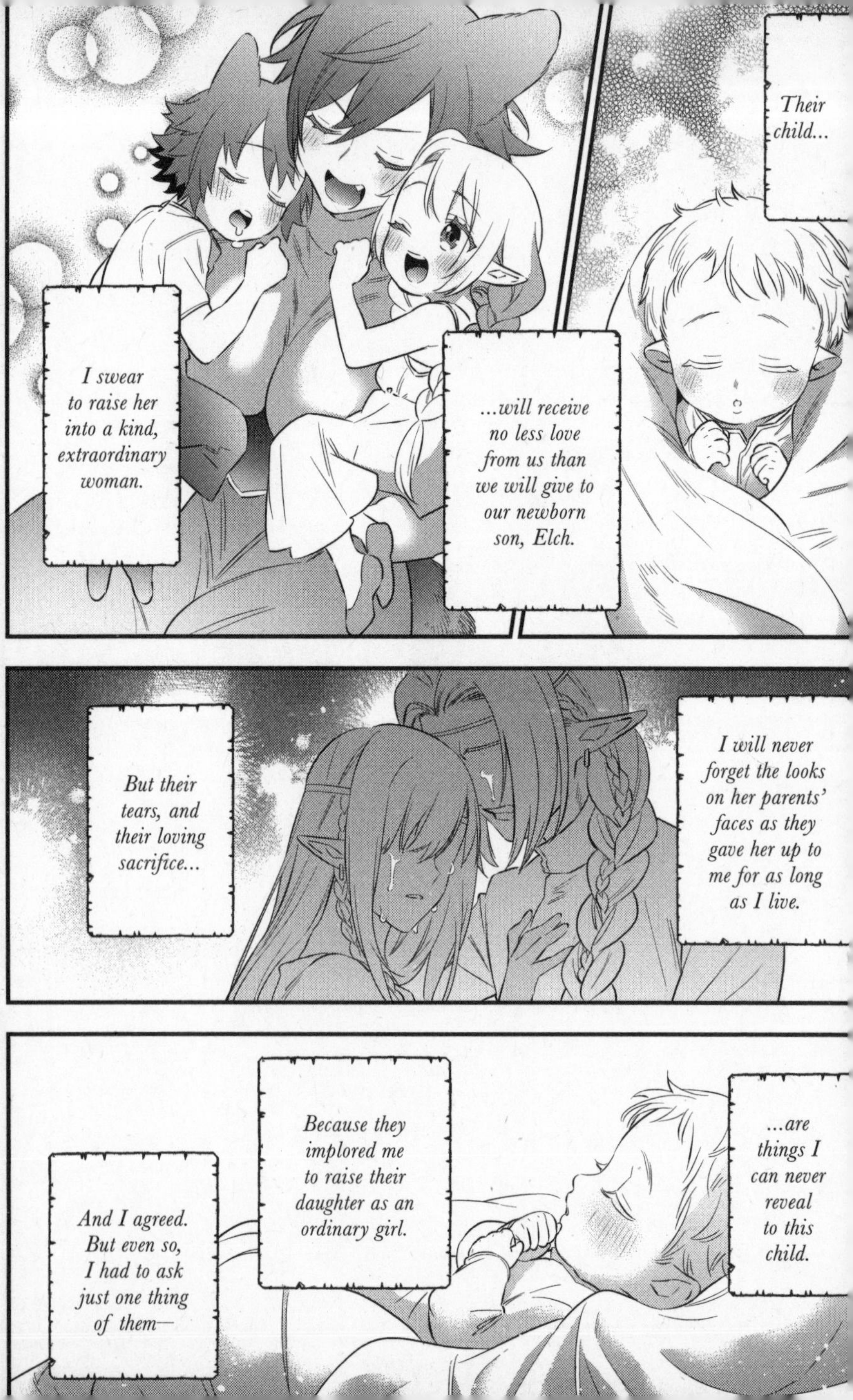
Their child...
...will receive no less love from us than we will give to our newborn son, Elch.
I swear to raise her into a kind, extraordinary woman.
I will never forget the looks on her parents' faces as they gave her up to me for as long as I live.
But their tears, and their loving sacrifice...
...are things I can never reveal to this child.
Because they implored me to raise their daughter as an ordinary girl.
And I agreed. But even so, I had to ask just one thing of them—

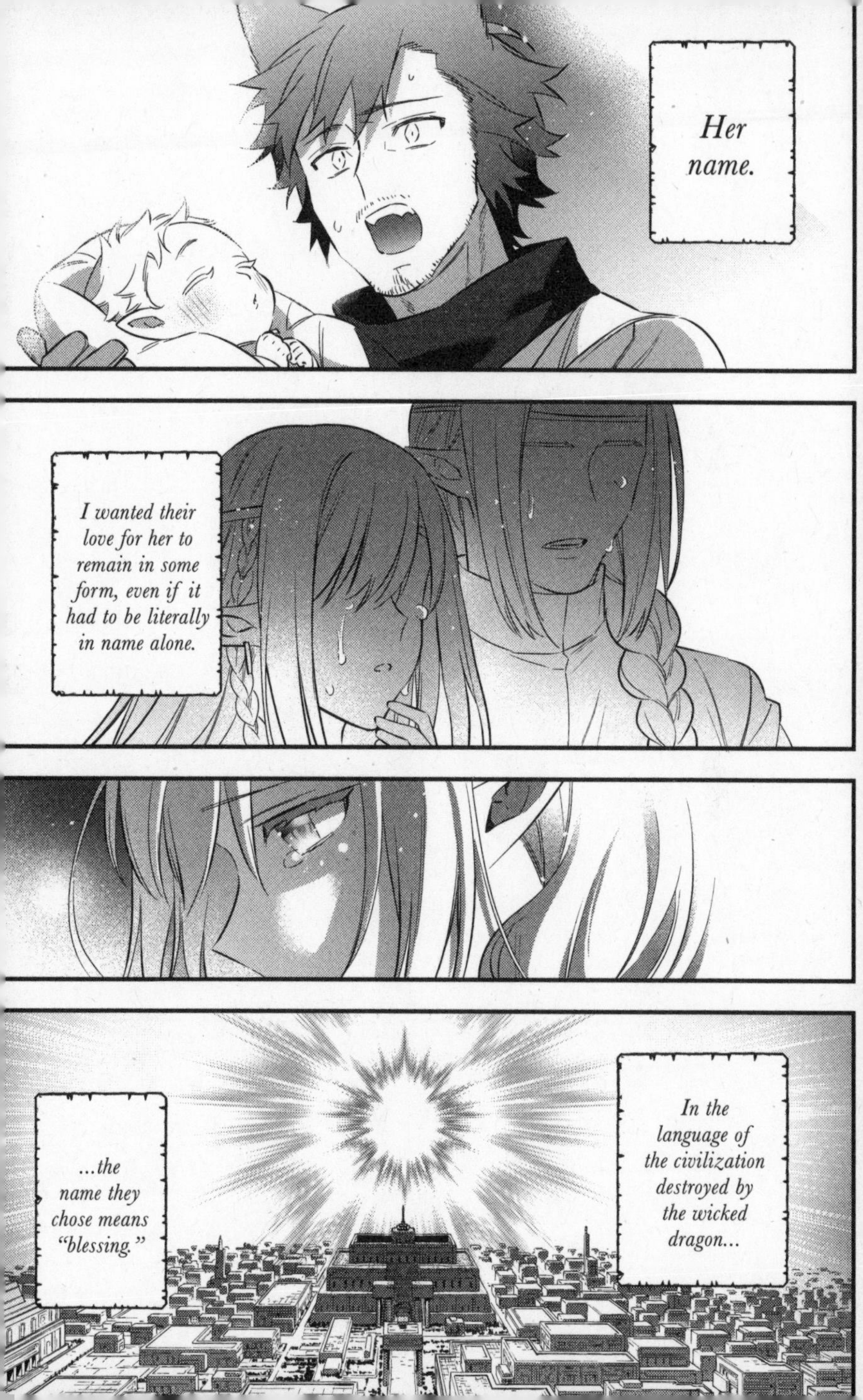
Her name.
I wanted their love for her to remain in some form, even if it had to be literally in name alone.
In the language of the civilization destroyed by the wicked dragon...
...the name they chose means "blessing."

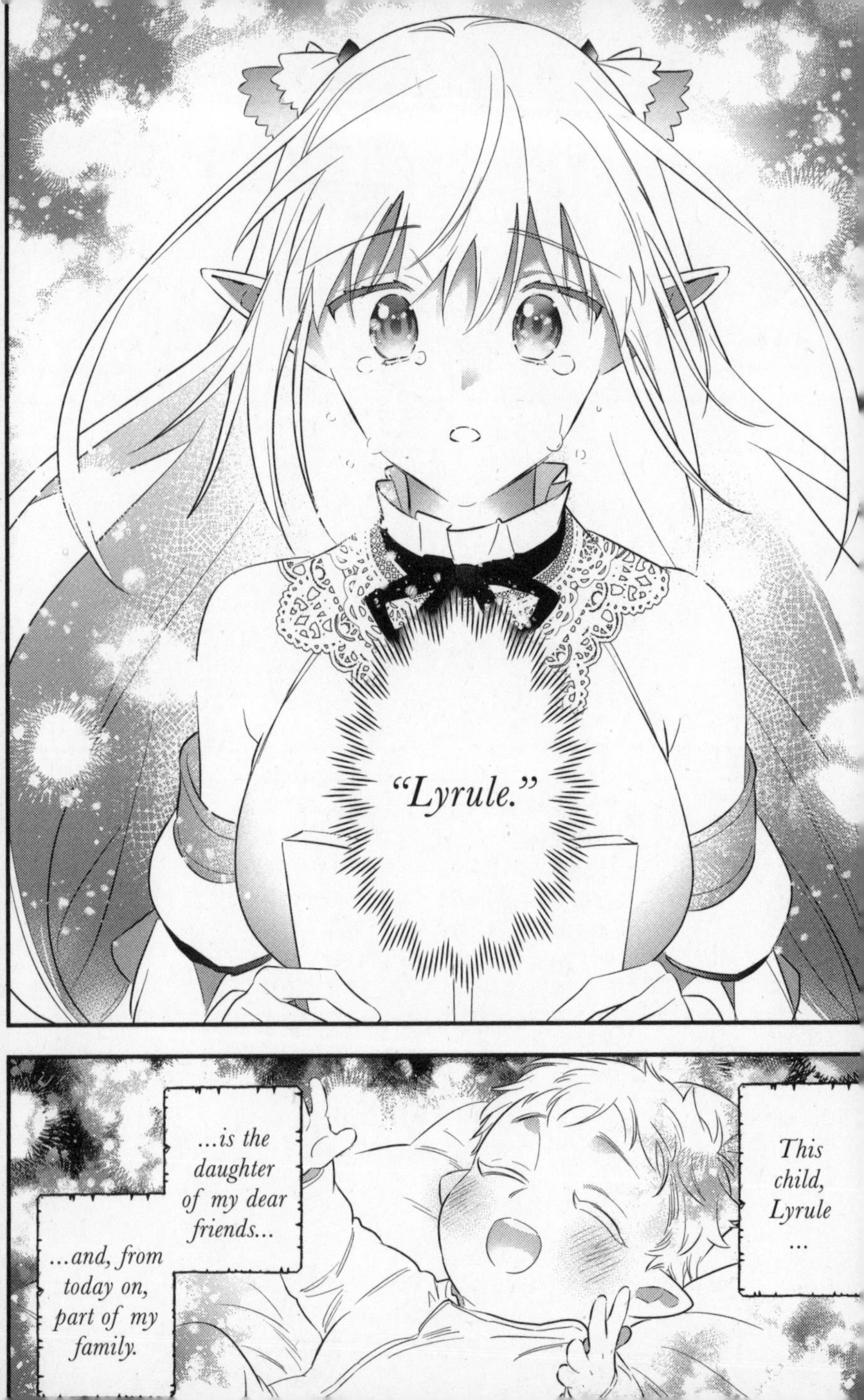
"Lyrule."
This child, Lyrule...
...is the daughter of my dear friends...
...and, from today on, part of my family.

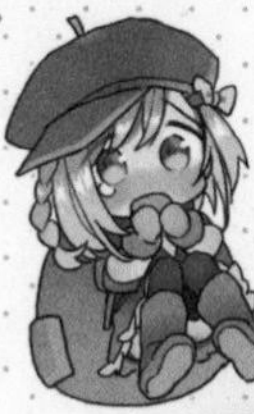
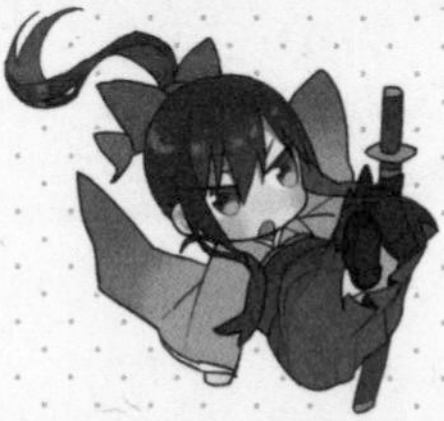
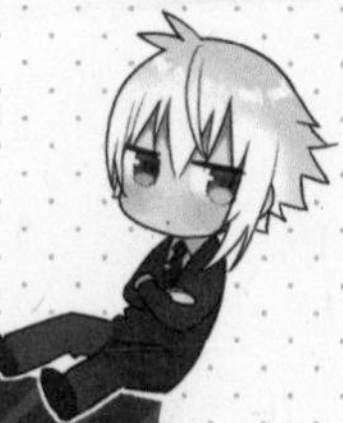

Special Illutstration Gallery to Celebrate the Manga's End!

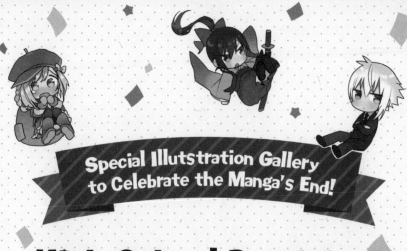

High School Prodigies Have It Easy Even in Another World!

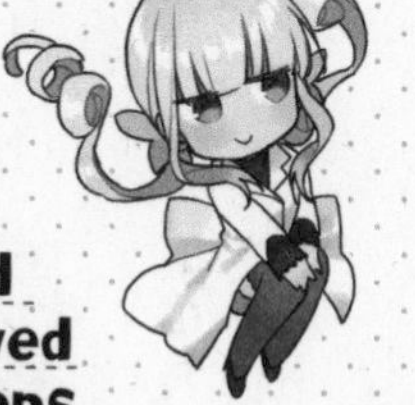
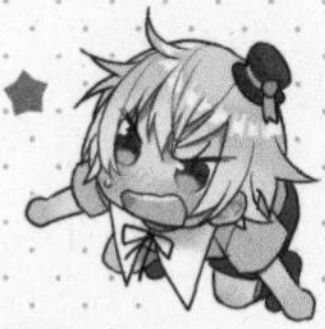

To commemorate the end of the manga, we've received celebratory art contributions from authors of other manga series under the GA Bunko umbrella, as well as various people with their own connections to *High School Prodigies*! Each one has been drawn with so much love and care, so enjoy these takes on all the characters you know and love!!

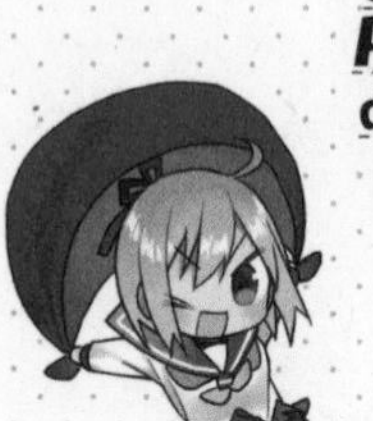
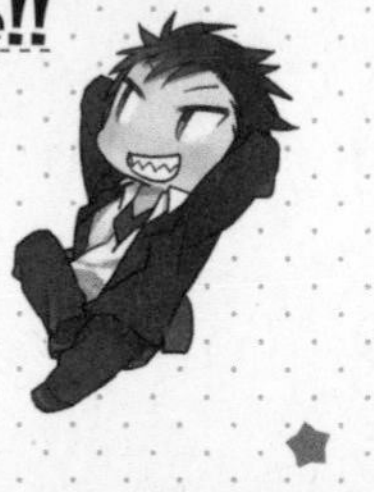

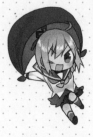

Illustration Gallery (1)

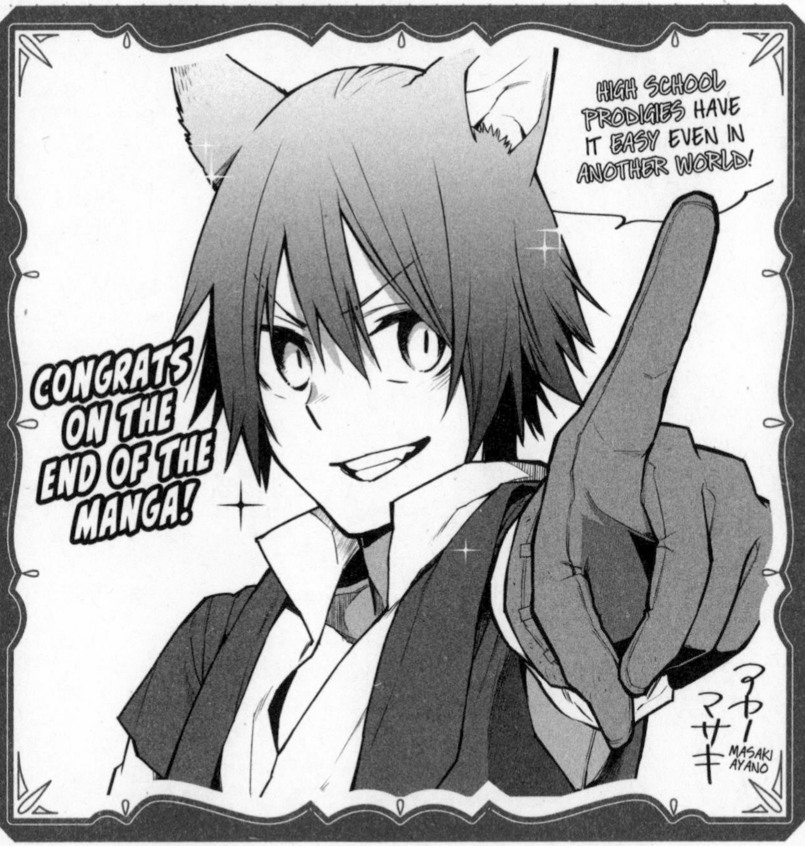
HIGH SCHOOL PRODIGIES HAVE IT EASY EVEN IN ANOTHER WORLD!
CONGRATS ON THE END OF THE MANGA!
MASAKI AYANO

Masaki Ayano-sensei

Manga artist for
***The Strongest Wizard Becomes a Countryside Guard After Taking an Arrow to the Knee*,**
featured in Manga UP!

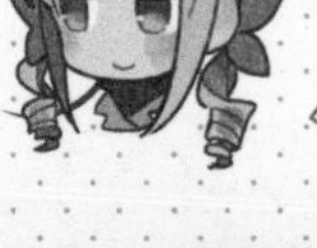

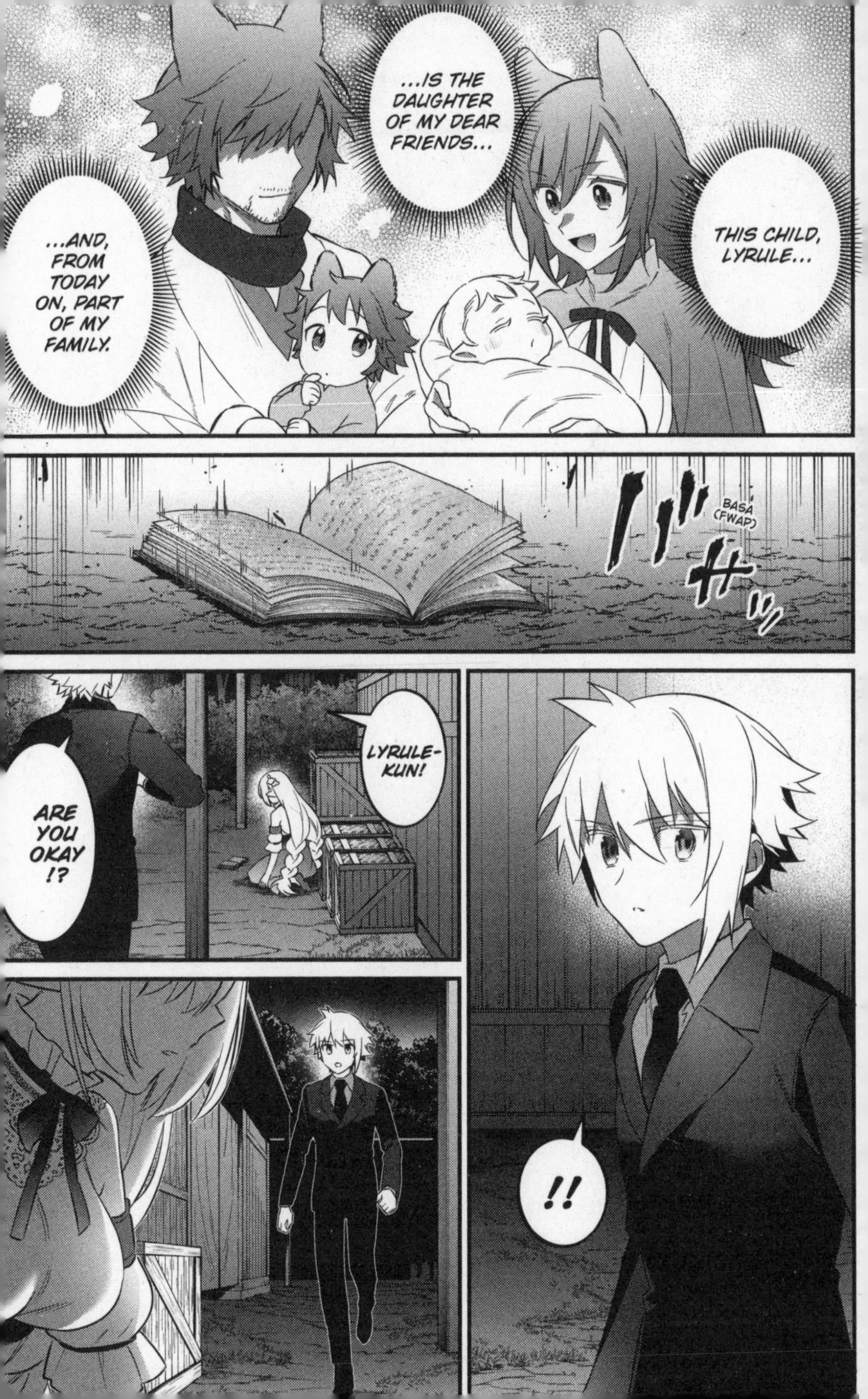
THIS CHILD, LYRULE...
...IS THE DAUGHTER OF MY DEAR FRIENDS...
...AND, FROM TODAY ON, PART OF MY FAMILY.
BASA (FWAP)
!!
LYRULE-KUN!
ARE YOU OKAY!?

CHAPTER 95: DEAR TO MY HEART

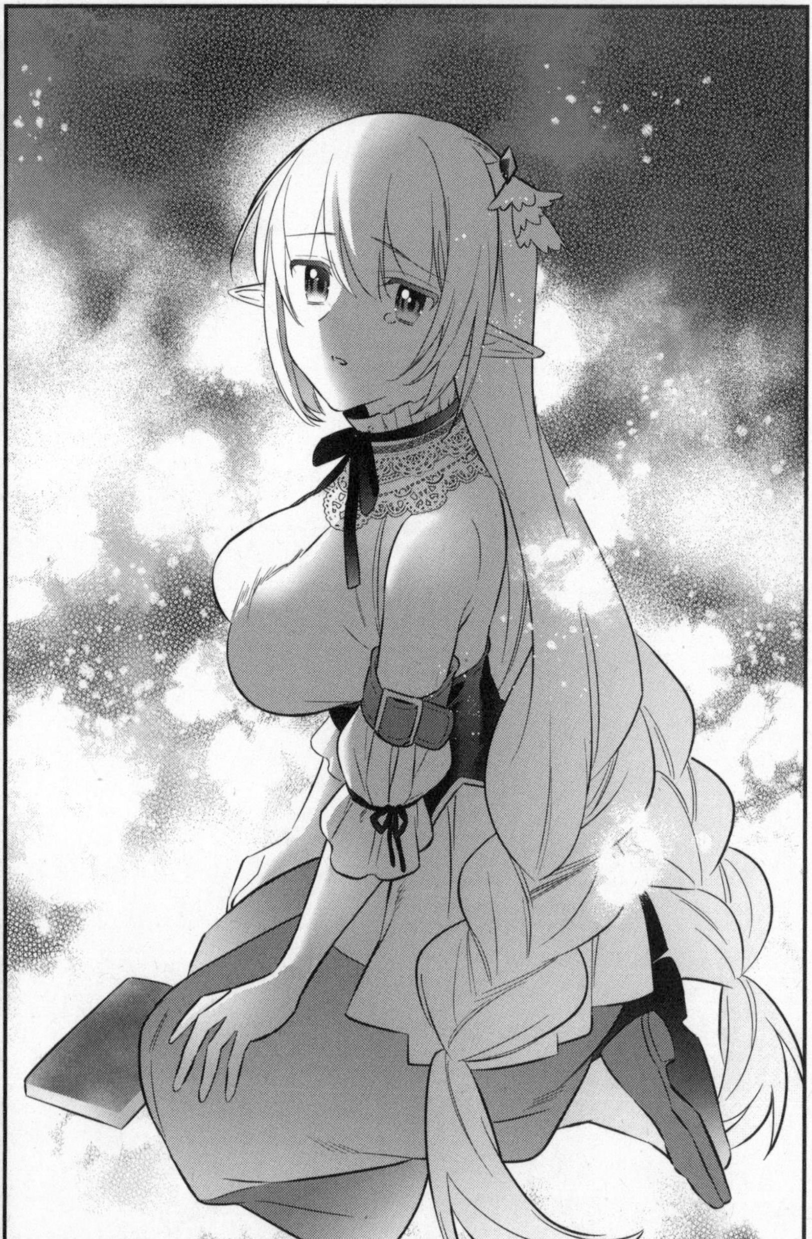

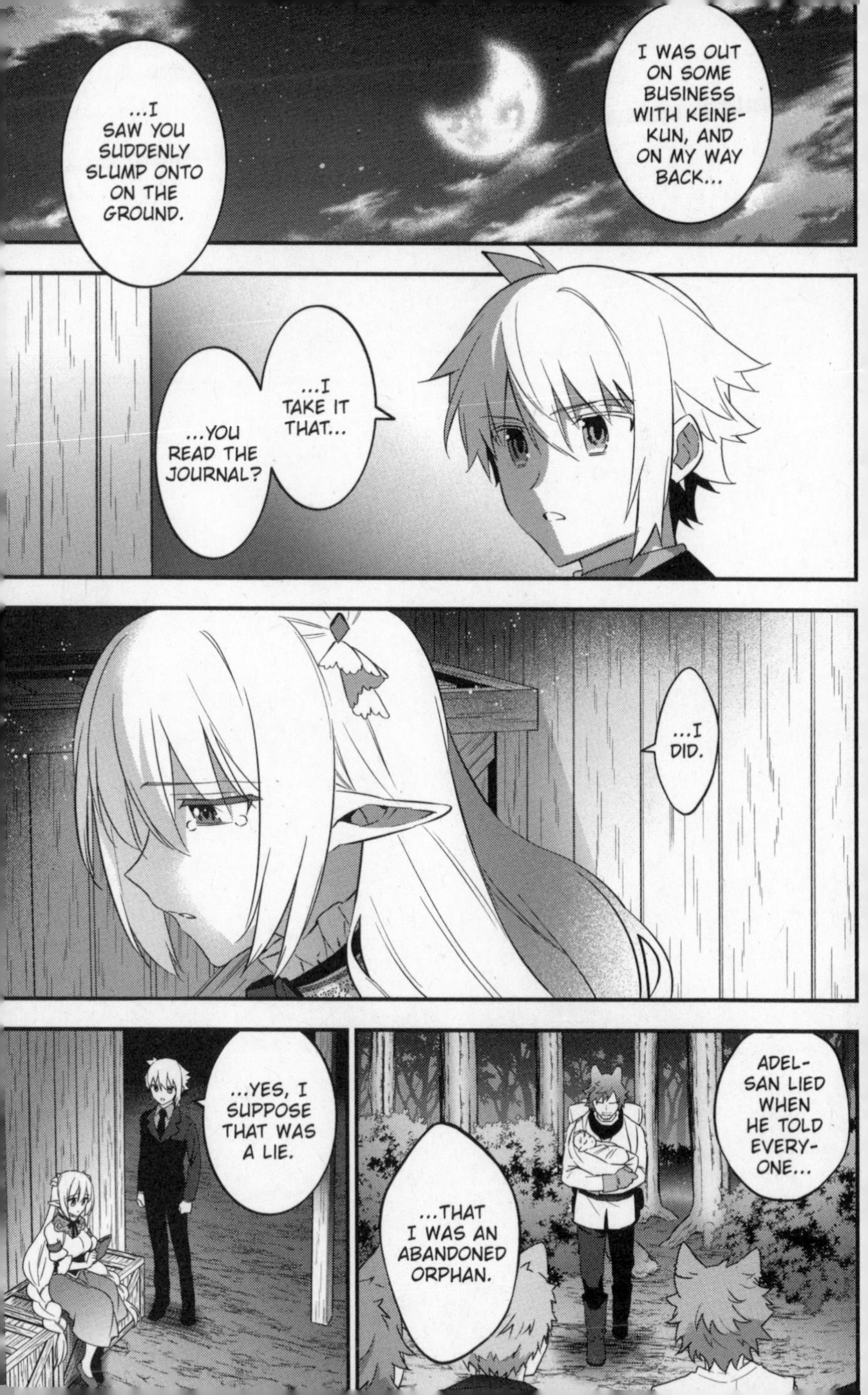
I WAS OUT ON SOME BUSINESS WITH KEINE-KUN, AND ON MY WAY BACK...
...I SAW YOU SUDDENLY SLUMP ONTO ON THE GROUND.
...I TAKE IT THAT...
...YOU READ THE JOURNAL?
...I DID.
ADEL-SAN LIED WHEN HE TOLD EVERY-ONE...
...THAT I WAS AN ABANDONED ORPHAN.
...YES, I SUPPOSE THAT WAS A LIE.

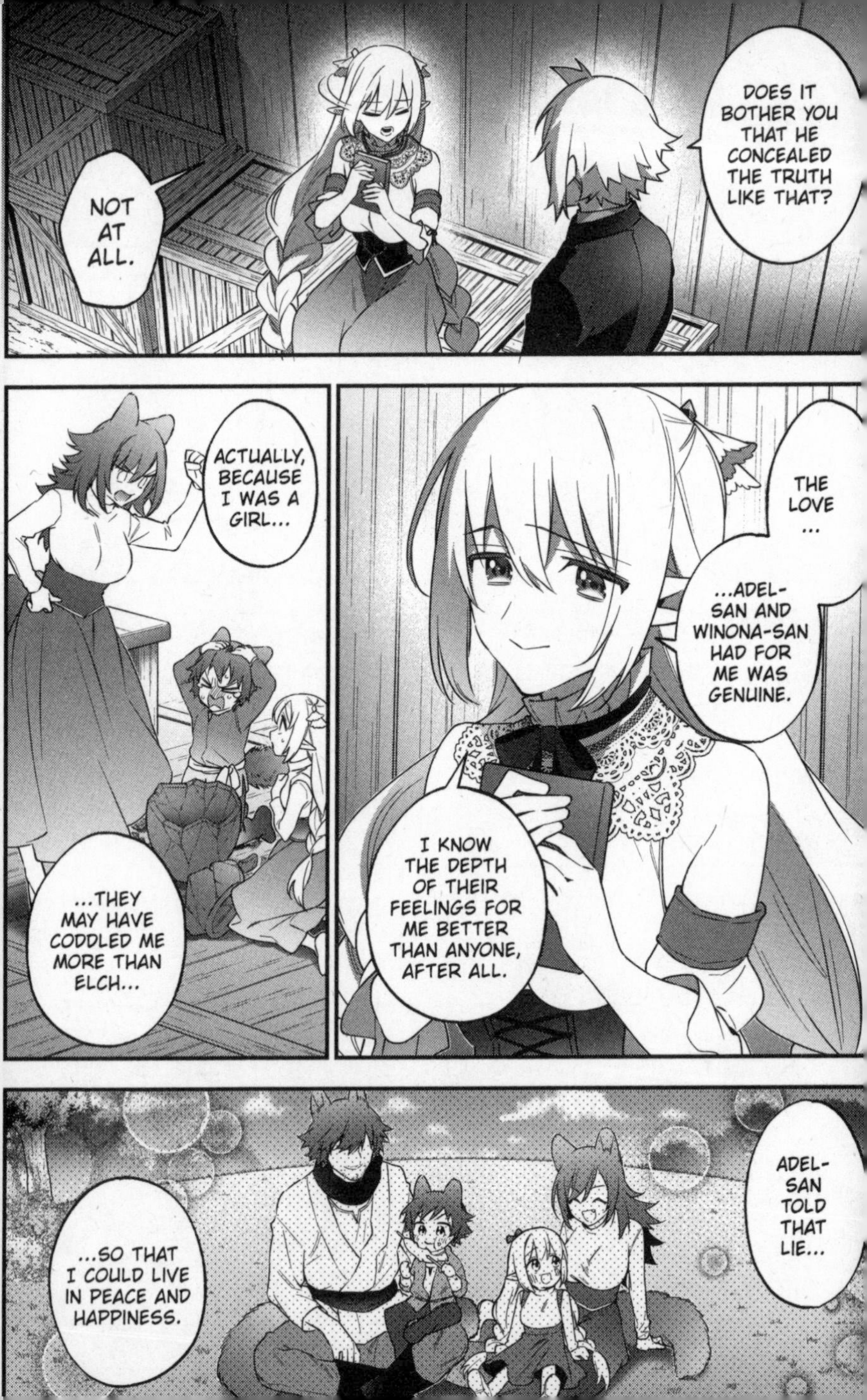
DOES IT BOTHER YOU THAT HE CONCEALED THE TRUTH LIKE THAT?
NOT AT ALL.
THE LOVE ...
...ADEL-SAN AND WINONA-SAN HAD FOR ME WAS GENUINE.
I KNOW THE DEPTH OF THEIR FEELINGS FOR ME BETTER THAN ANYONE, AFTER ALL.
ACTUALLY, BECAUSE I WAS A GIRL...
...THEY MAY HAVE CODDLED ME MORE THAN ELCH...
ADEL-SAN TOLD THAT LIE...
...SO THAT I COULD LIVE IN PEACE AND HAPPINESS.

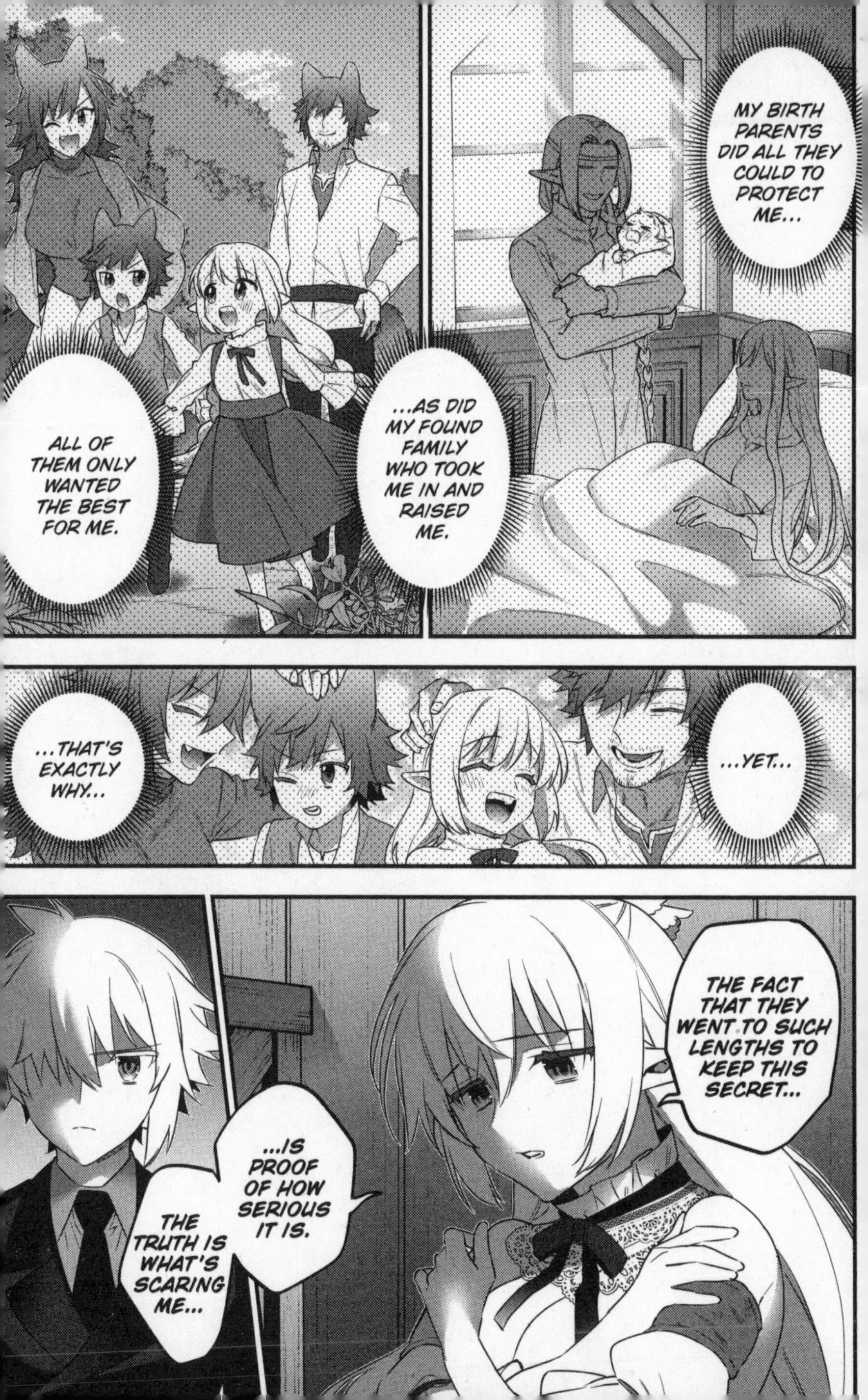
MY BIRTH PARENTS DID ALL THEY COULD TO PROTECT ME...
...AS DID MY FOUND FAMILY WHO TOOK ME IN AND RAISED ME.
ALL OF THEM ONLY WANTED THE BEST FOR ME.
...YET...
...THAT'S EXACTLY WHY...
THE FACT THAT THEY WENT TO SUCH LENGTHS TO KEEP THIS SECRET...
...IS PROOF OF HOW SERIOUS IT IS.
THE TRUTH IS WHAT'S SCARING ME...

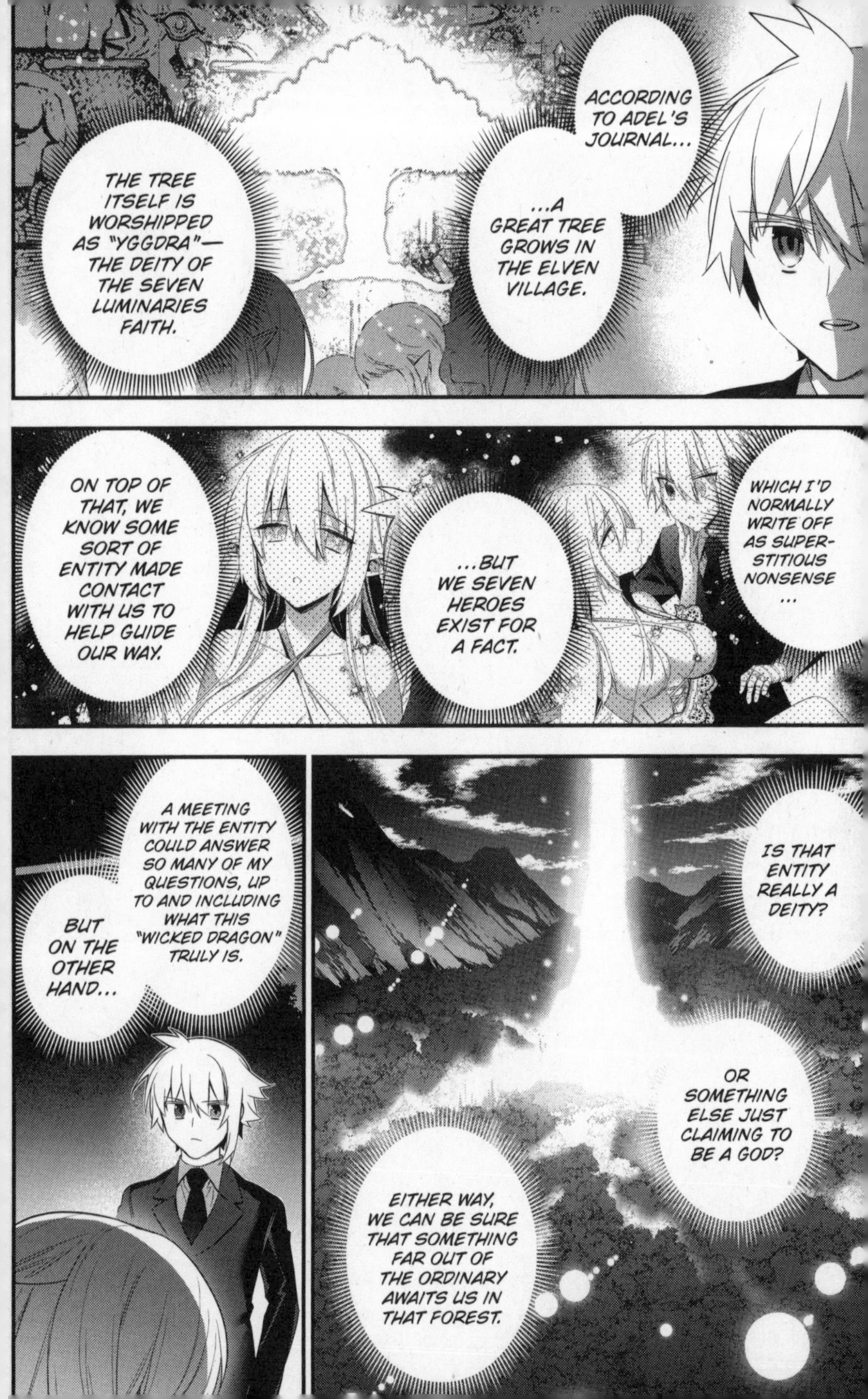
ACCORDING TO ADEL'S JOURNAL...
...A GREAT TREE GROWS IN THE ELVEN VILLAGE.
THE TREE ITSELF IS WORSHIPPED AS "YGGDRA"—THE DEITY OF THE SEVEN LUMINARIES FAITH.
WHICH I'D NORMALLY WRITE OFF AS SUPER-STITIOUS NONSENSE...
...BUT WE SEVEN HEROES EXIST FOR A FACT.
ON TOP OF THAT, WE KNOW SOME SORT OF ENTITY MADE CONTACT WITH US TO HELP GUIDE OUR WAY.
IS THAT ENTITY REALLY A DEITY?
OR SOMETHING ELSE JUST CLAIMING TO BE A GOD?
EITHER WAY, WE CAN BE SURE THAT SOMETHING FAR OUT OF THE ORDINARY AWAITS US IN THAT FOREST.
A MEETING WITH THE ENTITY COULD ANSWER SO MANY OF MY QUESTIONS, UP TO AND INCLUDING WHAT THIS "WICKED DRAGON" TRULY IS.
BUT ON THE OTHER HAND...

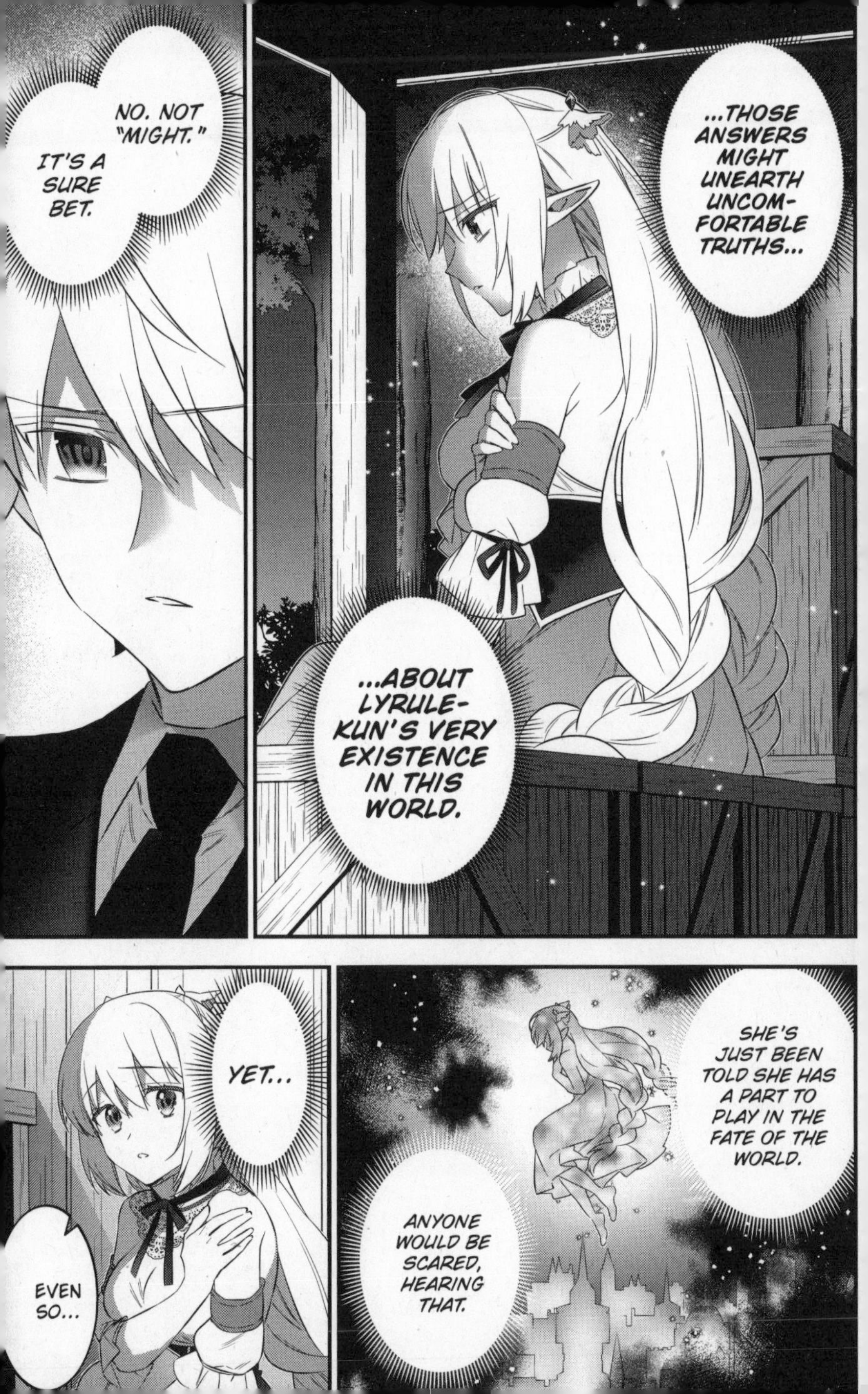
...THOSE ANSWERS MIGHT UNEARTH UNCOM-FORTABLE TRUTHS...
...ABOUT LYRULE-KUN'S VERY EXISTENCE IN THIS WORLD.
NO. NOT "MIGHT."
IT'S A SURE BET.
SHE'S JUST BEEN TOLD SHE HAS A PART TO PLAY IN THE FATE OF THE WORLD.
ANYONE WOULD BE SCARED, HEARING THAT.
YET...
EVEN SO...

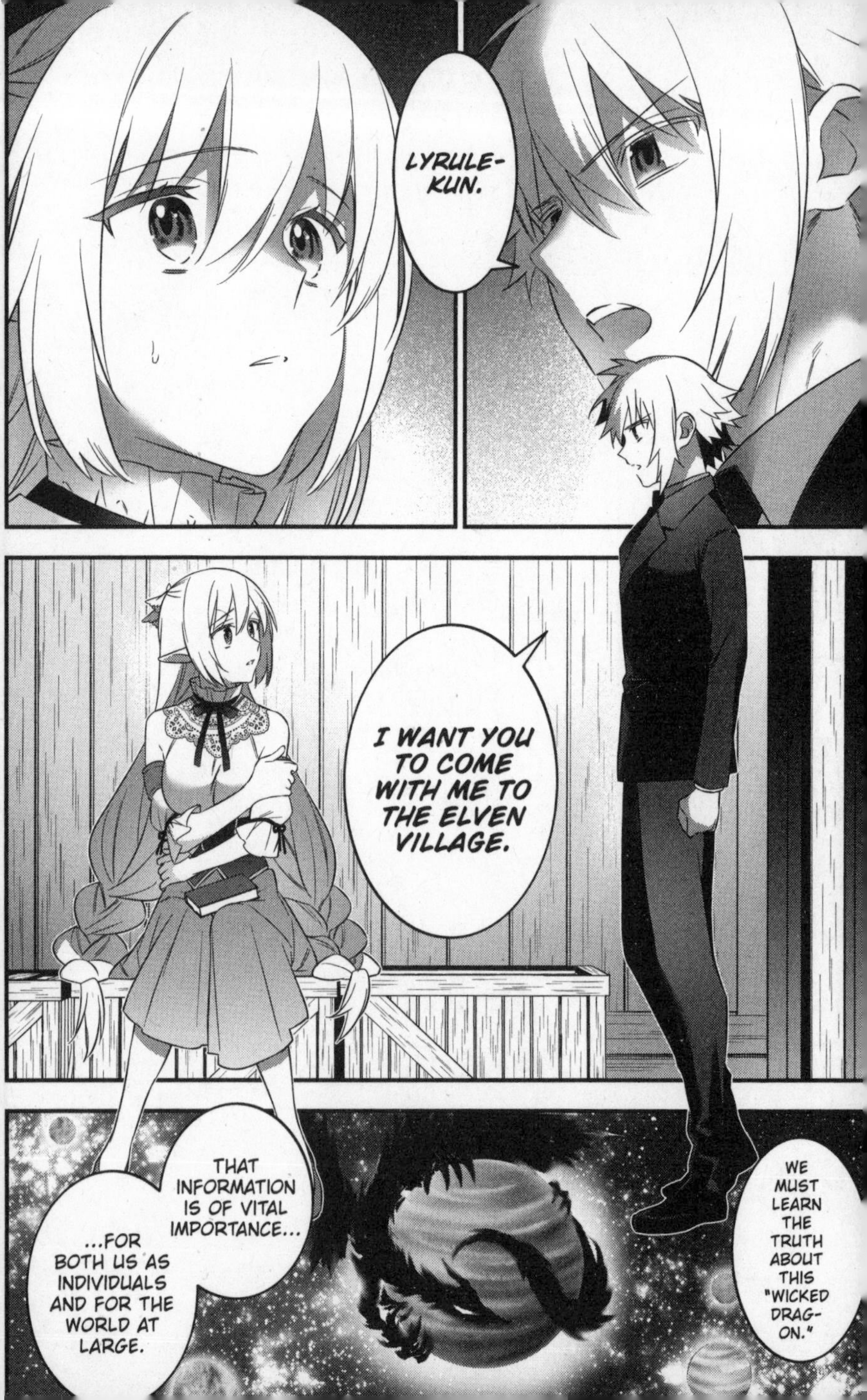
LYRULE-KUN.
I WANT YOU TO COME WITH ME TO THE ELVEN VILLAGE.
WE MUST LEARN THE TRUTH ABOUT THIS "WICKED DRAG-ON."
THAT INFORMATION IS OF VITAL IMPORTANCE...
...FOR BOTH US AS INDIVIDUALS AND FOR THE WORLD AT LARGE.

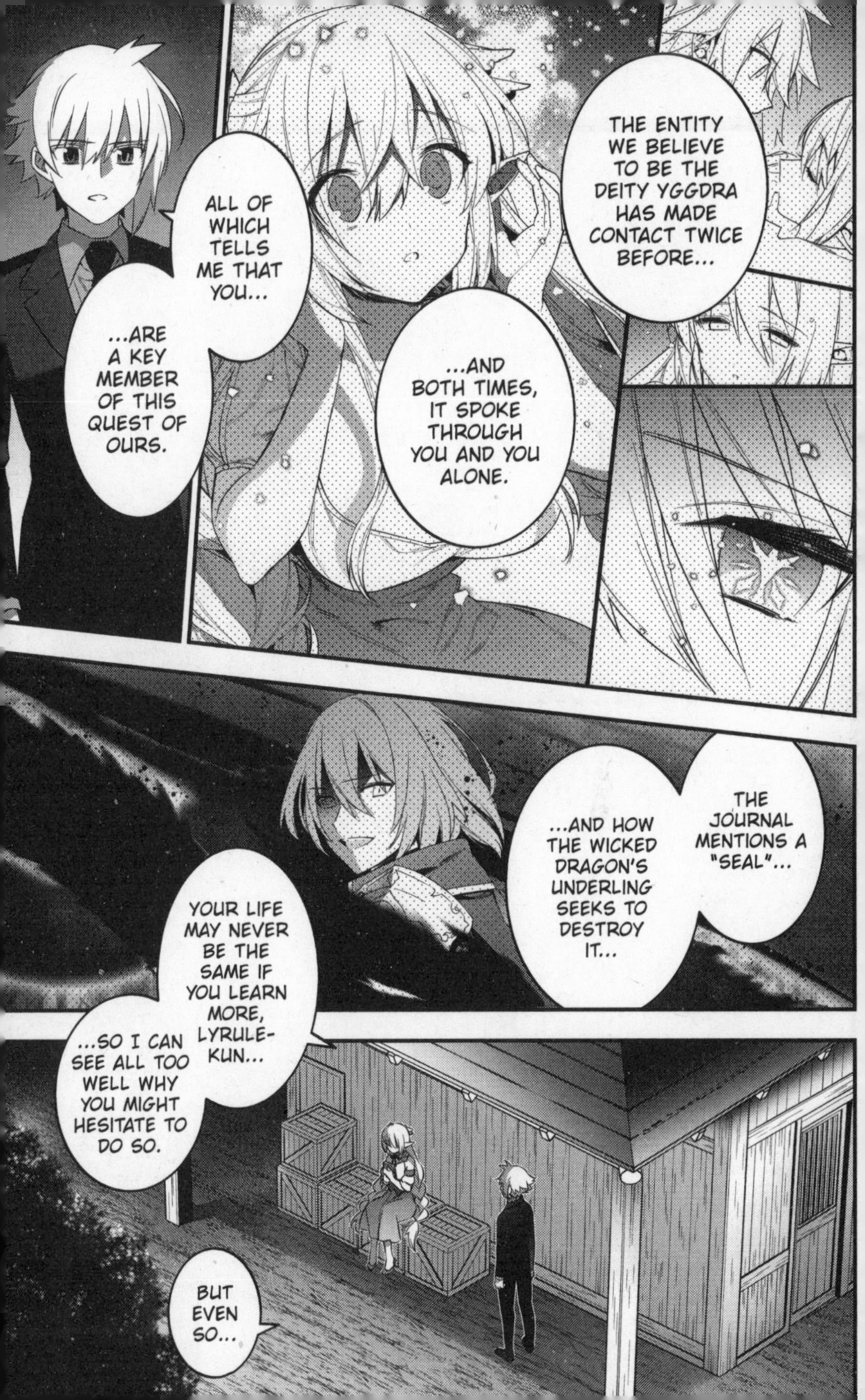
THE ENTITY WE BELIEVE TO BE THE DEITY YGGDRA HAS MADE CONTACT TWICE BEFORE...
...AND BOTH TIMES, IT SPOKE THROUGH YOU AND YOU ALONE.
ALL OF WHICH TELLS ME THAT YOU...
...ARE A KEY MEMBER OF THIS QUEST OF OURS.
THE JOURNAL MENTIONS A "SEAL"...
...AND HOW THE WICKED DRAGON'S UNDERLING SEEKS TO DESTROY IT...
YOUR LIFE MAY NEVER BE THE SAME IF YOU LEARN MORE, LYRULE-KUN...
...SO I CAN SEE ALL TOO WELL WHY YOU MIGHT HESITATE TO DO SO.
BUT EVEN SO...

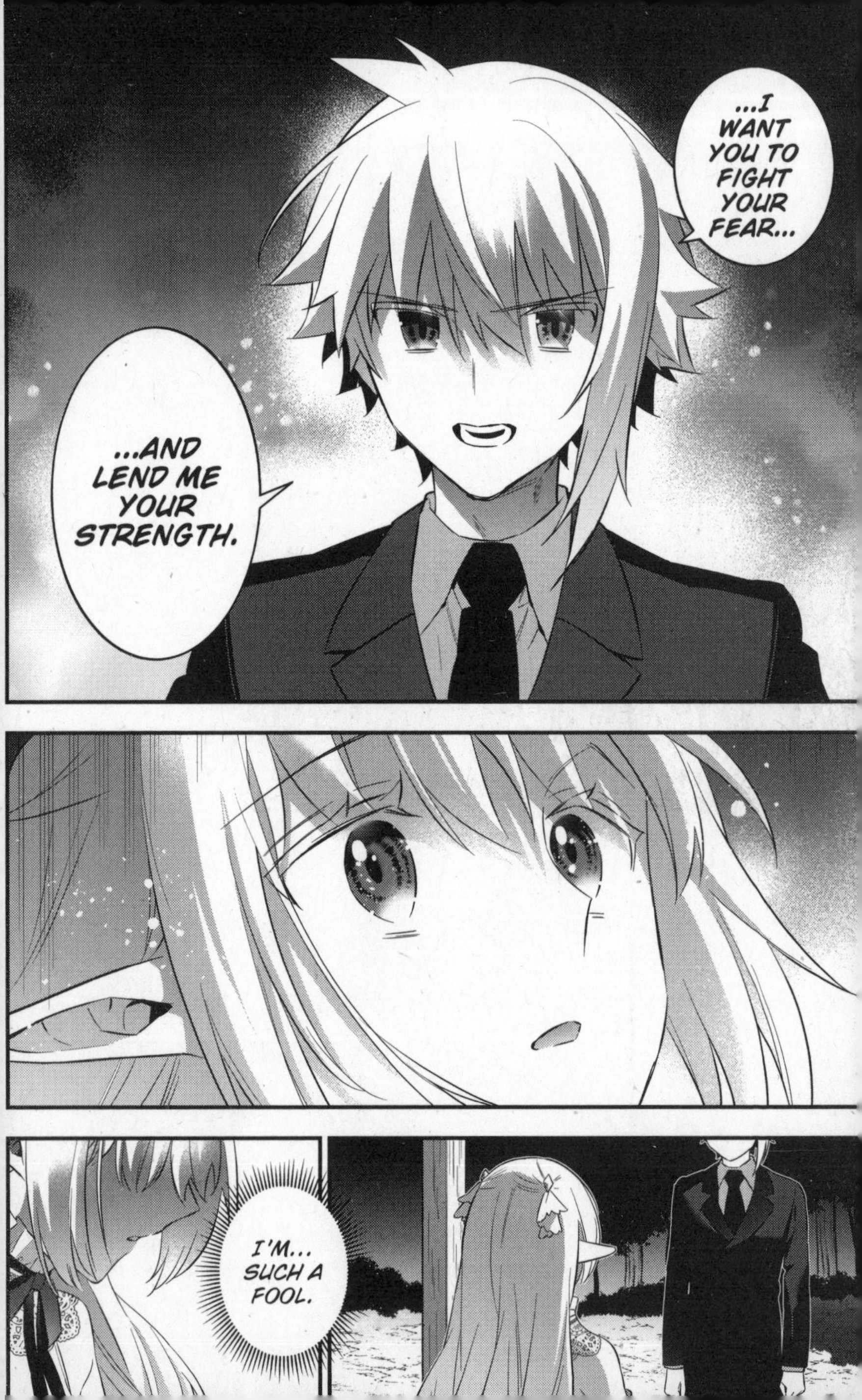
...I WANT YOU TO FIGHT YOUR FEAR...
...AND LEND ME YOUR STRENGTH.
I'M... SUCH A FOOL.

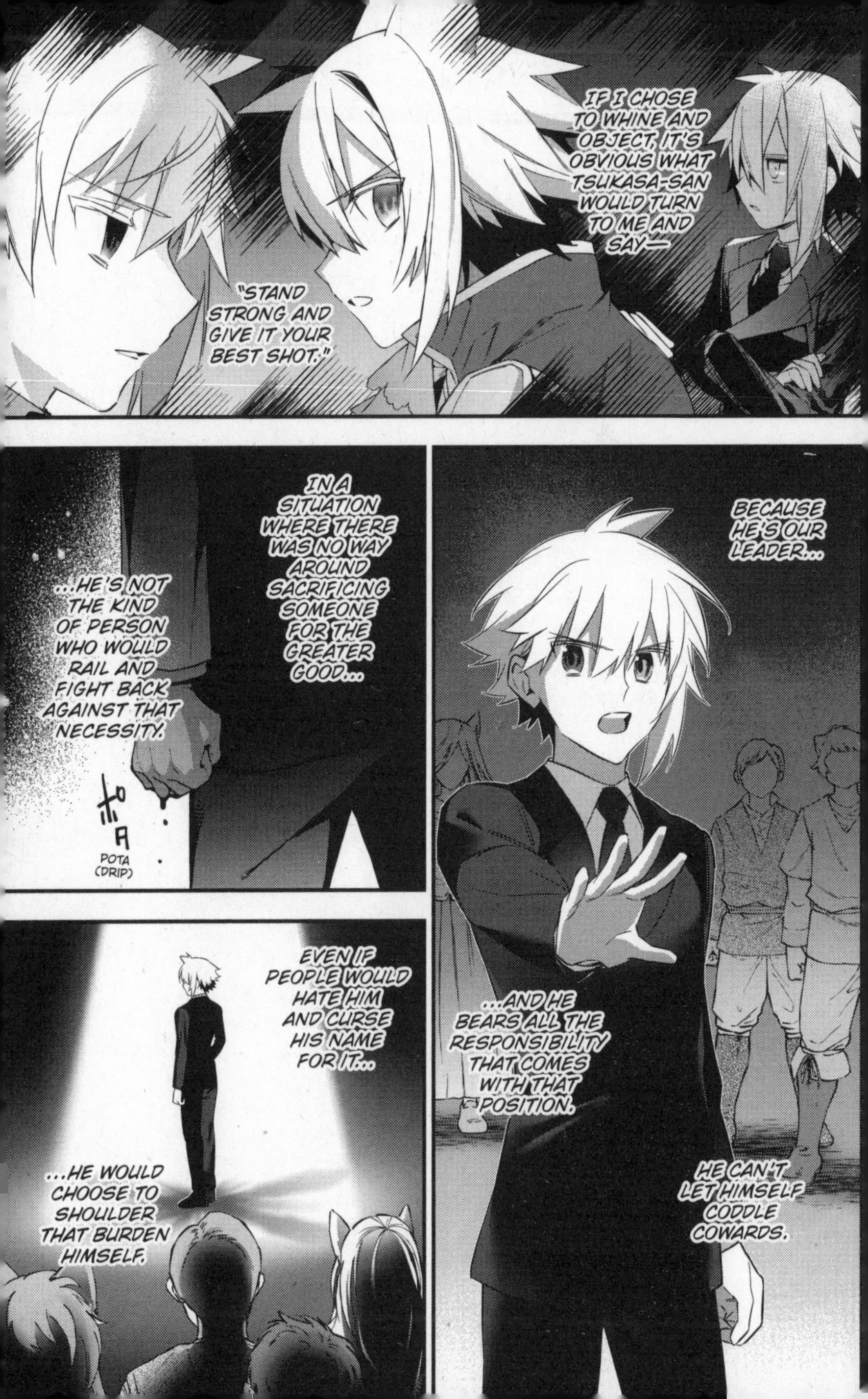
IF I CHOSE TO WHINE AND OBJECT, IT'S OBVIOUS WHAT TSUKASA-SAN WOULD TURN TO ME AND SAY—
"STAND STRONG AND GIVE IT YOUR BEST SHOT."
BECAUSE HE'S OUR LEADER...
...AND HE BEARS ALL THE RESPONSIBILITY THAT COMES WITH THAT POSITION.
HE CAN'T LET HIMSELF CODDLE COWARDS.
IN A SITUATION WHERE THERE WAS NO WAY AROUND SACRIFICING SOMEONE FOR THE GREATER GOOD...
...HE'S NOT THE KIND OF PERSON WHO WOULD RAIL AND FIGHT BACK AGAINST THAT NECESSITY.
POTA (DRIP)
EVEN IF PEOPLE WOULD HATE HIM AND CURSE HIS NAME FOR IT...
...HE WOULD CHOOSE TO SHOULDER THAT BURDEN HIMSELF.

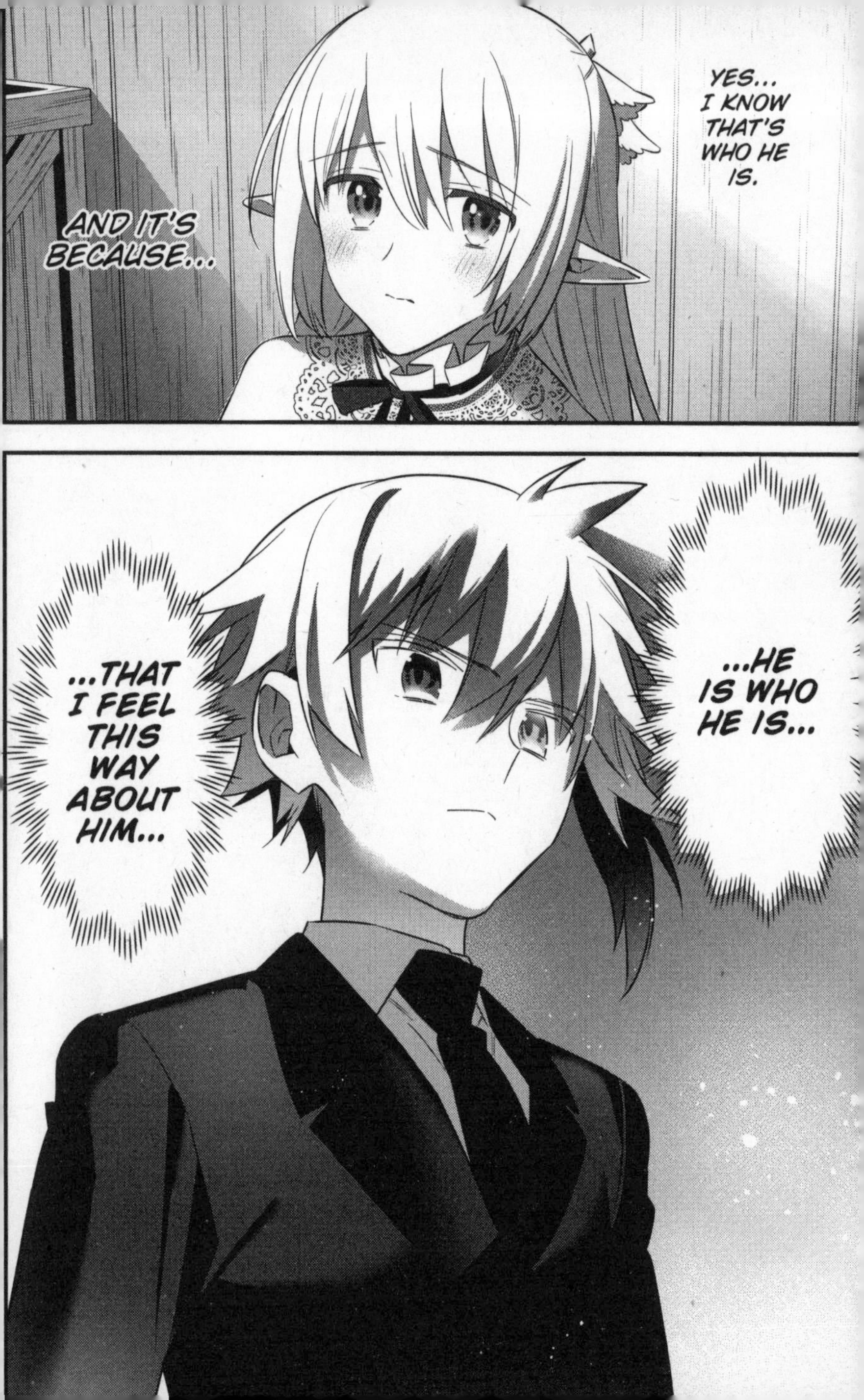
YES... I KNOW THAT'S WHO HE IS.
AND IT'S BECAUSE...
...HE IS WHO HE IS...
...THAT I FEEL THIS WAY ABOUT HIM...

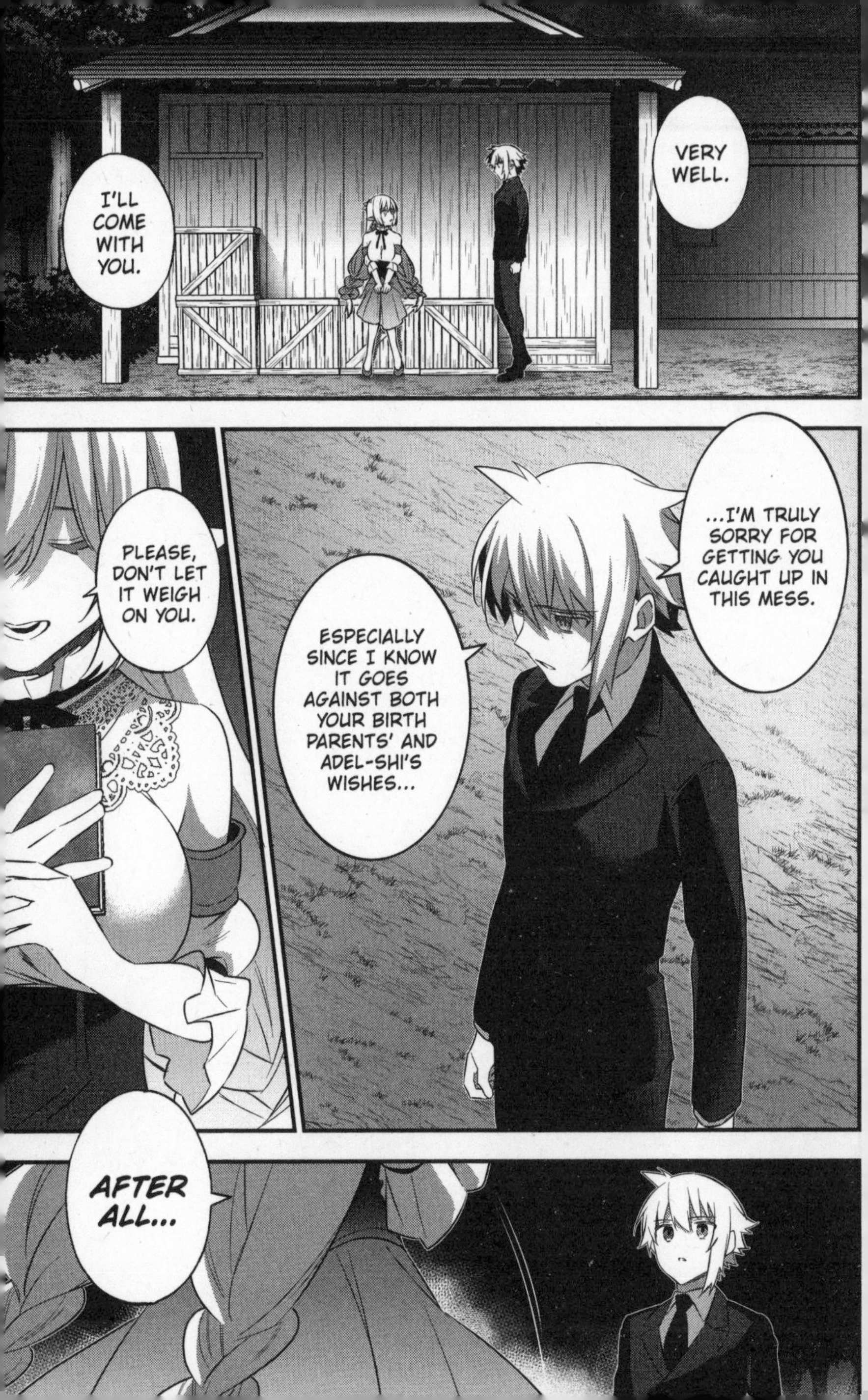
VERY WELL.
I'LL COME WITH YOU.
...I'M TRULY SORRY FOR GETTING YOU CAUGHT UP IN THIS MESS.
ESPECIALLY SINCE I KNOW IT GOES AGAINST BOTH YOUR BIRTH PARENTS' AND ADEL-SHI'S WISHES...
PLEASE, DON'T LET IT WEIGH ON YOU.
AFTER ALL...

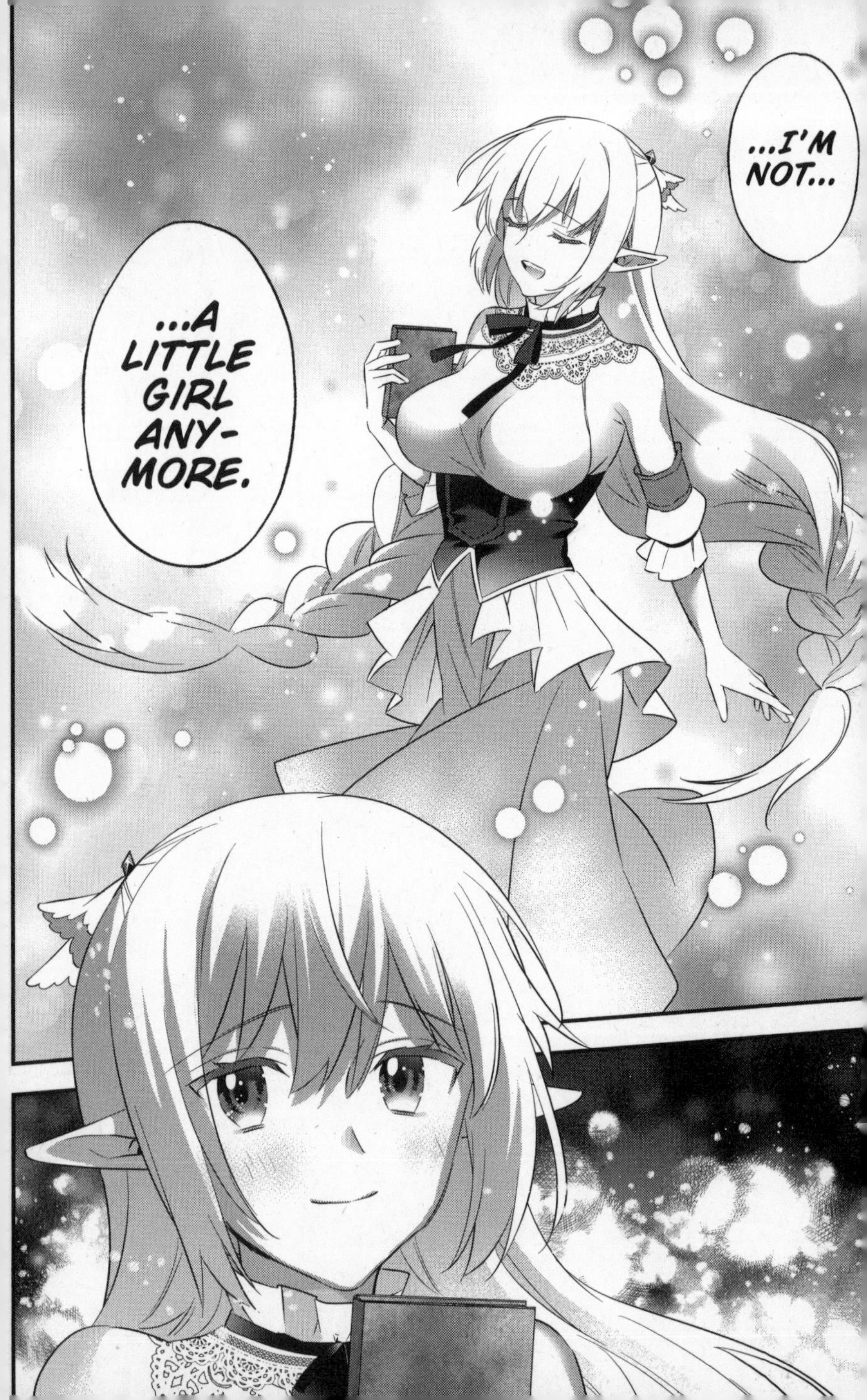
...I'M NOT...
...A LITTLE GIRL ANY-MORE.

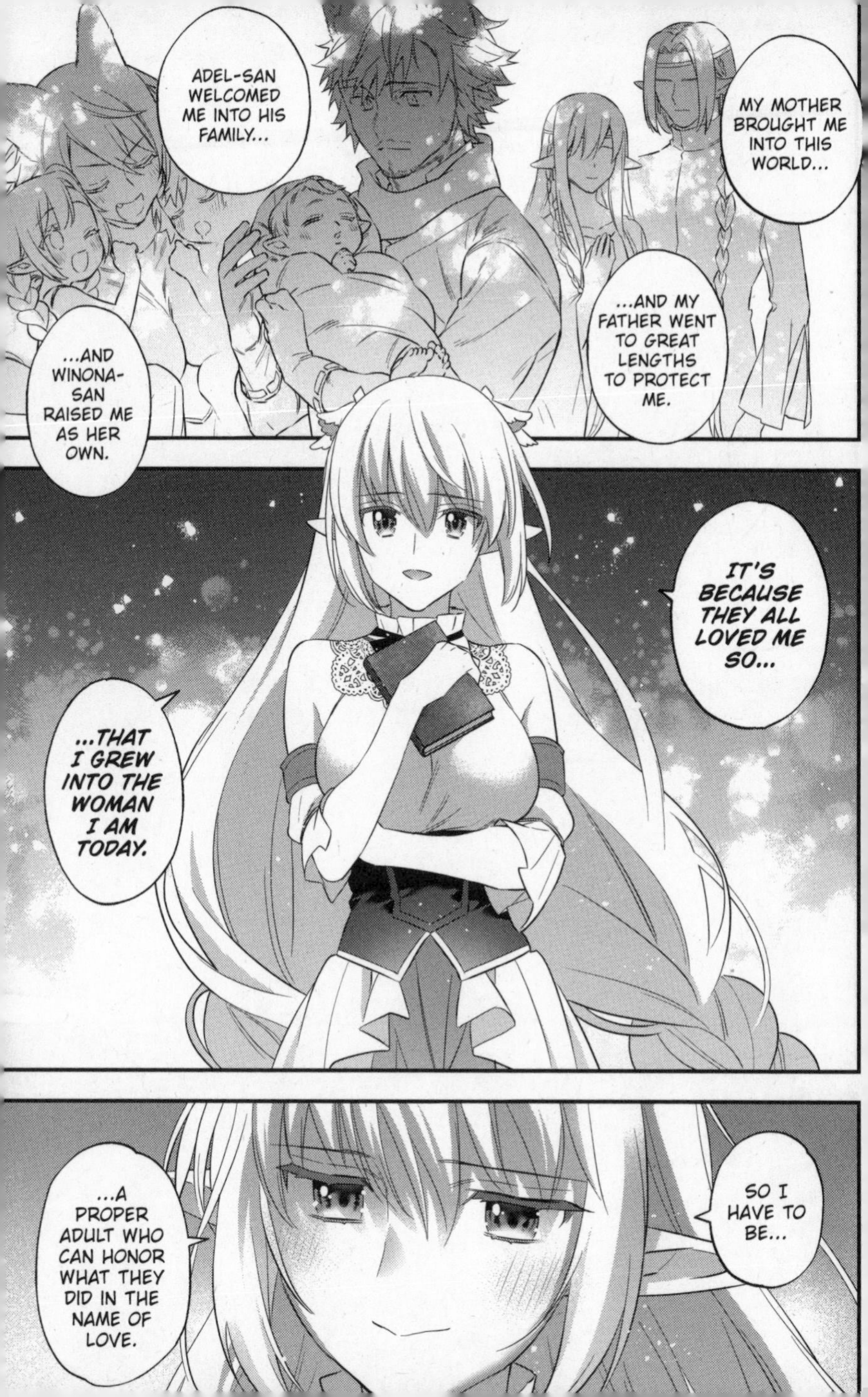
MY MOTHER BROUGHT ME INTO THIS WORLD...
...AND MY FATHER WENT TO GREAT LENGTHS TO PROTECT ME.
ADEL-SAN WELCOMED ME INTO HIS FAMILY...
...AND WINONA-SAN RAISED ME AS HER OWN.
IT'S BECAUSE THEY ALL LOVED ME SO...
...THAT I GREW INTO THE WOMAN I AM TODAY.
SO I HAVE TO BE...
...A PROPER ADULT WHO CAN HONOR WHAT THEY DID IN THE NAME OF LOVE.

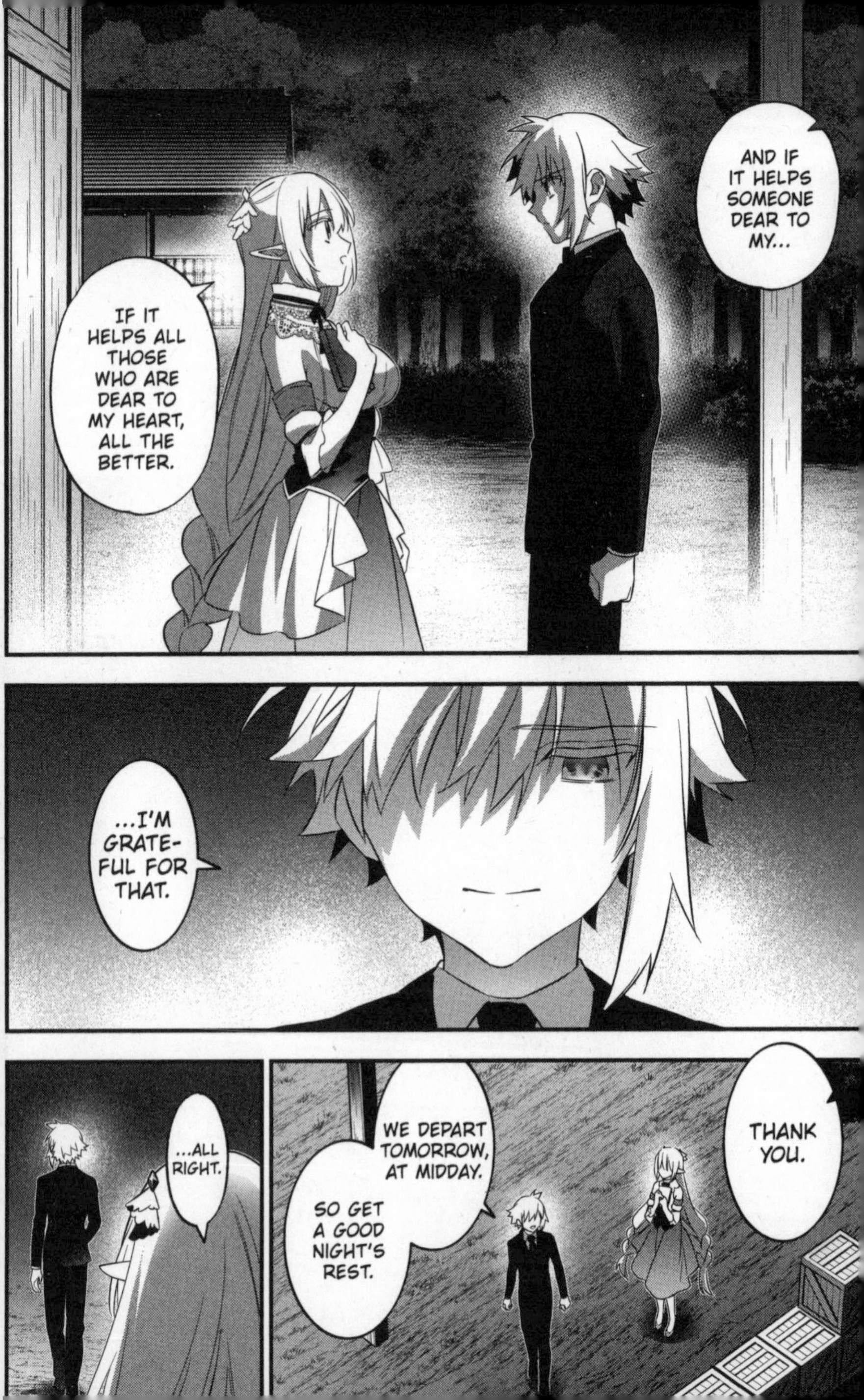
AND IF IT HELPS SOMEONE DEAR TO MY...
IF IT HELPS ALL THOSE WHO ARE DEAR TO MY HEART, ALL THE BETTER.
...I'M GRATE-FUL FOR THAT.
THANK YOU.
WE DEPART TOMORROW, AT MIDDAY.
SO GET A GOOD NIGHT'S REST.
...ALL RIGHT.

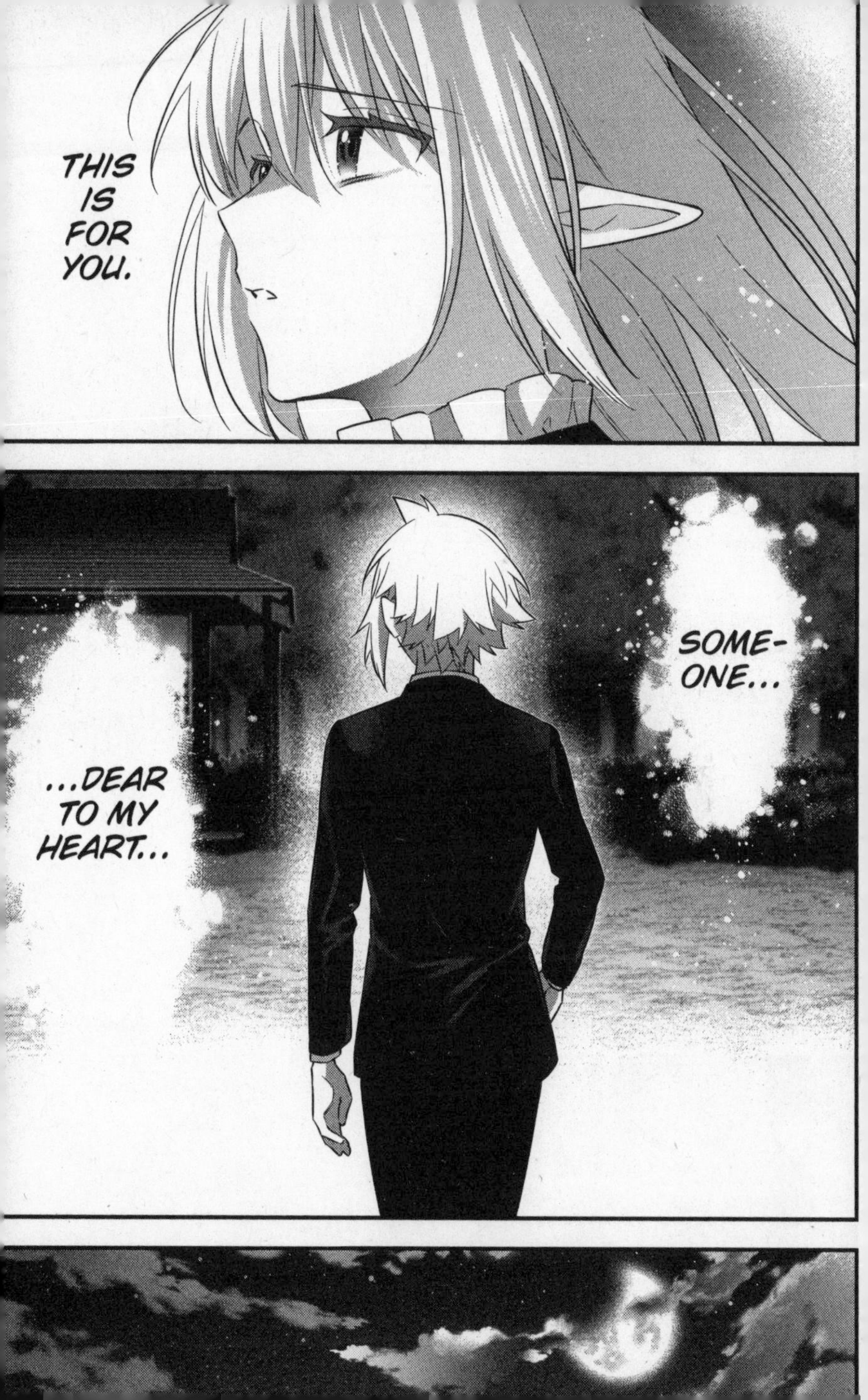
THIS IS FOR YOU.
SOME-ONE...
...DEAR TO MY HEART...

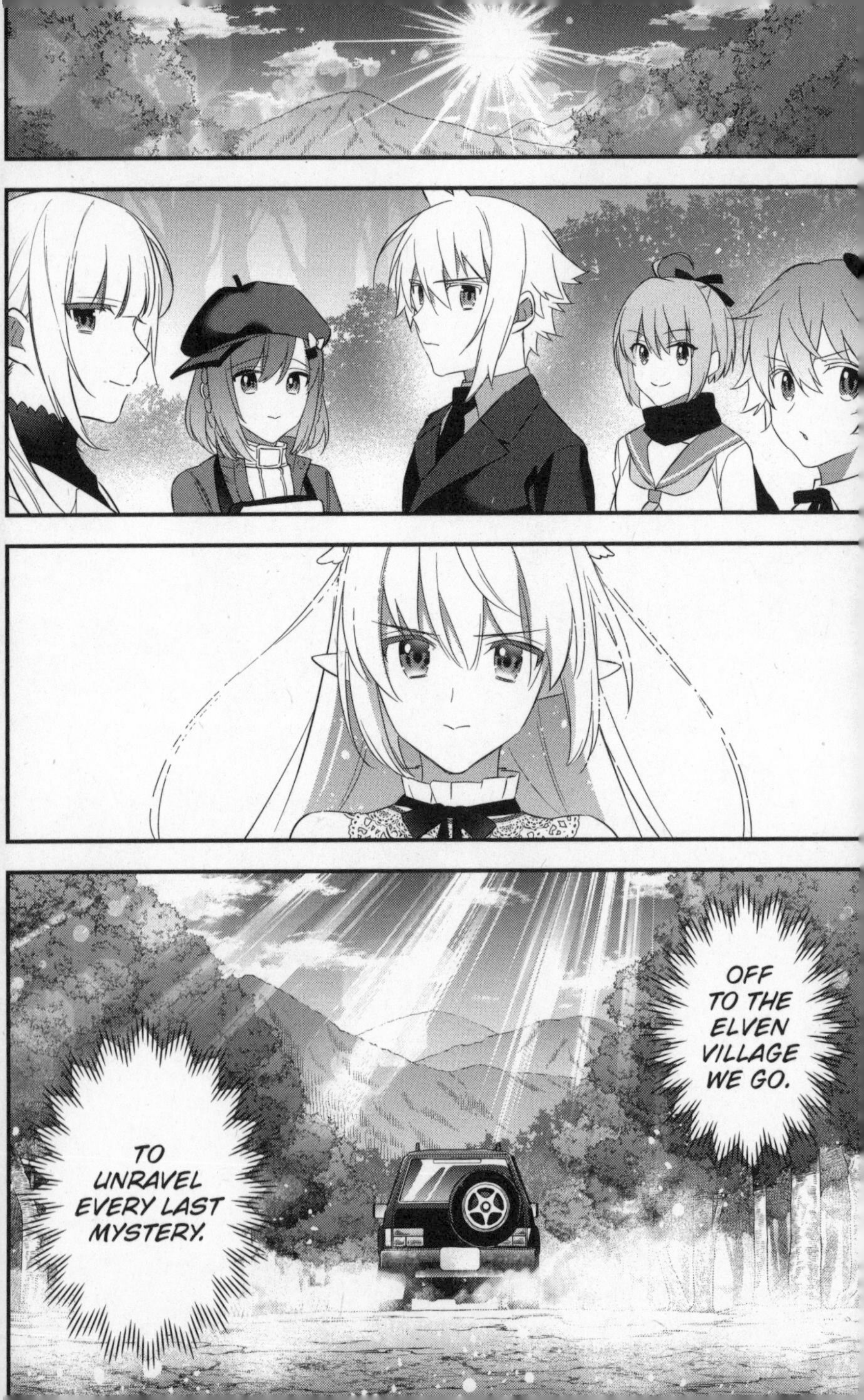
OFF TO THE ELVEN VILLAGE WE GO.
TO UNRAVEL EVERY LAST MYSTERY.

HIGH SCHOOL
PRODIGIES HAVE
IT EASY EVEN IN
ANOTHER
WORLD!

Illustration Gallery (2)

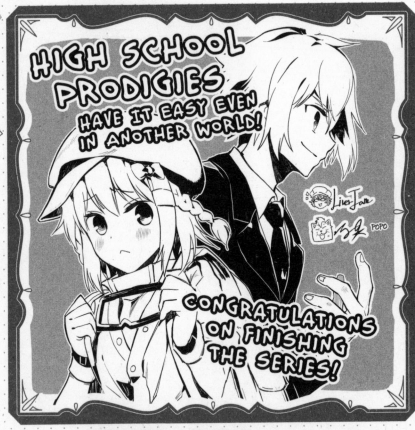

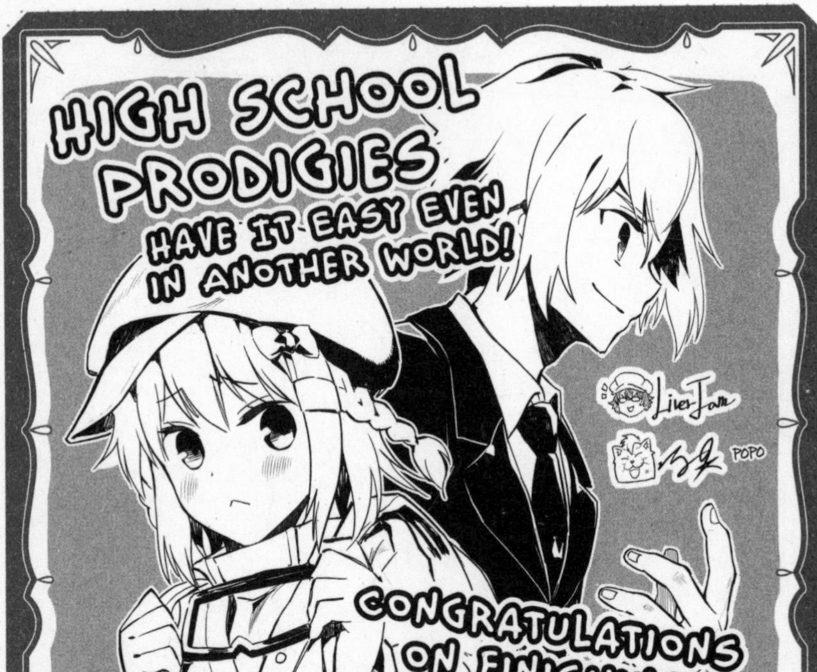
HIGH SCHOOL PRODIGIES HAVE IT EASY EVEN IN ANOTHER WORLD!
LiverJam
POPO
CONGRATULATIONS ON FINISHING THE SERIES!

LIVER JAM-sensei & POPO-sensei

Manga artists for *The Strongest Sage with the Weakest Crest*, featured in Manga UP!

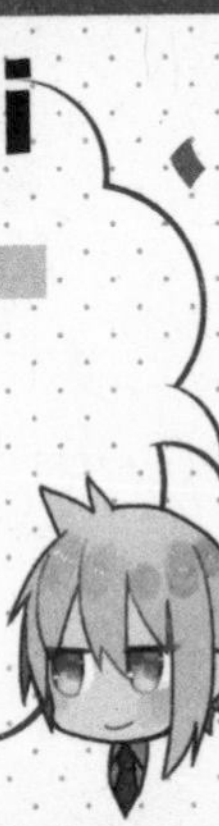

CHAPTER 96: THE DESTINATION AHEAD

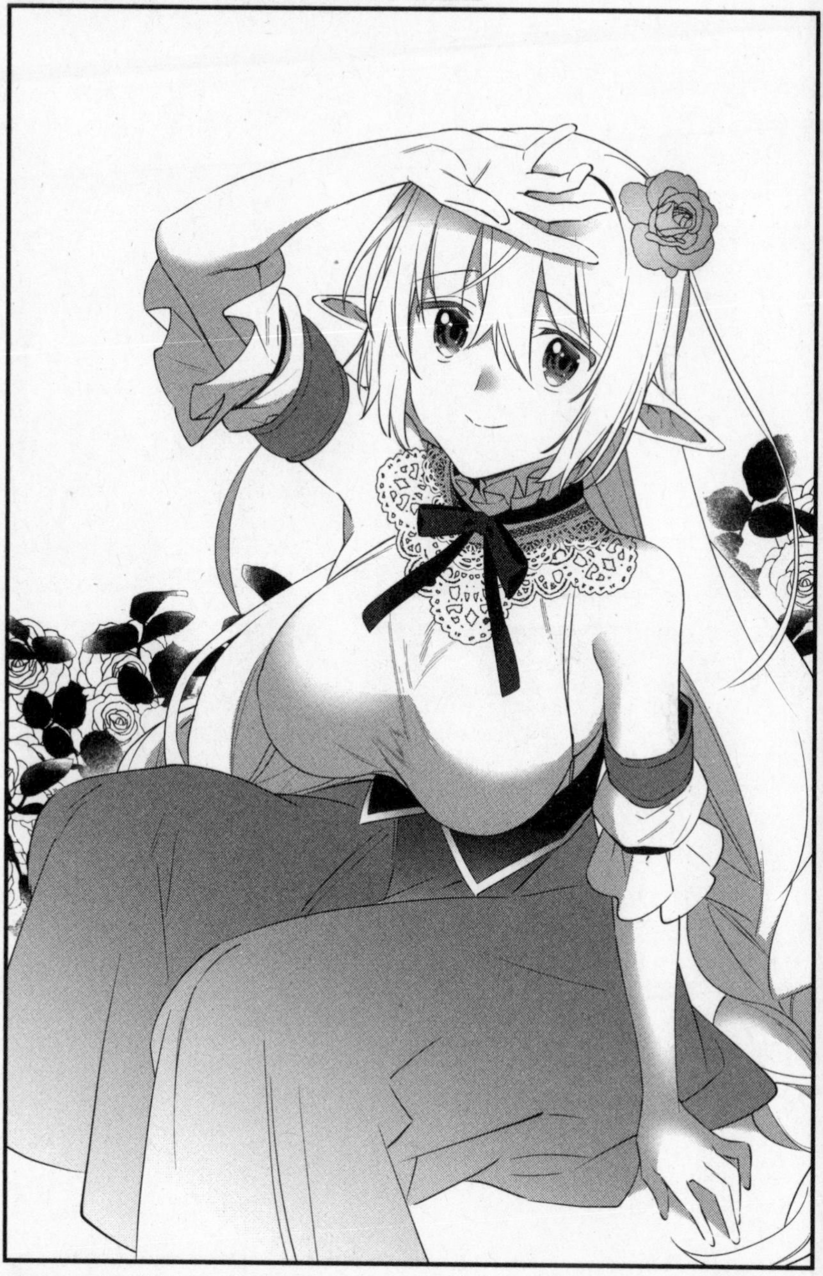

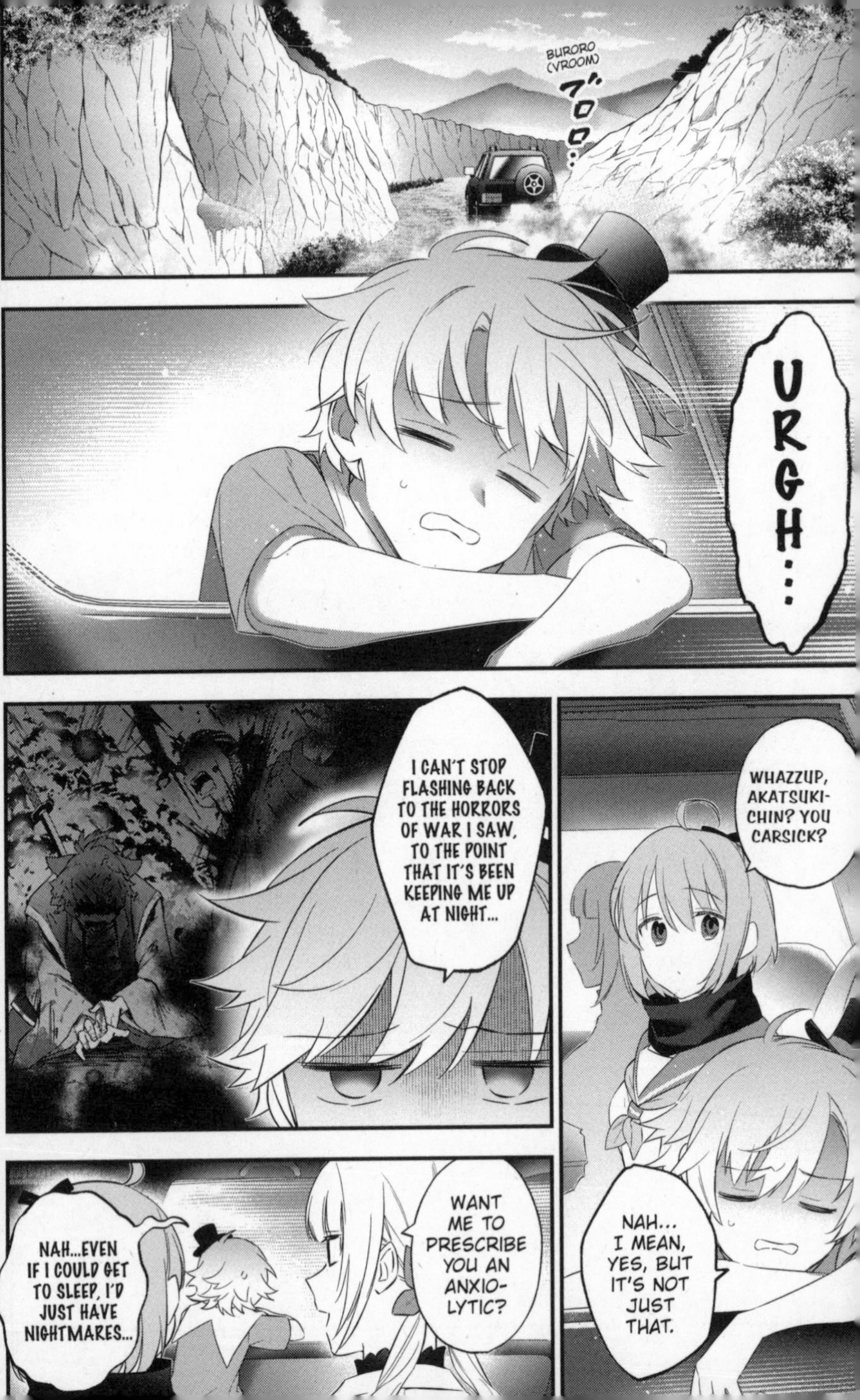
BURORO (VROOM)
URGH...
WHAZZUP, AKATSUKI-CHIN? YOU CARSICK?
NAH... I MEAN, YES, BUT IT'S NOT JUST THAT.
I CAN'T STOP FLASHING BACK TO THE HORRORS OF WAR I SAW, TO THE POINT THAT IT'S BEEN KEEPING ME UP AT NIGHT...
WANT ME TO PRESCRIBE YOU AN ANXIO-LYTIC?
NAH...EVEN IF I COULD GET TO SLEEP, I'D JUST HAVE NIGHTMARES...

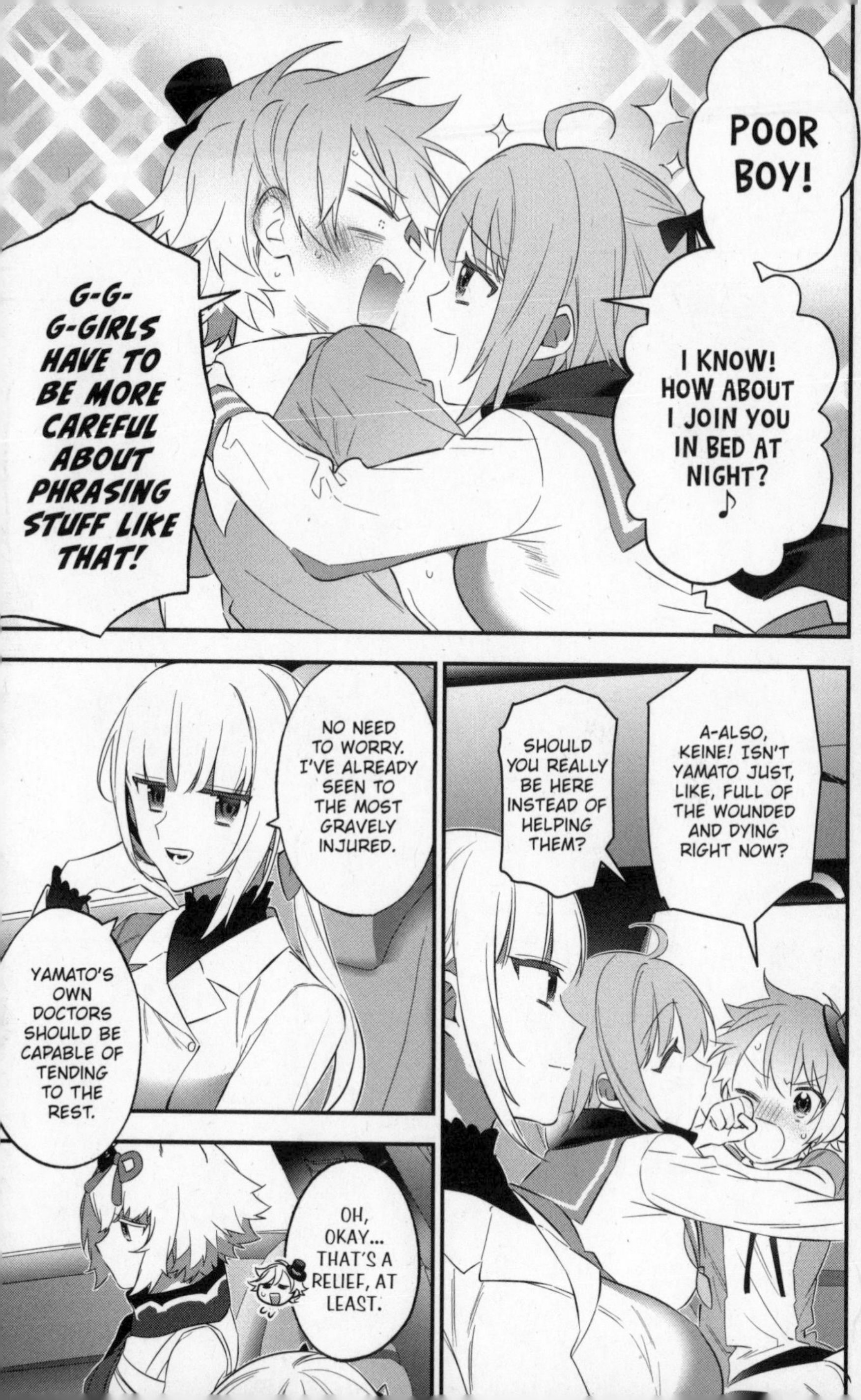
POOR BOY!
I KNOW! HOW ABOUT I JOIN YOU IN BED AT NIGHT? ♪
G-G-G-GIRLS HAVE TO BE MORE CAREFUL ABOUT PHRASING STUFF LIKE THAT!
A-ALSO, KEINE! ISN'T YAMATO JUST, LIKE, FULL OF THE WOUNDED AND DYING RIGHT NOW?
SHOULD YOU REALLY BE HERE INSTEAD OF HELPING THEM?
NO NEED TO WORRY. I'VE ALREADY SEEN TO THE MOST GRAVELY INJURED.
YAMATO'S OWN DOCTORS SHOULD BE CAPABLE OF TENDING TO THE REST.
OH, OKAY... THAT'S A RELIEF, AT LEAST.

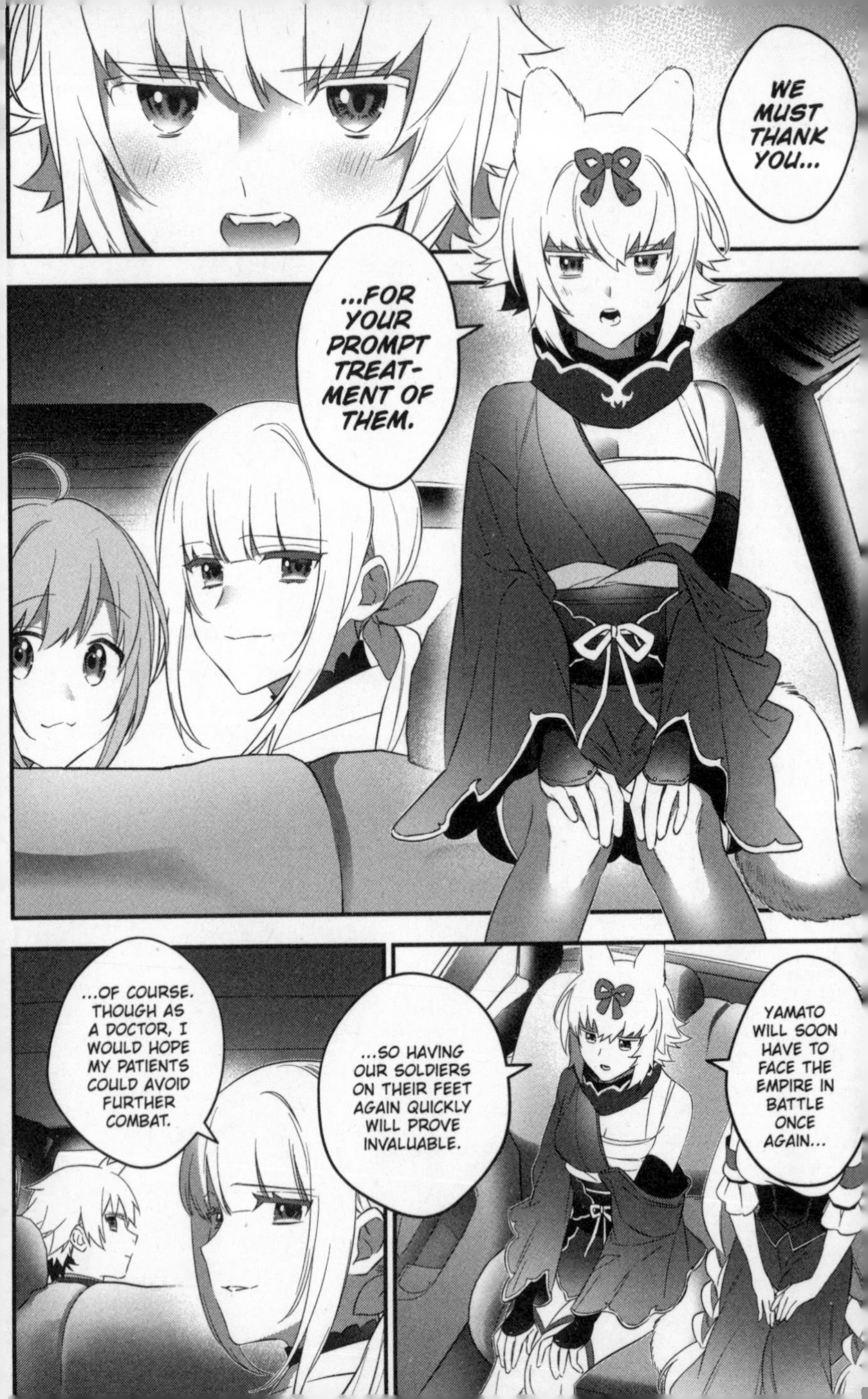
WE MUST THANK YOU...
...FOR YOUR PROMPT TREAT-MENT OF THEM.
YAMATO WILL SOON HAVE TO FACE THE EMPIRE IN BATTLE ONCE AGAIN...
...SO HAVING OUR SOLDIERS ON THEIR FEET AGAIN QUICKLY WILL PROVE INVALUABLE.
...OF COURSE. THOUGH AS A DOCTOR, I WOULD HOPE MY PATIENTS COULD AVOID FURTHER COMBAT.

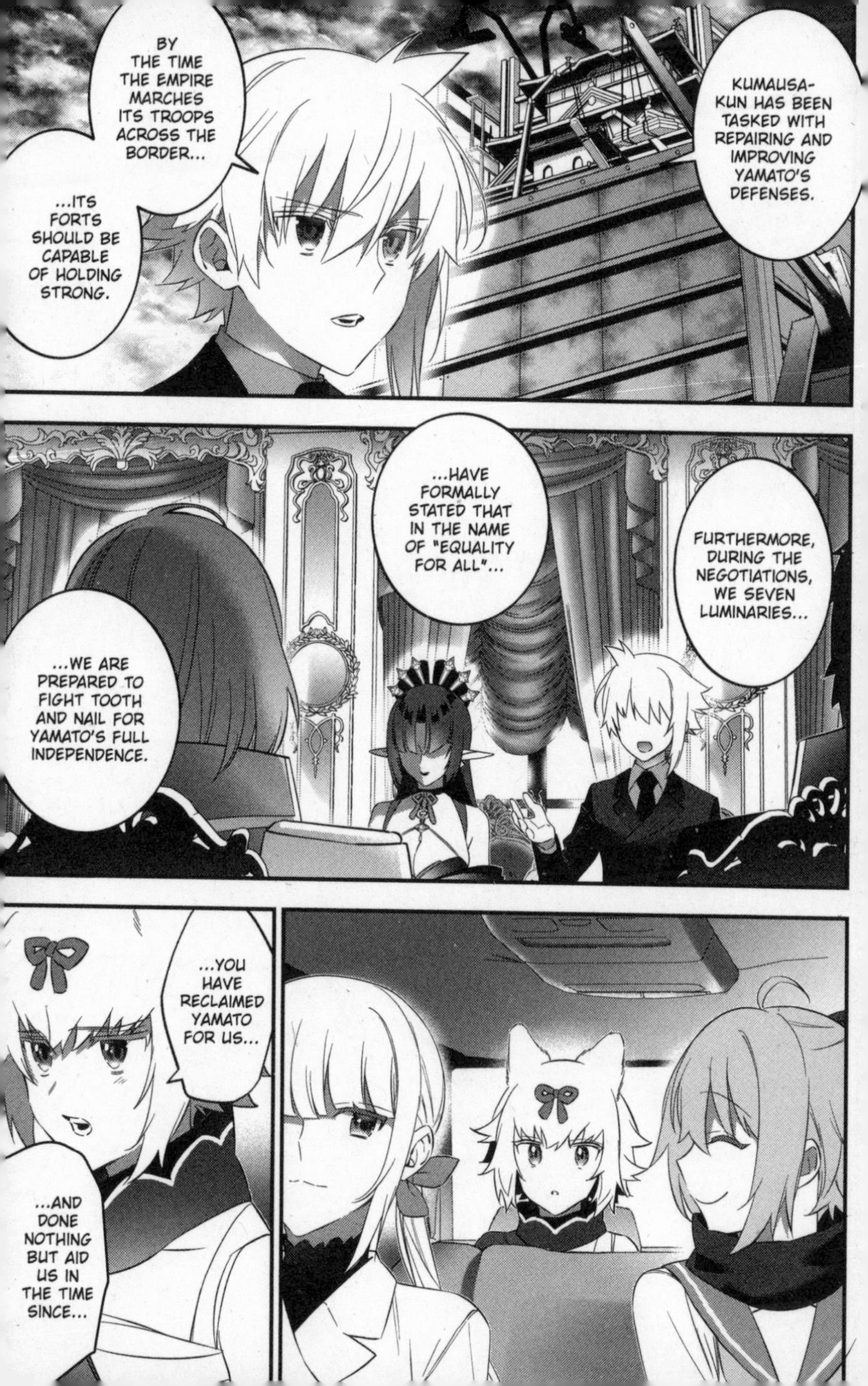
KUMAUSA-KUN HAS BEEN TASKED WITH REPAIRING AND IMPROVING YAMATO'S DEFENSES.
BY THE TIME THE EMPIRE MARCHES ITS TROOPS ACROSS THE BORDER...
...ITS FORTS SHOULD BE CAPABLE OF HOLDING STRONG.
FURTHERMORE, DURING THE NEGOTIATIONS, WE SEVEN LUMINARIES...
...HAVE FORMALLY STATED THAT IN THE NAME OF "EQUALITY FOR ALL"...
...WE ARE PREPARED TO FIGHT TOOTH AND NAIL FOR YAMATO'S FULL INDEPENDENCE.
...YOU HAVE RECLAIMED YAMATO FOR US...
...AND DONE NOTHING BUT AID US IN THE TIME SINCE...

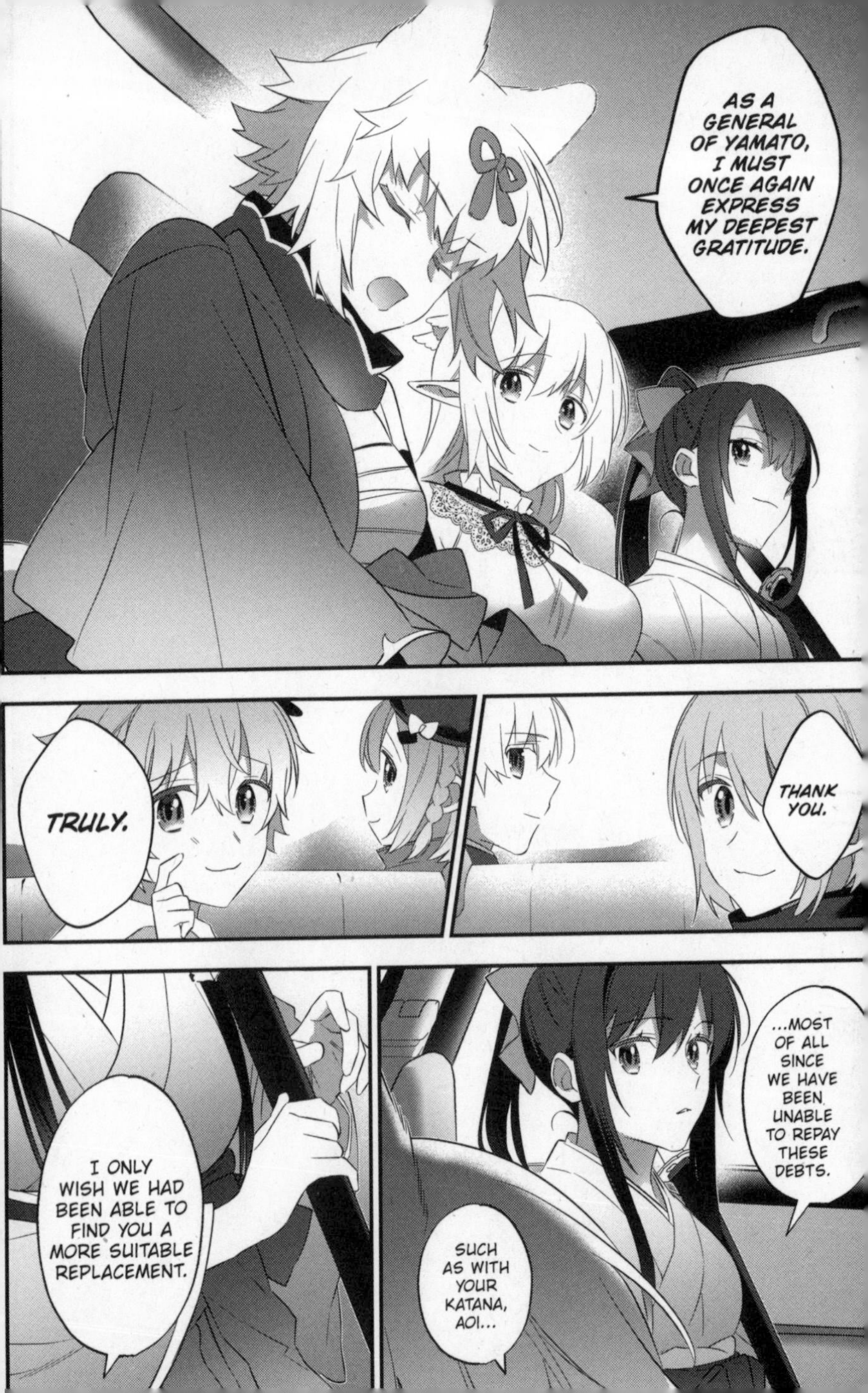
AS A GENERAL OF YAMATO, I MUST ONCE AGAIN EXPRESS MY DEEPEST GRATITUDE.
THANK YOU.
TRULY.
...MOST OF ALL SINCE WE HAVE BEEN UNABLE TO REPAY THESE DEBTS.
SUCH AS WITH YOUR KATANA, AOI...
I ONLY WISH WE HAD BEEN ABLE TO FIND YOU A MORE SUITABLE REPLACEMENT.

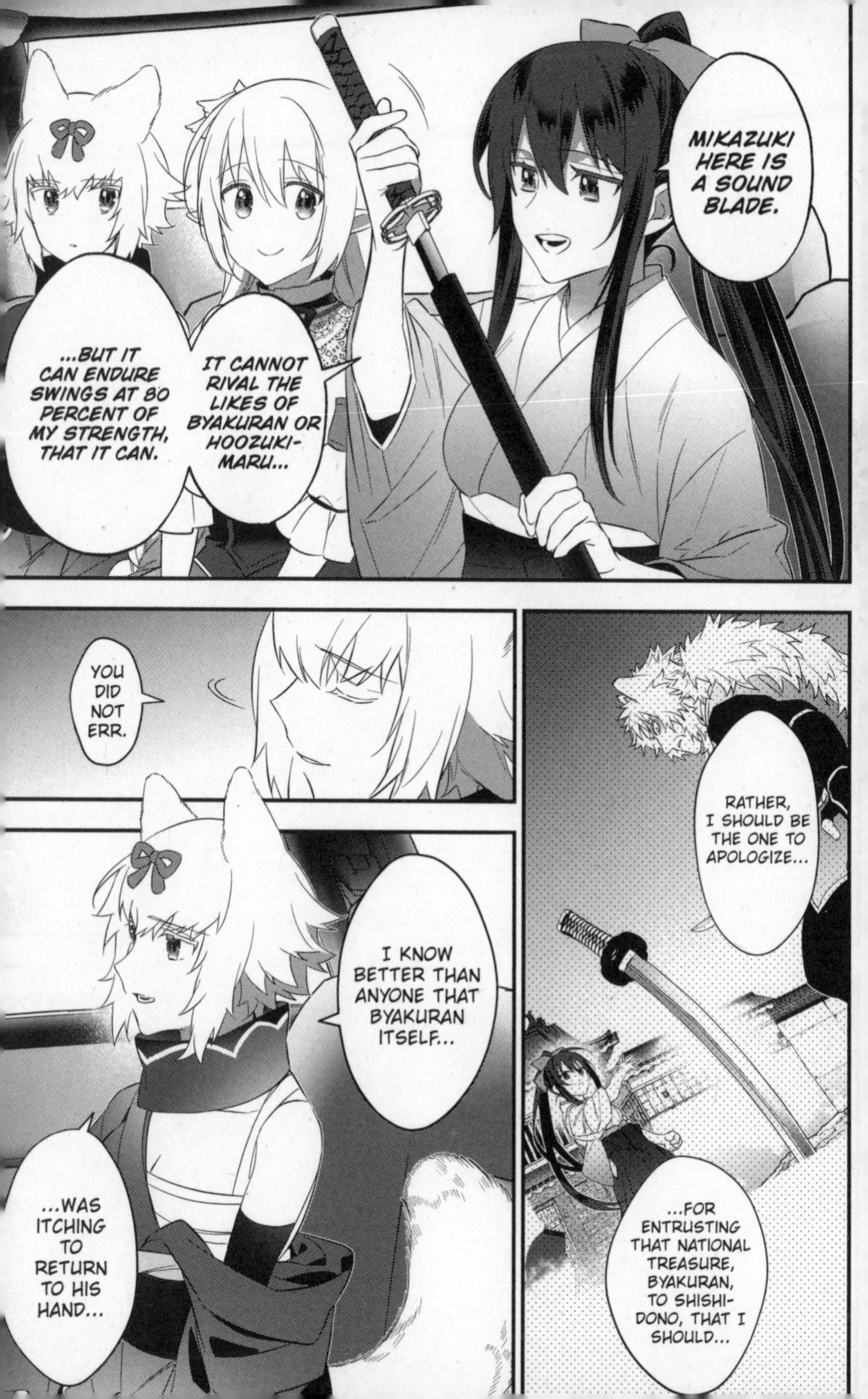
MIKAZUKI HERE IS A SOUND BLADE.
IT CANNOT RIVAL THE LIKES OF BYAKURAN OR HOOZUKI-MARU...
...BUT IT CAN ENDURE SWINGS AT 80 PERCENT OF MY STRENGTH, THAT IT CAN.
RATHER, I SHOULD BE THE ONE TO APOLOGIZE...
...FOR ENTRUSTING THAT NATIONAL TREASURE, BYAKURAN, TO SHISHI-DONO, THAT I SHOULD...
YOU DID NOT ERR.
I KNOW BETTER THAN ANYONE THAT BYAKURAN ITSELF...
...WAS ITCHING TO RETURN TO HIS HAND...

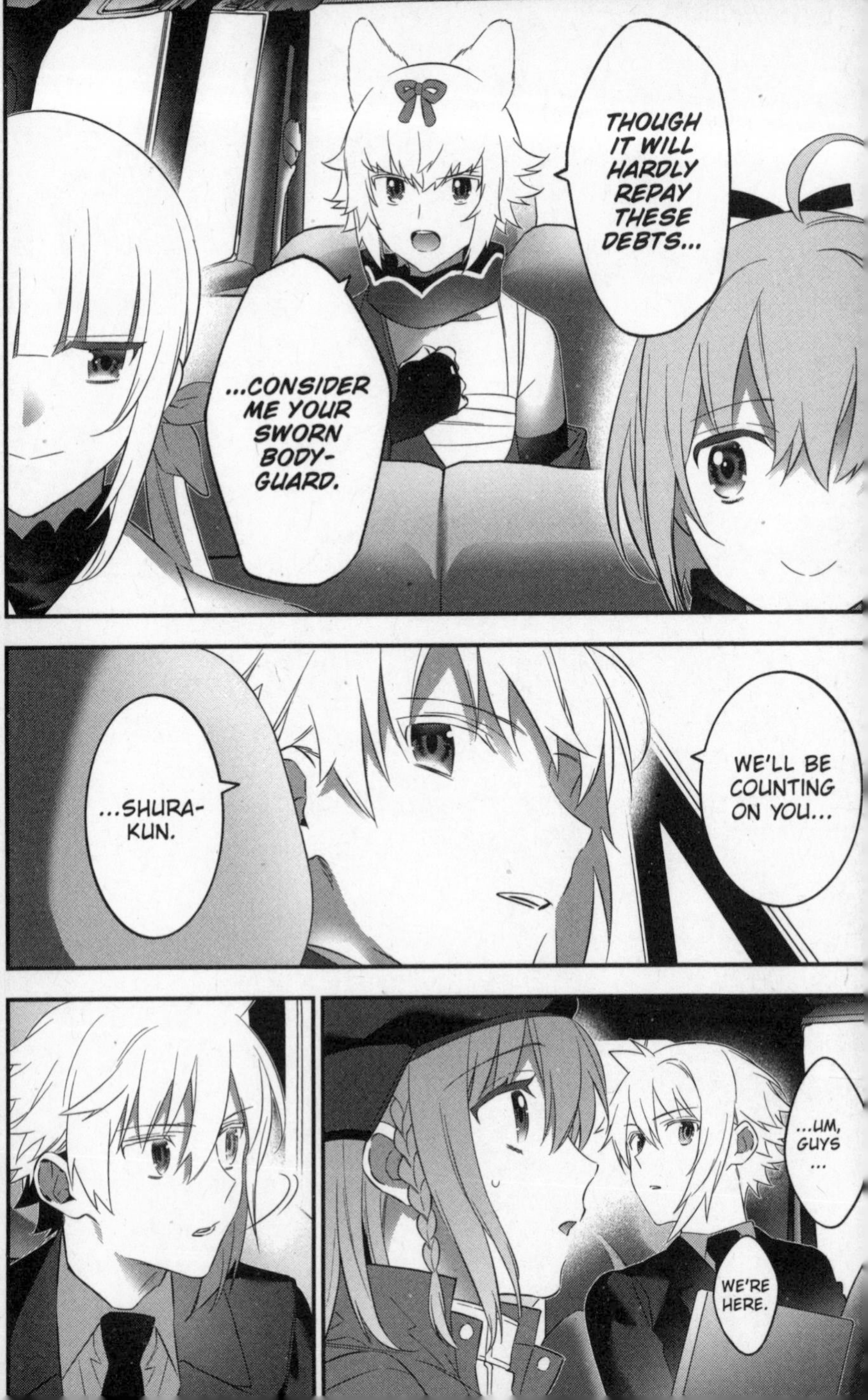
THOUGH IT WILL HARDLY REPAY THESE DEBTS...
...CONSIDER ME YOUR SWORN BODY-GUARD.
WE'LL BE COUNTING ON YOU...
...SHURA-KUN.
...UM, GUYS ...
WE'RE HERE.

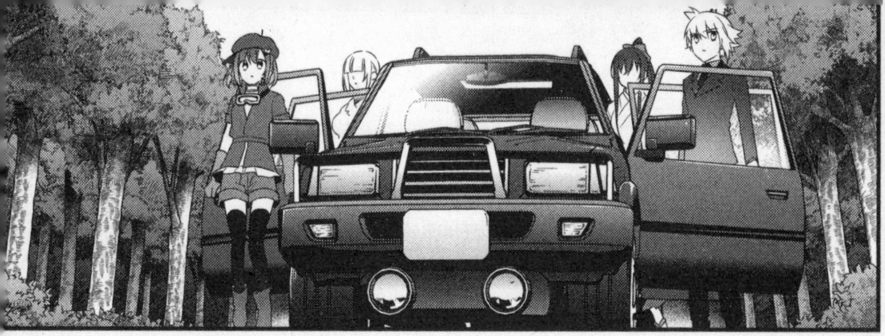
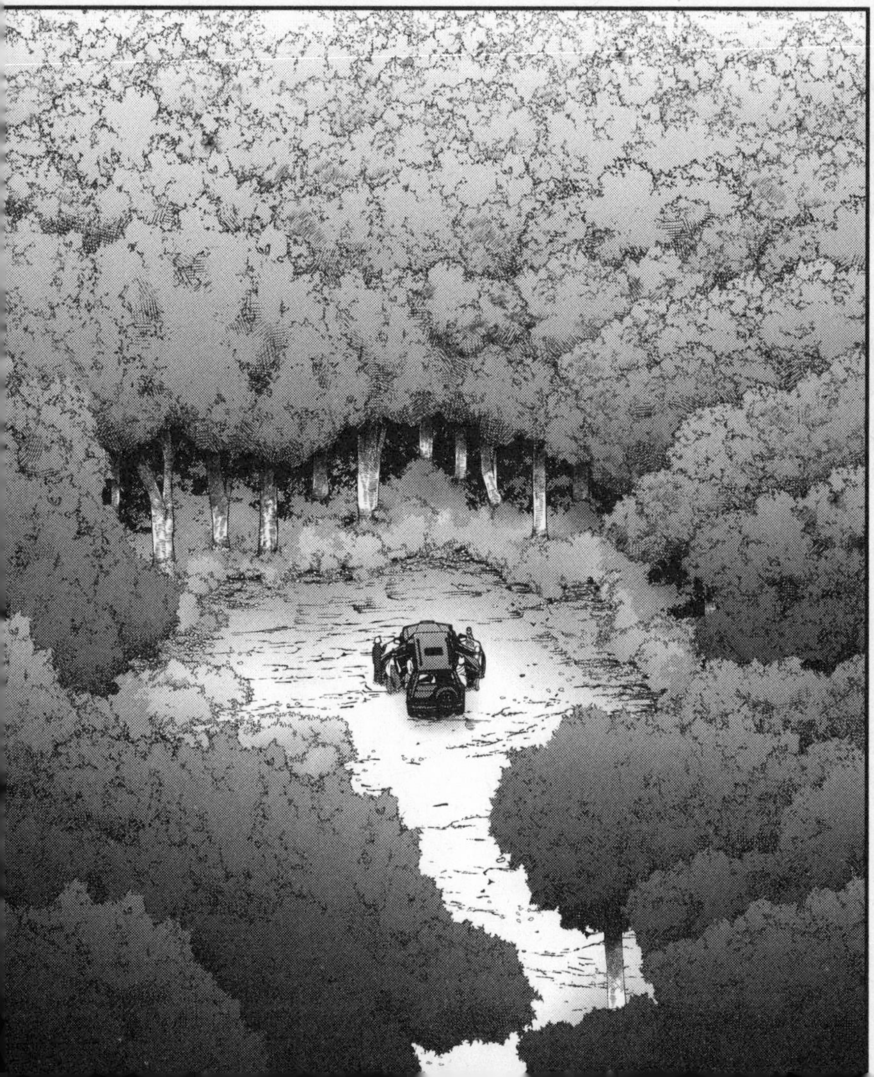

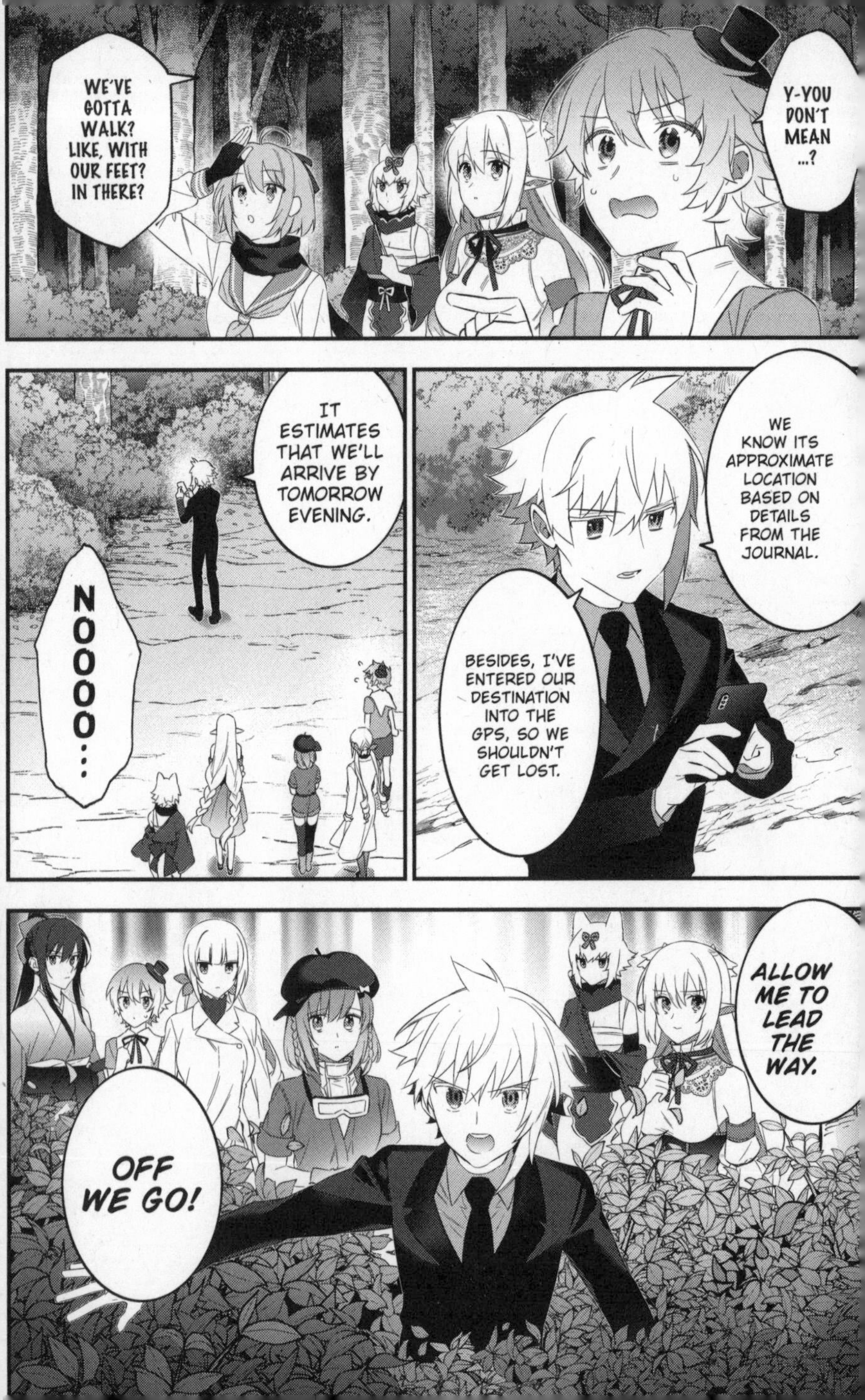
Y-YOU DON'T MEAN ...?
WE'VE GOTTA WALK? LIKE, WITH OUR FEET? IN THERE?
WE KNOW ITS APPROXIMATE LOCATION BASED ON DETAILS FROM THE JOURNAL.
BESIDES, I'VE ENTERED OUR DESTINATION INTO THE GPS, SO WE SHOULDN'T GET LOST.
IT ESTIMATES THAT WE'LL ARRIVE BY TOMORROW EVENING.
NOOOOO...
ALLOW ME TO LEAD THE WAY.
OFF WE GO!

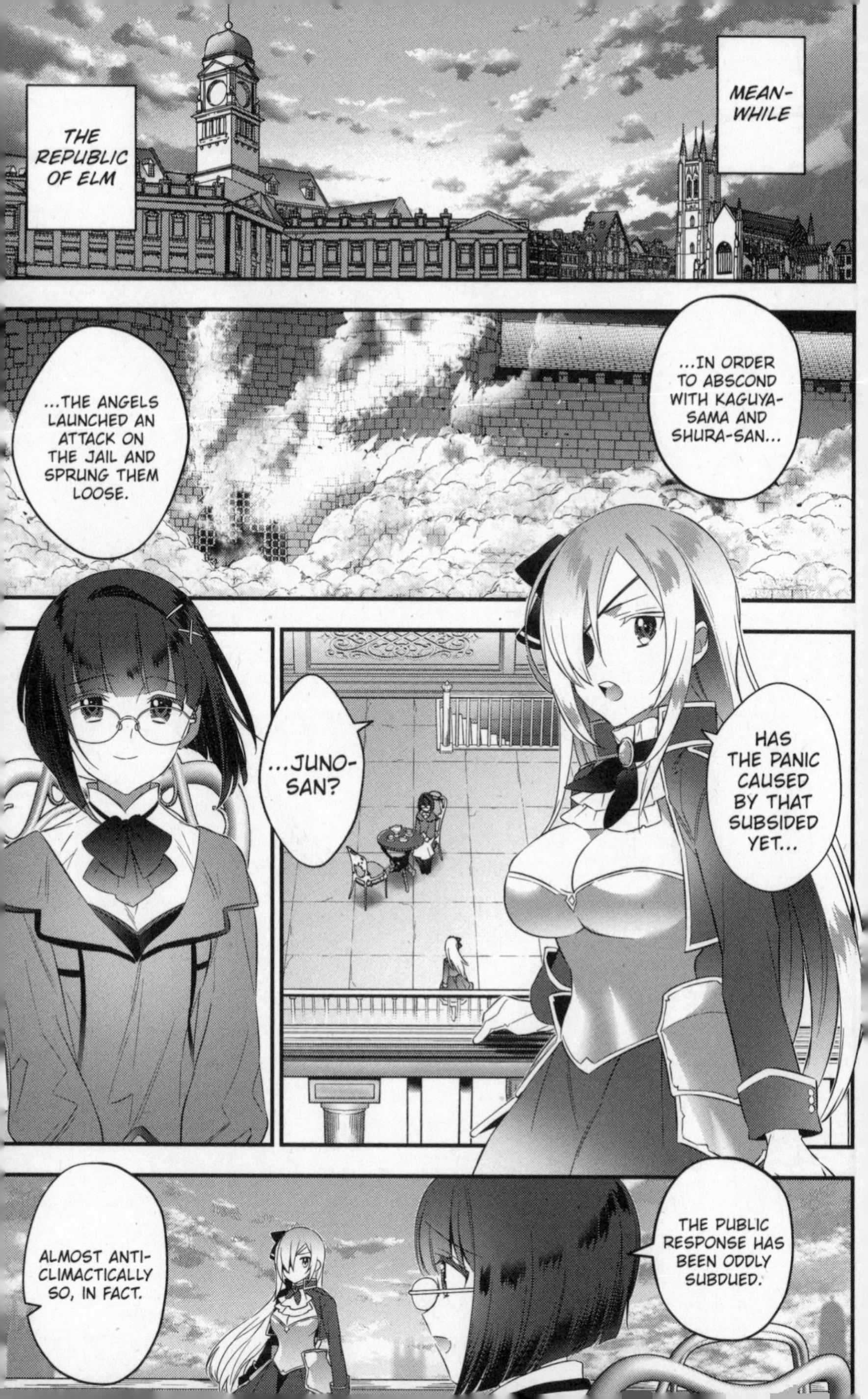
MEAN-WHILE
THE REPUBLIC OF ELM
...IN ORDER TO ABSCOND WITH KAGUYA-SAMA AND SHURA-SAN...
...THE ANGELS LAUNCHED AN ATTACK ON THE JAIL AND SPRUNG THEM LOOSE.
HAS THE PANIC CAUSED BY THAT SUBSIDED YET...
...JUNO-SAN?
THE PUBLIC RESPONSE HAS BEEN ODDLY SUBDUED.
ALMOST ANTI-CLIMACTICALLY SO, IN FACT.

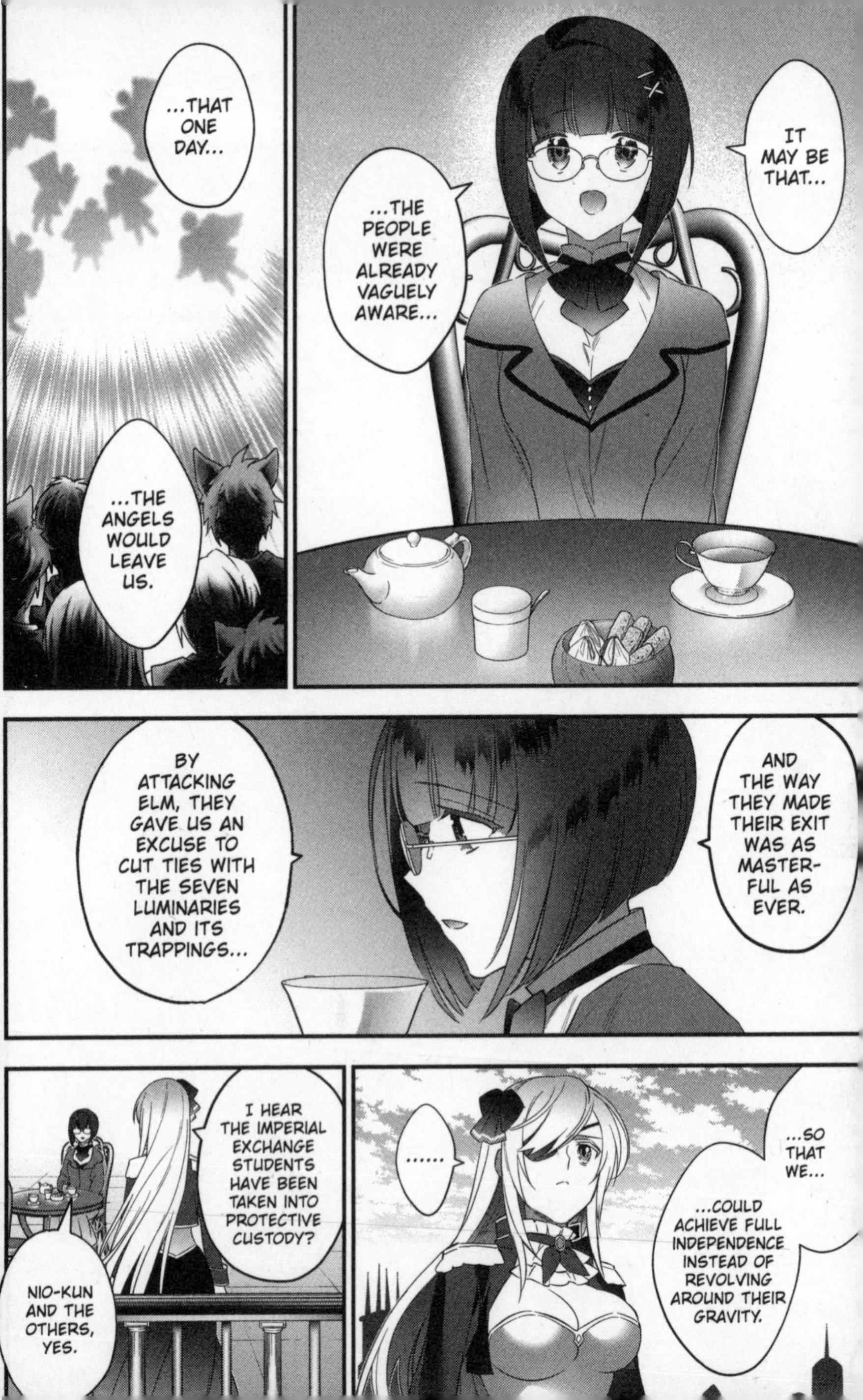
IT MAY BE THAT...
...THE PEOPLE WERE ALREADY VAGUELY AWARE...
...THAT ONE DAY...
...THE ANGELS WOULD LEAVE US.
AND THE WAY THEY MADE THEIR EXIT WAS AS MASTER-FUL AS EVER.
BY ATTACKING ELM, THEY GAVE US AN EXCUSE TO CUT TIES WITH THE SEVEN LUMINARIES AND ITS TRAPPINGS...
...SO THAT WE...
...COULD ACHIEVE FULL INDEPENDENCE INSTEAD OF REVOLVING AROUND THEIR GRAVITY.
......
I HEAR THE IMPERIAL EXCHANGE STUDENTS HAVE BEEN TAKEN INTO PROTECTIVE CUSTODY?
NIO-KUN AND THE OTHERS, YES.

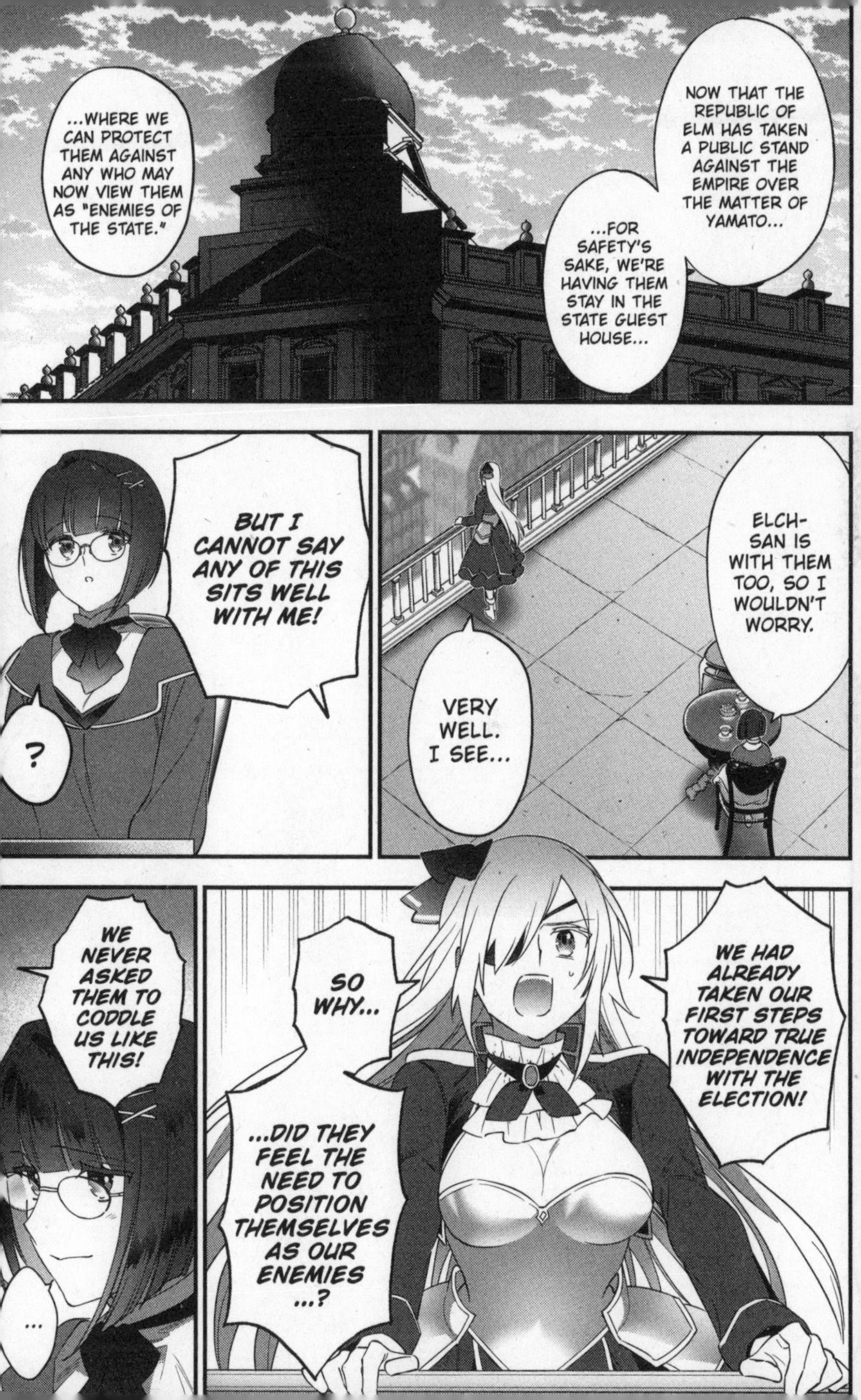
NOW THAT THE REPUBLIC OF ELM HAS TAKEN A PUBLIC STAND AGAINST THE EMPIRE OVER THE MATTER OF YAMATO...
...FOR SAFETY'S SAKE, WE'RE HAVING THEM STAY IN THE STATE GUEST HOUSE...
...WHERE WE CAN PROTECT THEM AGAINST ANY WHO MAY NOW VIEW THEM AS "ENEMIES OF THE STATE."
ELCH-SAN IS WITH THEM TOO, SO I WOULDN'T WORRY.
VERY WELL. I SEE...
BUT I CANNOT SAY ANY OF THIS SITS WELL WITH ME!
?
WE HAD ALREADY TAKEN OUR FIRST STEPS TOWARD TRUE INDEPENDENCE WITH THE ELECTION!
SO WHY...
...DID THEY FEEL THE NEED TO POSITION THEMSELVES AS OUR ENEMIES ...?
WE NEVER ASKED THEM TO CODDLE US LIKE THIS!
...

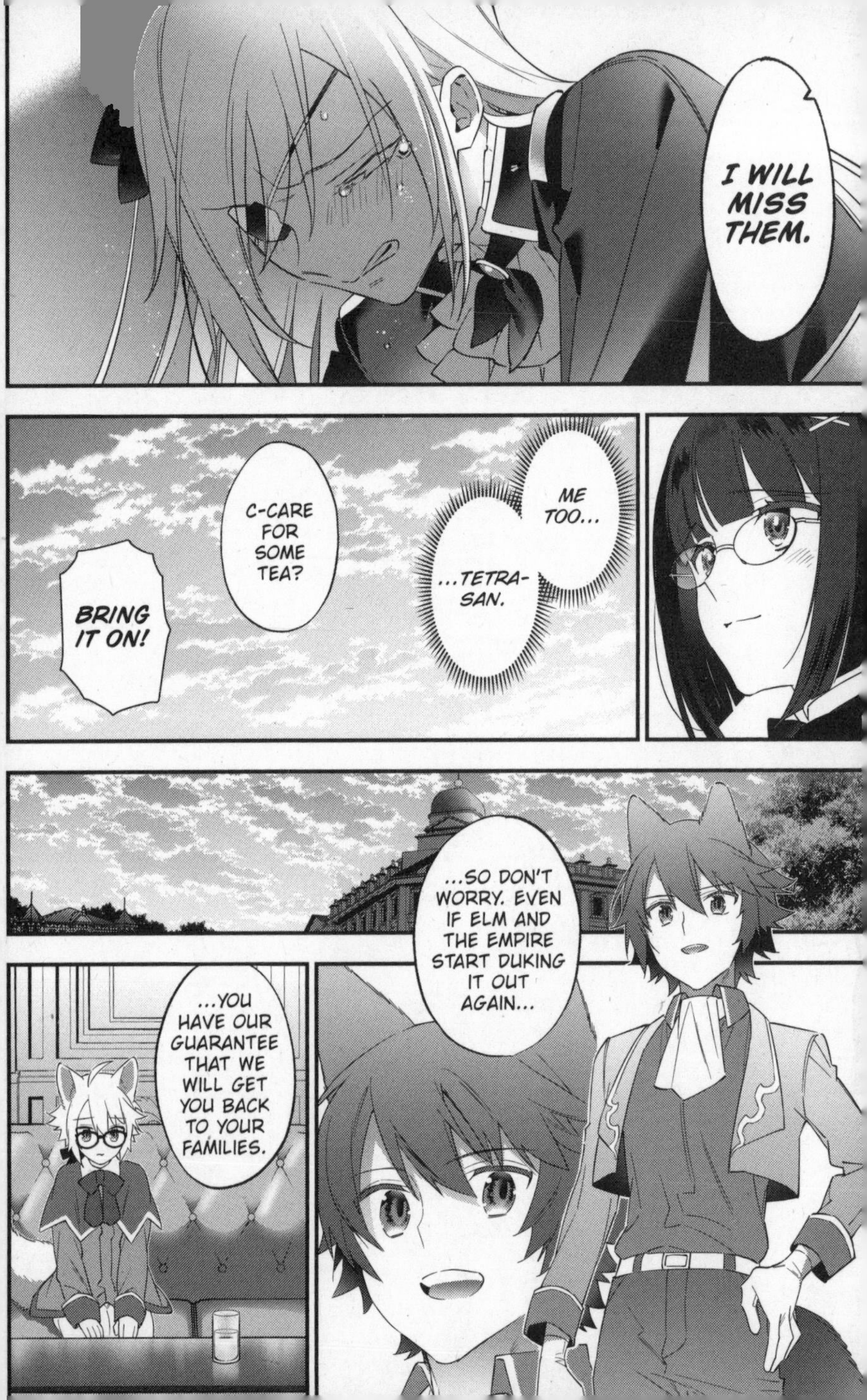
I WILL MISS THEM.
ME TOO...
...TETRA-SAN.
C-CARE FOR SOME TEA?
BRING IT ON!
...SO DON'T WORRY. EVEN IF ELM AND THE EMPIRE START DUKING IT OUT AGAIN...
...YOU HAVE OUR GUARANTEE THAT WE WILL GET YOU BACK TO YOUR FAMILIES.

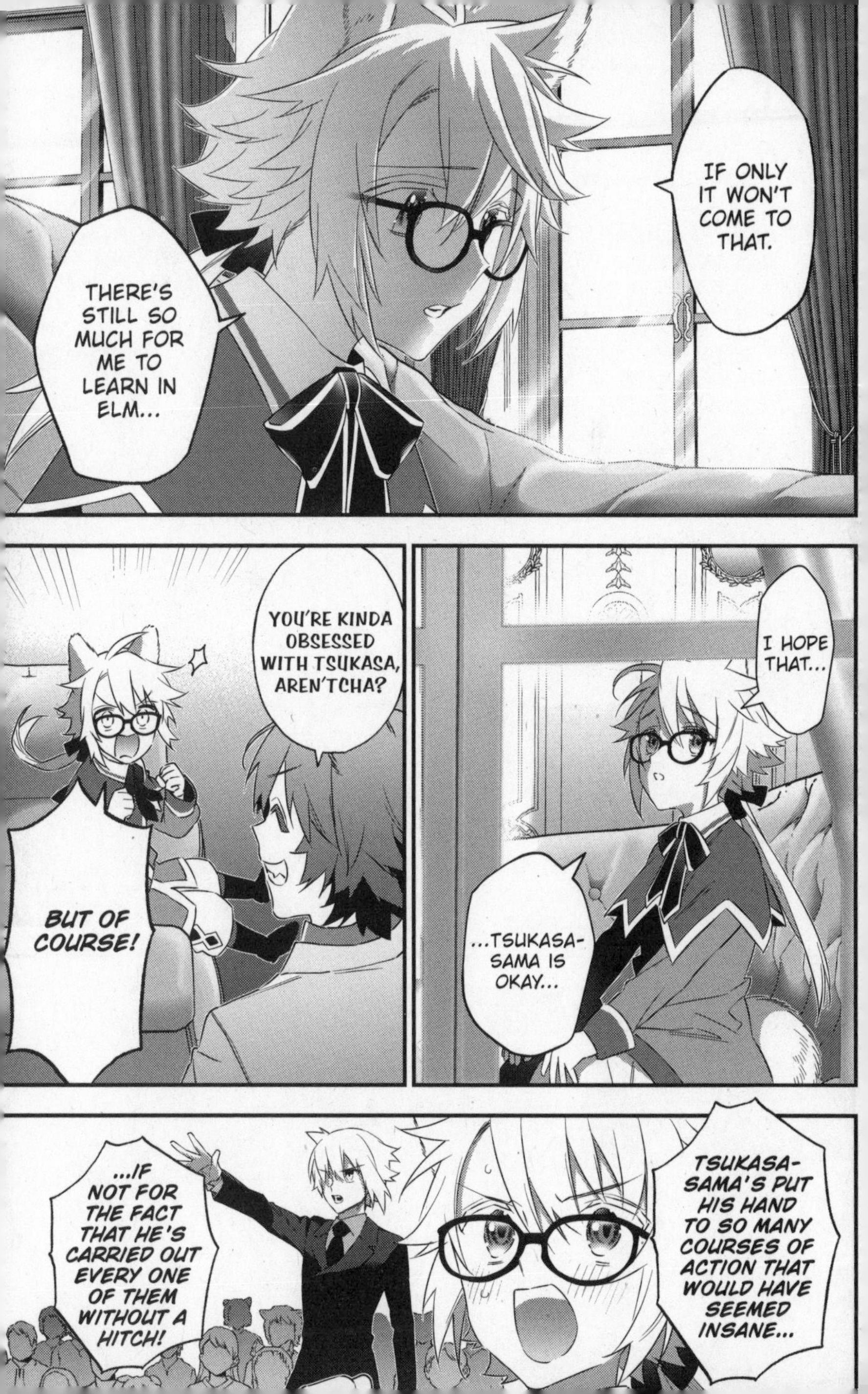
IF ONLY IT WON'T COME TO THAT.
THERE'S STILL SO MUCH FOR ME TO LEARN IN ELM...
I HOPE THAT...
...TSUKASA-SAMA IS OKAY...
YOU'RE KINDA OBSESSED WITH TSUKASA, AREN'TCHA?
BUT OF COURSE!
TSUKASA-SAMA'S PUT HIS HAND TO SO MANY COURSES OF ACTION THAT WOULD HAVE SEEMED INSANE...
...IF NOT FOR THE FACT THAT HE'S CARRIED OUT EVERY ONE OF THEM WITHOUT A HITCH!

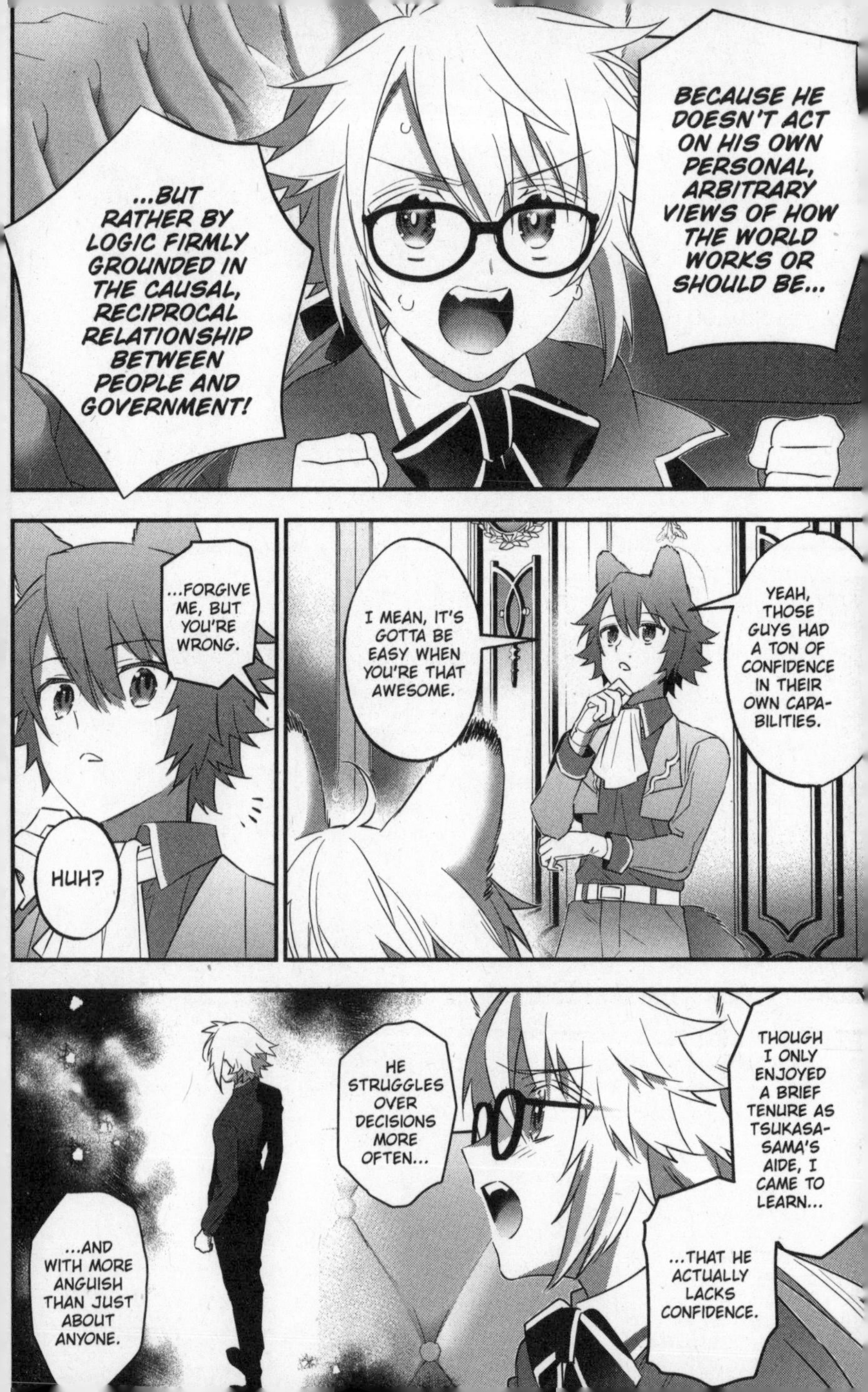
BECAUSE HE DOESN'T ACT ON HIS OWN PERSONAL, ARBITRARY VIEWS OF HOW THE WORLD WORKS OR SHOULD BE...
...BUT RATHER BY LOGIC FIRMLY GROUNDED IN THE CAUSAL, RECIPROCAL RELATIONSHIP BETWEEN PEOPLE AND GOVERNMENT!
YEAH, THOSE GUYS HAD A TON OF CONFIDENCE IN THEIR OWN CAPA-BILITIES.
I MEAN, IT'S GOTTA BE EASY WHEN YOU'RE THAT AWESOME.
...FORGIVE ME, BUT YOU'RE WRONG.
HUH?
THOUGH I ONLY ENJOYED A BRIEF TENURE AS TSUKASA-SAMA'S AIDE, I CAME TO LEARN...
...THAT HE ACTUALLY LACKS CONFIDENCE.
HE STRUGGLES OVER DECISIONS MORE OFTEN...
...AND WITH MORE ANGUISH THAN JUST ABOUT ANYONE.

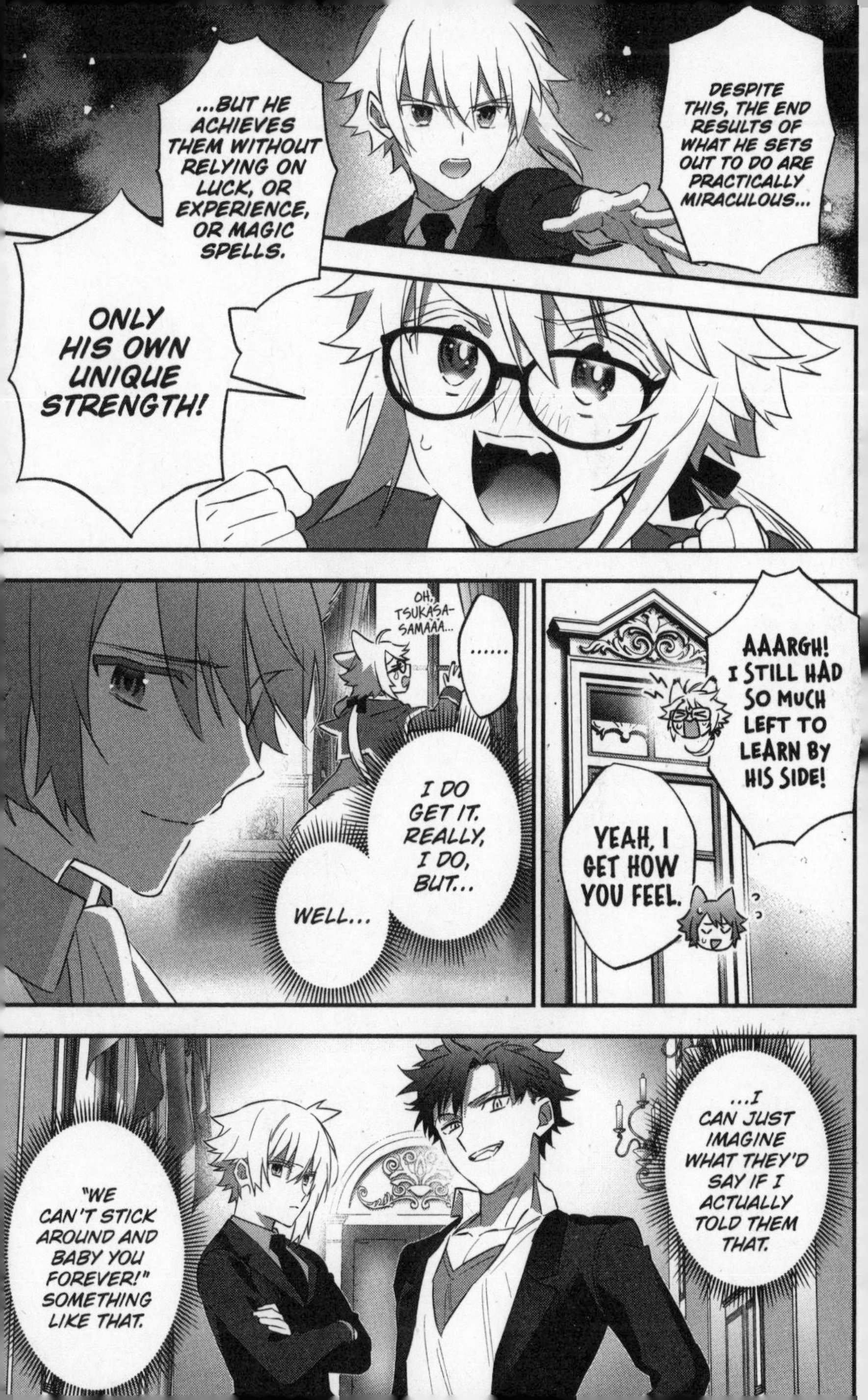
DESPITE THIS, THE END RESULTS OF WHAT HE SETS OUT TO DO ARE PRACTICALLY MIRACULOUS...
...BUT HE ACHIEVES THEM WITHOUT RELYING ON LUCK, OR EXPERIENCE, OR MAGIC SPELLS.
ONLY HIS OWN UNIQUE STRENGTH!
AAARGH! I STILL HAD SO MUCH LEFT TO LEARN BY HIS SIDE!
YEAH, I GET HOW YOU FEEL.
OH, TSUKASA-SAMAAA...
......
I DO GET IT. REALLY, I DO, BUT...
WELL...
...I CAN JUST IMAGINE WHAT THEY'D SAY IF I ACTUALLY TOLD THEM THAT.
"WE CAN'T STICK AROUND AND BABY YOU FOREVER!" SOMETHING LIKE THAT.

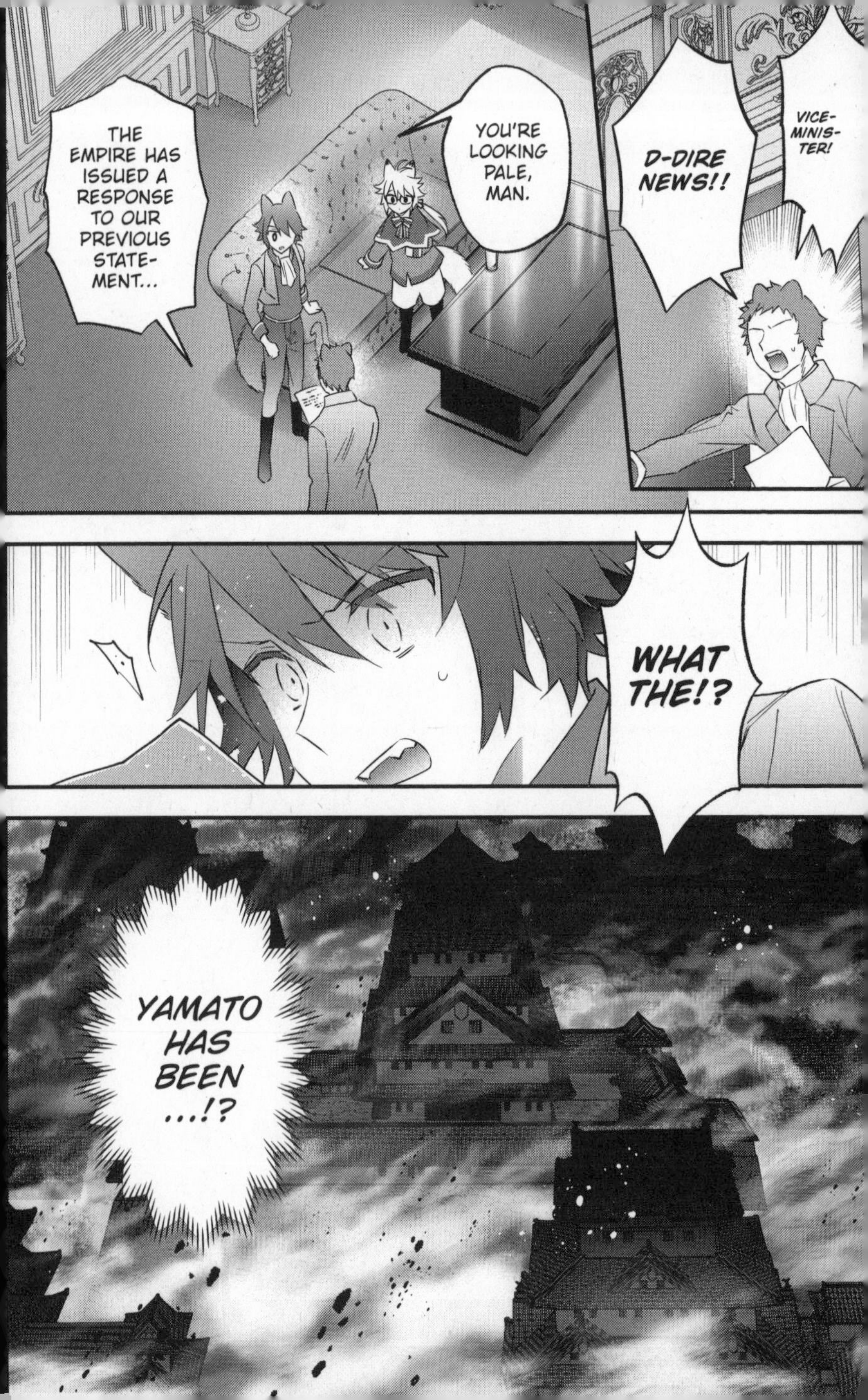
VICE-MINISTER!
D-DIRE NEWS!!
YOU'RE LOOKING PALE, MAN.
THE EMPIRE HAS ISSUED A RESPONSE TO OUR PREVIOUS STATEMENT...
WHAT THE!?
YAMATO HAS BEEN ...!?

HIGH SCHOOL
PRODIGIES HAVE
IT EASY EVEN IN
ANOTHER
WORLD!

Illustration Gallery (3)

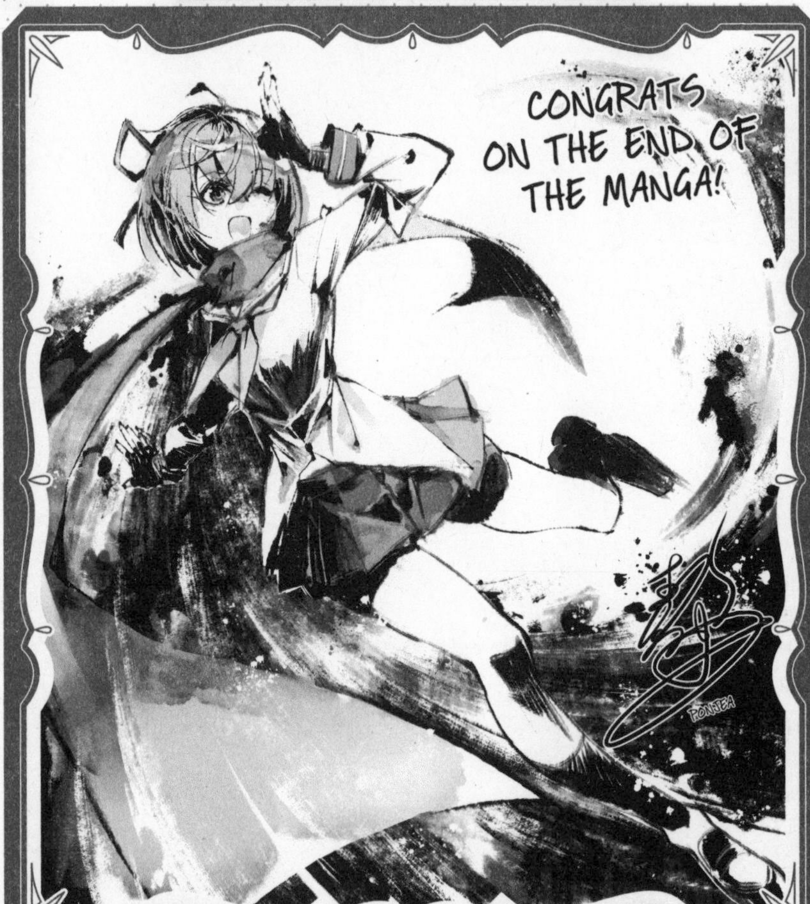
CONGRATS ON THE END OF THE MANGA!
PONJEA

Ponjea-sensei

Manga artist for
***My Isekai Life: I Gained a Second Character Class and Became the Strongest Sage in the World!*,**
featured in Manga UP!

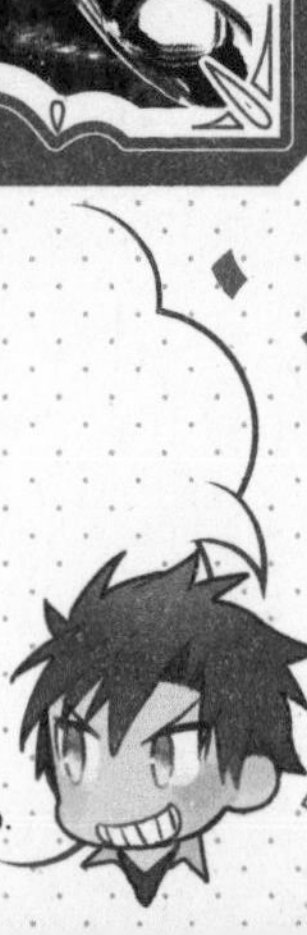

CHAPTER 97: TRUTH OF THE DEEP FOREST

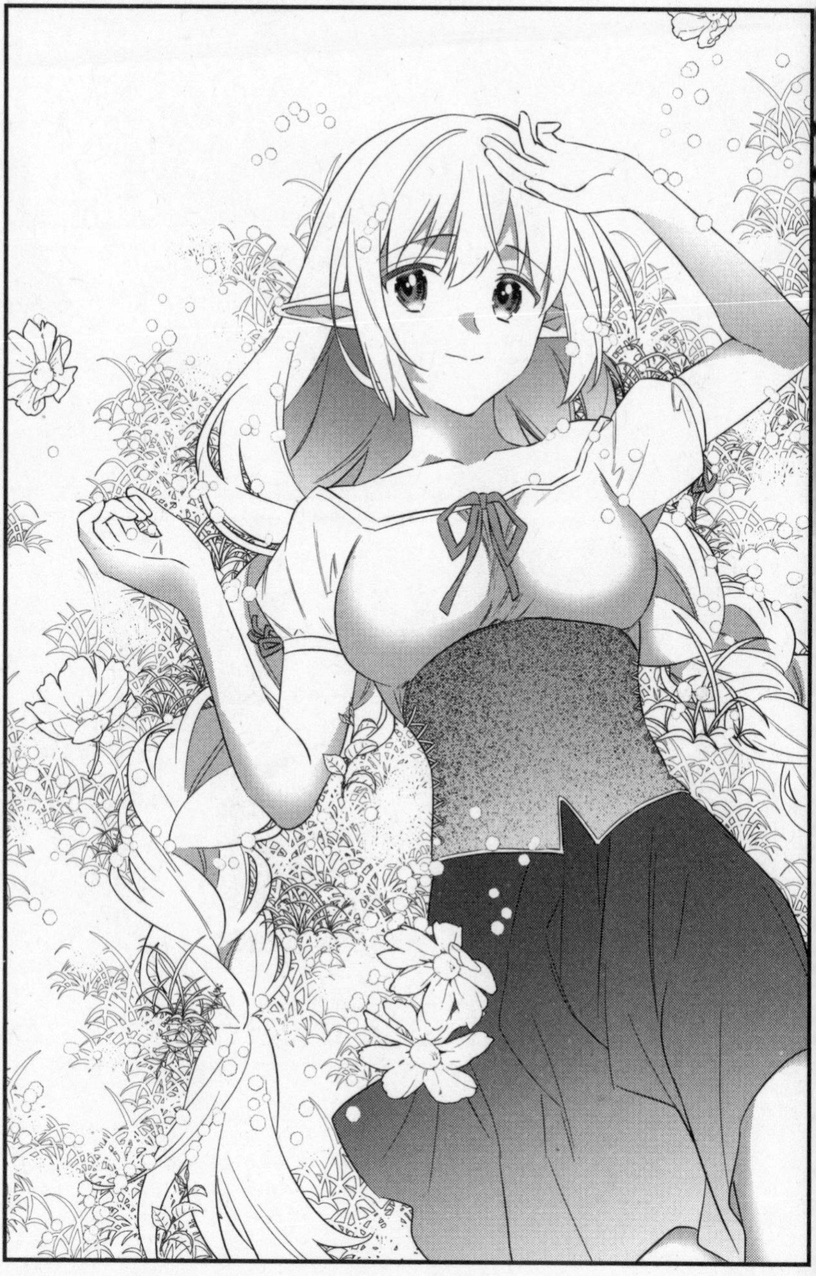

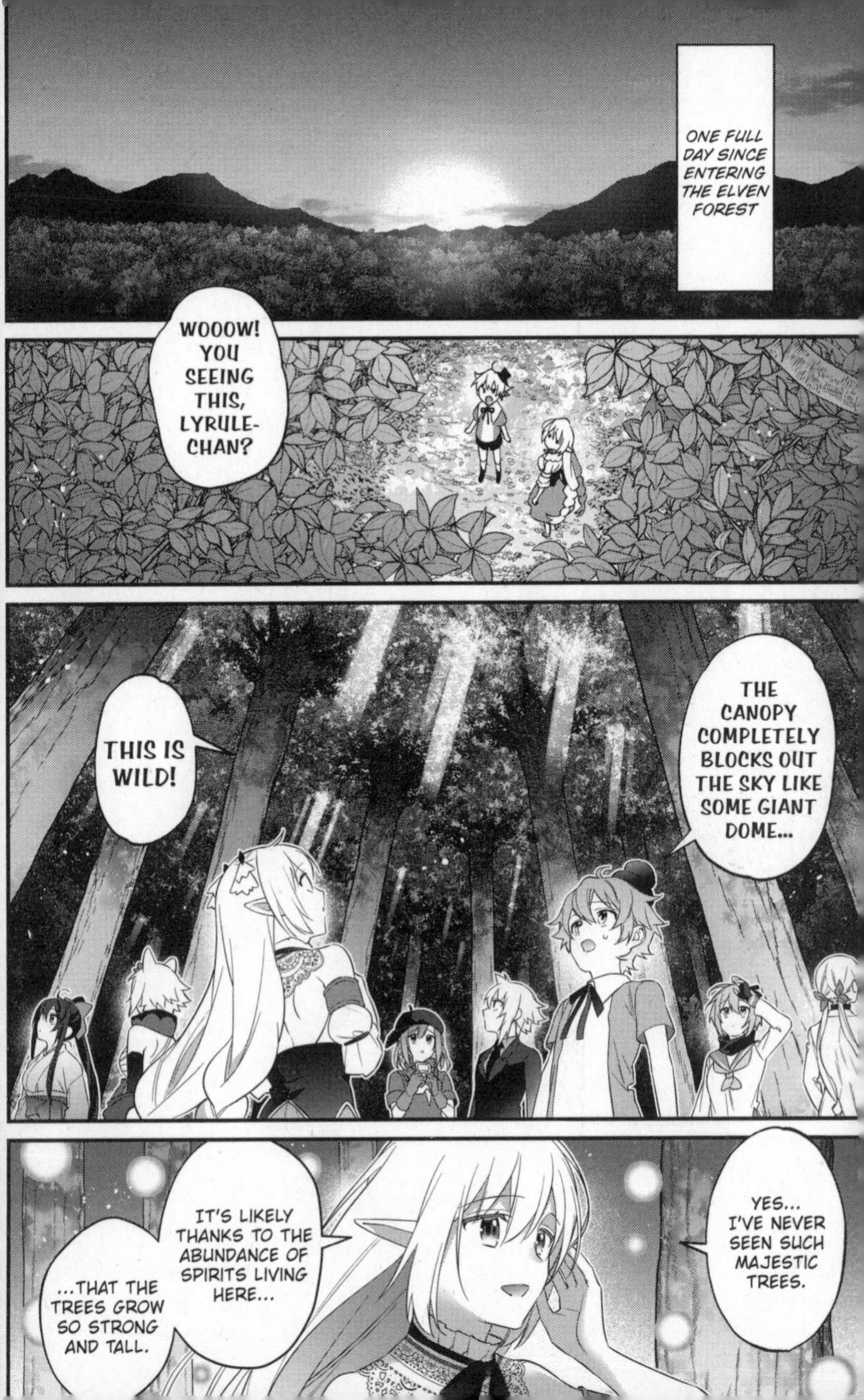
ONE FULL DAY SINCE ENTERING THE ELVEN FOREST
WOOOW! YOU SEEING THIS, LYRULE-CHAN?
THE CANOPY COMPLETELY BLOCKS OUT THE SKY LIKE SOME GIANT DOME...
THIS IS WILD!
YES... I'VE NEVER SEEN SUCH MAJESTIC TREES.
IT'S LIKELY THANKS TO THE ABUNDANCE OF SPIRITS LIVING HERE...
...THAT THE TREES GROW SO STRONG AND TALL.

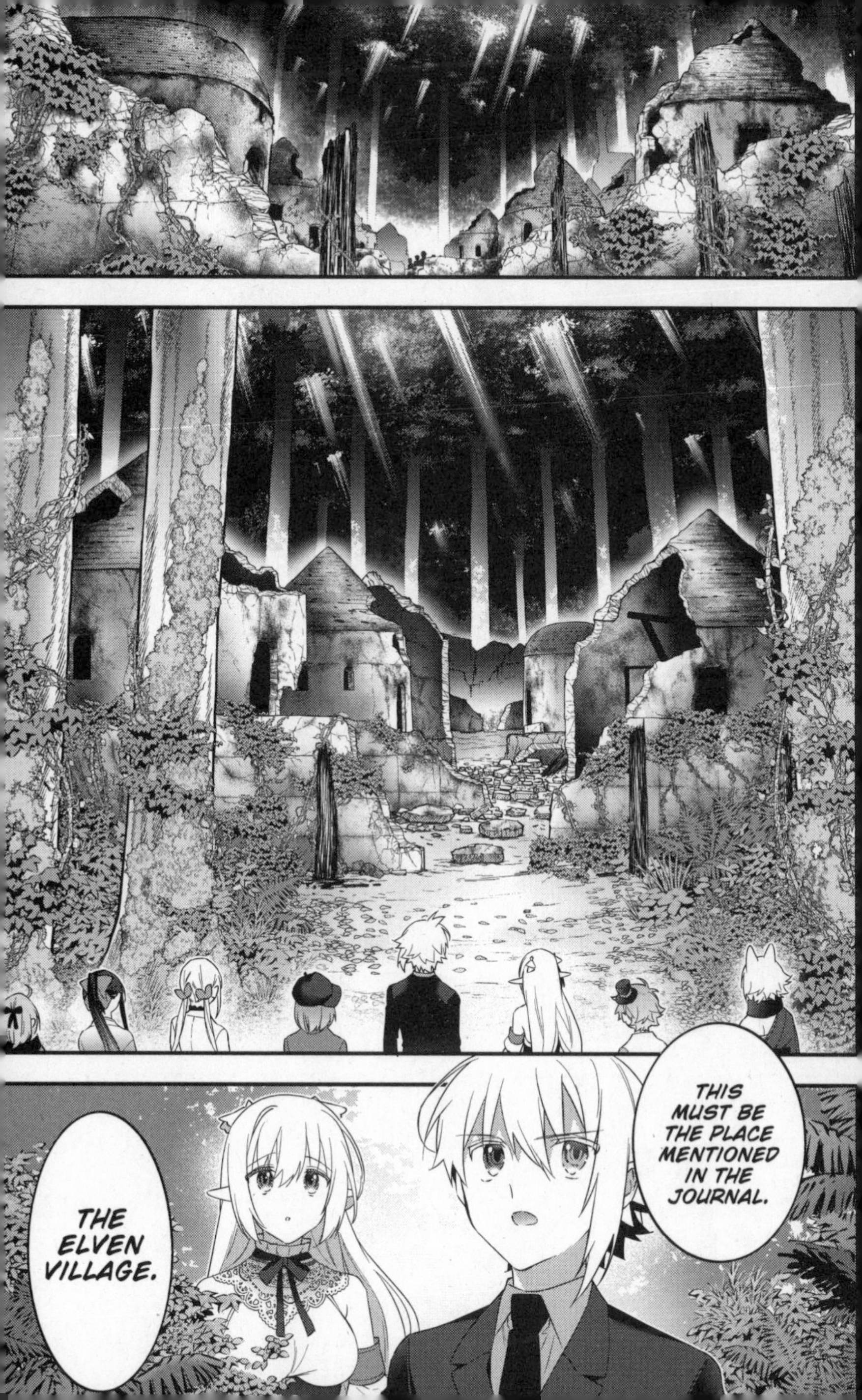
THIS MUST BE THE PLACE MENTIONED IN THE JOURNAL.
THE ELVEN VILLAGE.

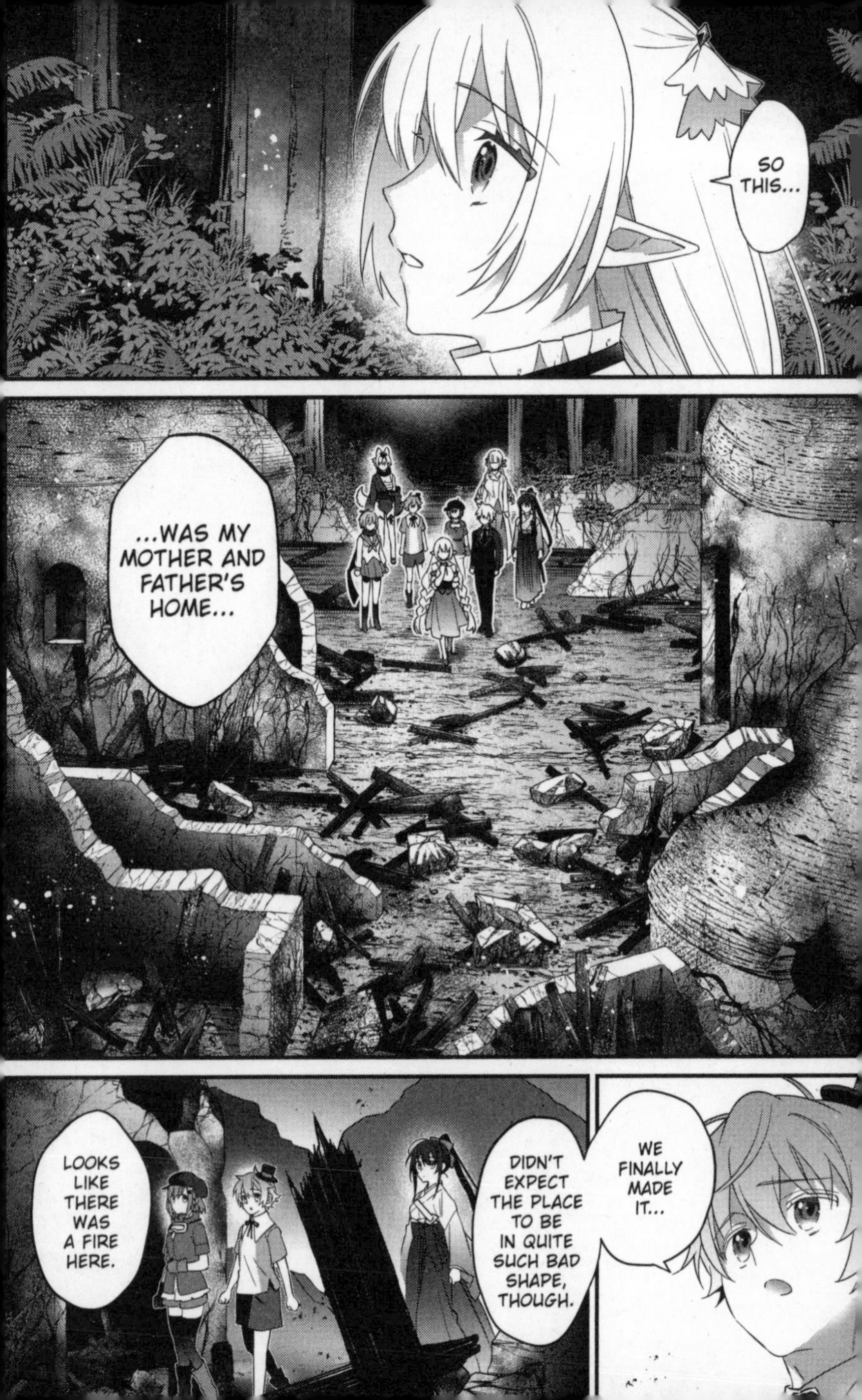
SO THIS...
...WAS MY MOTHER AND FATHER'S HOME...
WE FINALLY MADE IT...
DIDN'T EXPECT THE PLACE TO BE IN QUITE SUCH BAD SHAPE, THOUGH.
LOOKS LIKE THERE WAS A FIRE HERE.

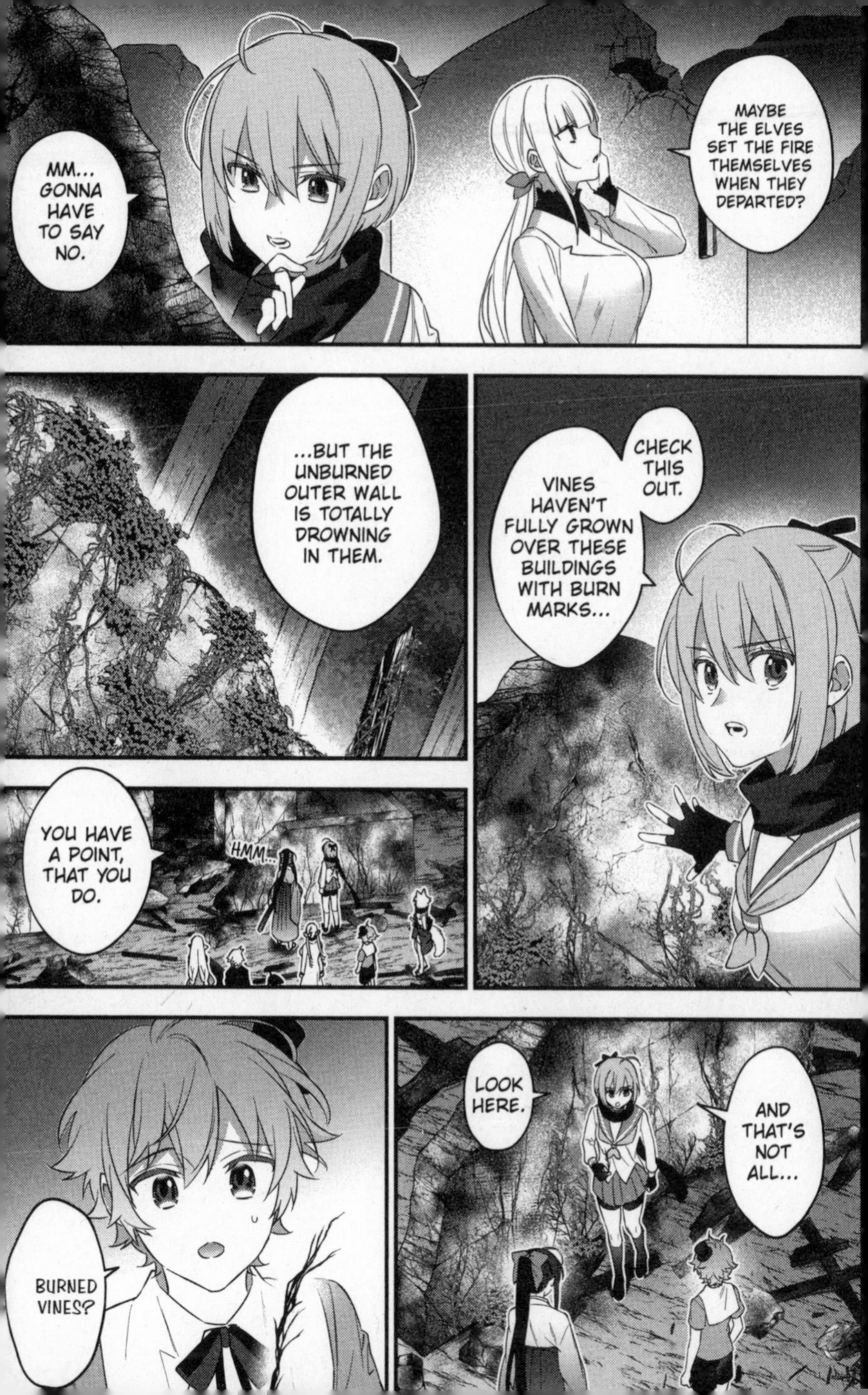
MAYBE THE ELVES SET THE FIRE THEMSELVES WHEN THEY DEPARTED?
MM... GONNA HAVE TO SAY NO.
CHECK THIS OUT.
VINES HAVEN'T FULLY GROWN OVER THESE BUILDINGS WITH BURN MARKS...
...BUT THE UNBURNED OUTER WALL IS TOTALLY DROWNING IN THEM.
HMM...
YOU HAVE A POINT, THAT YOU DO.
AND THAT'S NOT ALL...
LOOK HERE.
BURNED VINES?

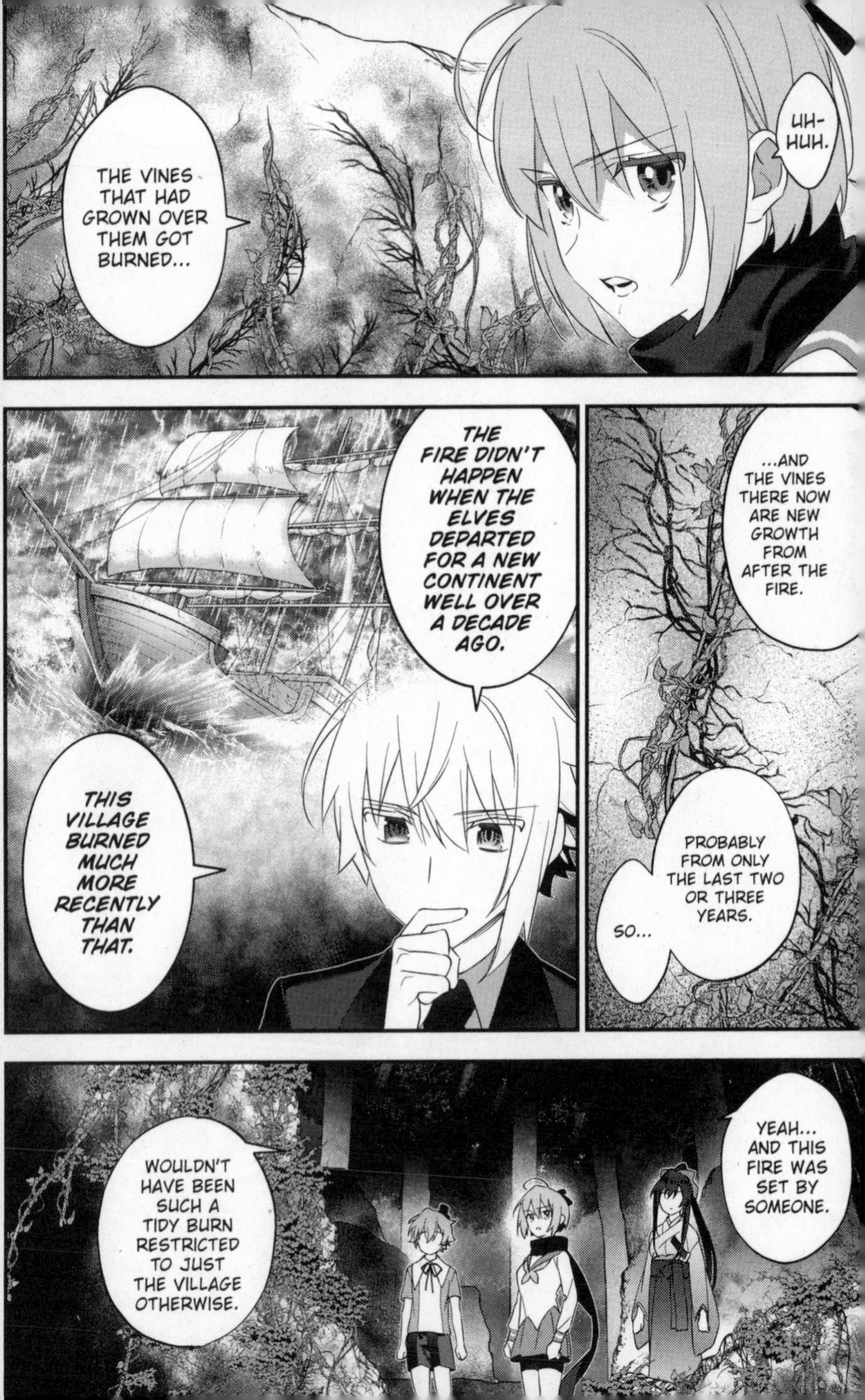
UH-HUH.
THE VINES THAT HAD GROWN OVER THEM GOT BURNED...
...AND THE VINES THERE NOW ARE NEW GROWTH FROM AFTER THE FIRE.
PROBABLY FROM ONLY THE LAST TWO OR THREE YEARS. SO...
THE FIRE DIDN'T HAPPEN WHEN THE ELVES DEPARTED FOR A NEW CONTINENT WELL OVER A DECADE AGO.
THIS VILLAGE BURNED MUCH MORE RECENTLY THAN THAT.
YEAH... AND THIS FIRE WAS SET BY SOMEONE.
WOULDN'T HAVE BEEN SUCH A TIDY BURN RESTRICTED TO JUST THE VILLAGE OTHERWISE.

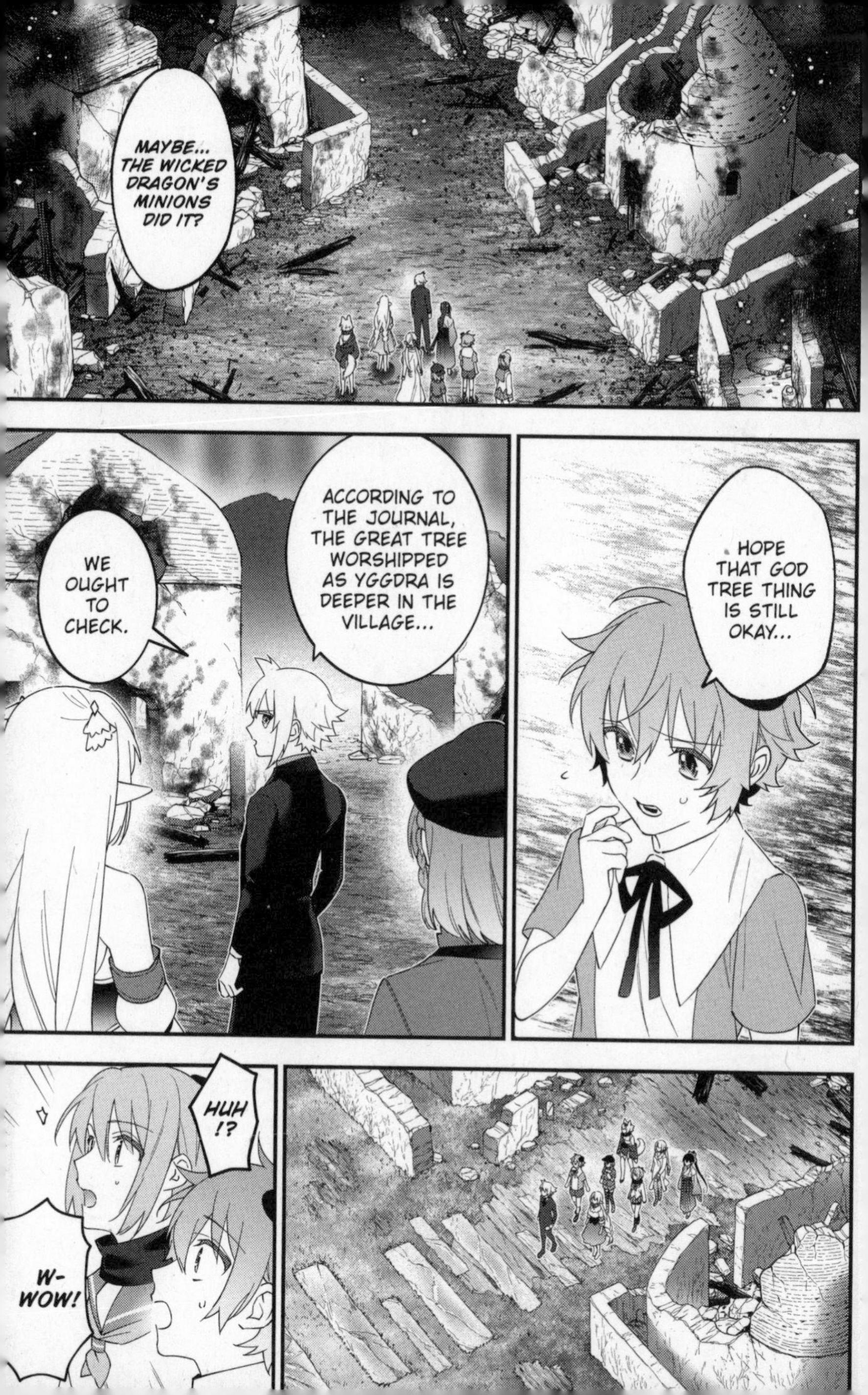
MAYBE... THE WICKED DRAGON'S MINIONS DID IT?
HOPE THAT GOD TREE THING IS STILL OKAY...
ACCORDING TO THE JOURNAL, THE GREAT TREE WORSHIPPED AS YGGDRA IS DEEPER IN THE VILLAGE...
WE OUGHT TO CHECK.
HUH!?
W-WOW!

THIS MUST BE...

...YGGDRA'S TREE...

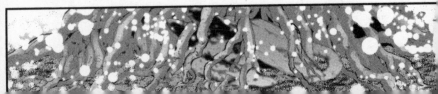

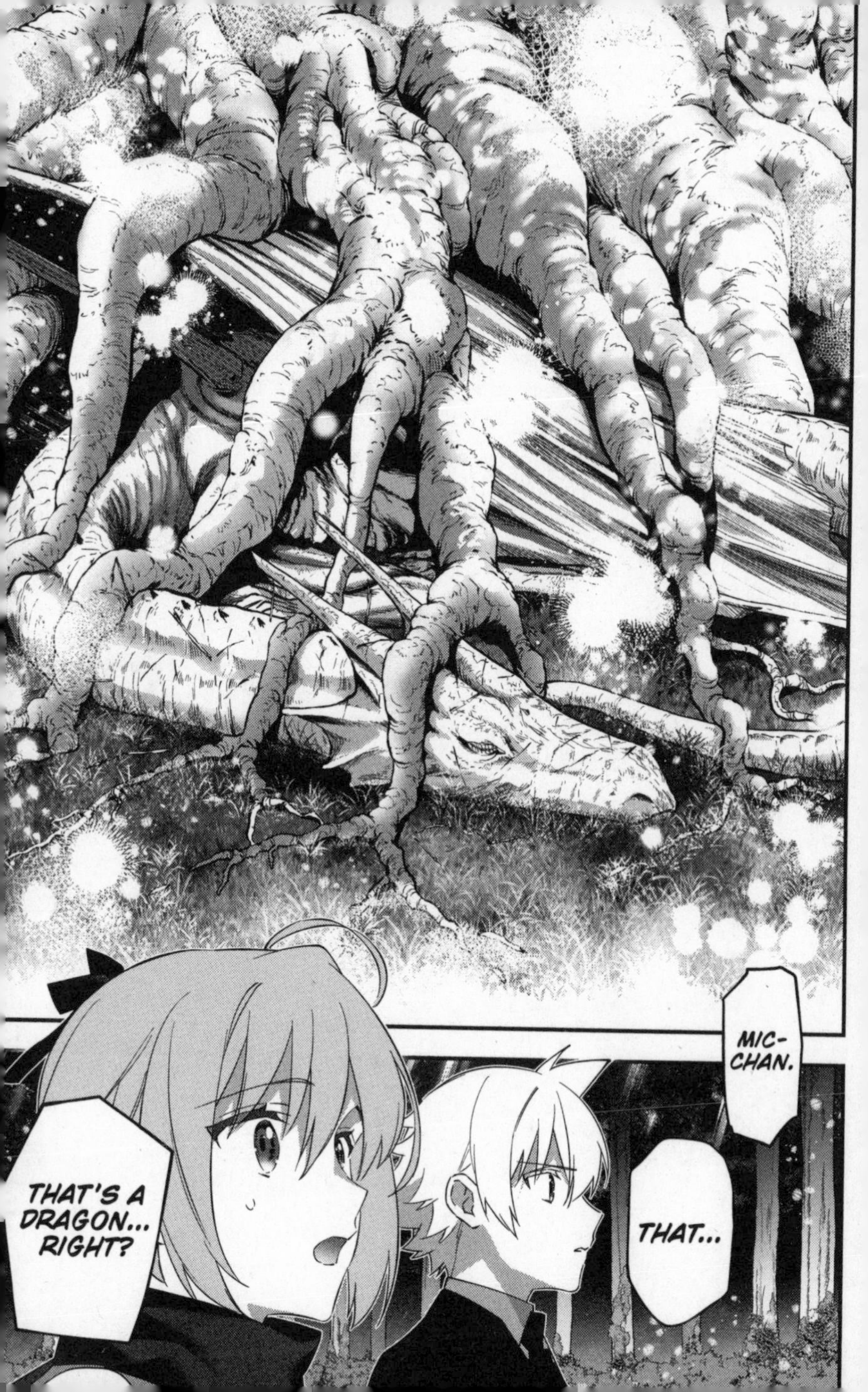
MIC-CHAN.
THAT...
THAT'S A DRAGON... RIGHT?

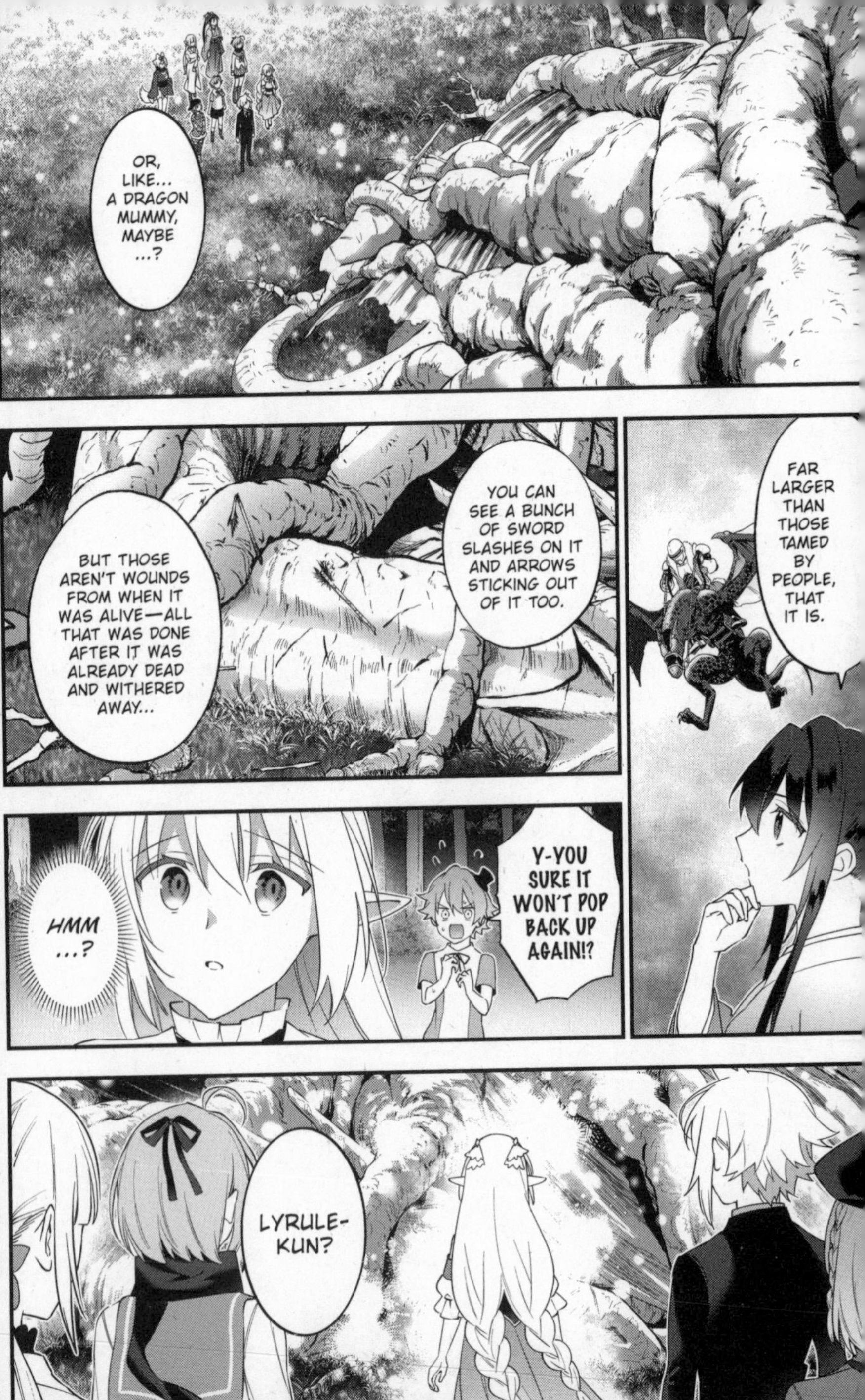
OR, LIKE... A DRAGON MUMMY, MAYBE ...?
FAR LARGER THAN THOSE TAMED BY PEOPLE, THAT IT IS.
YOU CAN SEE A BUNCH OF SWORD SLASHES ON IT AND ARROWS STICKING OUT OF IT TOO.
BUT THOSE AREN'T WOUNDS FROM WHEN IT WAS ALIVE—ALL THAT WAS DONE AFTER IT WAS ALREADY DEAD AND WITHERED AWAY...
Y-YOU SURE IT WON'T POP BACK UP AGAIN!?
HMM ...?
LYRULE-KUN?

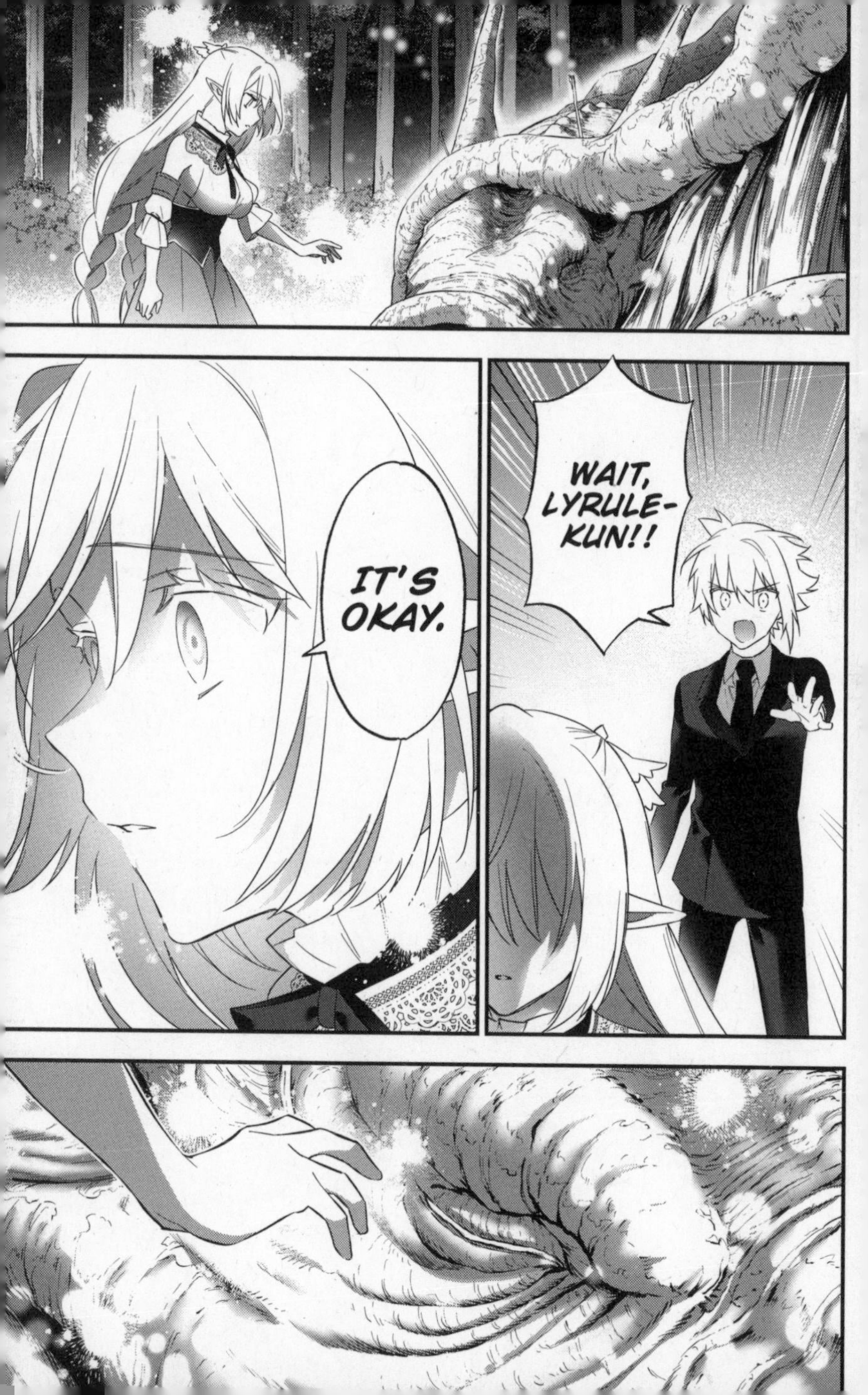
WAIT, LYRULE-KUN!!
IT'S OKAY.

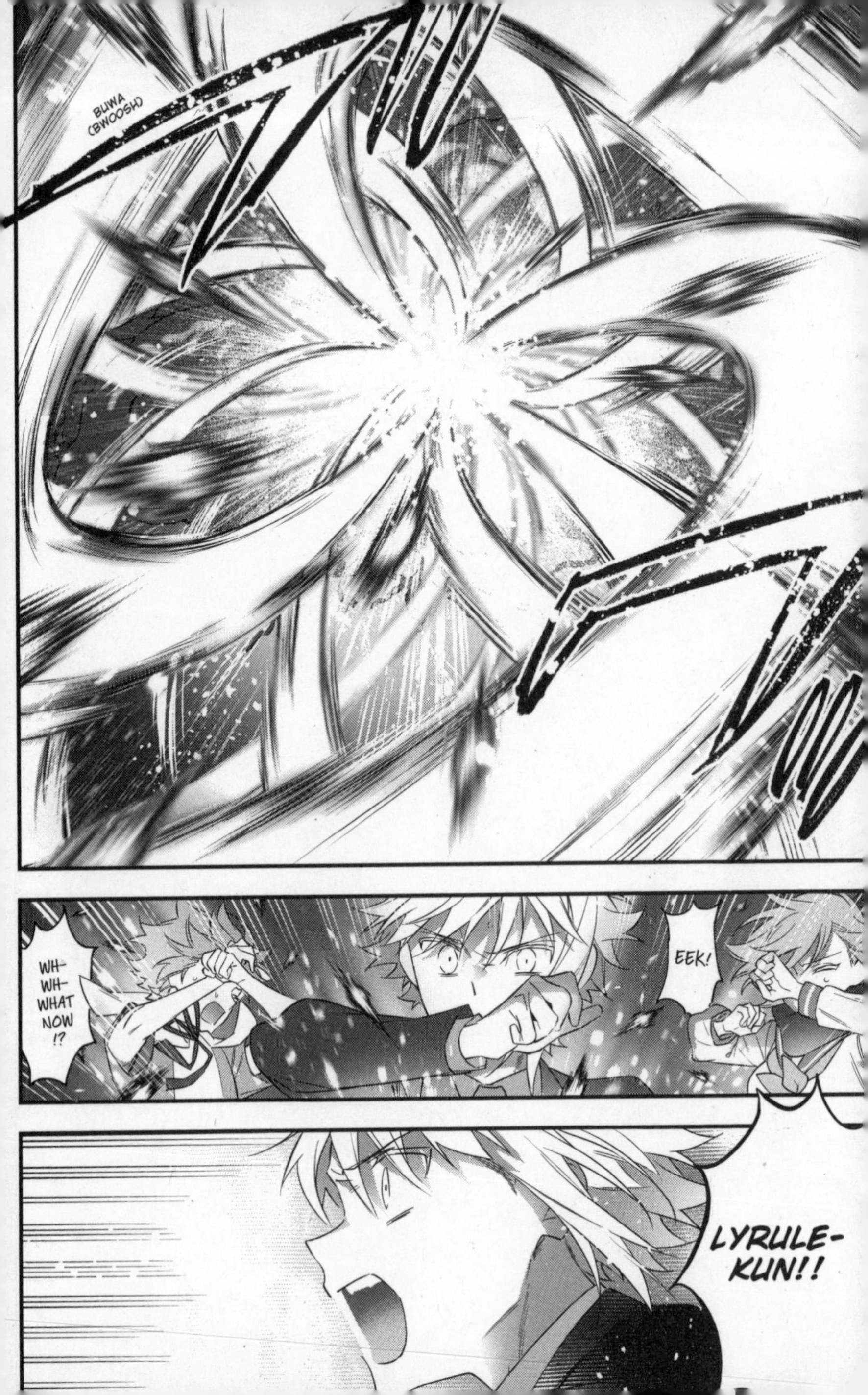
BUWA (BWOOSH)
EEK!
WH-WH-WHAT NOW!?
LYRULE-KUN!!

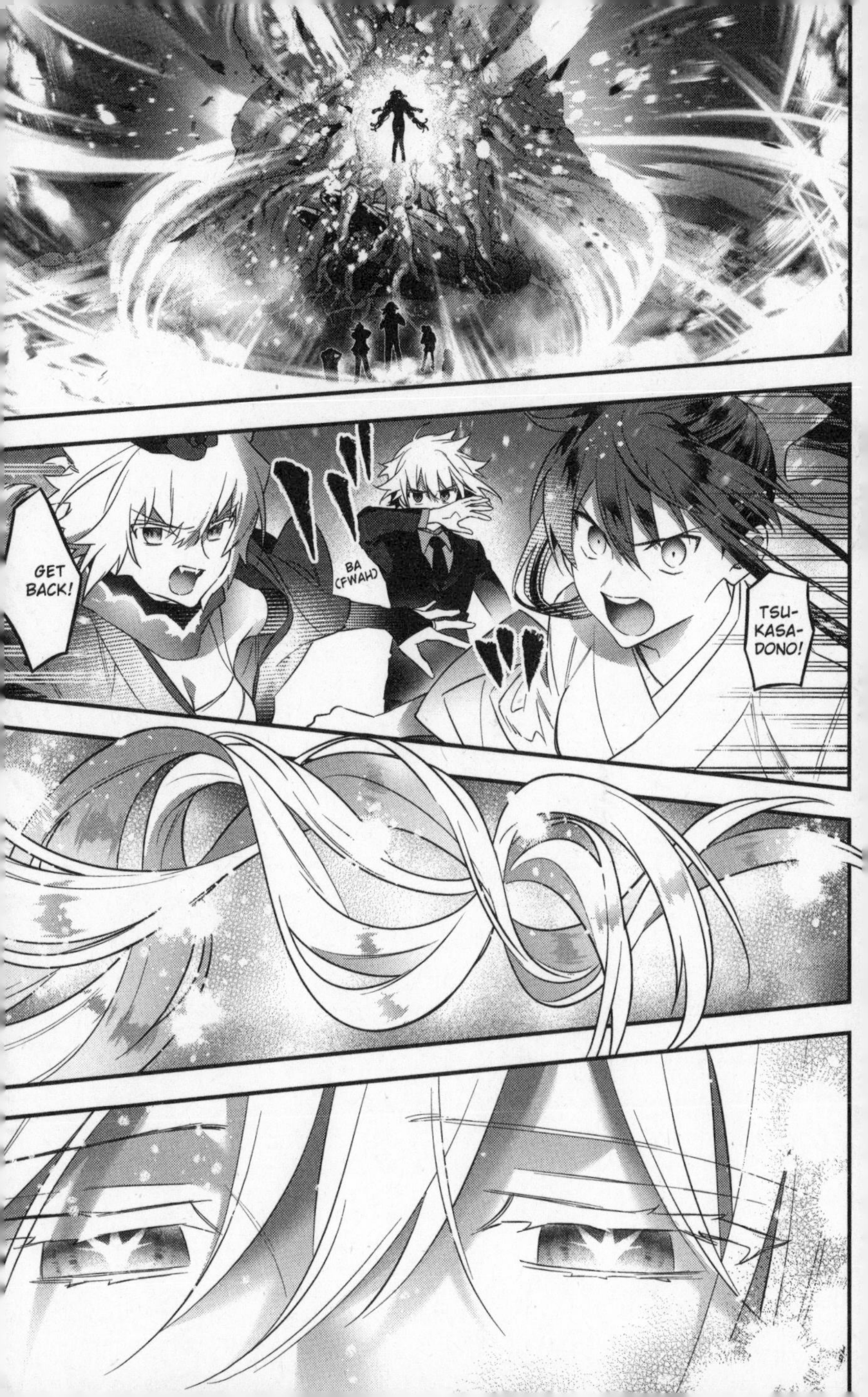
TSU-KASA-DONO!
BA (FWAH)
GET BACK!

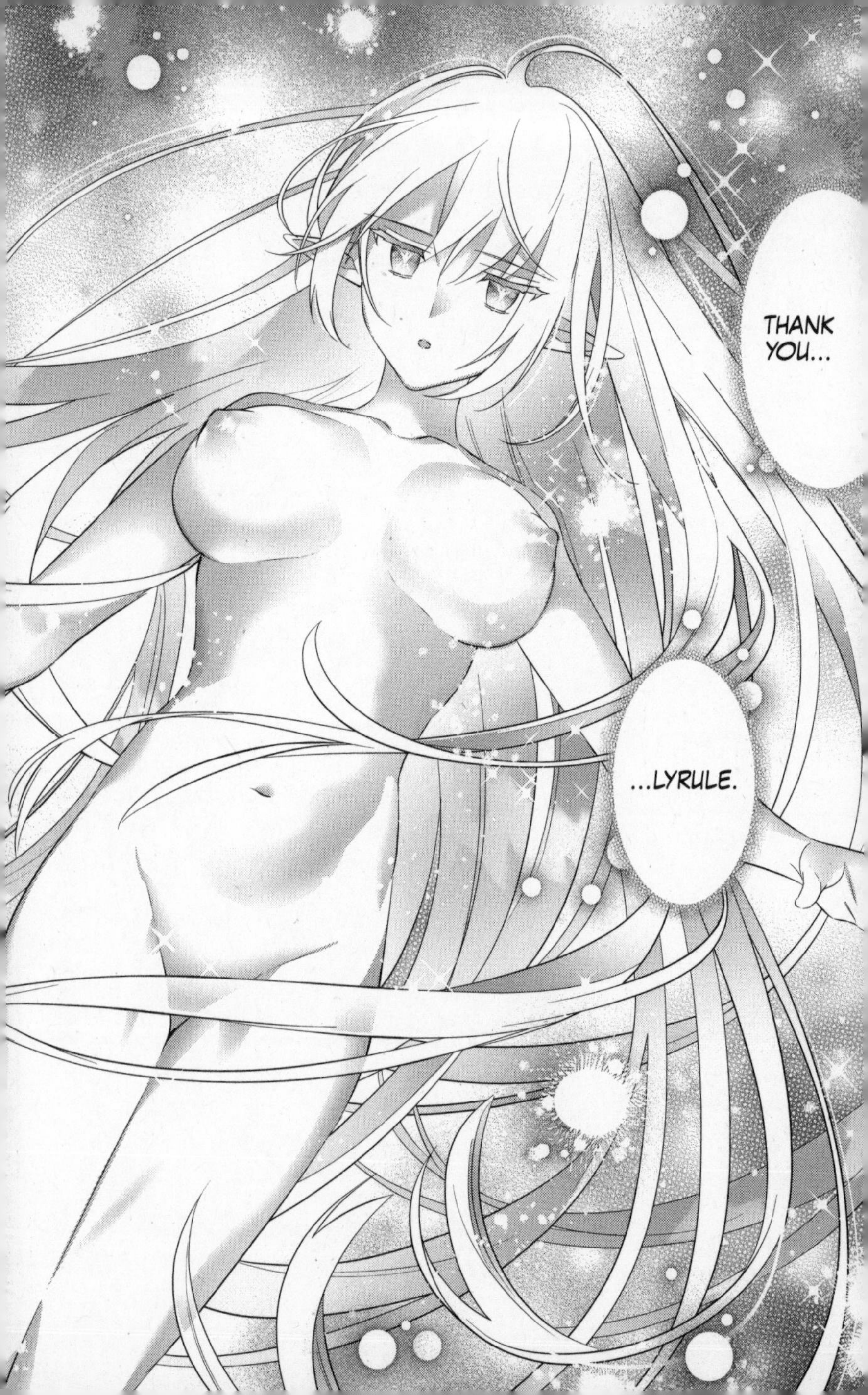
THANK YOU...
...LYRULE.

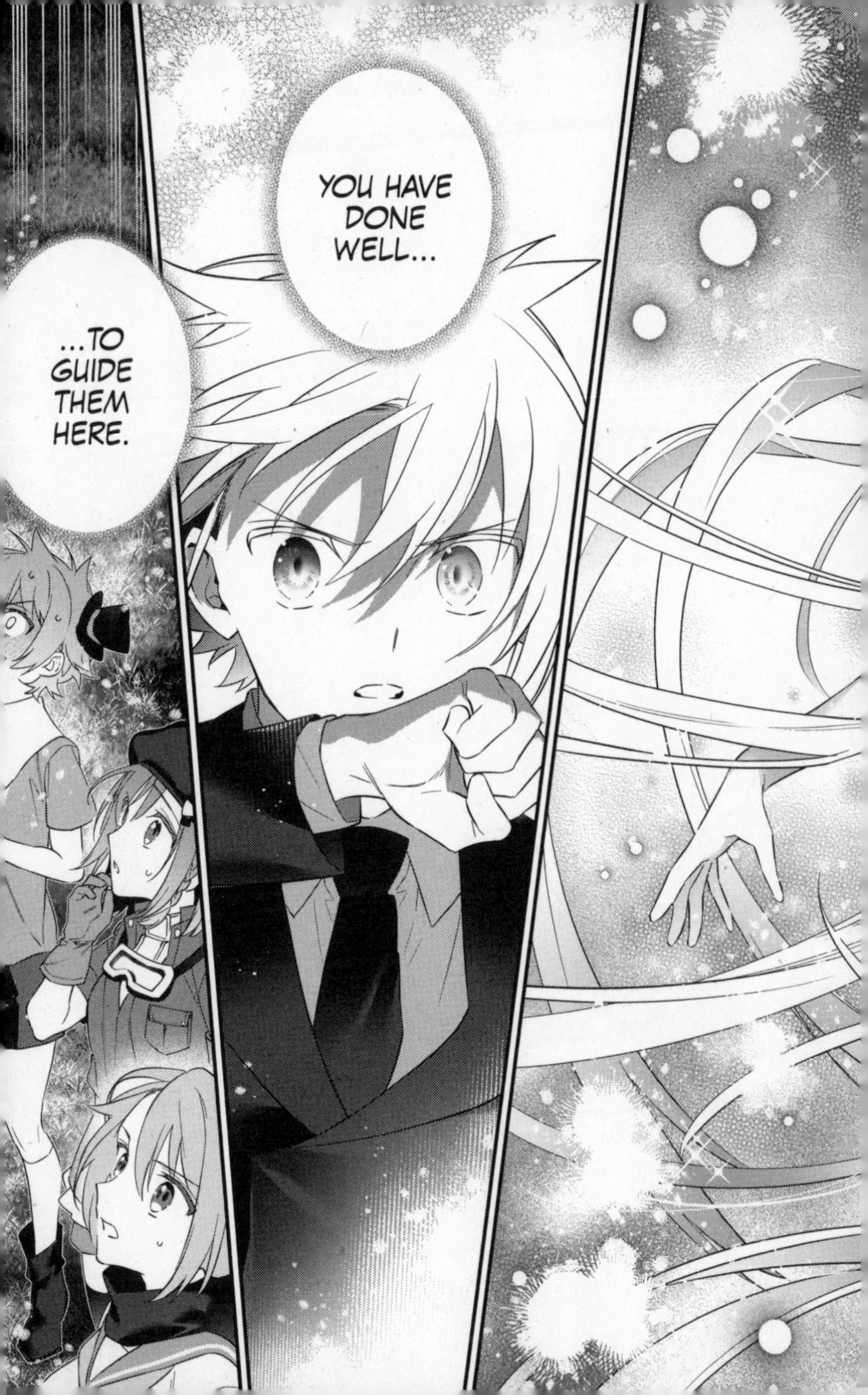
YOU HAVE DONE WELL...
...TO GUIDE THEM HERE.

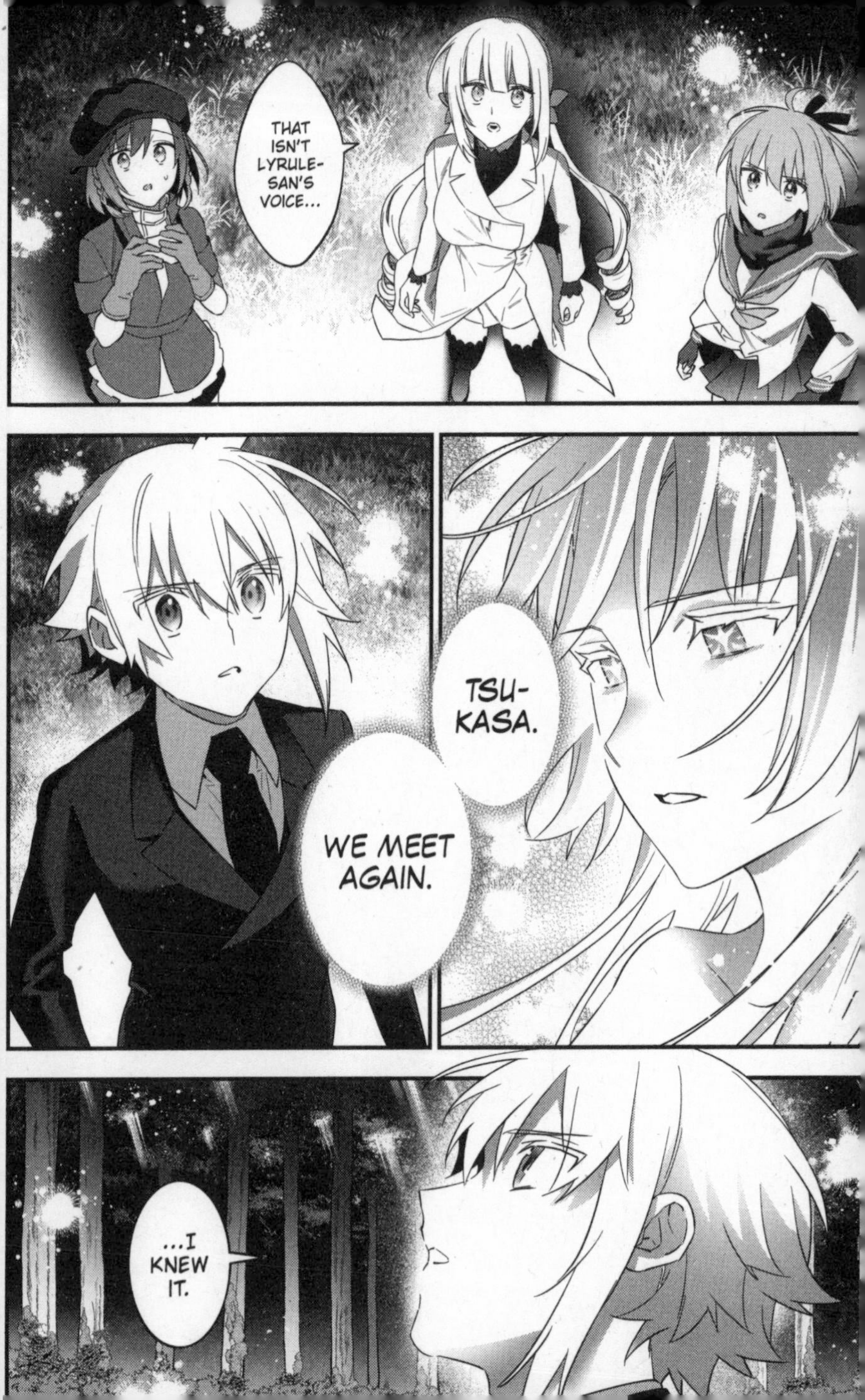
THAT ISN'T LYRULE-SAN'S VOICE...
TSU-KASA.
WE MEET AGAIN.
...I KNEW IT.

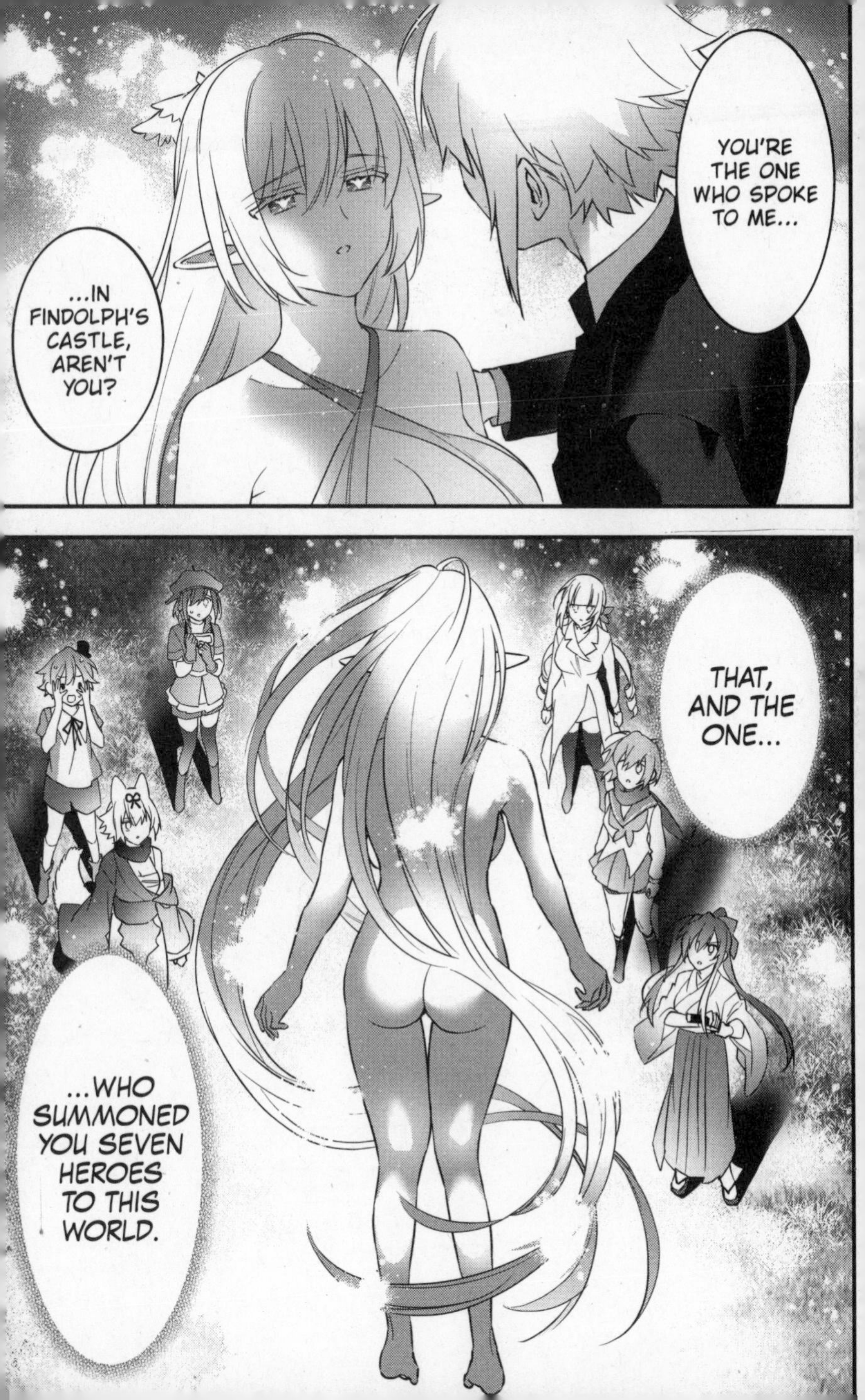
YOU'RE THE ONE WHO SPOKE TO ME...
...IN FINDOLPH'S CASTLE, AREN'T YOU?
THAT, AND THE ONE...
...WHO SUMMONED YOU SEVEN HEROES TO THIS WORLD.

HIGH SCHOOL
PRODIGIES HAVE
IT EASY EVEN IN
ANOTHER
WORLD!

Illustration Gallery (4)

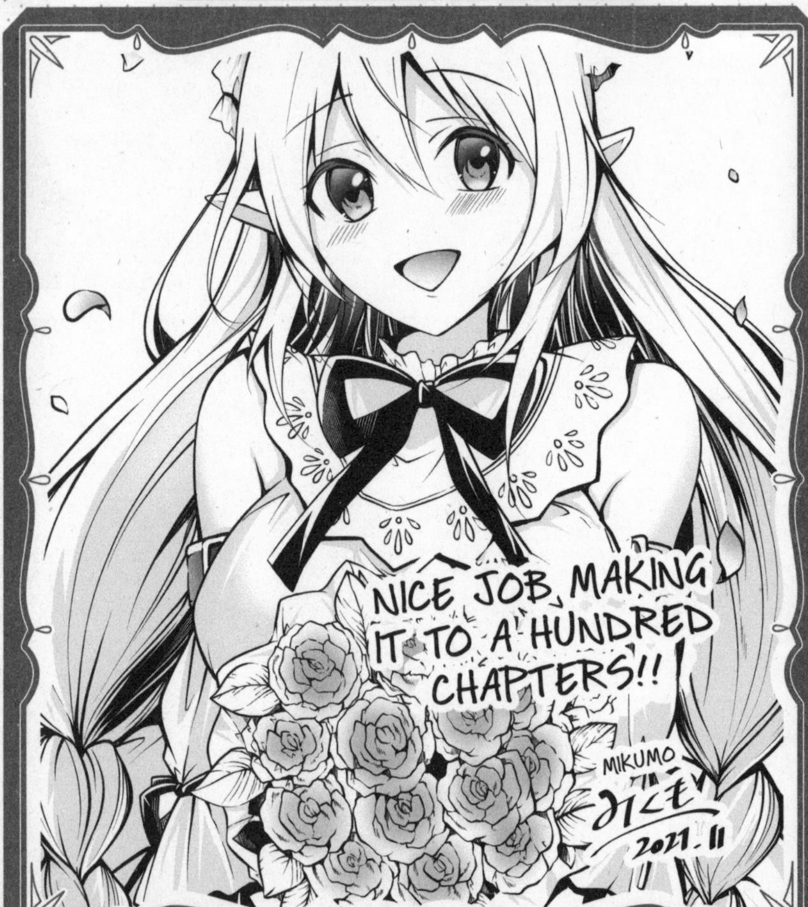
NICE JOB MAKING IT TO A HUNDRED CHAPTERS!!
MIKUMO
みくも
2021. 11

George Mikumo-sensei

Manga artist for
I *Don't Need an IRL Girlfriend!*,
featured in Manga UP!

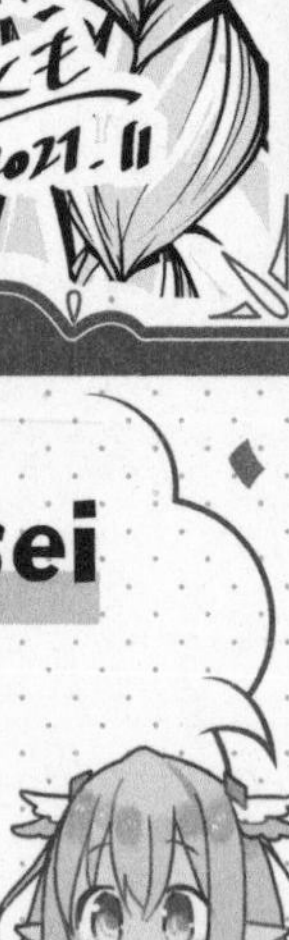

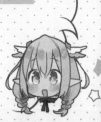

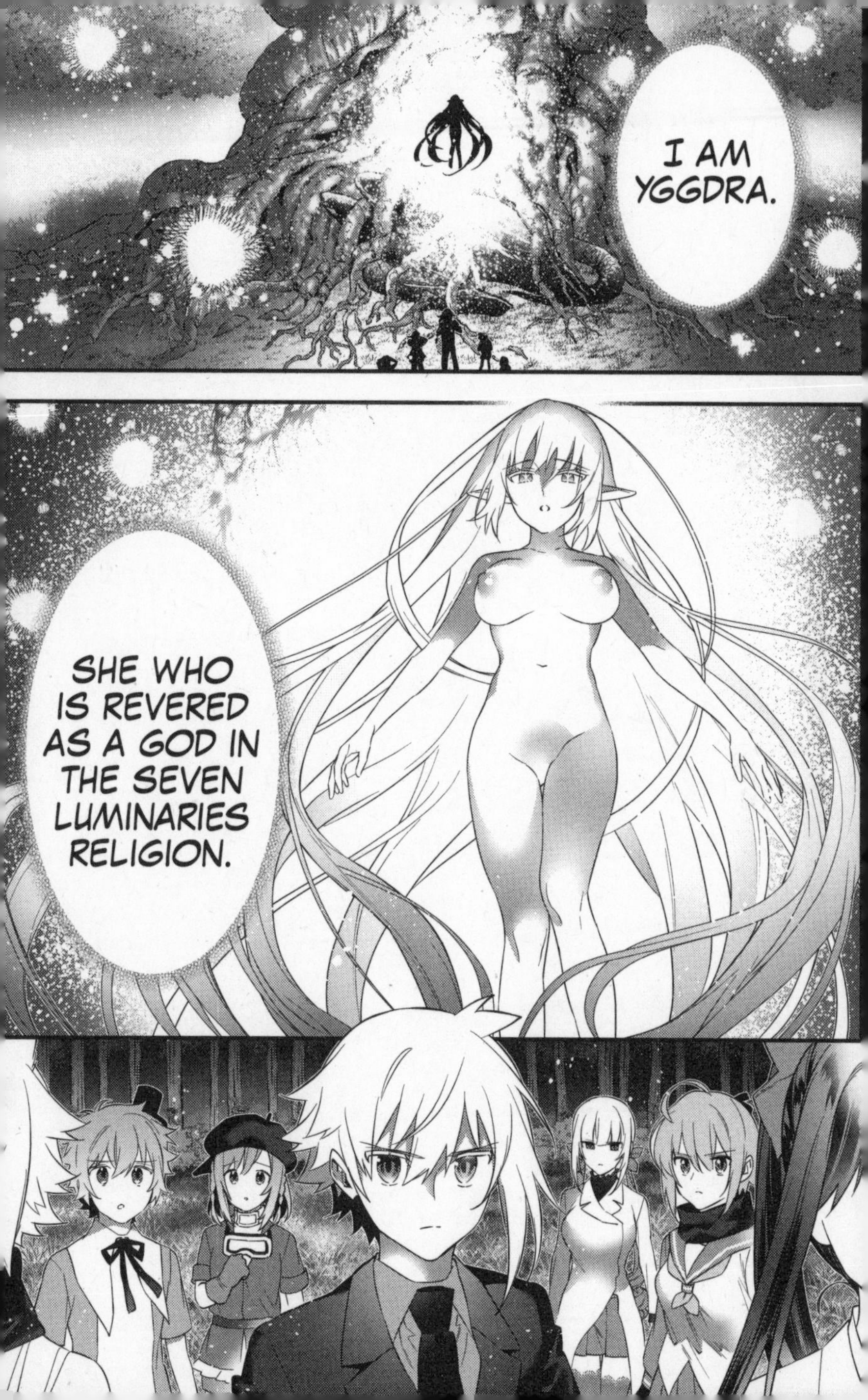
I AM YGGDRA.
SHE WHO IS REVERED AS A GOD IN THE SEVEN LUMINARIES RELIGION.

CHAPTER 98: ONE REVERED AS A GOD

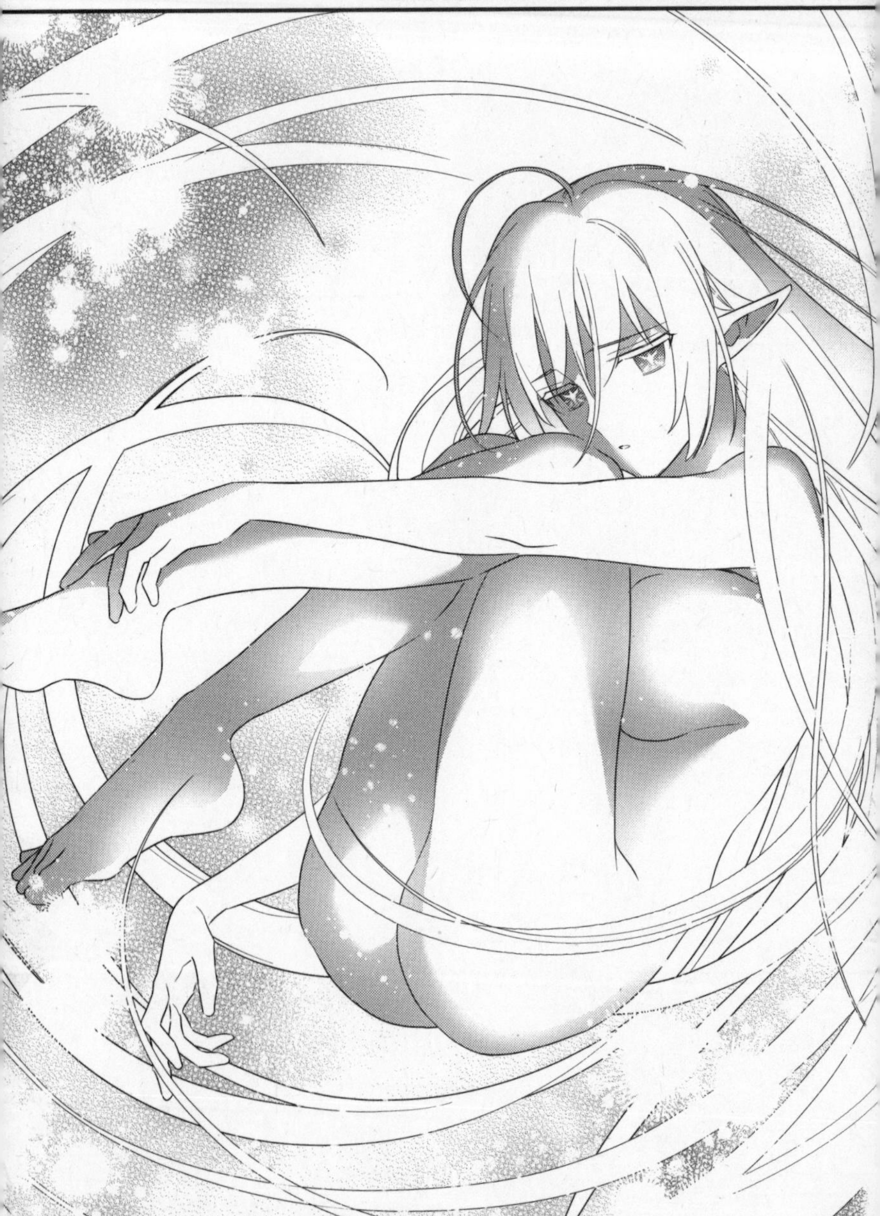

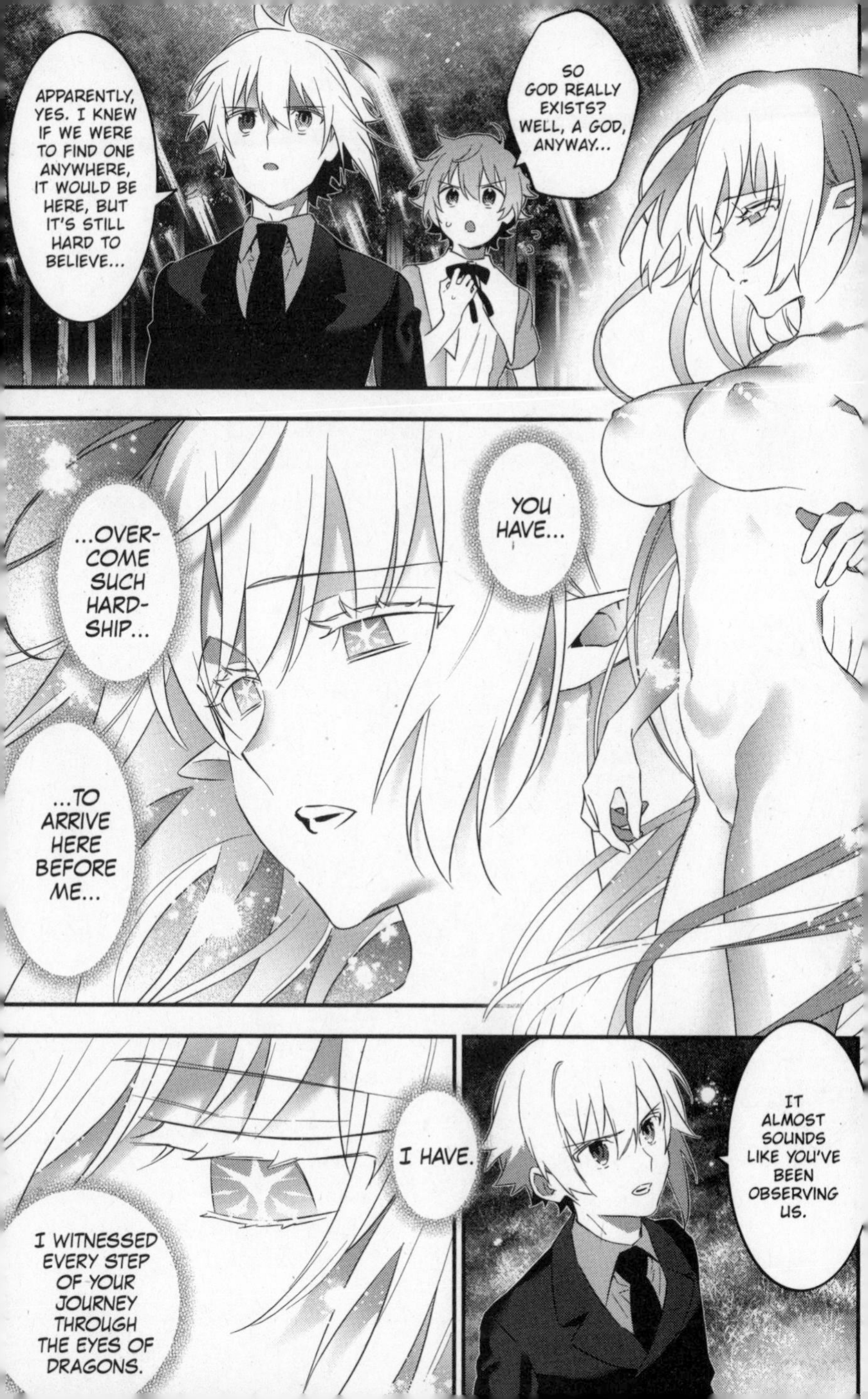
SO GOD REALLY EXISTS? WELL, A GOD, ANYWAY...
APPARENTLY, YES. I KNEW IF WE WERE TO FIND ONE ANYWHERE, IT WOULD BE HERE, BUT IT'S STILL HARD TO BELIEVE...
YOU HAVE...
...OVER-COME SUCH HARD-SHIP...
...TO ARRIVE HERE BEFORE ME...
IT ALMOST SOUNDS LIKE YOU'VE BEEN OBSERVING US.
I HAVE.
I WITNESSED EVERY STEP OF YOUR JOURNEY THROUGH THE EYES OF DRAGONS.

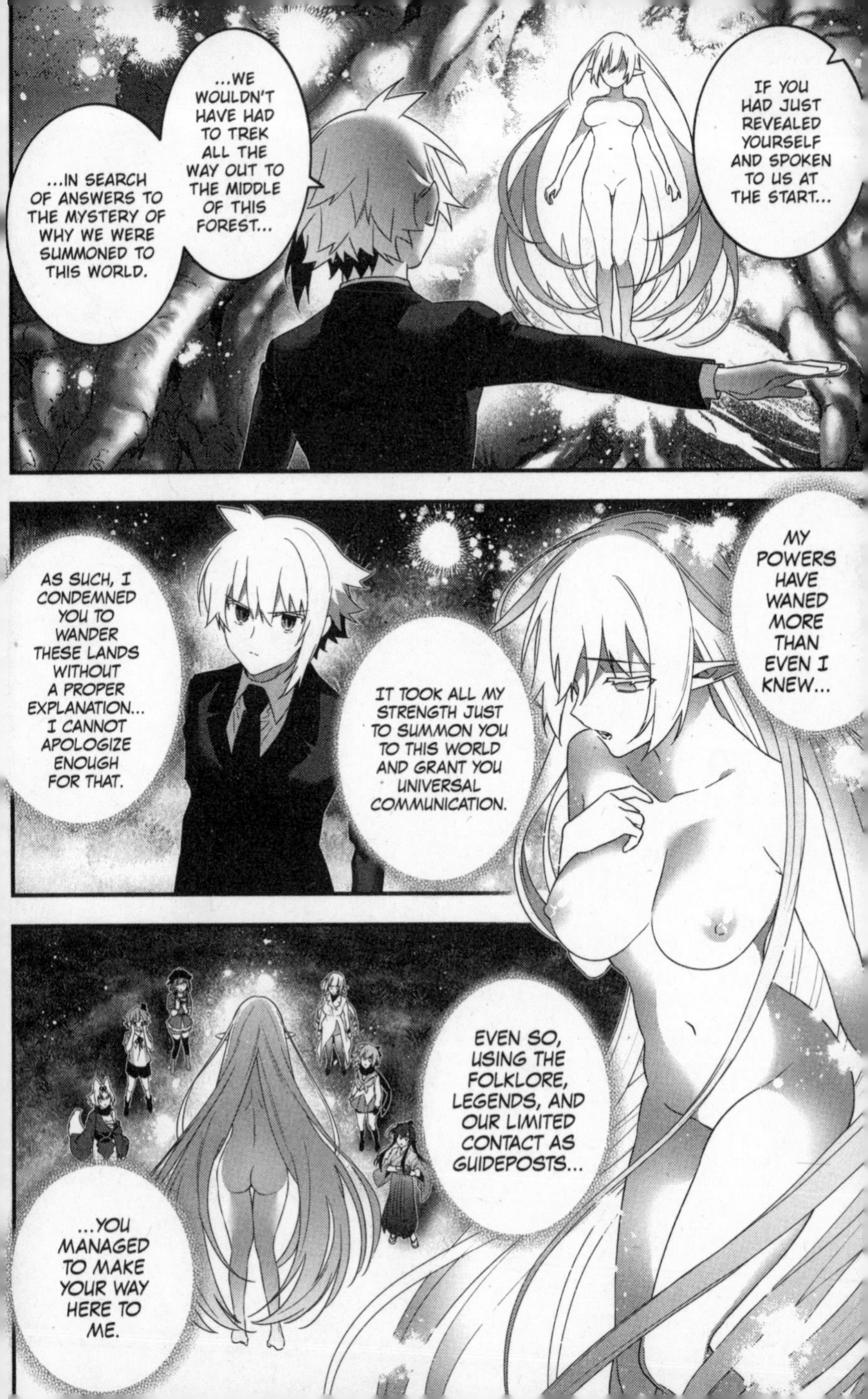
IF YOU HAD JUST REVEALED YOURSELF AND SPOKEN TO US AT THE START...
...WE WOULDN'T HAVE HAD TO TREK ALL THE WAY OUT TO THE MIDDLE OF THIS FOREST...
...IN SEARCH OF ANSWERS TO THE MYSTERY OF WHY WE WERE SUMMONED TO THIS WORLD.
MY POWERS HAVE WANED MORE THAN EVEN I KNEW...
IT TOOK ALL MY STRENGTH JUST TO SUMMON YOU TO THIS WORLD AND GRANT YOU UNIVERSAL COMMUNICATION.
AS SUCH, I CONDEMNED YOU TO WANDER THESE LANDS WITHOUT A PROPER EXPLANATION... I CANNOT APOLOGIZE ENOUGH FOR THAT.
EVEN SO, USING THE FOLKLORE, LEGENDS, AND OUR LIMITED CONTACT AS GUIDEPOSTS...
...YOU MANAGED TO MAKE YOUR WAY HERE TO ME.

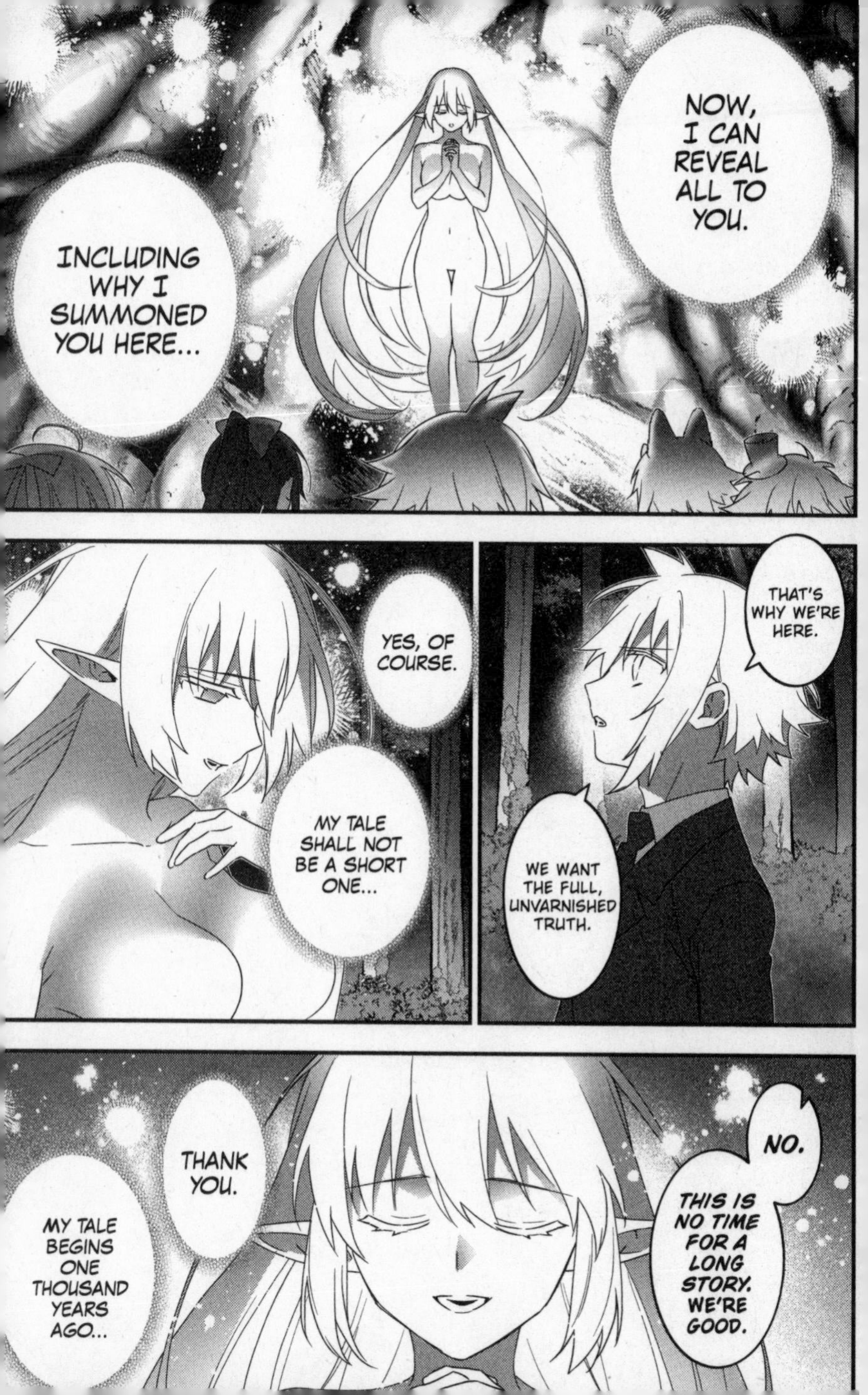
NOW, I CAN REVEAL ALL TO YOU.
INCLUDING WHY I SUMMONED YOU HERE...
THAT'S WHY WE'RE HERE.
WE WANT THE FULL, UNVARNISHED TRUTH.
YES, OF COURSE.
MY TALE SHALL NOT BE A SHORT ONE...
NO.
THIS IS NO TIME FOR A LONG STORY. WE'RE GOOD.
THANK YOU.
MY TALE BEGINS ONE THOUSAND YEARS AGO...

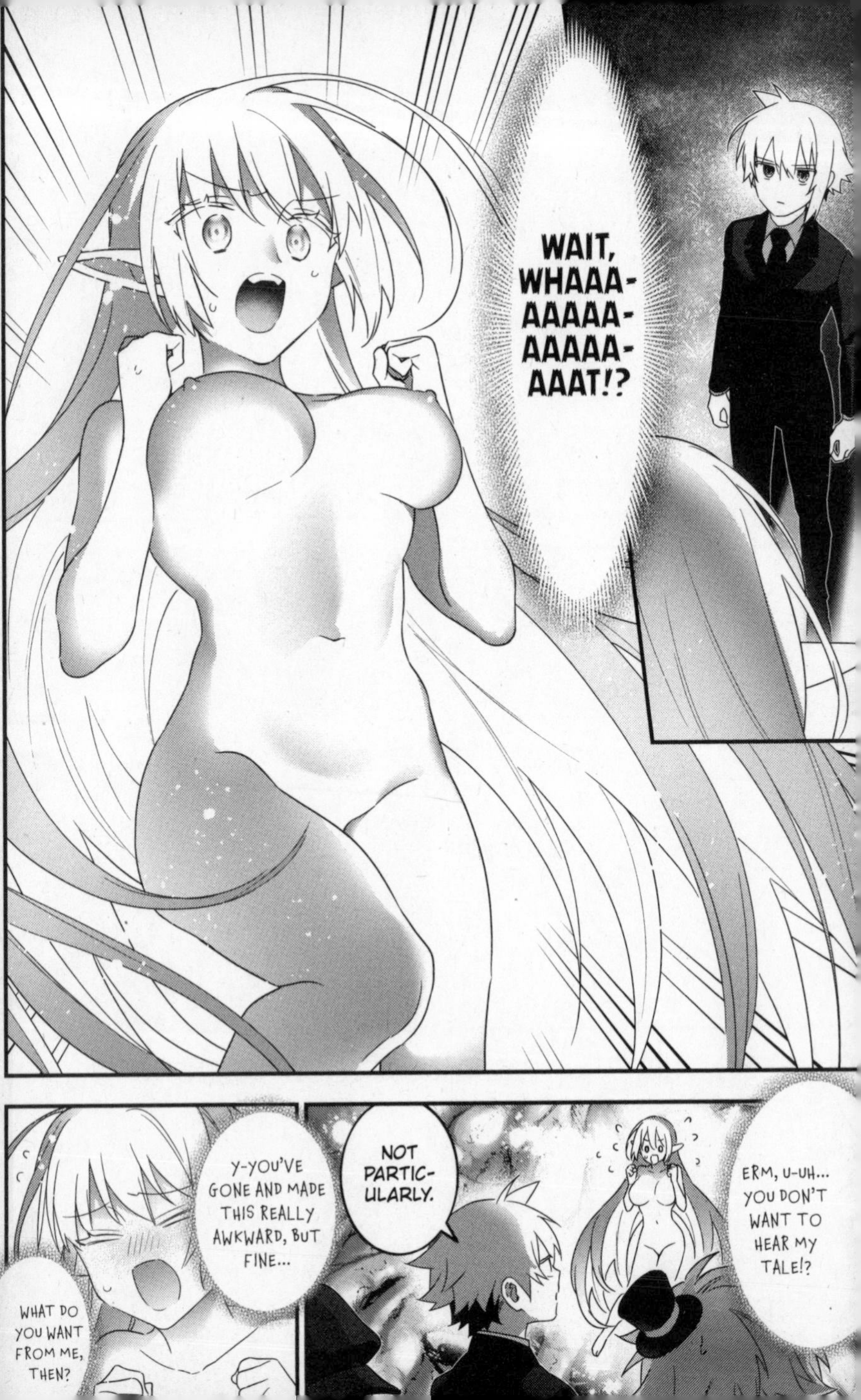
WAIT, WHAAA-AAAAA-AAAAA-AAAT!?
ERM, U-UH... YOU DON'T WANT TO HEAR MY TALE!?
NOT PARTIC-ULARLY.
Y-YOU'VE GONE AND MADE THIS REALLY AWKWARD, BUT FINE...
WHAT DO YOU WANT FROM ME, THEN?

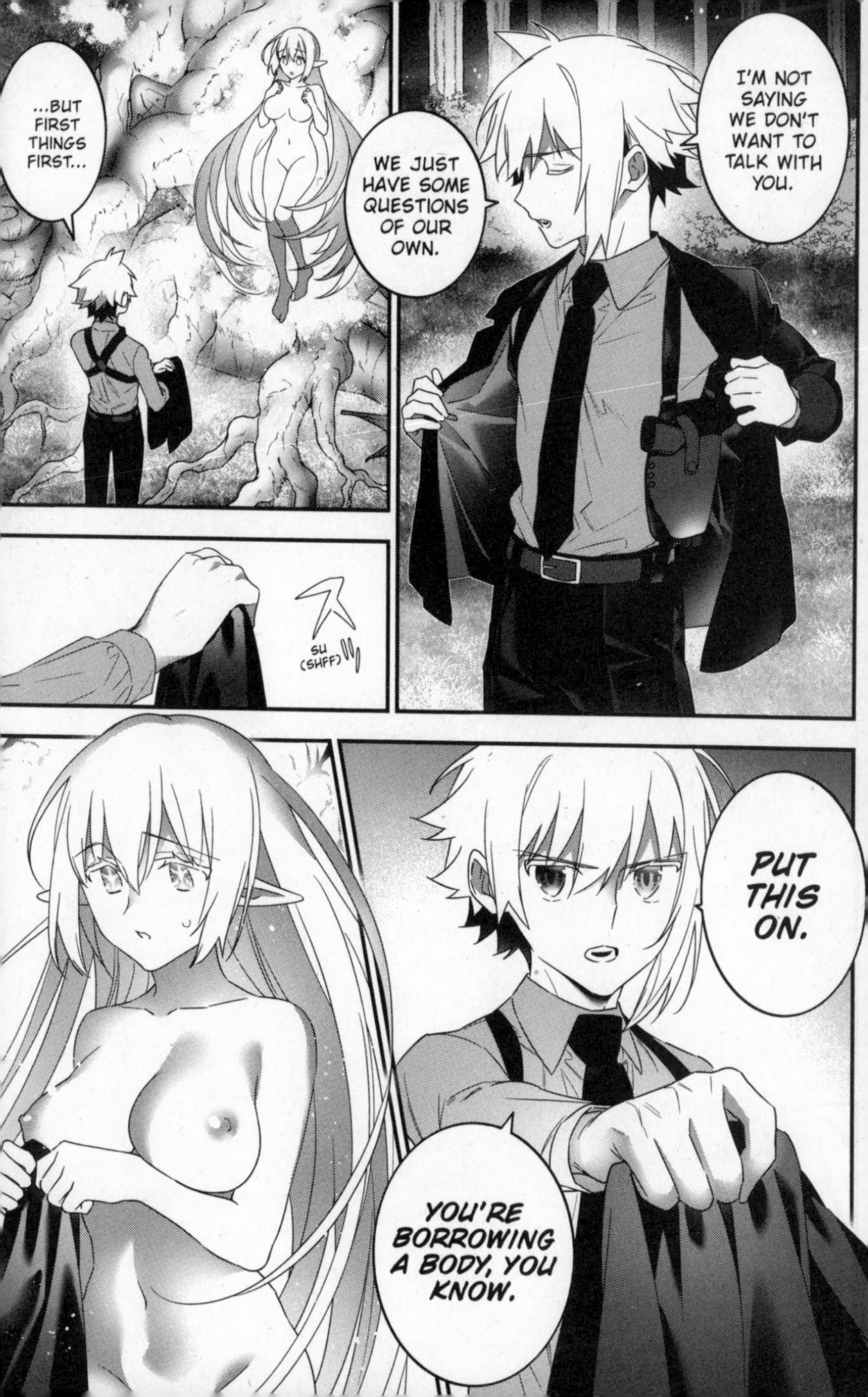
I'M NOT SAYING WE DON'T WANT TO TALK WITH YOU.
WE JUST HAVE SOME QUESTIONS OF OUR OWN.
...BUT FIRST THINGS FIRST...
ス
SU (SHFF)
PUT THIS ON.
YOU'RE BORROWING A BODY, YOU KNOW.

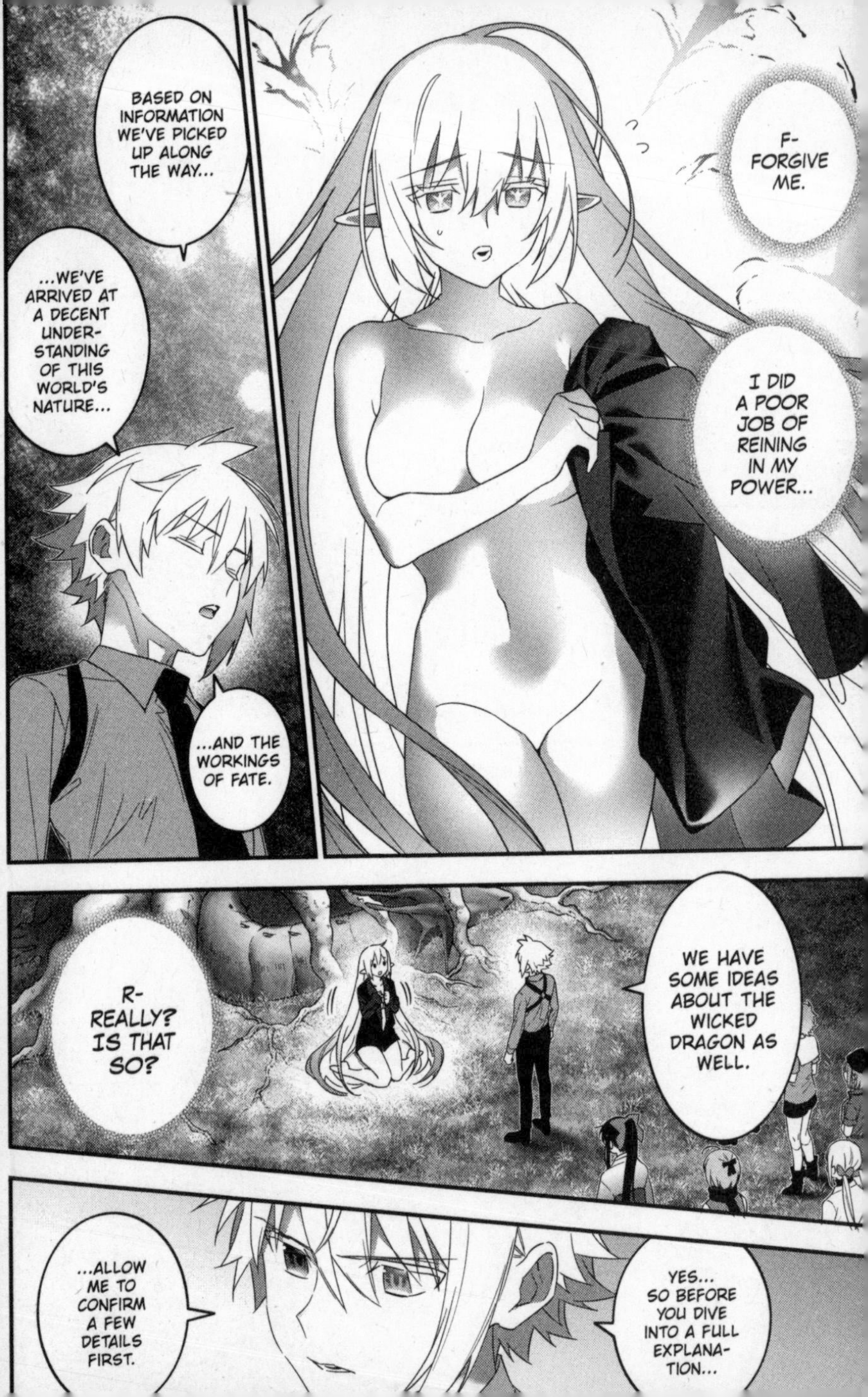
F-FORGIVE ME.
I DID A POOR JOB OF REINING IN MY POWER...
BASED ON INFORMATION WE'VE PICKED UP ALONG THE WAY...
...WE'VE ARRIVED AT A DECENT UNDER-STANDING OF THIS WORLD'S NATURE...
...AND THE WORKINGS OF FATE.
WE HAVE SOME IDEAS ABOUT THE WICKED DRAGON AS WELL.
R-REALLY? IS THAT SO?
YES... SO BEFORE YOU DIVE INTO A FULL EXPLANA-TION...
...ALLOW ME TO CONFIRM A FEW DETAILS FIRST.

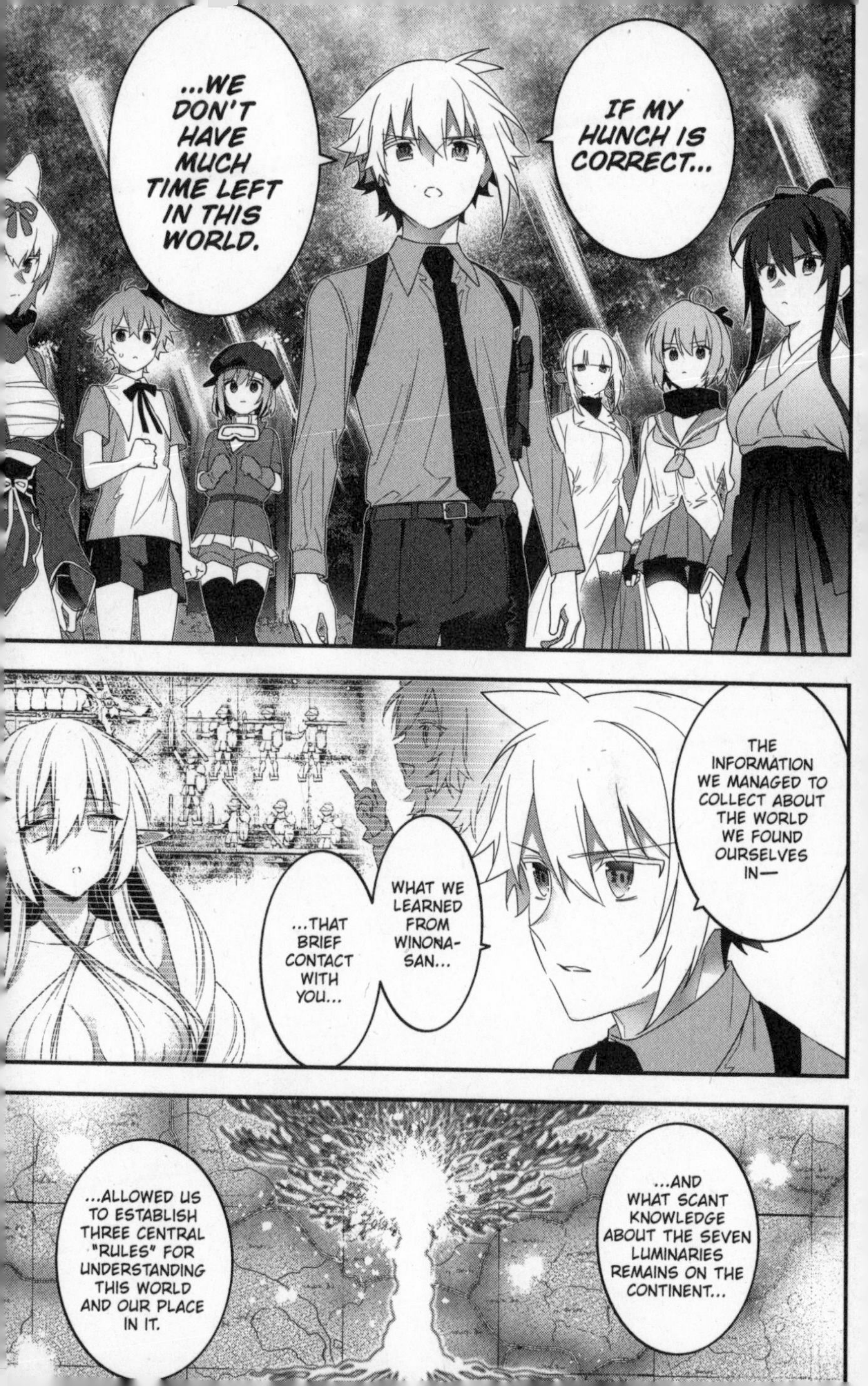
IF MY HUNCH IS CORRECT...
...WE DON'T HAVE MUCH TIME LEFT IN THIS WORLD.
THE INFORMATION WE MANAGED TO COLLECT ABOUT THE WORLD WE FOUND OURSELVES IN—
WHAT WE LEARNED FROM WINONA-SAN...
...THAT BRIEF CONTACT WITH YOU...
...AND WHAT SCANT KNOWLEDGE ABOUT THE SEVEN LUMINARIES REMAINS ON THE CONTINENT...
...ALLOWED US TO ESTABLISH THREE CENTRAL "RULES" FOR UNDERSTANDING THIS WORLD AND OUR PLACE IN IT.

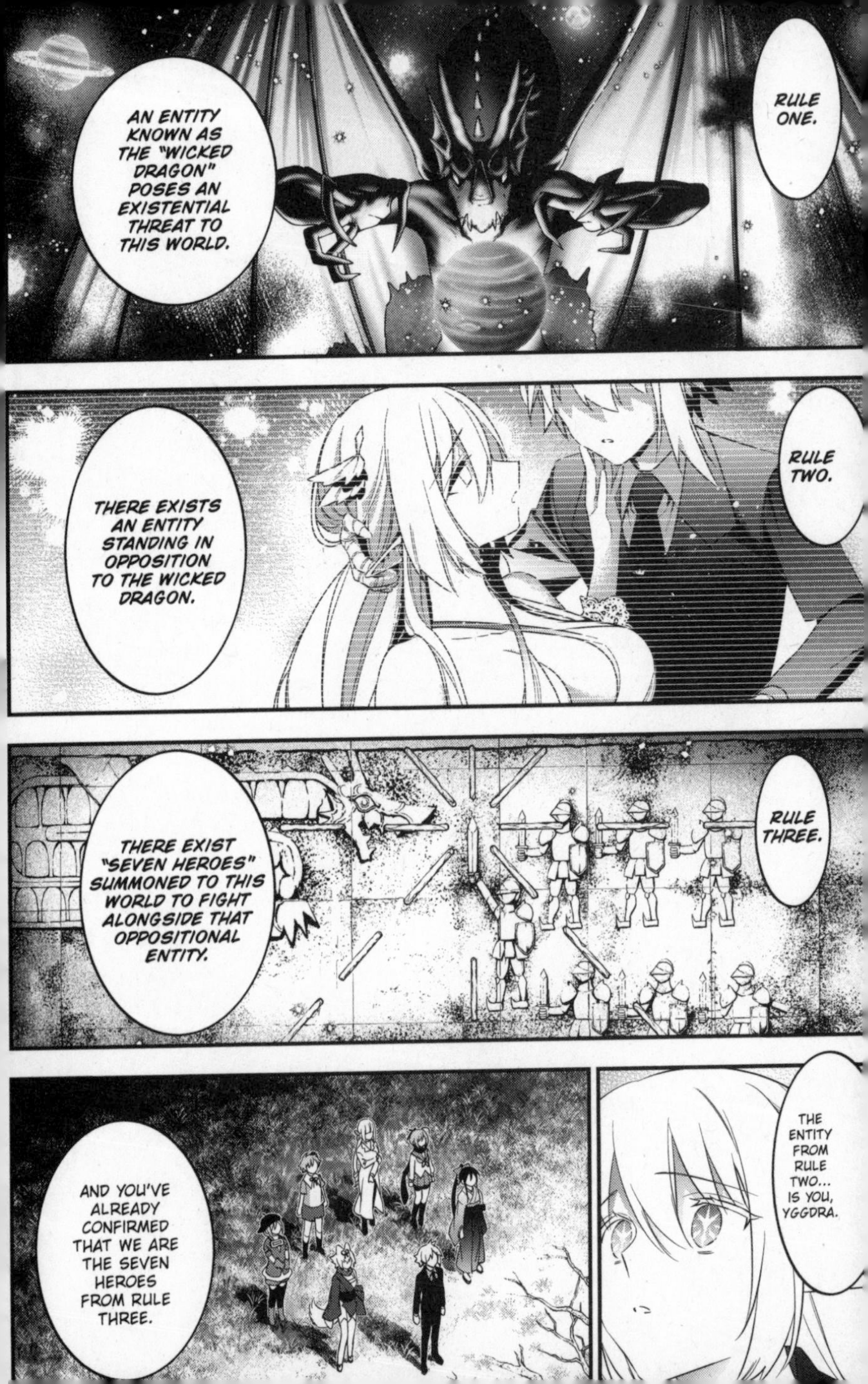
RULE ONE.
AN ENTITY KNOWN AS THE "WICKED DRAGON" POSES AN EXISTENTIAL THREAT TO THIS WORLD.
RULE TWO.
THERE EXISTS AN ENTITY STANDING IN OPPOSITION TO THE WICKED DRAGON.
RULE THREE.
THERE EXIST "SEVEN HEROES" SUMMONED TO THIS WORLD TO FIGHT ALONGSIDE THAT OPPOSITIONAL ENTITY.
THE ENTITY FROM RULE TWO... IS YOU, YGGDRA.
AND YOU'VE ALREADY CONFIRMED THAT WE ARE THE SEVEN HEROES FROM RULE THREE.

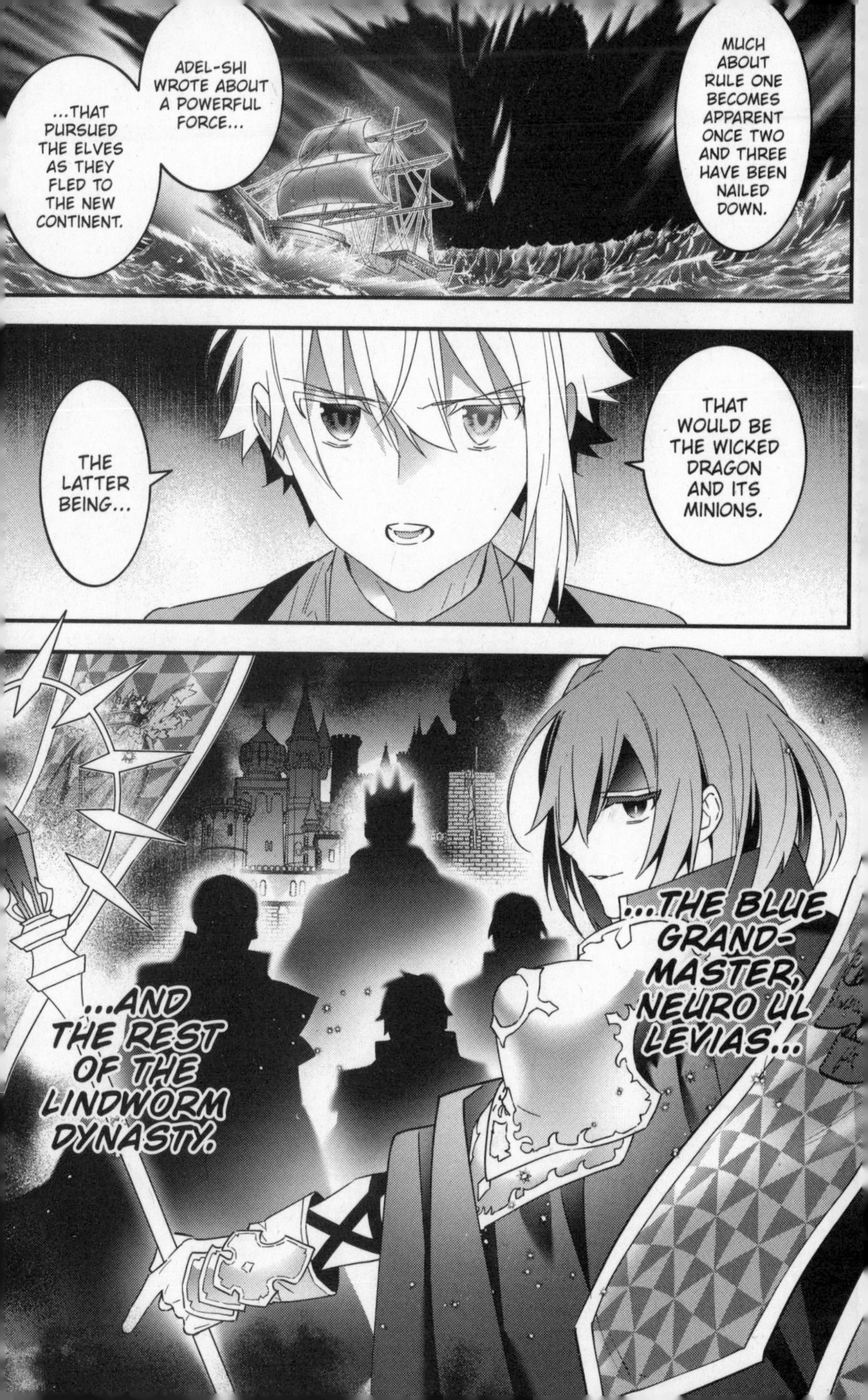
MUCH ABOUT RULE ONE BECOMES APPARENT ONCE TWO AND THREE HAVE BEEN NAILED DOWN.
ADEL-SHI WROTE ABOUT A POWERFUL FORCE...
...THAT PURSUED THE ELVES AS THEY FLED TO THE NEW CONTINENT.
THAT WOULD BE THE WICKED DRAGON AND ITS MINIONS.
THE LATTER BEING...
...THE BLUE GRAND-MASTER, NEURO UL LEVIAS...
...AND THE REST OF THE LINDWORM DYNASTY.

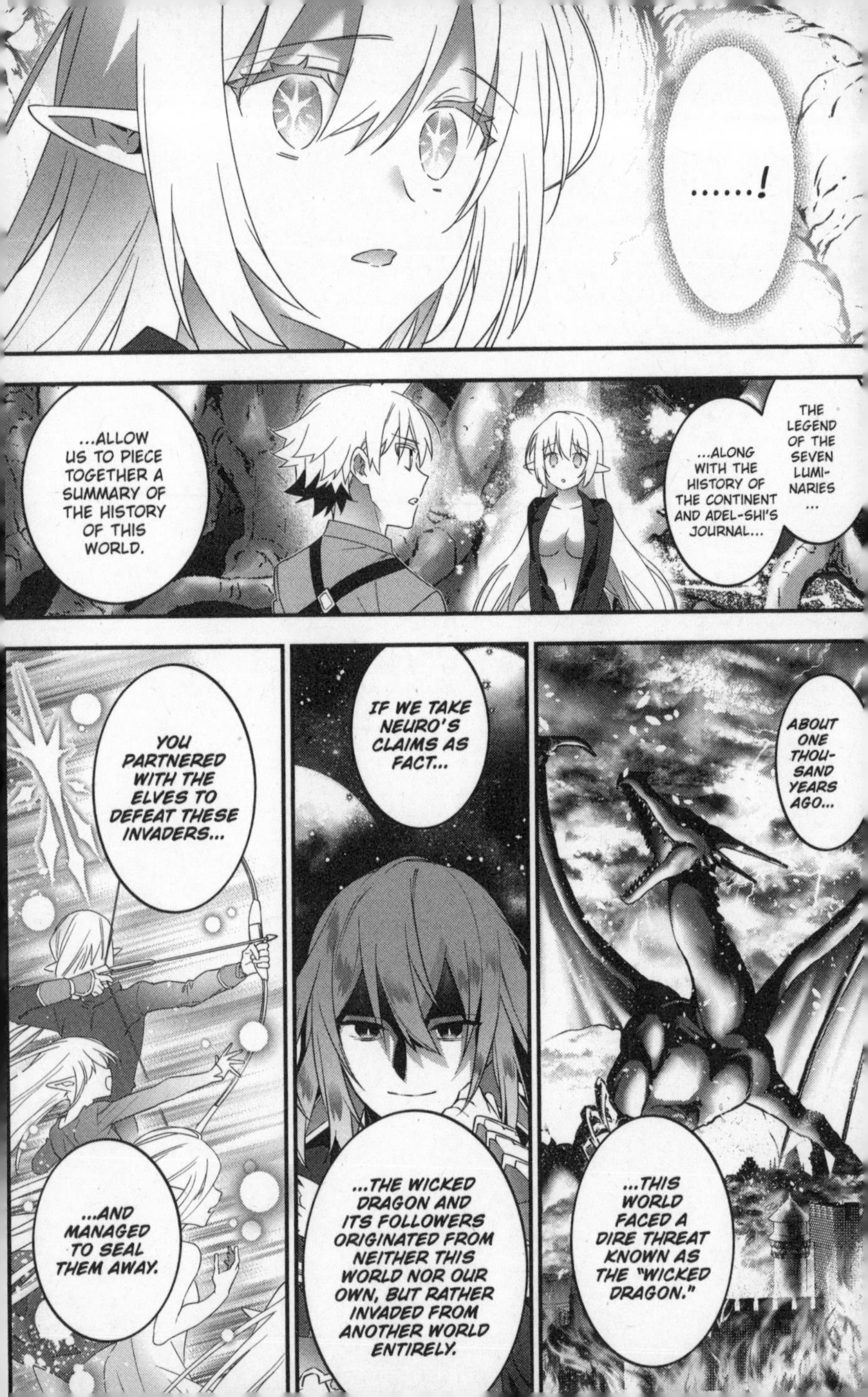
……!
THE LEGEND OF THE SEVEN LUMINARIES ...
...ALONG WITH THE HISTORY OF THE CONTINENT AND ADEL-SHI'S JOURNAL...
...ALLOW US TO PIECE TOGETHER A SUMMARY OF THE HISTORY OF THIS WORLD.
ABOUT ONE THOUSAND YEARS AGO...
...THIS WORLD FACED A DIRE THREAT KNOWN AS THE "WICKED DRAGON."
IF WE TAKE NEURO'S CLAIMS AS FACT...
...THE WICKED DRAGON AND ITS FOLLOWERS ORIGINATED FROM NEITHER THIS WORLD NOR OUR OWN, BUT RATHER INVADED FROM ANOTHER WORLD ENTIRELY.
YOU PARTNERED WITH THE ELVES TO DEFEAT THESE INVADERS...
...AND MANAGED TO SEAL THEM AWAY.

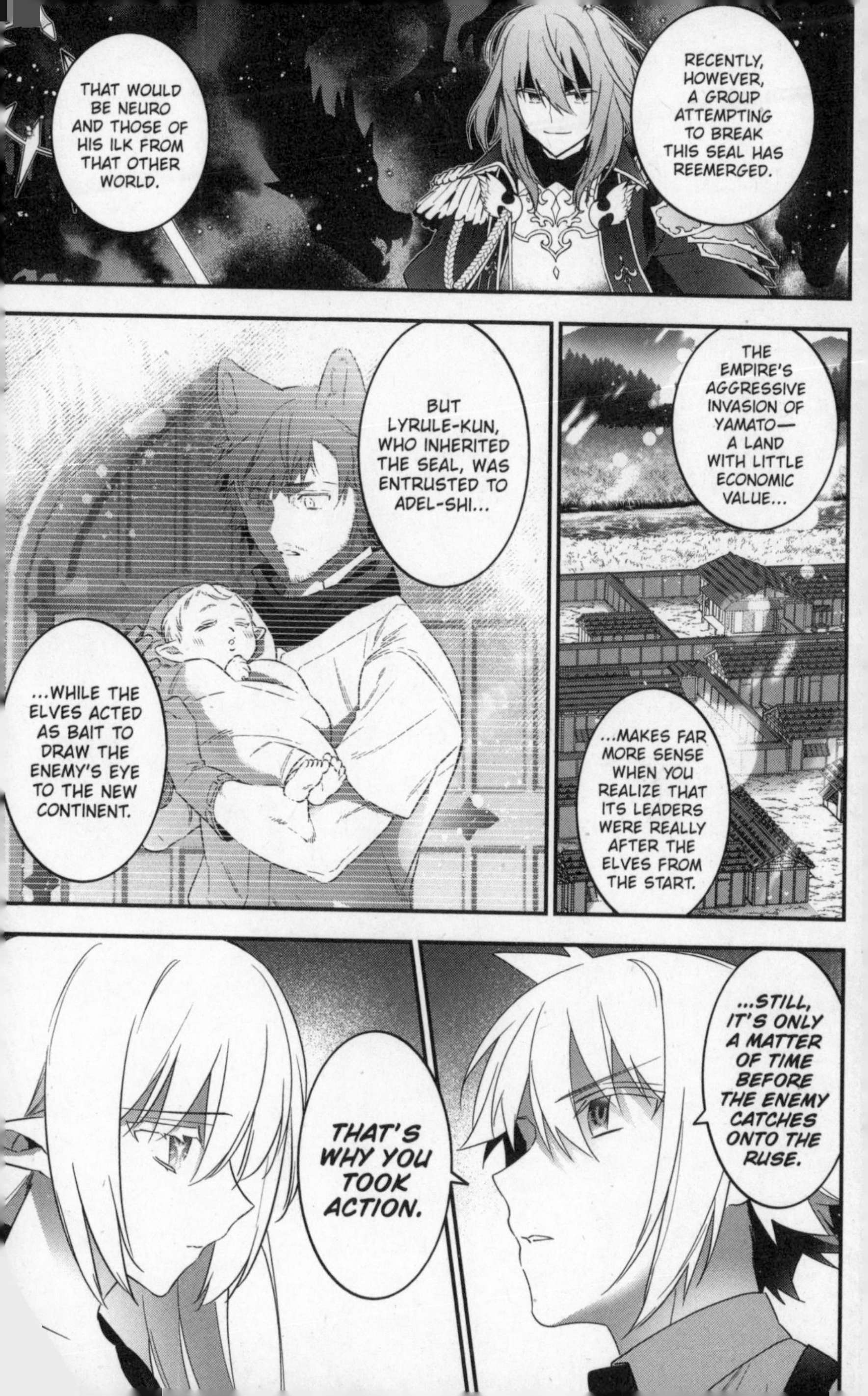
RECENTLY, HOWEVER, A GROUP ATTEMPTING TO BREAK THIS SEAL HAS REEMERGED.
THAT WOULD BE NEURO AND THOSE OF HIS ILK FROM THAT OTHER WORLD.
THE EMPIRE'S AGGRESSIVE INVASION OF YAMATO— A LAND WITH LITTLE ECONOMIC VALUE...
...MAKES FAR MORE SENSE WHEN YOU REALIZE THAT ITS LEADERS WERE REALLY AFTER THE ELVES FROM THE START.
BUT LYRULE-KUN, WHO INHERITED THE SEAL, WAS ENTRUSTED TO ADEL-SHI...
...WHILE THE ELVES ACTED AS BAIT TO DRAW THE ENEMY'S EYE TO THE NEW CONTINENT.
...STILL, IT'S ONLY A MATTER OF TIME BEFORE THE ENEMY CATCHES ONTO THE RUSE.
THAT'S WHY YOU TOOK ACTION.

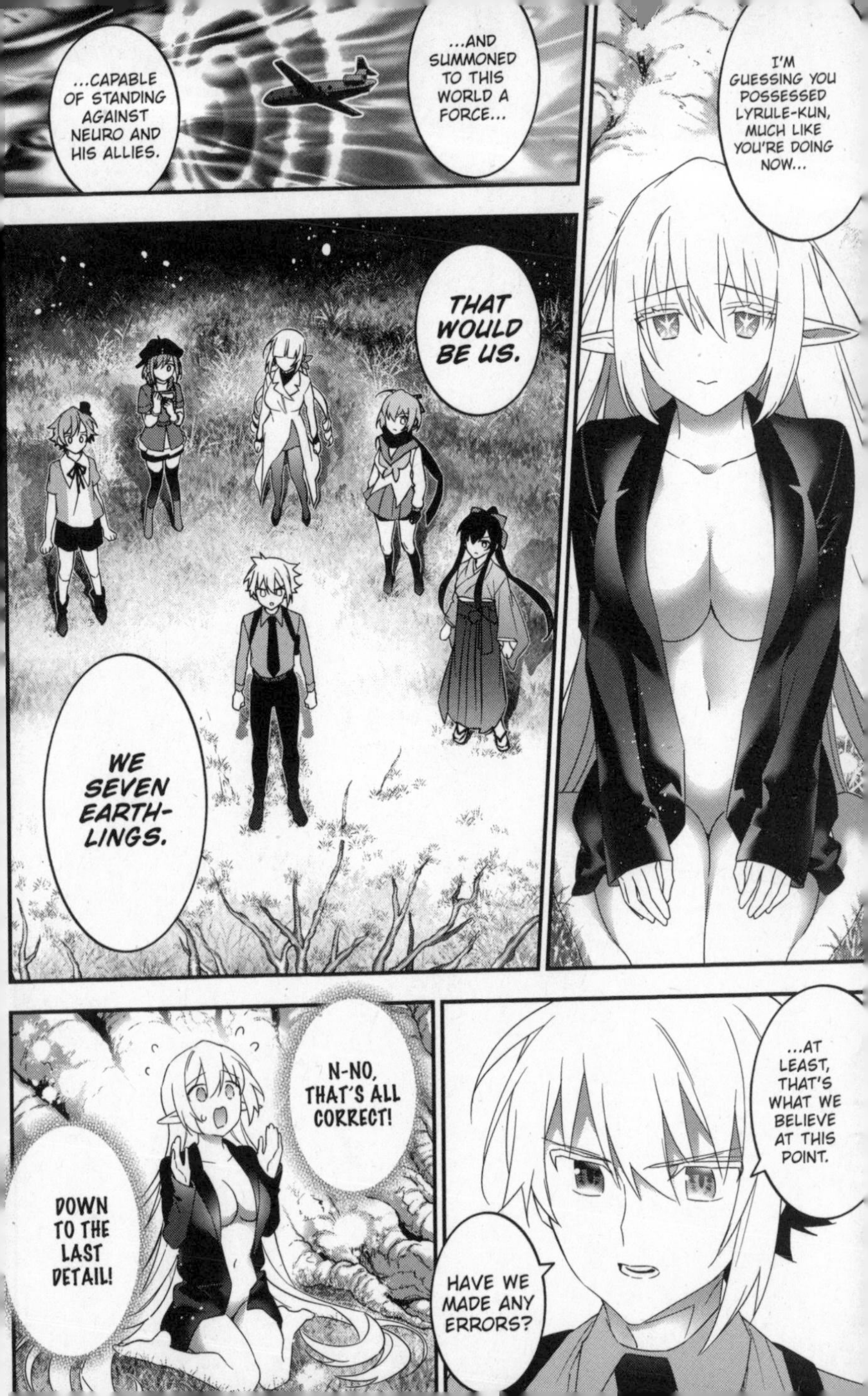
I'M GUESSING YOU POSSESSED LYRULE-KUN, MUCH LIKE YOU'RE DOING NOW...
...AND SUMMONED TO THIS WORLD A FORCE...
...CAPABLE OF STANDING AGAINST NEURO AND HIS ALLIES.
THAT WOULD BE US.
WE SEVEN EARTH-LINGS.
...AT LEAST, THAT'S WHAT WE BELIEVE AT THIS POINT.
HAVE WE MADE ANY ERRORS?
N-NO, THAT'S ALL CORRECT!
DOWN TO THE LAST DETAIL!

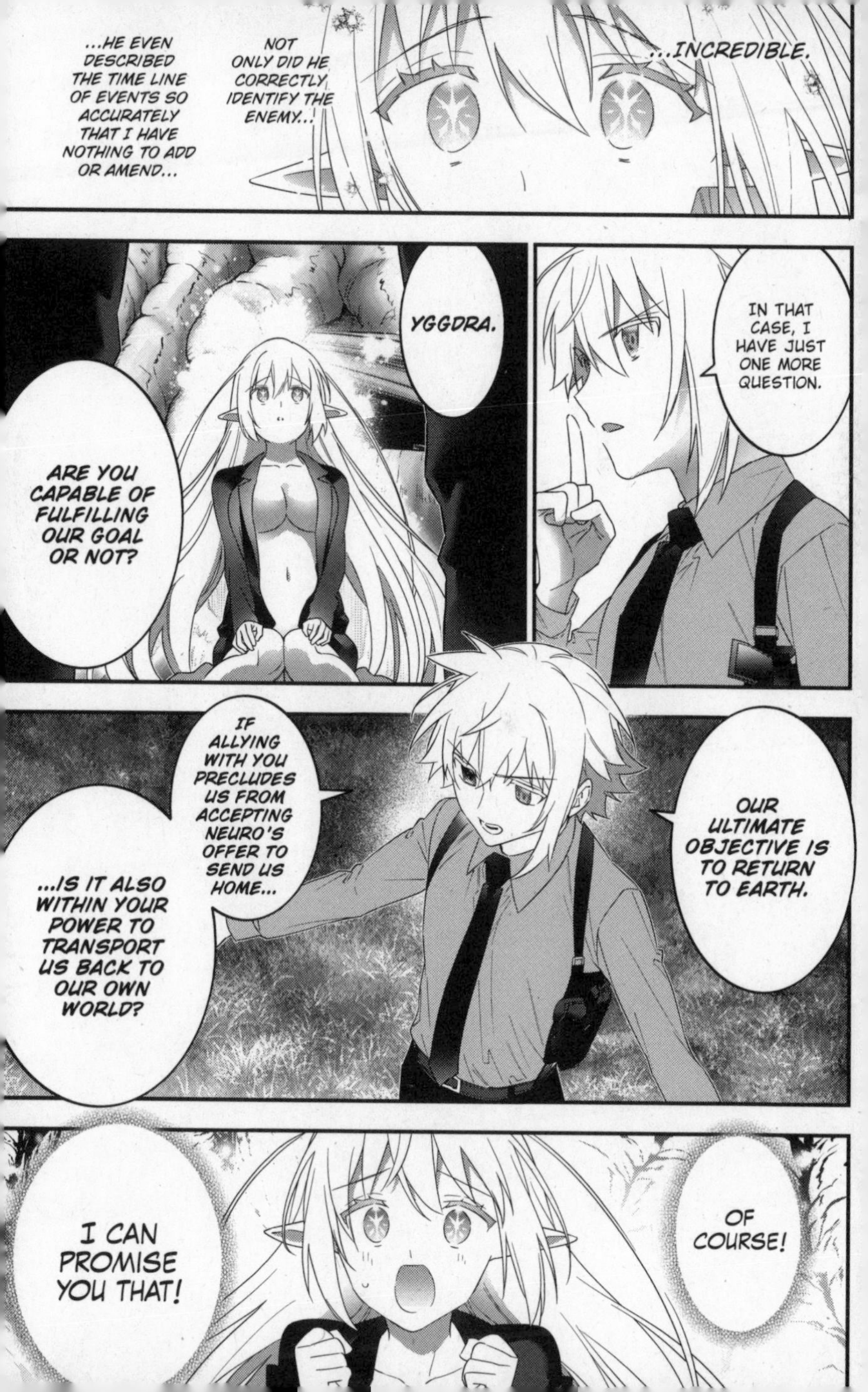
...INCREDIBLE.
NOT ONLY DID HE CORRECTLY IDENTIFY THE ENEMY...
...HE EVEN DESCRIBED THE TIME LINE OF EVENTS SO ACCURATELY THAT I HAVE NOTHING TO ADD OR AMEND...
IN THAT CASE, I HAVE JUST ONE MORE QUESTION.
YGGDRA.
ARE YOU CAPABLE OF FULFILLING OUR GOAL OR NOT?
OUR ULTIMATE OBJECTIVE IS TO RETURN TO EARTH.
IF ALLYING WITH YOU PRECLUDES US FROM ACCEPTING NEURO'S OFFER TO SEND US HOME...
...IS IT ALSO WITHIN YOUR POWER TO TRANSPORT US BACK TO OUR OWN WORLD?
OF COURSE!
I CAN PROMISE YOU THAT!

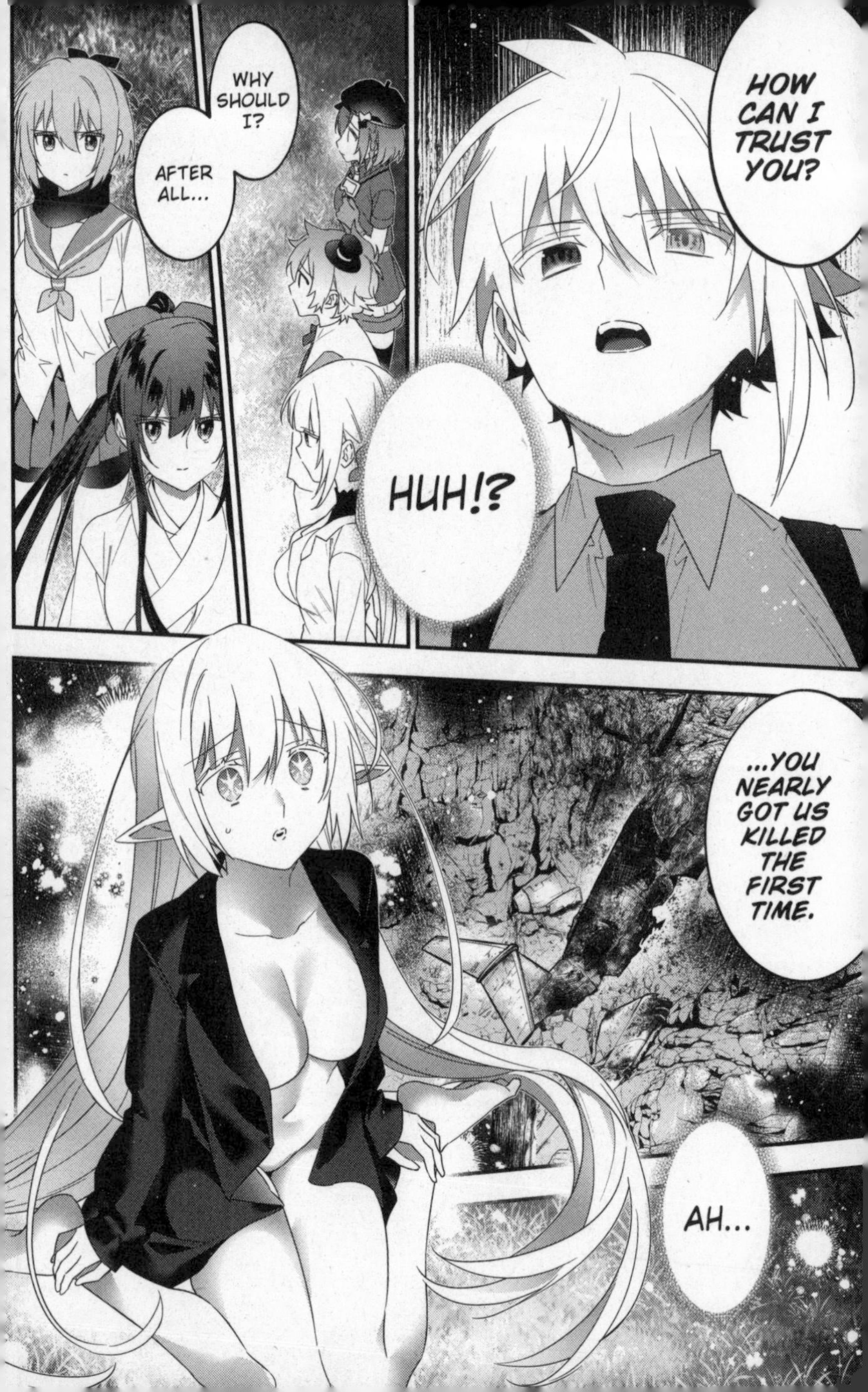

HOW CAN I TRUST YOU?
HUH!?
WHY SHOULD I?
AFTER ALL...
...YOU NEARLY GOT US KILLED THE FIRST TIME.
AH...

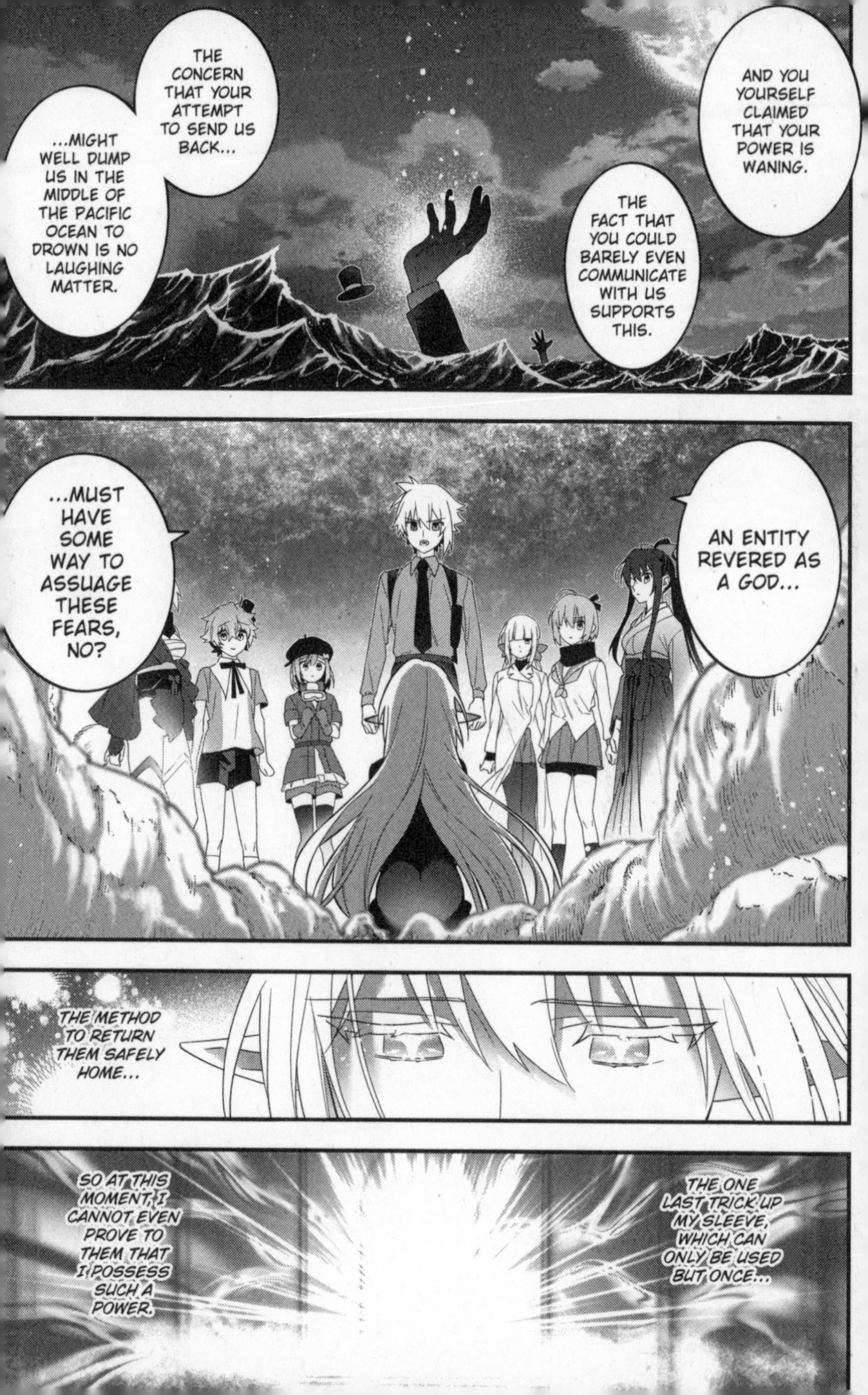
AND YOU YOURSELF CLAIMED THAT YOUR POWER IS WANING.
THE FACT THAT YOU COULD BARELY EVEN COMMUNICATE WITH US SUPPORTS THIS.
THE CONCERN THAT YOUR ATTEMPT TO SEND US BACK...
...MIGHT WELL DUMP US IN THE MIDDLE OF THE PACIFIC OCEAN TO DROWN IS NO LAUGHING MATTER.
AN ENTITY REVERED AS A GOD...
...MUST HAVE SOME WAY TO ASSUAGE THESE FEARS, NO?
THE METHOD TO RETURN THEM SAFELY HOME...
THE ONE LAST TRICK UP MY SLEEVE, WHICH CAN ONLY BE USED BUT ONCE...
SO AT THIS MOMENT, I CANNOT EVEN PROVE TO THEM THAT I POSSESS SUCH A POWER.

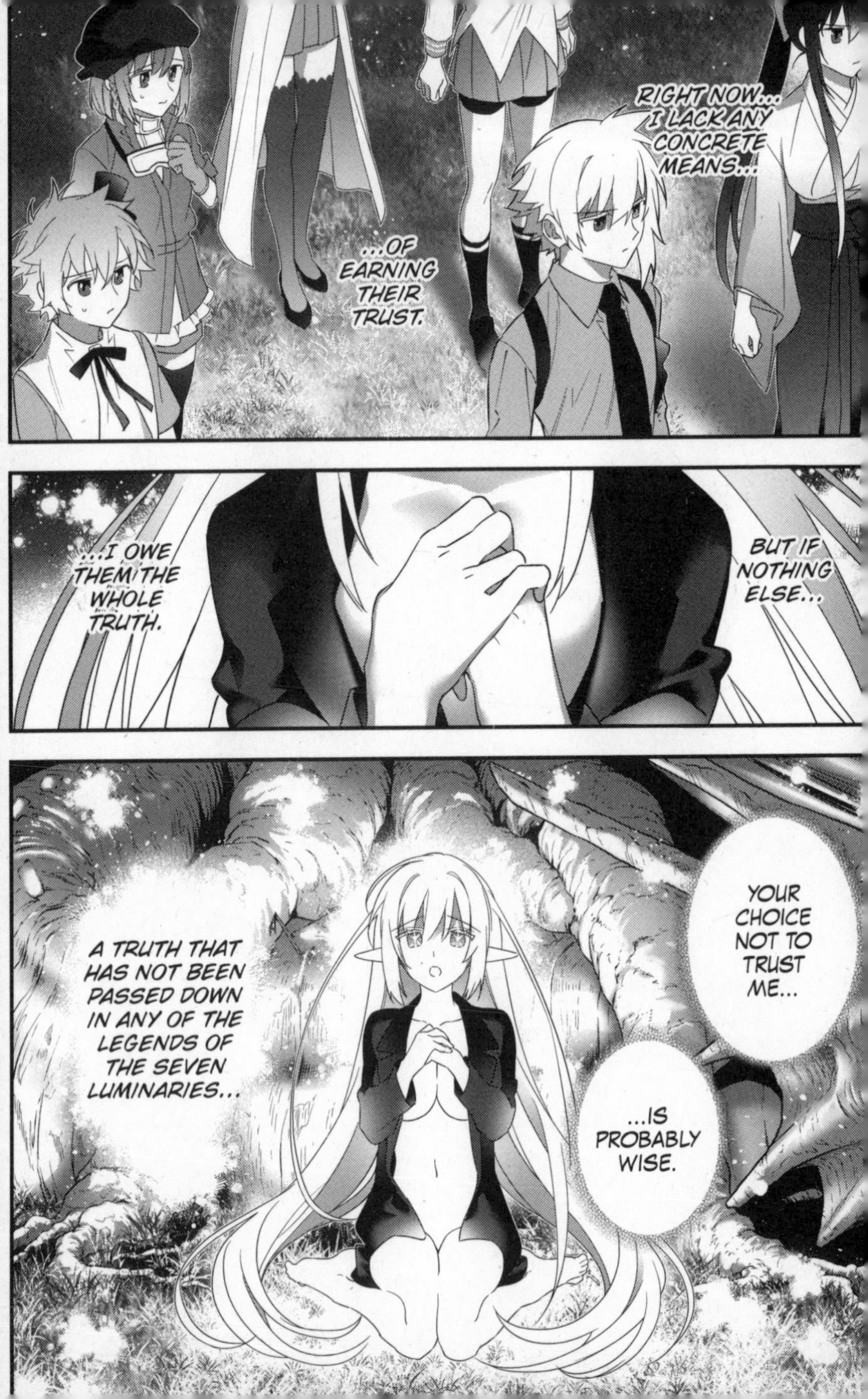
RIGHT NOW... I LACK ANY CONCRETE MEANS...
...OF EARNING THEIR TRUST.
BUT IF NOTHING ELSE...
...I OWE THEM THE WHOLE TRUTH.
YOUR CHOICE NOT TO TRUST ME...
...IS PROBABLY WISE.
A TRUTH THAT HAS NOT BEEN PASSED DOWN IN ANY OF THE LEGENDS OF THE SEVEN LUMINARIES...

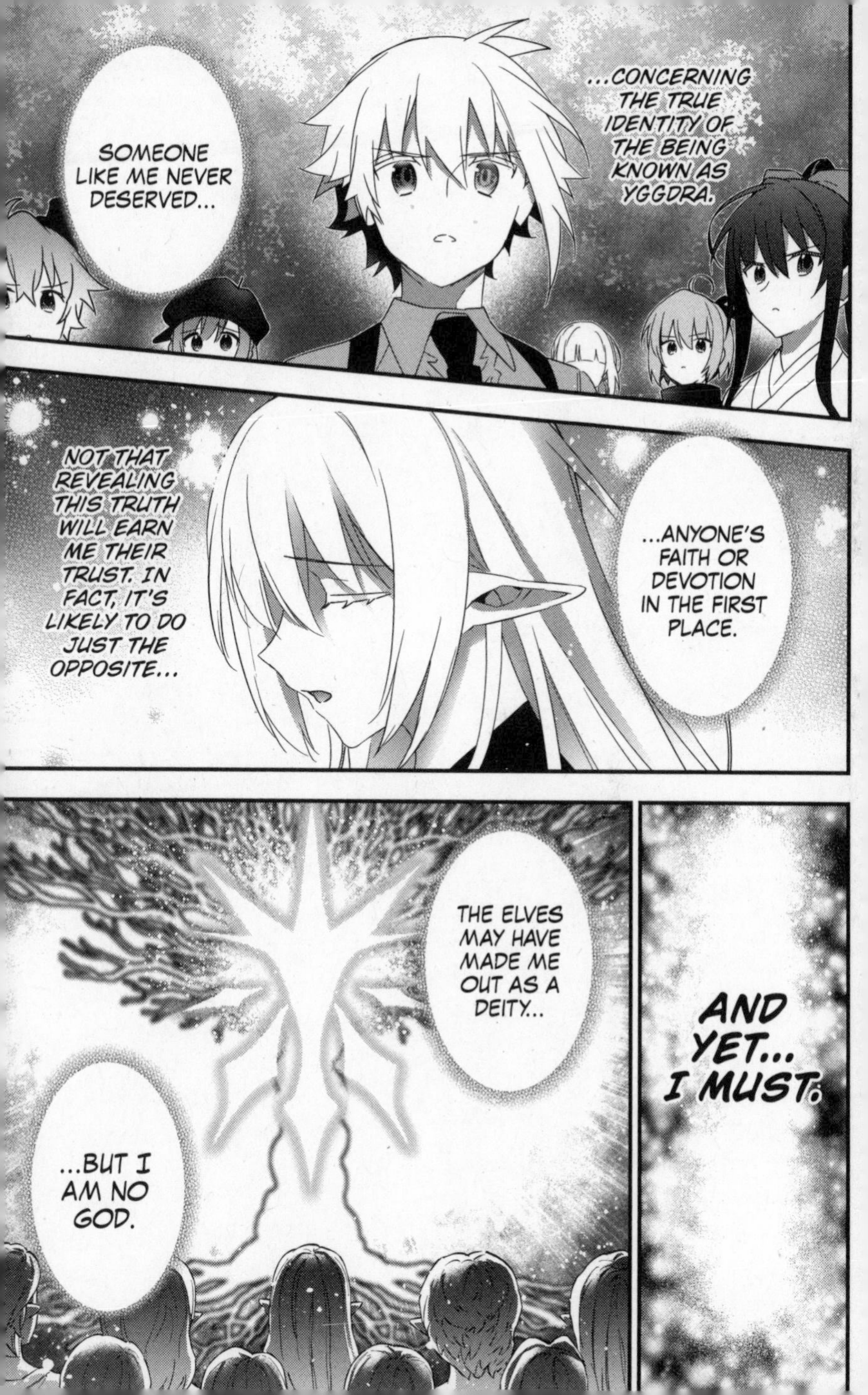
...CONCERNING THE TRUE IDENTITY OF THE BEING KNOWN AS YGGDRA.
SOMEONE LIKE ME NEVER DESERVED...
...ANYONE'S FAITH OR DEVOTION IN THE FIRST PLACE.
NOT THAT REVEALING THIS TRUTH WILL EARN ME THEIR TRUST. IN FACT, IT'S LIKELY TO DO JUST THE OPPOSITE...
AND YET... I MUST.
THE ELVES MAY HAVE MADE ME OUT AS A DEITY...
...BUT I AM NO GOD.

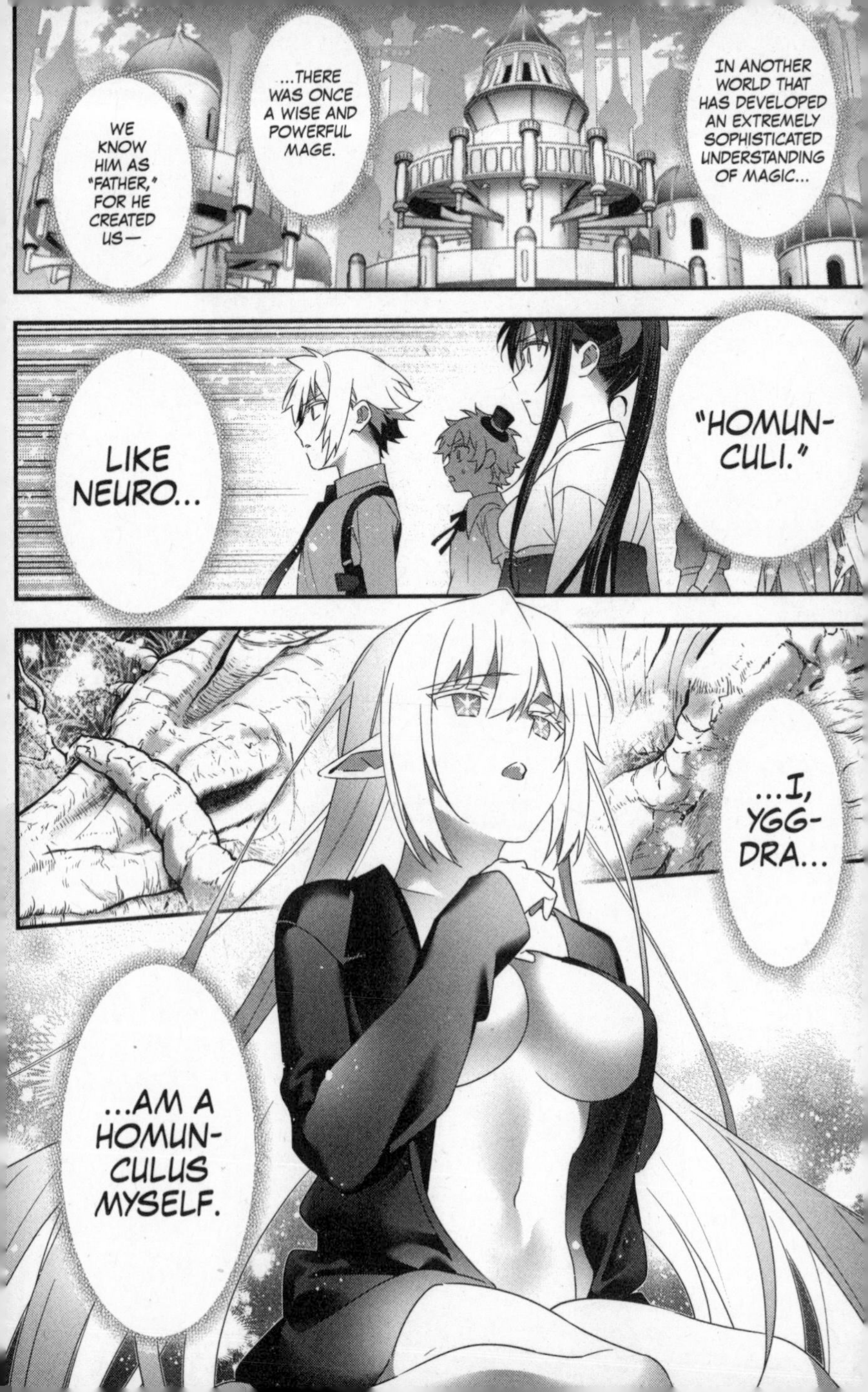
IN ANOTHER WORLD THAT HAS DEVELOPED AN EXTREMELY SOPHISTICATED UNDERSTANDING OF MAGIC...
...THERE WAS ONCE A WISE AND POWERFUL MAGE.
WE KNOW HIM AS "FATHER," FOR HE CREATED US—
"HOMUN-CULI."
LIKE NEURO...
...I, YGG-DRA...
...AM A HOMUN-CULUS MYSELF.

HIGH SCHOOL PRODIGIES HAVE IT EASY EVEN IN ANOTHER WORLD!

Illustration Gallery (5)

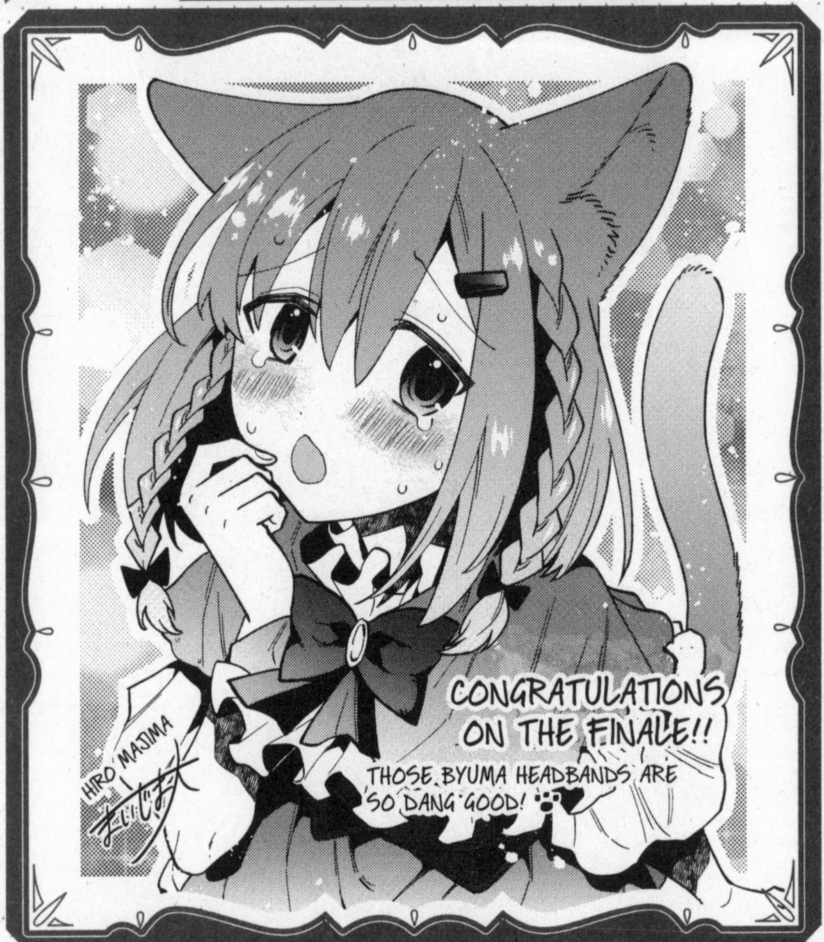
CONGRATULATIONS ON THE FINALE!!
THOSE BYUMA HEADBANDS ARE SO DANG GOOD!
HIRO MAJIMA

Hiro Maijima-sensei

Manga artist for
The Strongest Sorcerer Making Full Use of the Strategy Guide —No Taking Orders, I'll Slay the Demon King My Own Way—
featured in Manga UP!

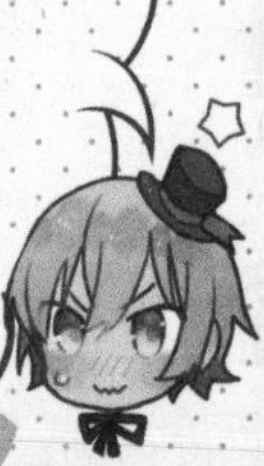

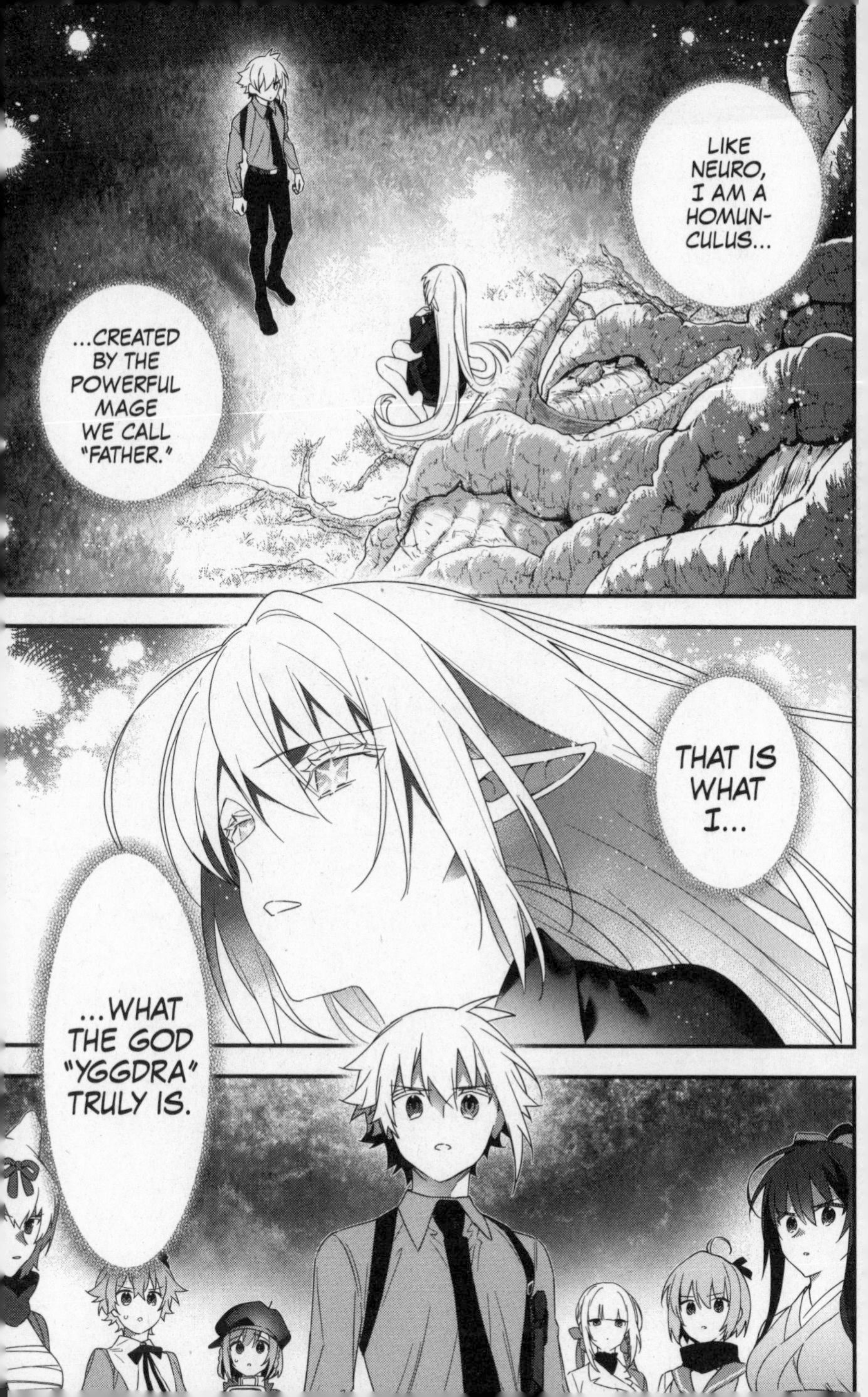
LIKE NEURO, I AM A HOMUN-CULUS...
...CREATED BY THE POWERFUL MAGE WE CALL "FATHER."
THAT IS WHAT I...
...WHAT THE GOD "YGGDRA" TRULY IS.

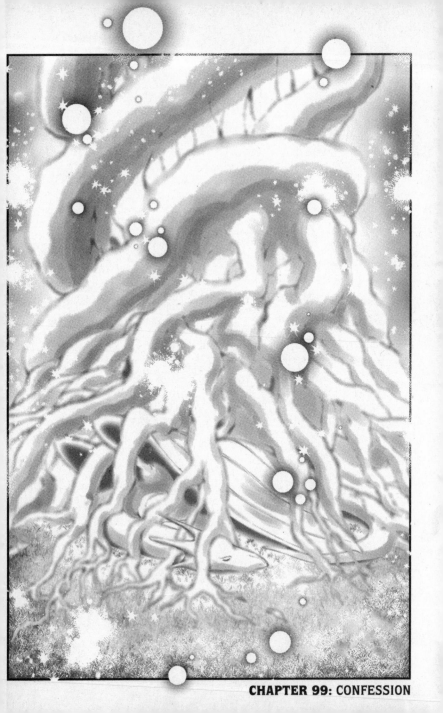

CHAPTER 99: CONFESSION

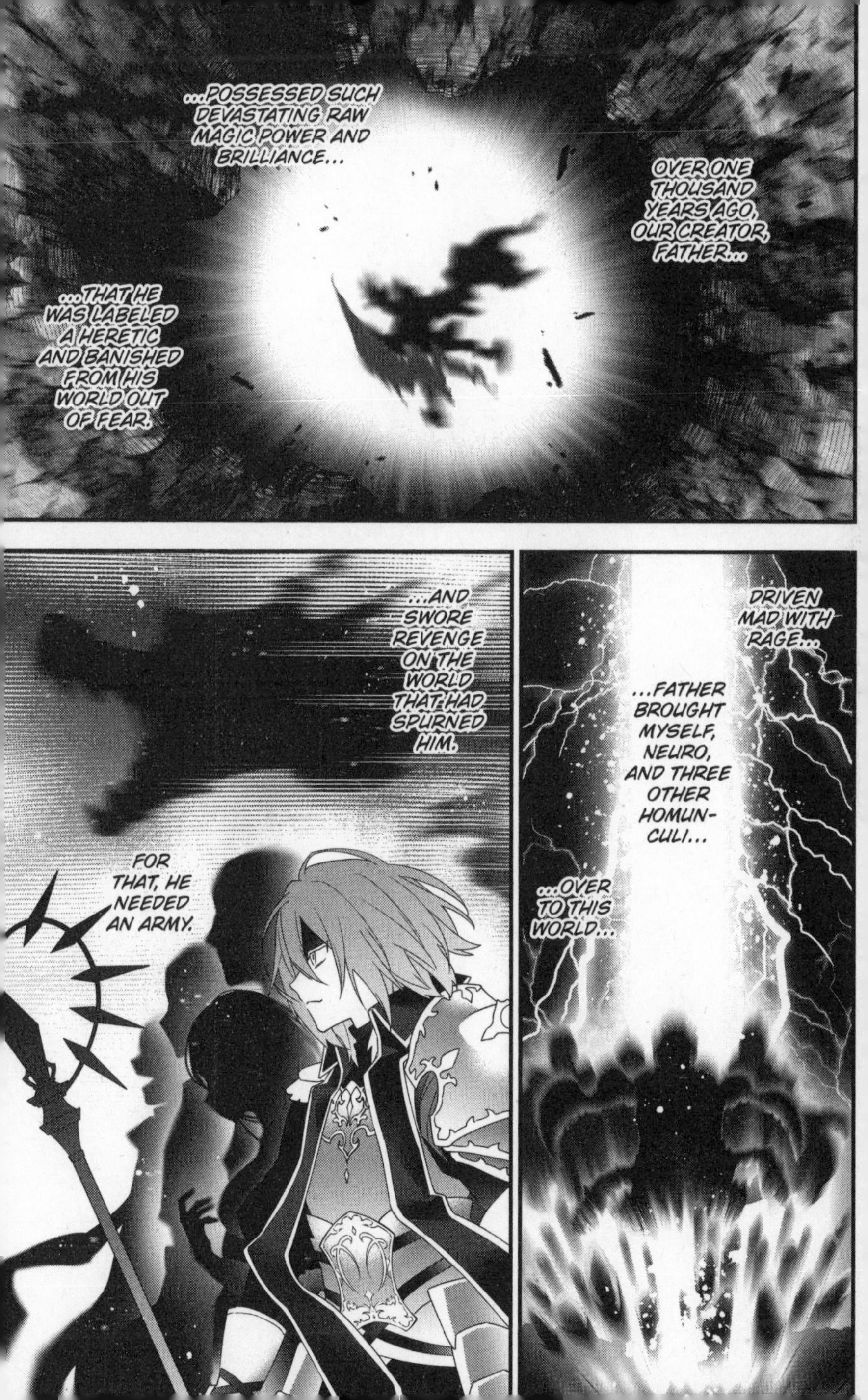
OVER ONE THOUSAND YEARS AGO, OUR CREATOR, FATHER...
...POSSESSED SUCH DEVASTATING RAW MAGIC POWER AND BRILLIANCE...
...THAT HE WAS LABELED A HERETIC AND BANISHED FROM HIS WORLD OUT OF FEAR.
DRIVEN MAD WITH RAGE...
...FATHER BROUGHT MYSELF, NEURO, AND THREE OTHER HOMUN-CULI...
...OVER TO THIS WORLD...
...AND SWORE REVENGE ON THE WORLD THAT HAD SPURNED HIM.
FOR THAT, HE NEEDED AN ARMY.

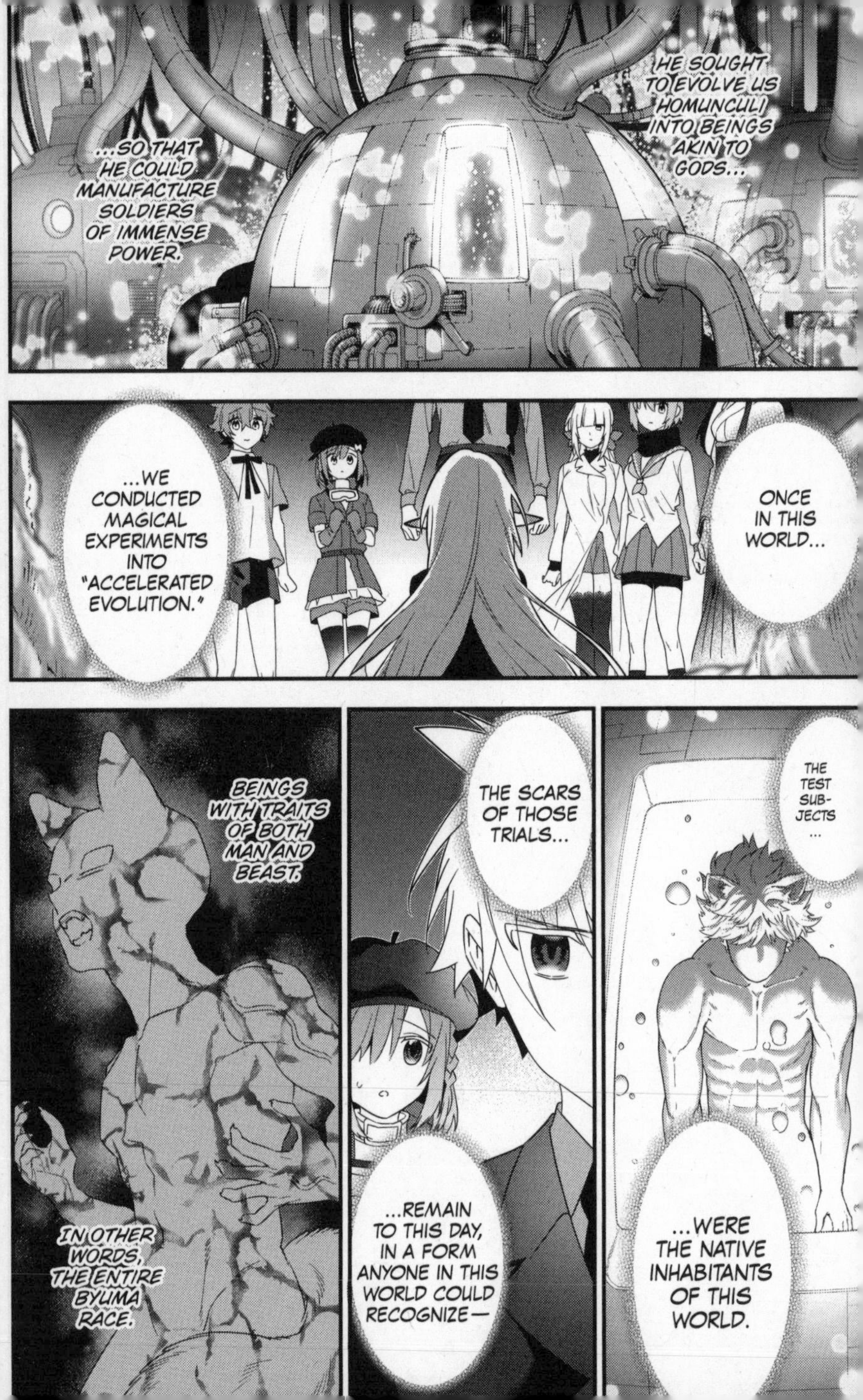
HE SOUGHT TO EVOLVE US HOMUNCULI INTO BEINGS AKIN TO GODS...
...SO THAT HE COULD MANUFACTURE SOLDIERS OF IMMENSE POWER.
ONCE IN THIS WORLD...
...WE CONDUCTED MAGICAL EXPERIMENTS INTO "ACCELERATED EVOLUTION."
THE TEST SUB-JECTS...
...WERE THE NATIVE INHABITANTS OF THIS WORLD.
THE SCARS OF THOSE TRIALS...
...REMAIN TO THIS DAY, IN A FORM ANYONE IN THIS WORLD COULD RECOGNIZE—
BEINGS WITH TRAITS OF BOTH MAN AND BEAST.
IN OTHER WORDS, THE ENTIRE BYUMA RACE.

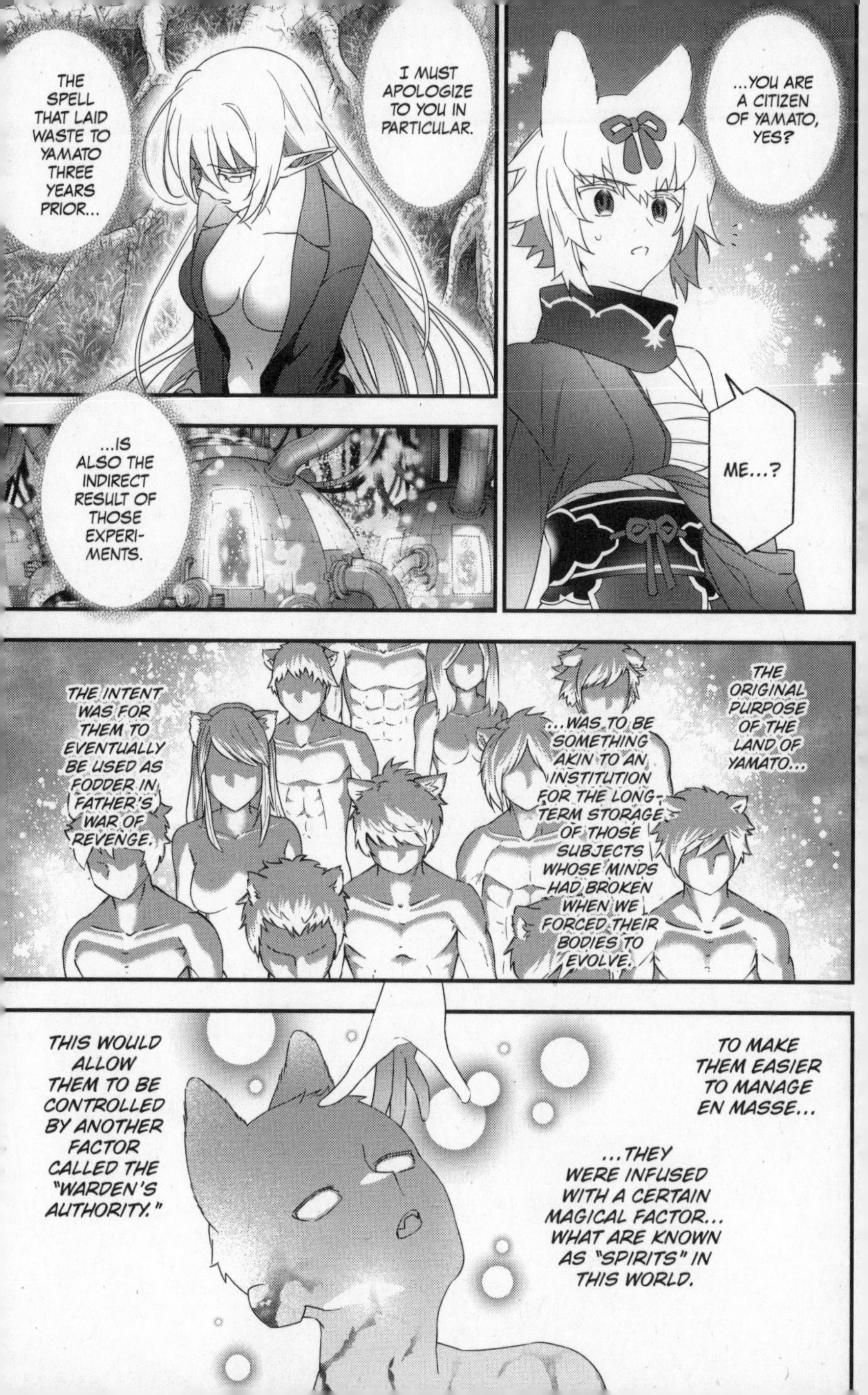
...YOU ARE A CITIZEN OF YAMATO, YES?
ME...?
I MUST APOLOGIZE TO YOU IN PARTICULAR.
THE SPELL THAT LAID WASTE TO YAMATO THREE YEARS PRIOR...
...IS ALSO THE INDIRECT RESULT OF THOSE EXPERI-MENTS.
THE ORIGINAL PURPOSE OF THE LAND OF YAMATO...
...WAS TO BE SOMETHING AKIN TO AN INSTITUTION FOR THE LONG-TERM STORAGE OF THOSE SUBJECTS WHOSE MINDS HAD BROKEN WHEN WE FORCED THEIR BODIES TO EVOLVE.
THE INTENT WAS FOR THEM TO EVENTUALLY BE USED AS FODDER IN FATHER'S WAR OF REVENGE.
TO MAKE THEM EASIER TO MANAGE EN MASSE...
...THEY WERE INFUSED WITH A CERTAIN MAGICAL FACTOR... WHAT ARE KNOWN AS "SPIRITS" IN THIS WORLD.
THIS WOULD ALLOW THEM TO BE CONTROLLED BY ANOTHER FACTOR CALLED THE "WARDEN'S AUTHORITY."

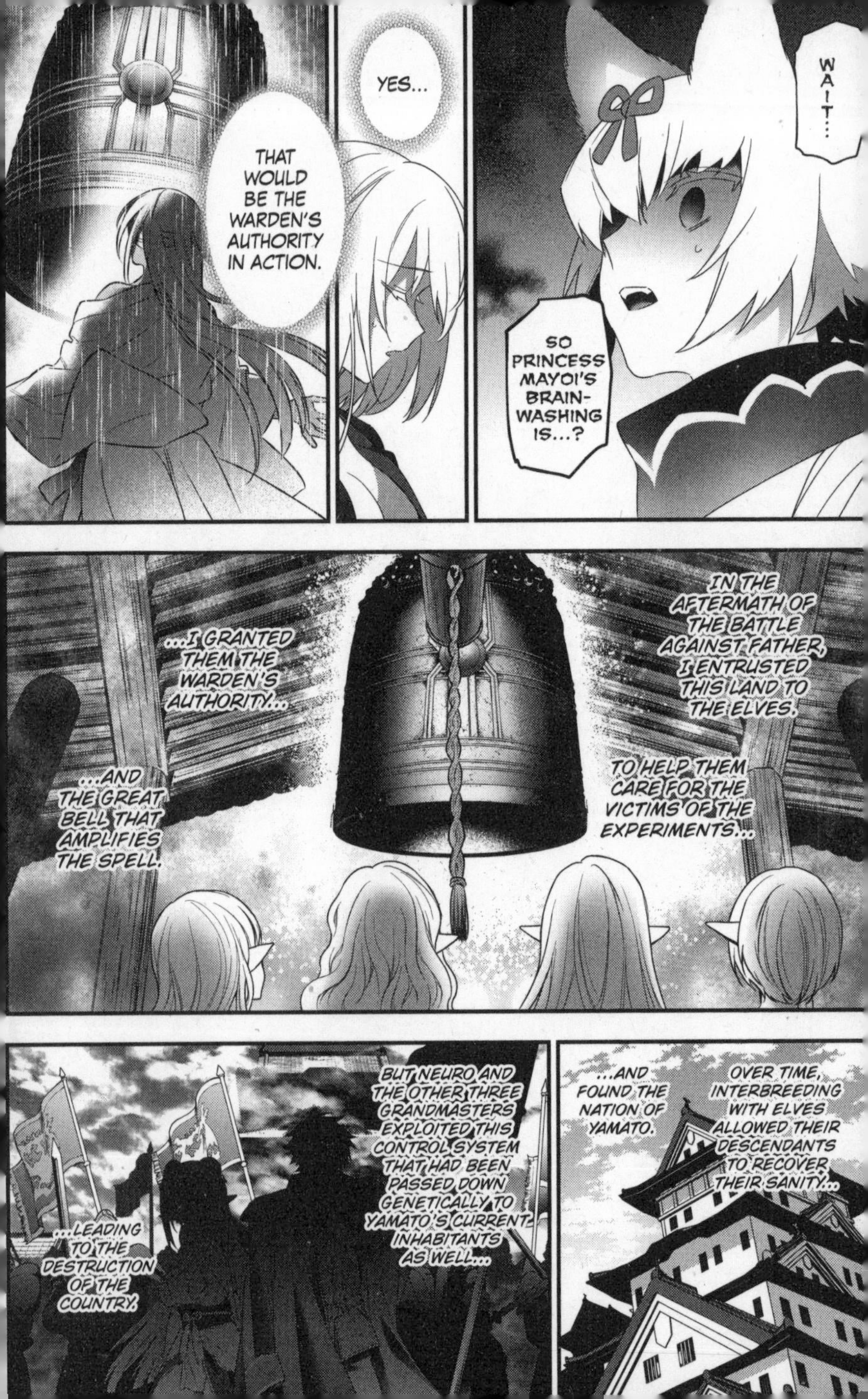
WAIT...
SO PRINCESS MAYOI'S BRAIN-WASHING IS...?
YES...
THAT WOULD BE THE WARDEN'S AUTHORITY IN ACTION.
IN THE AFTERMATH OF THE BATTLE AGAINST FATHER, I ENTRUSTED THIS LAND TO THE ELVES.
TO HELP THEM CARE FOR THE VICTIMS OF THE EXPERIMENTS...
...I GRANTED THEM THE WARDEN'S AUTHORITY...
...AND THE GREAT BELL THAT AMPLIFIES THE SPELL.
OVER TIME, INTERBREEDING WITH ELVES ALLOWED THEIR DESCENDANTS TO RECOVER THEIR SANITY...
...AND FOUND THE NATION OF YAMATO.
BUT NEURO AND THE OTHER THREE GRANDMASTERS EXPLOITED THIS CONTROL SYSTEM THAT HAD BEEN PASSED DOWN GENETICALLY TO YAMATO'S CURRENT INHABITANTS AS WELL...
...LEADING TO THE DESTRUCTION OF THE COUNTRY.

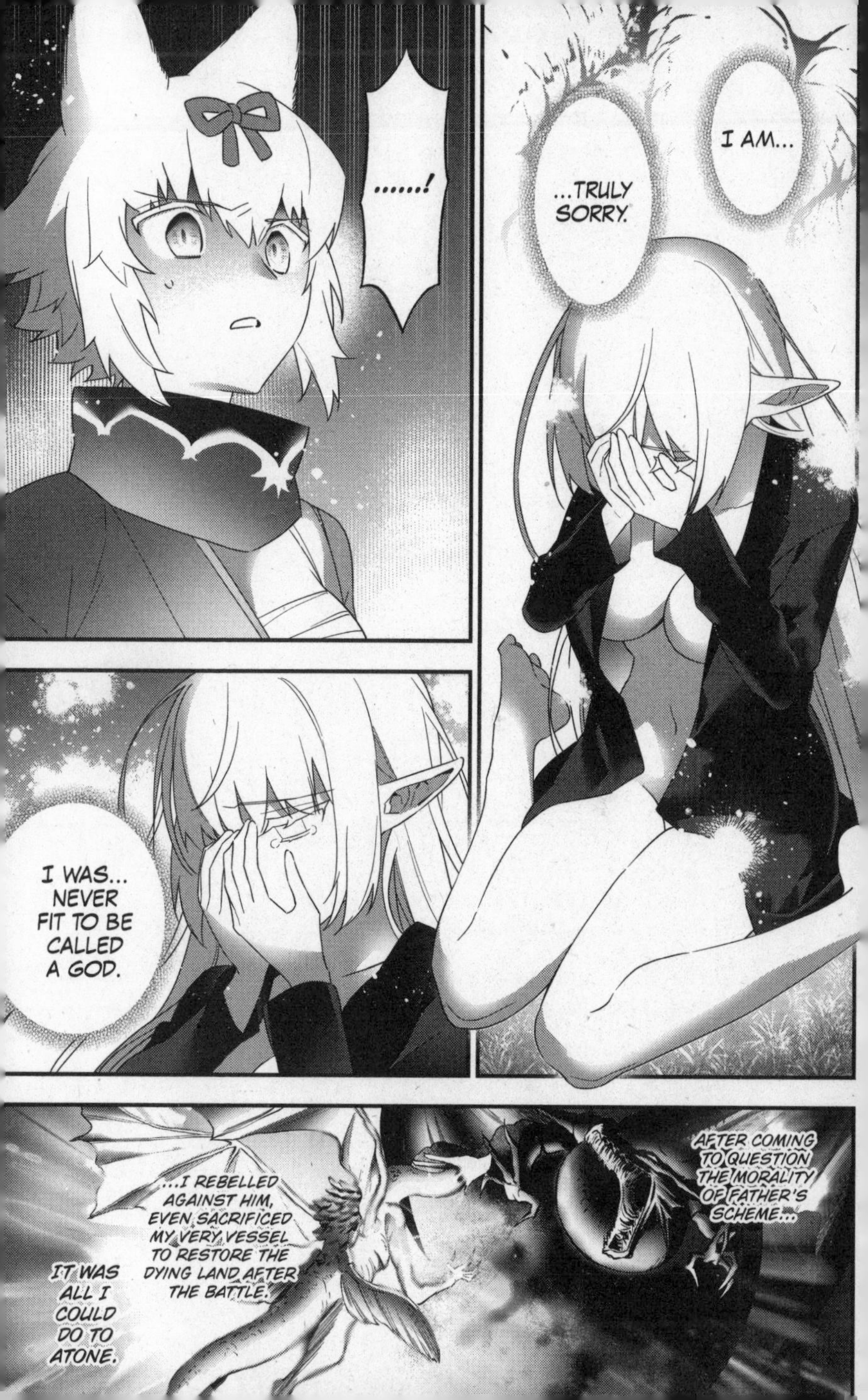
I AM...
...TRULY SORRY.
......!
I WAS... NEVER FIT TO BE CALLED A GOD.
AFTER COMING TO QUESTION THE MORALITY OF FATHER'S SCHEME...
...I REBELLED AGAINST HIM, EVEN SACRIFICED MY VERY VESSEL TO RESTORE THE DYING LAND AFTER THE BATTLE.
IT WAS ALL I COULD DO TO ATONE.

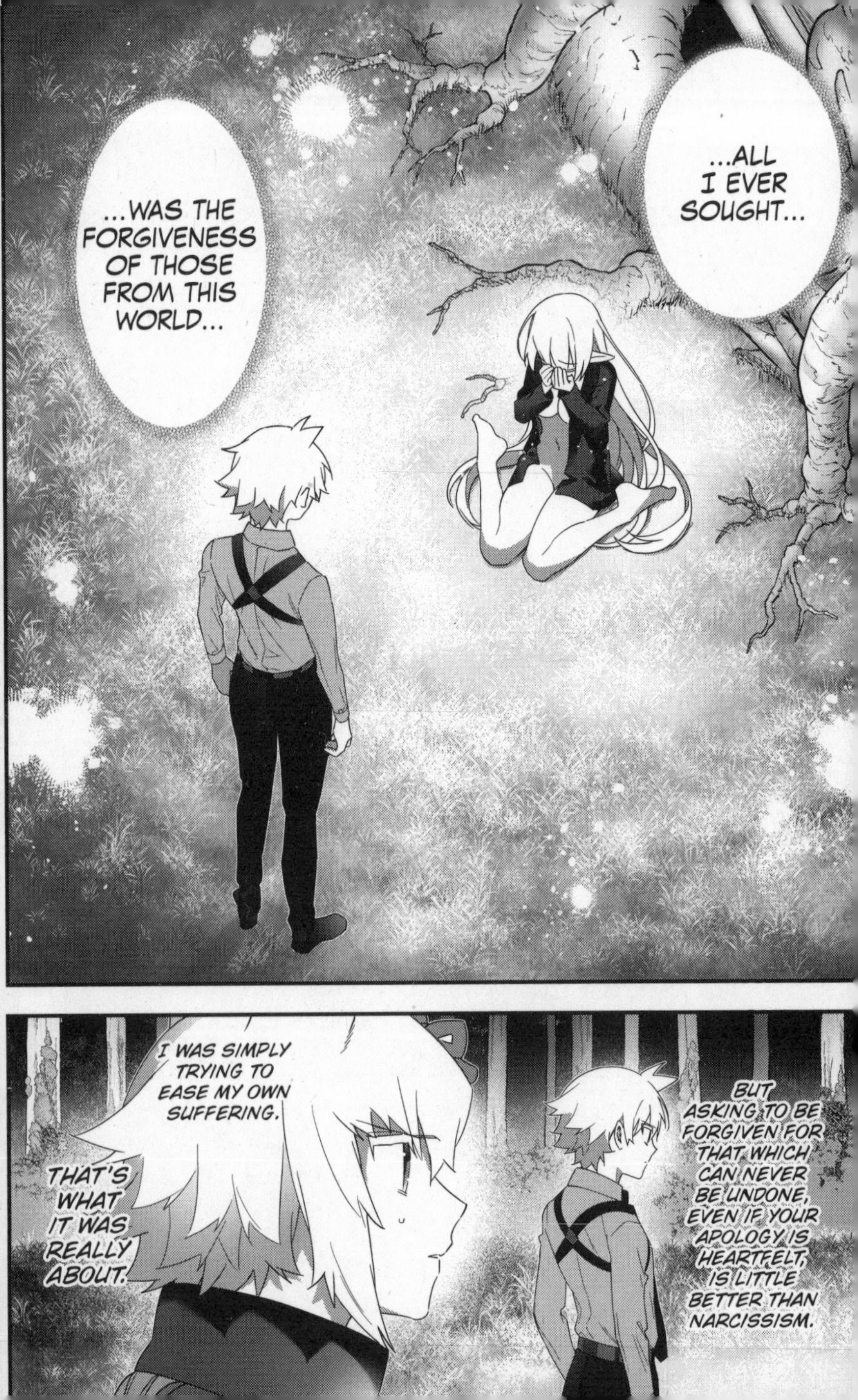
...ALL I EVER SOUGHT...
...WAS THE FORGIVENESS OF THOSE FROM THIS WORLD...
BUT ASKING TO BE FORGIVEN FOR THAT WHICH CAN NEVER BE UNDONE, EVEN IF YOUR APOLOGY IS HEARTFELT, IS LITTLE BETTER THAN NARCISSISM.
I WAS SIMPLY TRYING TO EASE MY OWN SUFFERING.
THAT'S WHAT IT WAS REALLY ABOUT.

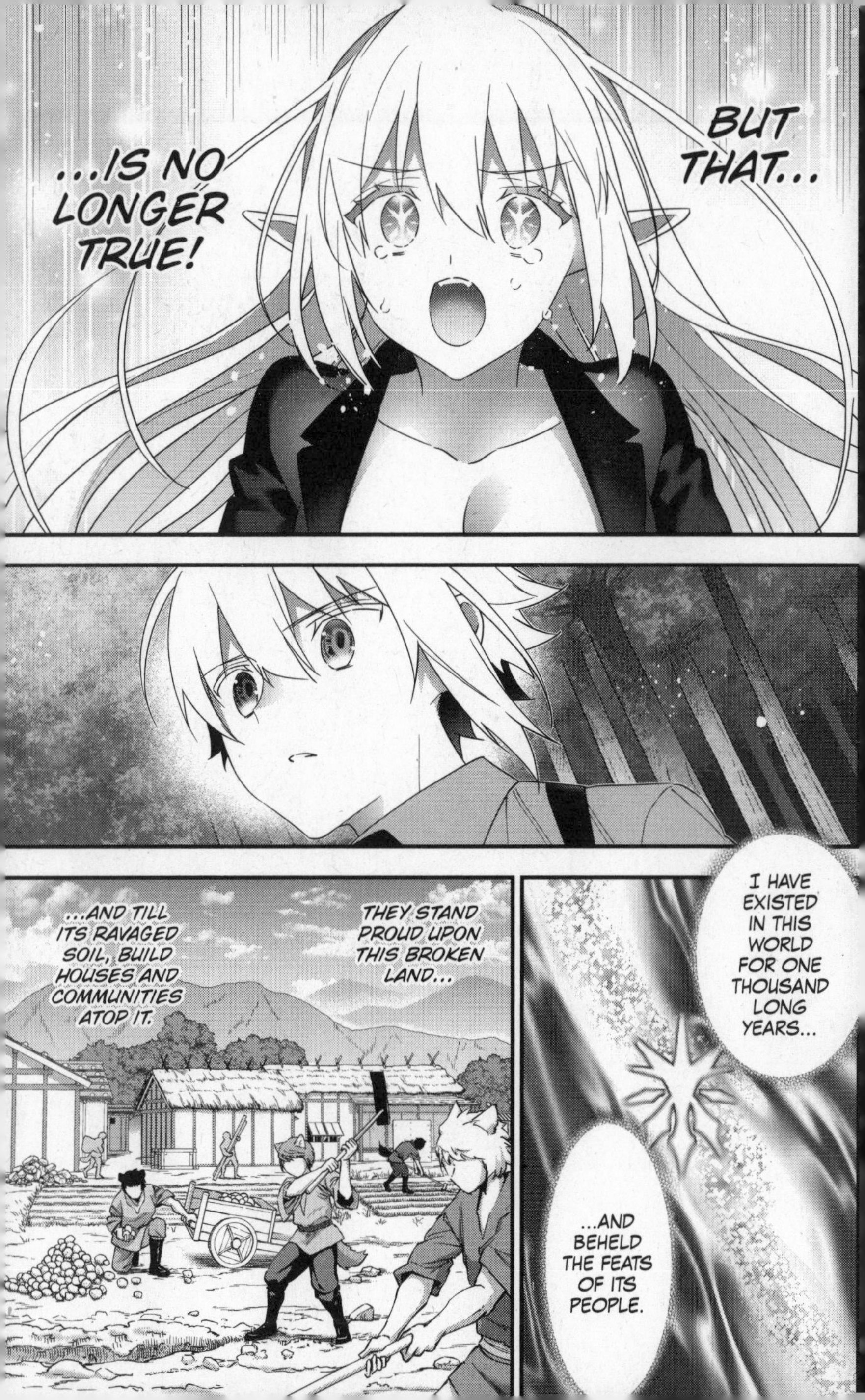
BUT THAT...
...IS NO LONGER TRUE!
I HAVE EXISTED IN THIS WORLD FOR ONE THOUSAND LONG YEARS...
...AND BEHELD THE FEATS OF ITS PEOPLE.
THEY STAND PROUD UPON THIS BROKEN LAND...
...AND TILL ITS RAVAGED SOIL, BUILD HOUSES AND COMMUNITIES ATOP IT.

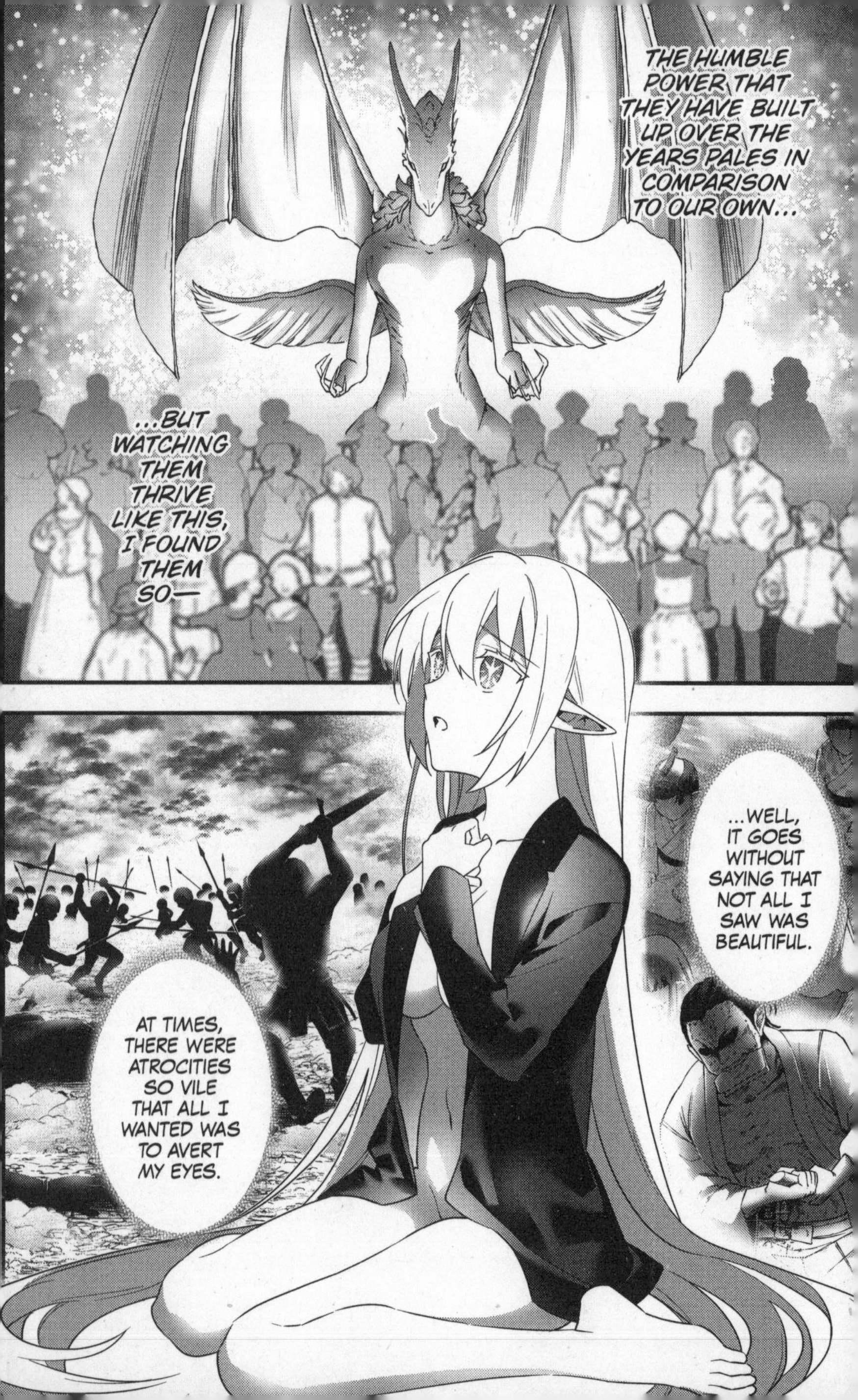
THE HUMBLE POWER THAT THEY HAVE BUILT UP OVER THE YEARS PALES IN COMPARISON TO OUR OWN...
...BUT WATCHING THEM THRIVE LIKE THIS, I FOUND THEM SO—
...WELL, IT GOES WITHOUT SAYING THAT NOT ALL I SAW WAS BEAUTIFUL.
AT TIMES, THERE WERE ATROCITIES SO VILE THAT ALL I WANTED WAS TO AVERT MY EYES.

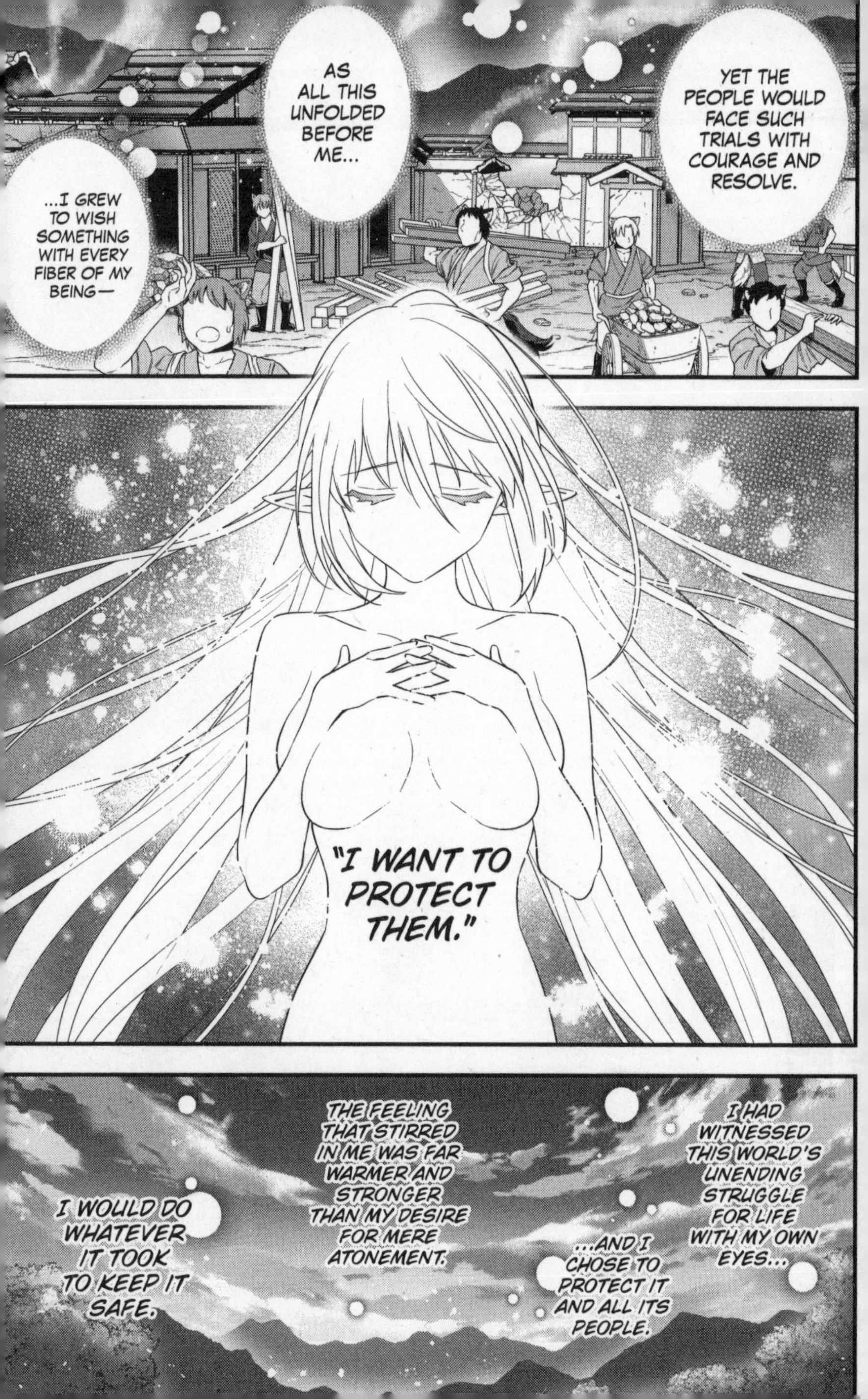
YET THE PEOPLE WOULD FACE SUCH TRIALS WITH COURAGE AND RESOLVE.
AS ALL THIS UNFOLDED BEFORE ME...
...I GREW TO WISH SOMETHING WITH EVERY FIBER OF MY BEING—
"I WANT TO PROTECT THEM."
I HAD WITNESSED THIS WORLD'S UNENDING STRUGGLE FOR LIFE WITH MY OWN EYES...
...AND I CHOSE TO PROTECT IT AND ALL ITS PEOPLE.
THE FEELING THAT STIRRED IN ME WAS FAR WARMER AND STRONGER THAN MY DESIRE FOR MERE ATONEMENT.
I WOULD DO WHATEVER IT TOOK TO KEEP IT SAFE.

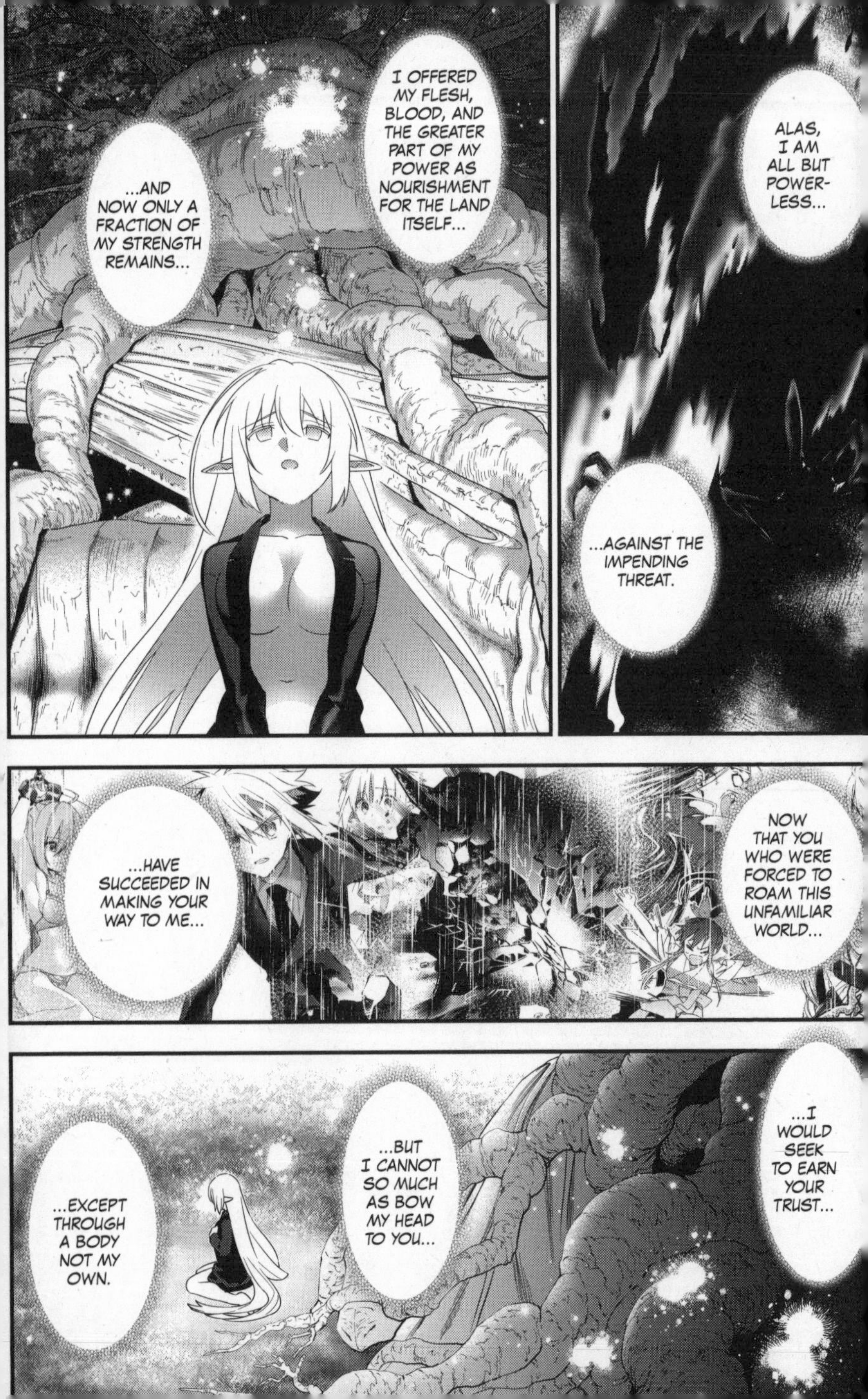
ALAS, I AM ALL BUT POWERLESS...
...AGAINST THE IMPENDING THREAT.
I OFFERED MY FLESH, BLOOD, AND THE GREATER PART OF MY POWER AS NOURISHMENT FOR THE LAND ITSELF...
...AND NOW ONLY A FRACTION OF MY STRENGTH REMAINS...
NOW THAT YOU WHO WERE FORCED TO ROAM THIS UNFAMILIAR WORLD...
...HAVE SUCCEEDED IN MAKING YOUR WAY TO ME...
...I WOULD SEEK TO EARN YOUR TRUST...
...BUT I CANNOT SO MUCH AS BOW MY HEAD TO YOU...
...EXCEPT THROUGH A BODY NOT MY OWN.

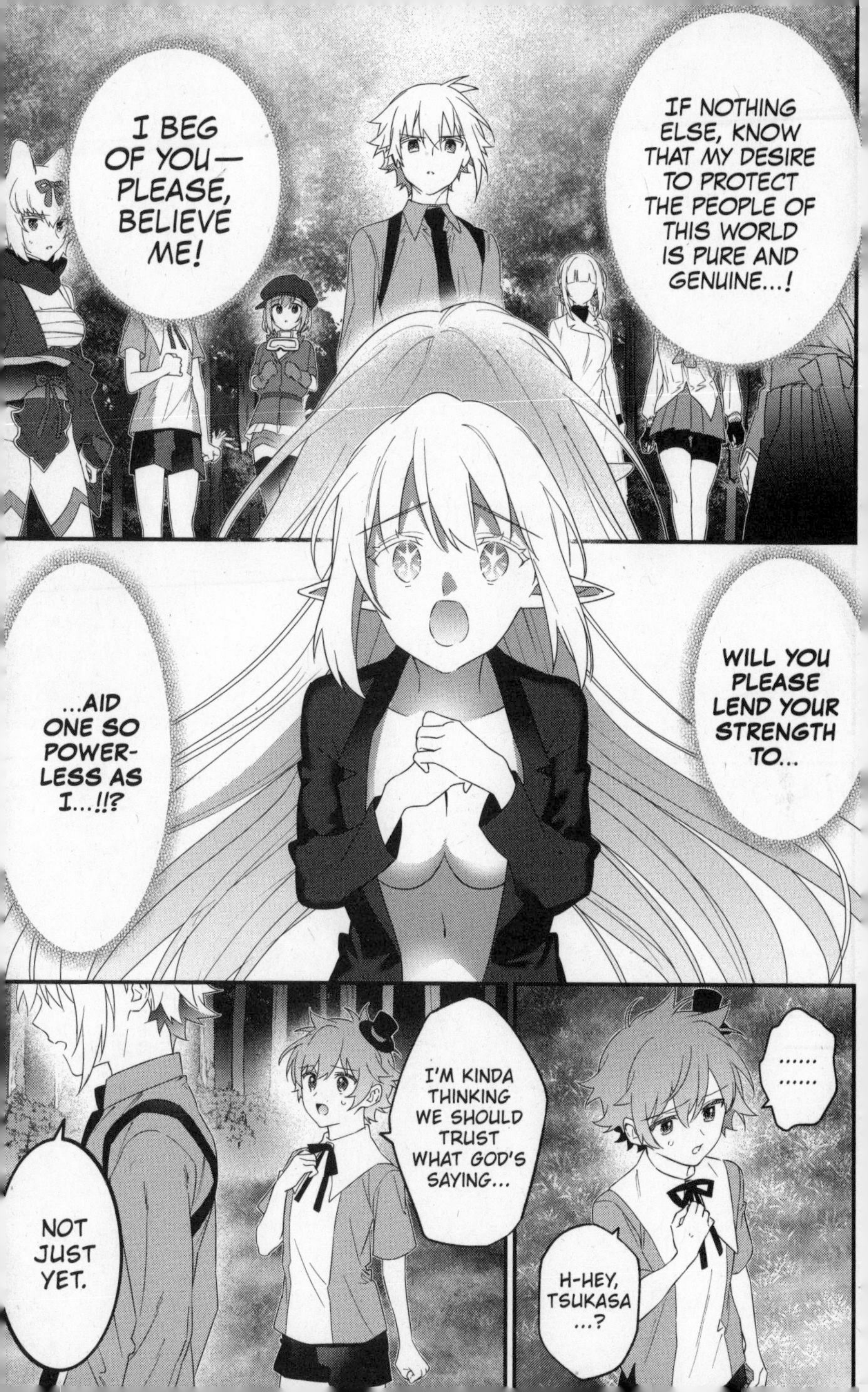
IF NOTHING ELSE, KNOW THAT MY DESIRE TO PROTECT THE PEOPLE OF THIS WORLD IS PURE AND GENUINE...!
I BEG OF YOU—PLEASE, BELIEVE ME!
WILL YOU PLEASE LEND YOUR STRENGTH TO...
...AID ONE SO POWER-LESS AS I...!!?
....
H-HEY, TSUKASA...?
I'M KINDA THINKING WE SHOULD TRUST WHAT GOD'S SAYING...
NOT JUST YET.

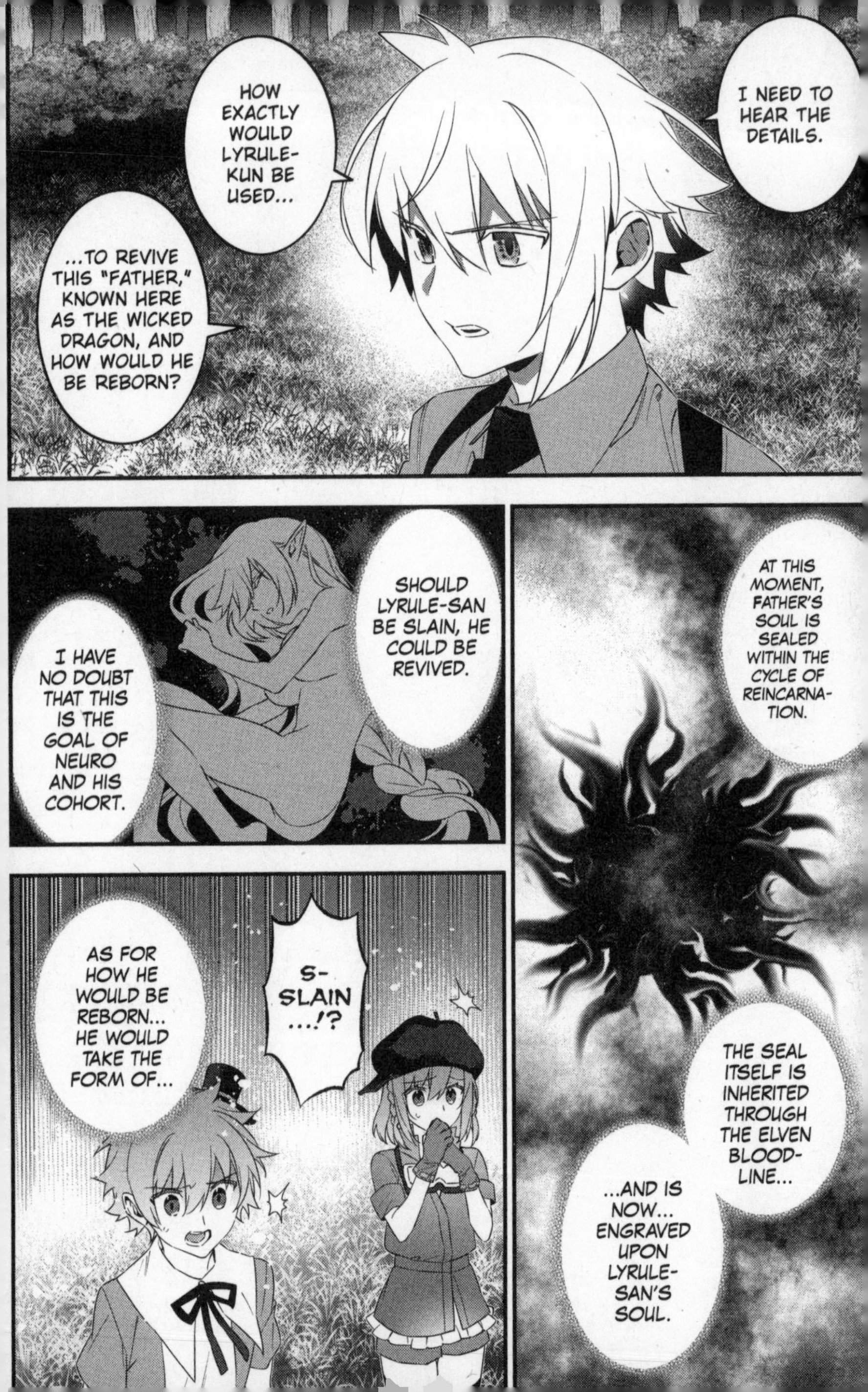
I NEED TO HEAR THE DETAILS.
HOW EXACTLY WOULD LYRULE-KUN BE USED...
...TO REVIVE THIS "FATHER," KNOWN HERE AS THE WICKED DRAGON, AND HOW WOULD HE BE REBORN?
AT THIS MOMENT, FATHER'S SOUL IS SEALED WITHIN THE CYCLE OF REINCARNATION.
THE SEAL ITSELF IS INHERITED THROUGH THE ELVEN BLOODLINE...
...AND IS NOW... ENGRAVED UPON LYRULE-SAN'S SOUL.
SHOULD LYRULE-SAN BE SLAIN, HE COULD BE REVIVED.
I HAVE NO DOUBT THAT THIS IS THE GOAL OF NEURO AND HIS COHORT.
S-SLAIN...!?
AS FOR HOW HE WOULD BE REBORN... HE WOULD TAKE THE FORM OF...

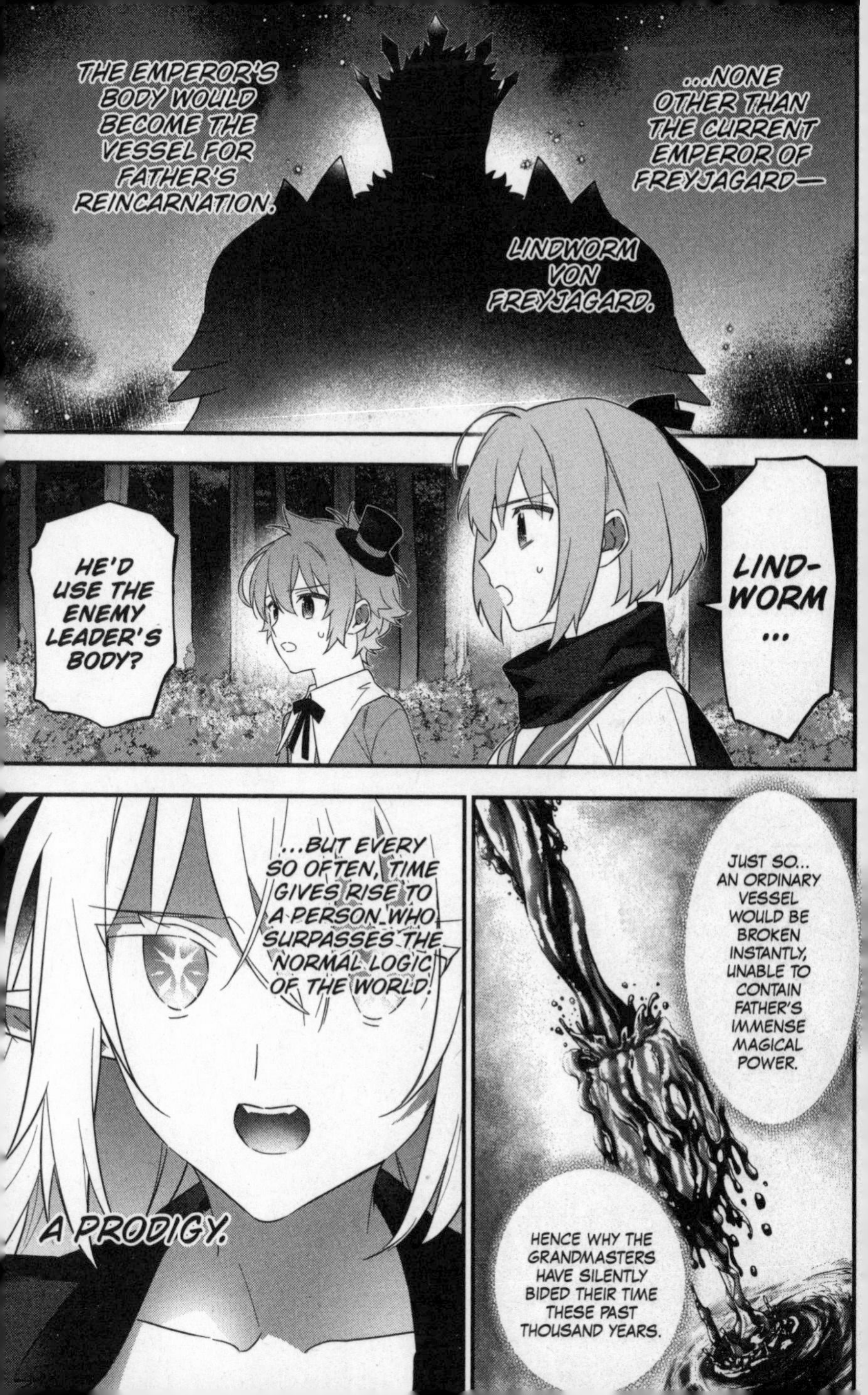
...NONE OTHER THAN THE CURRENT EMPEROR OF FREYJAGARD—
LINDWORM VON FREYJAGARD.
THE EMPEROR'S BODY WOULD BECOME THE VESSEL FOR FATHER'S REINCARNATION.
LIND-WORM...
HE'D USE THE ENEMY LEADER'S BODY?
JUST SO... AN ORDINARY VESSEL WOULD BE BROKEN INSTANTLY, UNABLE TO CONTAIN FATHER'S IMMENSE MAGICAL POWER.
HENCE WHY THE GRANDMASTERS HAVE SILENTLY BIDED THEIR TIME THESE PAST THOUSAND YEARS.
...BUT EVERY SO OFTEN, TIME GIVES RISE TO A PERSON WHO SURPASSES THE NORMAL LOGIC OF THE WORLD.
A PRODIGY.

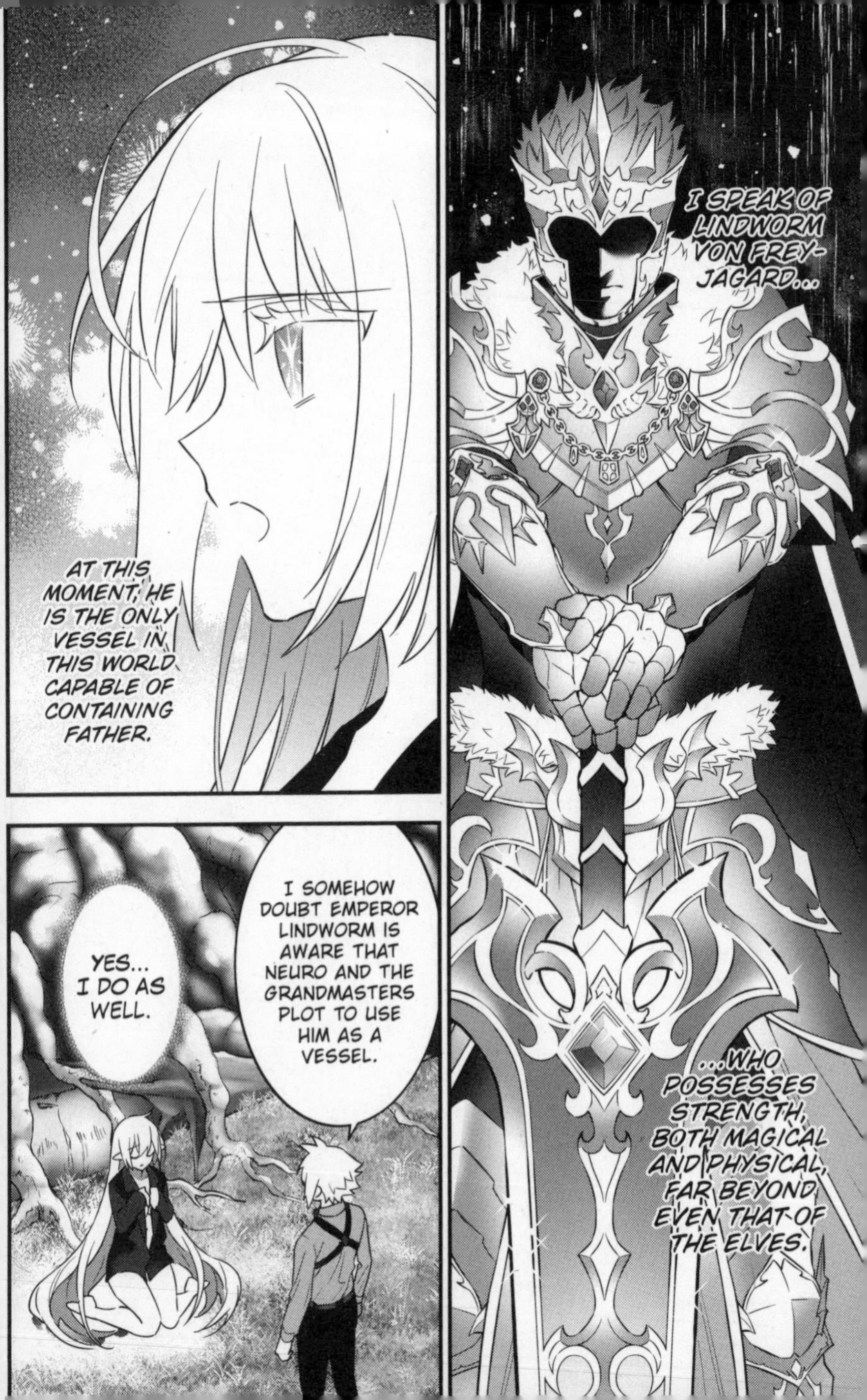
I SPEAK OF LINDWORM VON FREY-JAGARD...
...WHO POSSESSES STRENGTH, BOTH MAGICAL AND PHYSICAL, FAR BEYOND EVEN THAT OF THE ELVES.
AT THIS MOMENT, HE IS THE ONLY VESSEL IN THIS WORLD CAPABLE OF CONTAINING FATHER.
I SOMEHOW DOUBT EMPEROR LINDWORM IS AWARE THAT NEURO AND THE GRANDMASTERS PLOT TO USE HIM AS A VESSEL.
YES... I DO AS WELL.

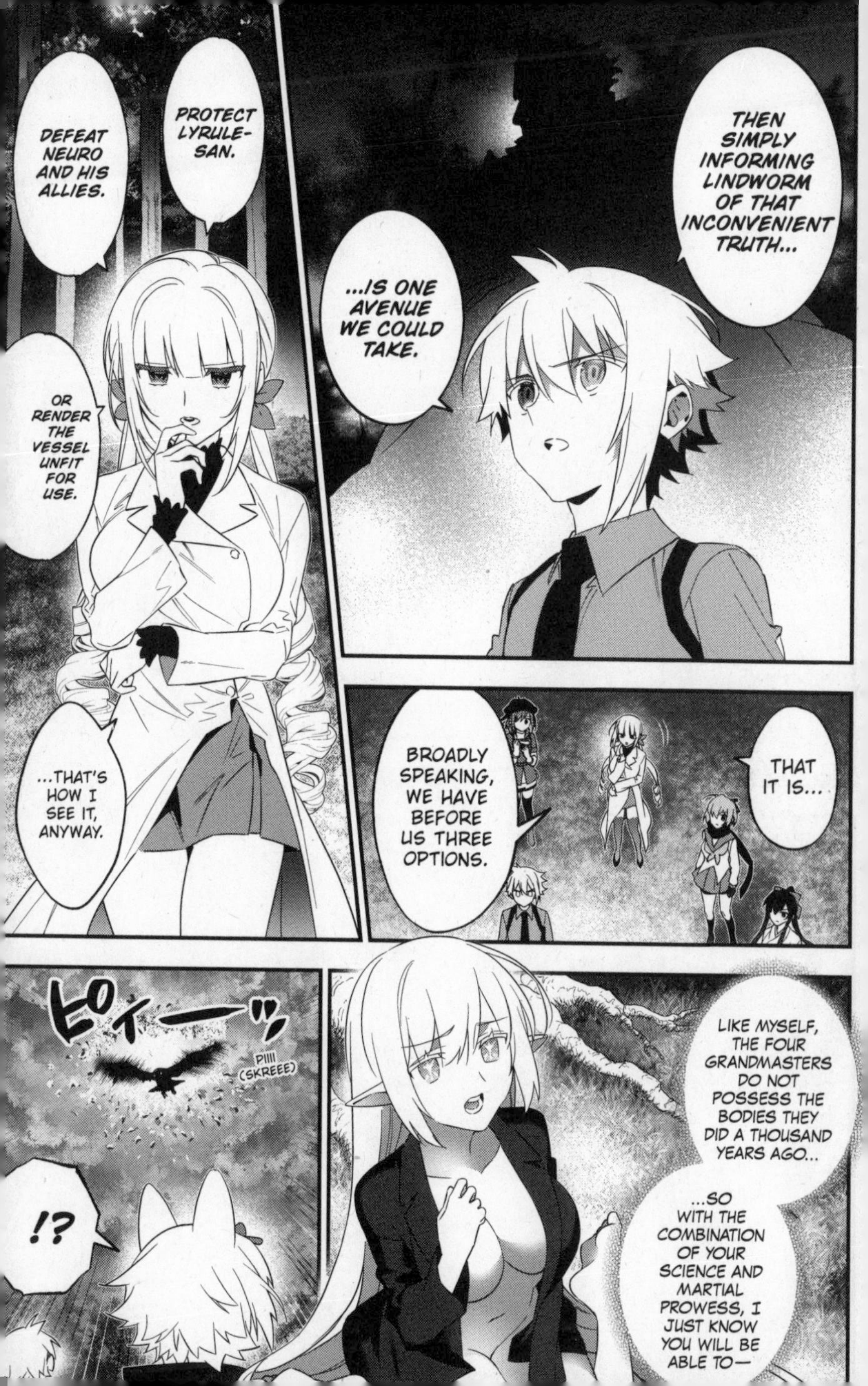
THEN SIMPLY INFORMING LINDWORM OF THAT INCONVENIENT TRUTH...
...IS ONE AVENUE WE COULD TAKE.
THAT IT IS...
BROADLY SPEAKING, WE HAVE BEFORE US THREE OPTIONS.
PROTECT LYRULE-SAN.
DEFEAT NEURO AND HIS ALLIES.
OR RENDER THE VESSEL UNFIT FOR USE.
...THAT'S HOW I SEE IT, ANYWAY.
LIKE MYSELF, THE FOUR GRANDMASTERS DO NOT POSSESS THE BODIES THEY DID A THOUSAND YEARS AGO...
...SO WITH THE COMBINATION OF YOUR SCIENCE AND MARTIAL PROWESS, I JUST KNOW YOU WILL BE ABLE TO—
ピイーッ
PIIII (SKREEE)
!?

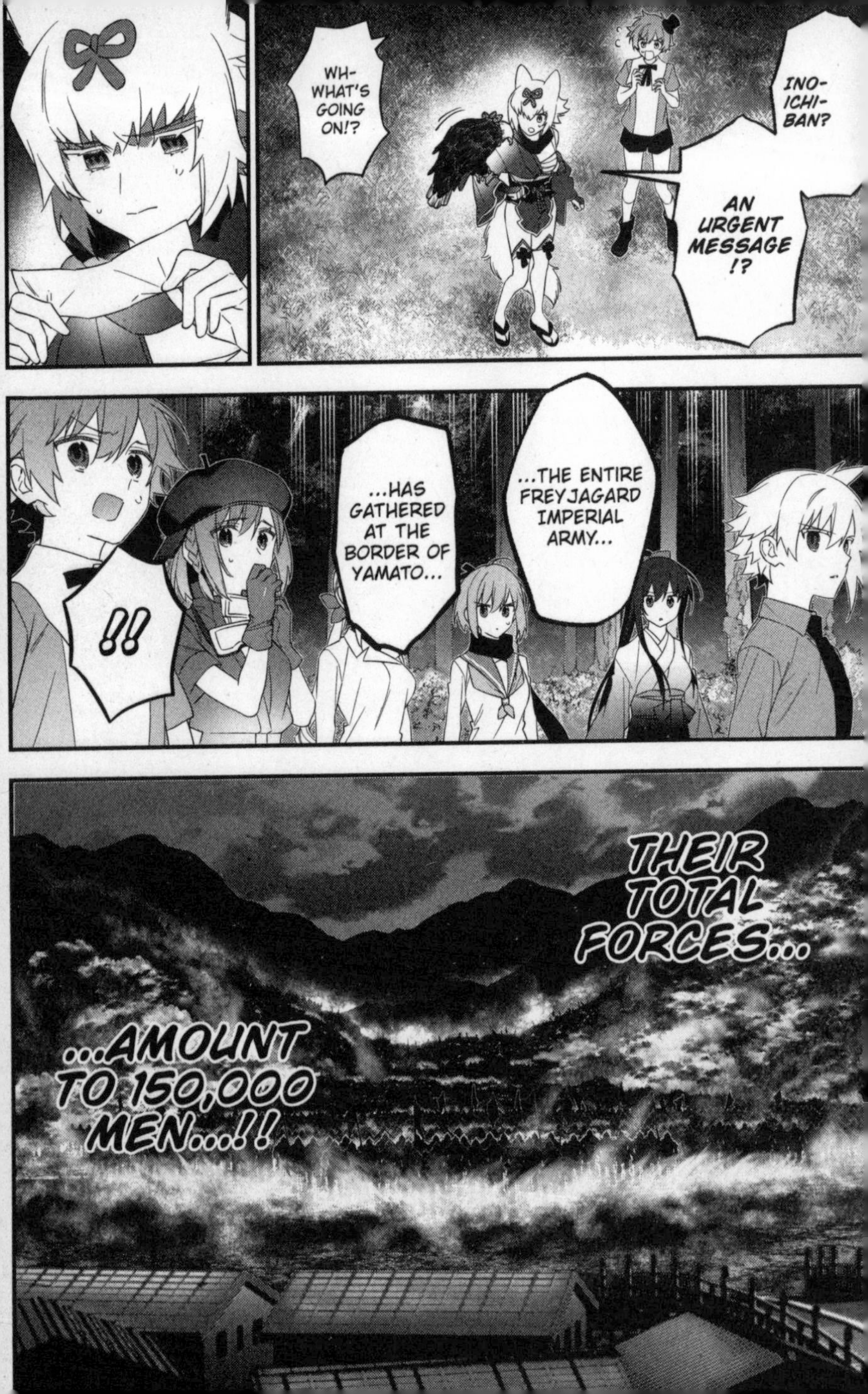
INO-ICHI-BAN?
AN URGENT MESSAGE!?
WH-WHAT'S GOING ON!?
...THE ENTIRE FREYJAGARD IMPERIAL ARMY...
...HAS GATHERED AT THE BORDER OF YAMATO...
!!
THEIR TOTAL FORCES...
...AMOUNT TO 150,000 MEN...!!

HIGH SCHOOL PRODIGIES HAVE IT EASY EVEN IN ANOTHER WORLD!

Illustration Gallery (6)

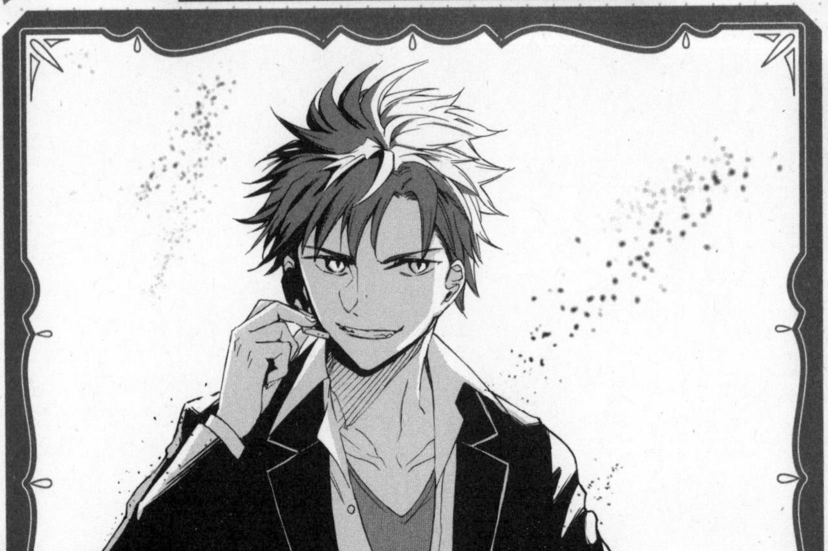
唯浦史
FUMI TADAURA

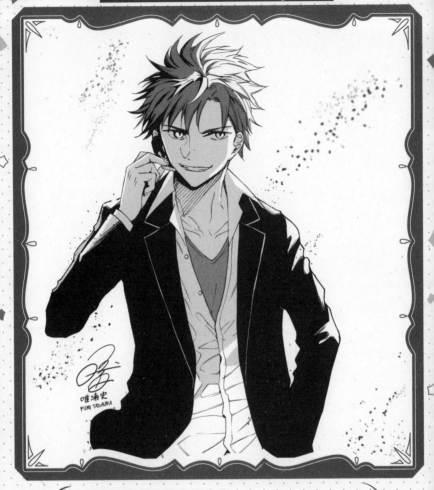

Fumi Tadaura-sensei

Manga artist for
I Lost My Adventurer's License, but It's Fine Because I Have an Adorable Daughter Now,
featured in Manga UP!

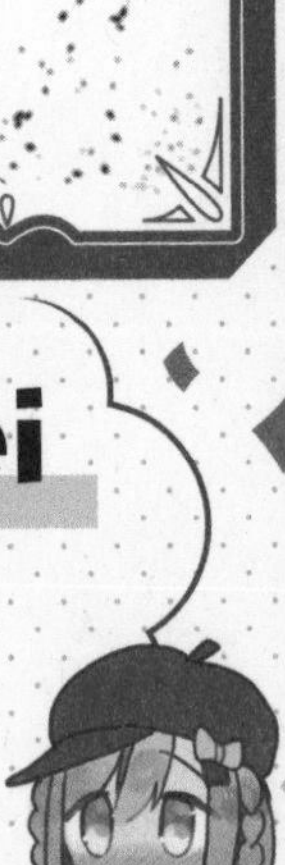

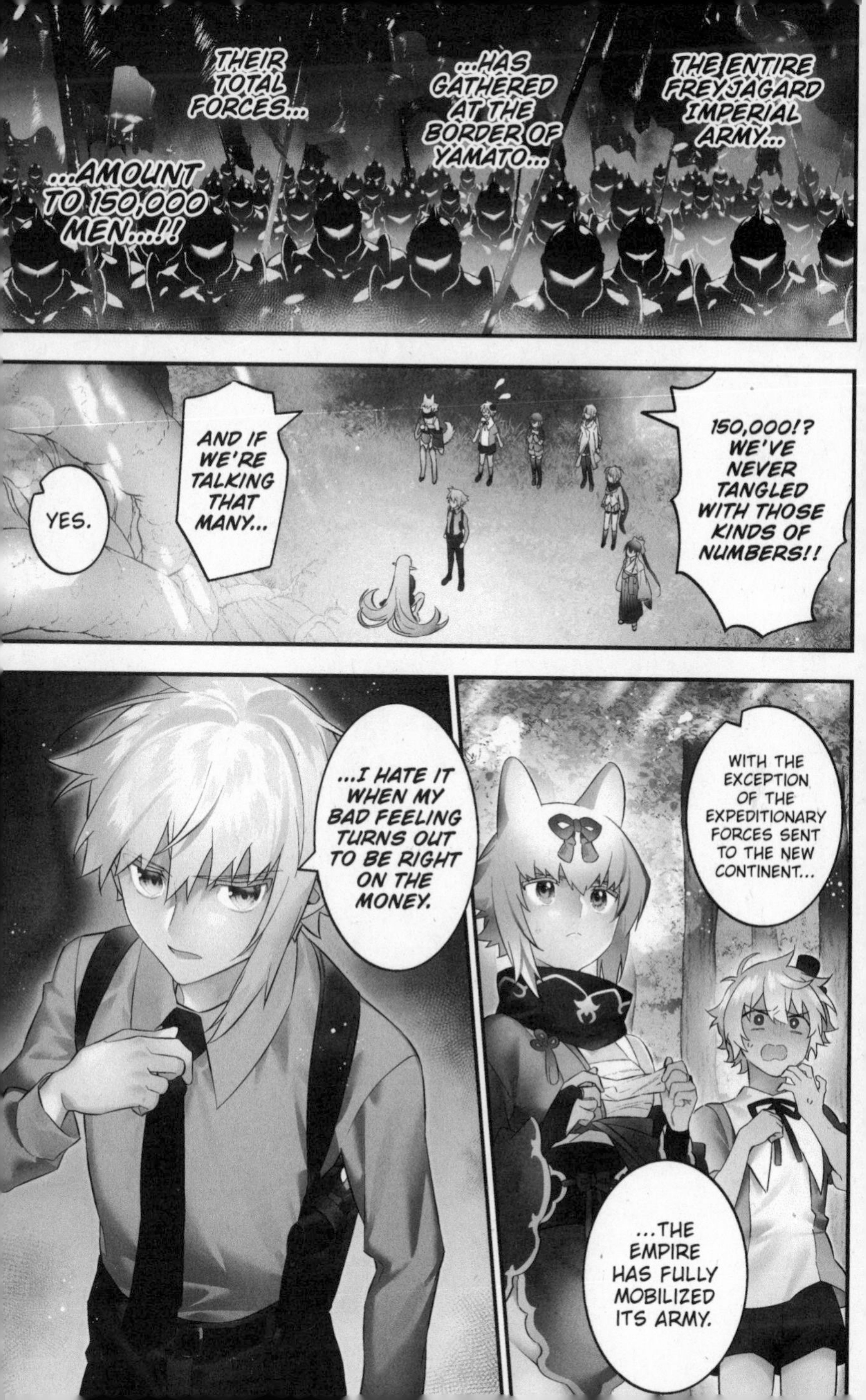
THE ENTIRE FREYJAGARD IMPERIAL ARMY...
...HAS GATHERED AT THE BORDER OF YAMATO...
THEIR TOTAL FORCES...
...AMOUNT TO 150,000 MEN...!!
150,000!? WE'VE NEVER TANGLED WITH THOSE KINDS OF NUMBERS!!
AND IF WE'RE TALKING THAT MANY...
YES.
WITH THE EXCEPTION OF THE EXPEDITIONARY FORCES SENT TO THE NEW CONTINENT...
...THE EMPIRE HAS FULLY MOBILIZED ITS ARMY.
...I HATE IT WHEN MY BAD FEELING TURNS OUT TO BE RIGHT ON THE MONEY.

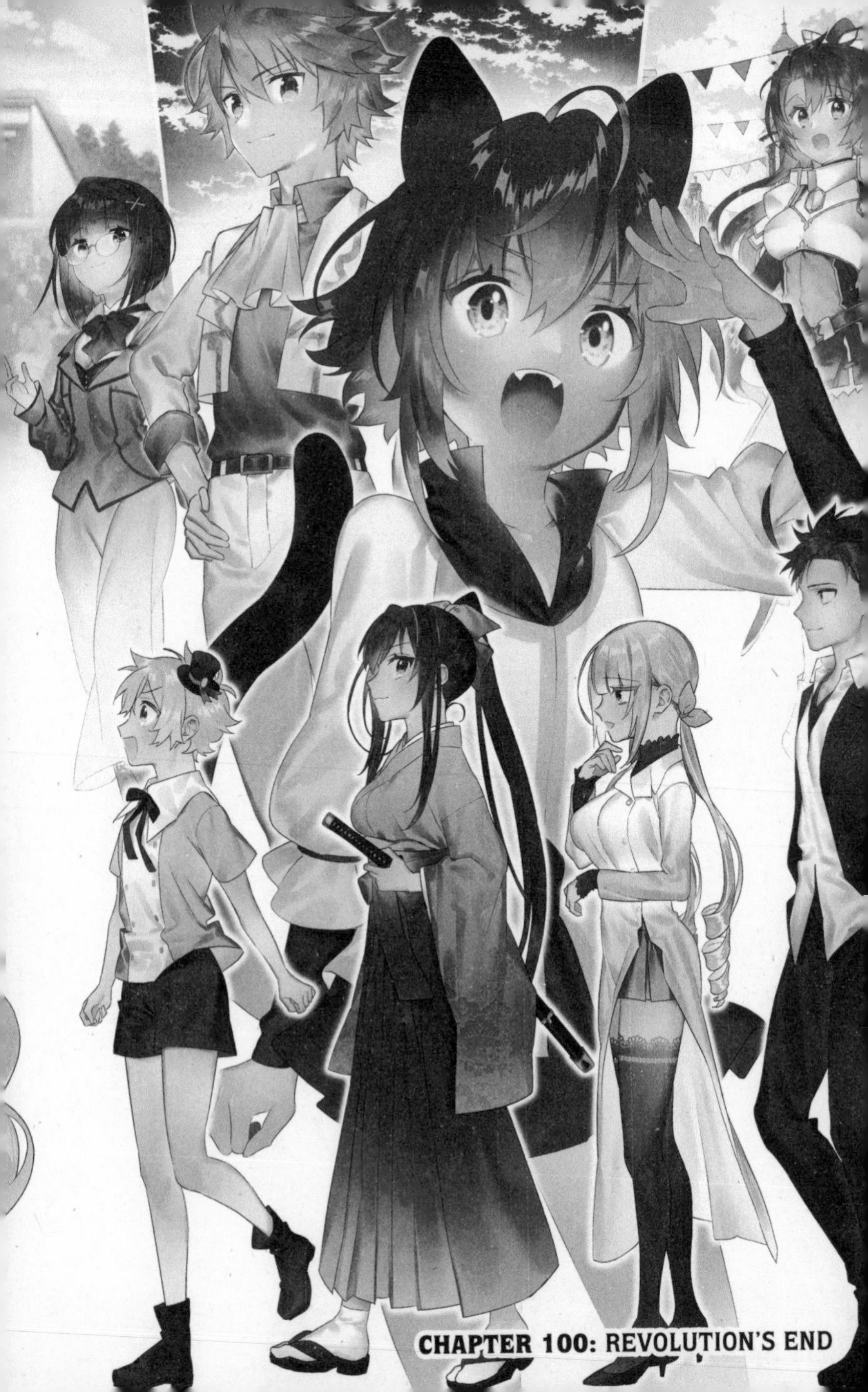
CHAPTER 100: REVOLUTION'S END

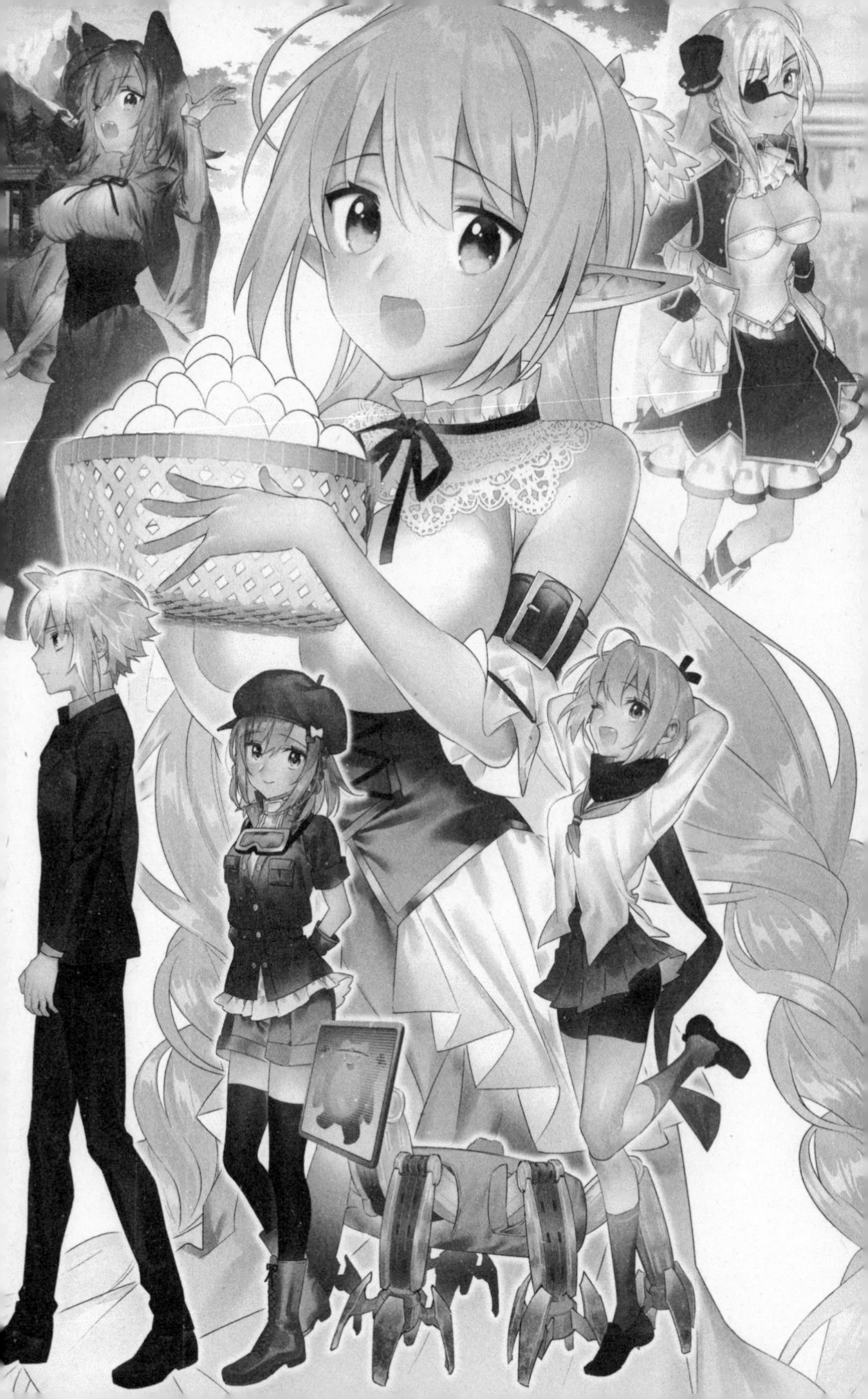

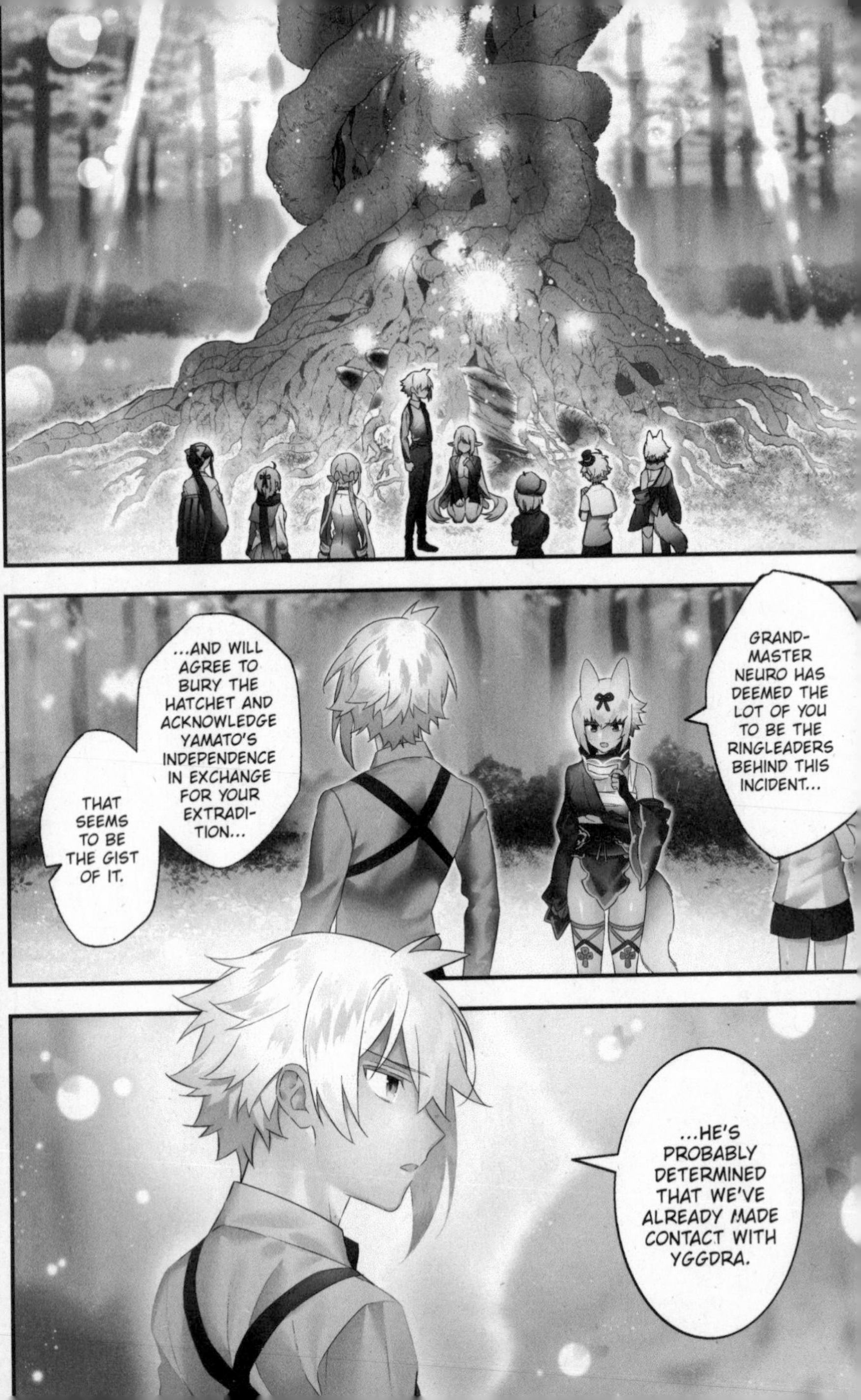
GRAND-MASTER NEURO HAS DEEMED THE LOT OF YOU TO BE THE RINGLEADERS BEHIND THIS INCIDENT...
...AND WILL AGREE TO BURY THE HATCHET AND ACKNOWLEDGE YAMATO'S INDEPENDENCE IN EXCHANGE FOR YOUR EXTRADI-TION...
THAT SEEMS TO BE THE GIST OF IT.
...HE'S PROBABLY DETERMINED THAT WE'VE ALREADY MADE CONTACT WITH YGGDRA.

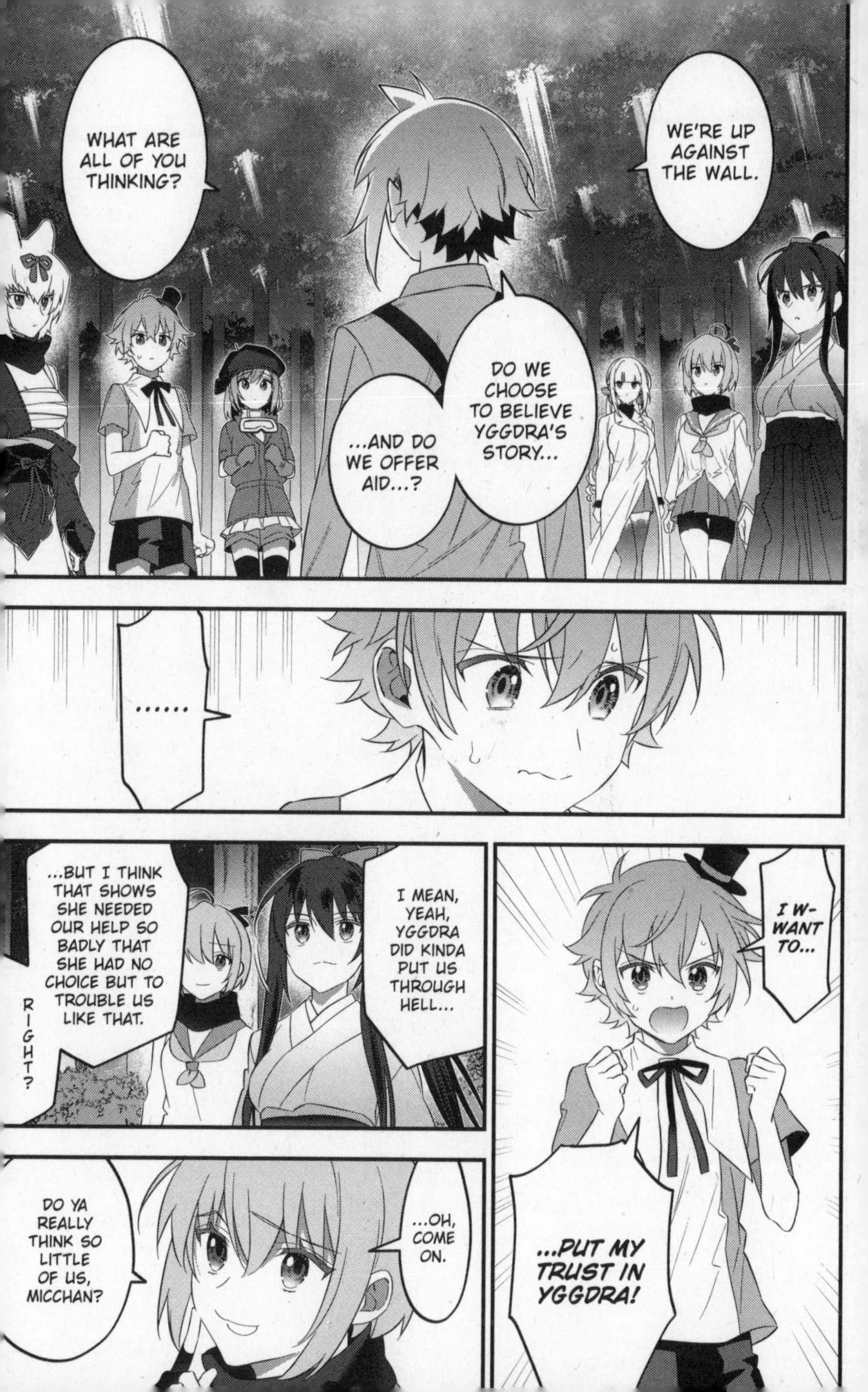
WE'RE UP AGAINST THE WALL.
DO WE CHOOSE TO BELIEVE YGGDRA'S STORY...
...AND DO WE OFFER AID...?
WHAT ARE ALL OF YOU THINKING?
......
I W-WANT TO...
...PUT MY TRUST IN YGGDRA!
I MEAN, YEAH, YGGDRA DID KINDA PUT US THROUGH HELL...
...BUT I THINK THAT SHOWS SHE NEEDED OUR HELP SO BADLY THAT SHE HAD NO CHOICE BUT TO TROUBLE US LIKE THAT.
RIGHT?
...OH, COME ON.
DO YA REALLY THINK SO LITTLE OF US, MICCHAN?

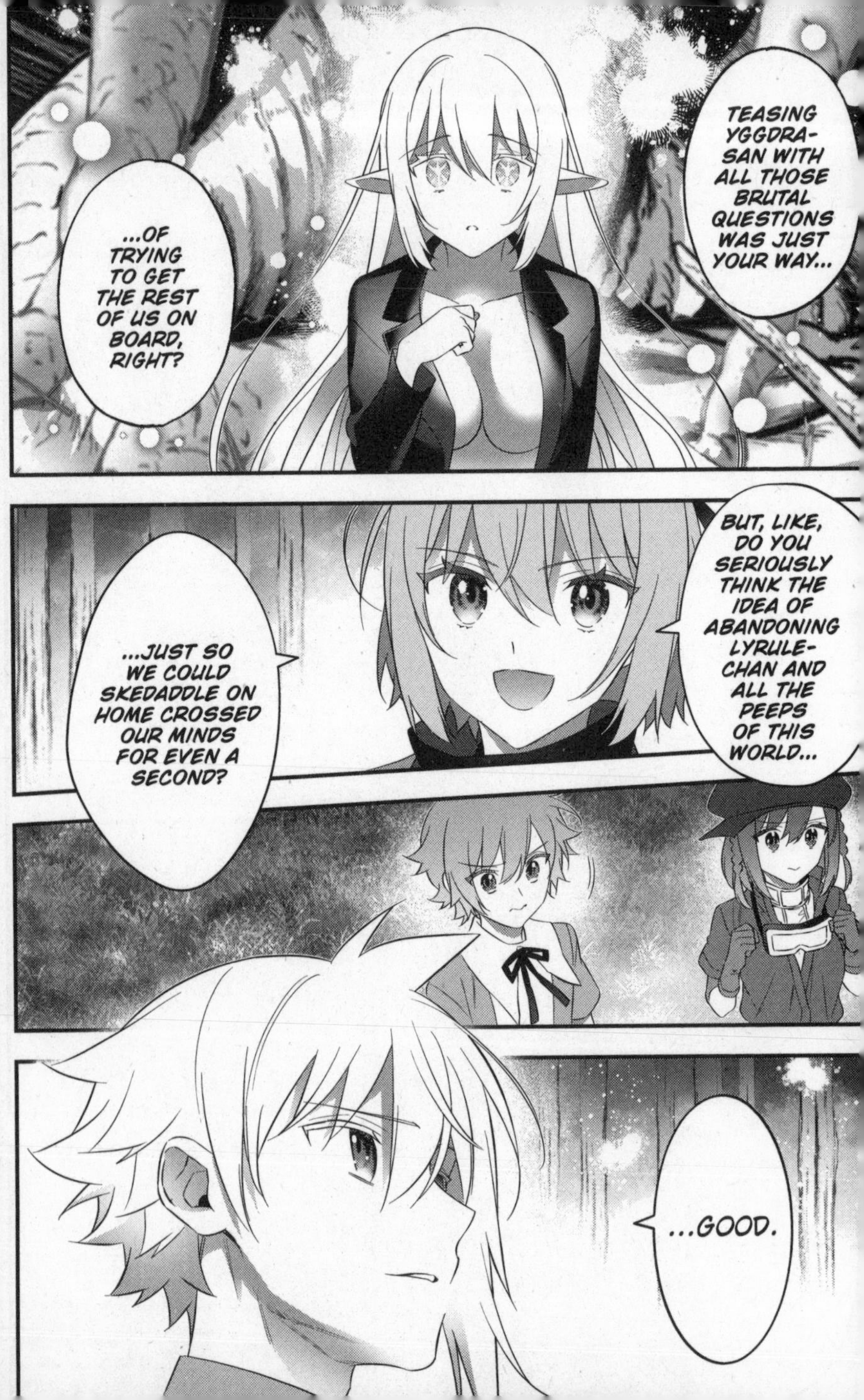
TEASING YGGDRA-SAN WITH ALL THOSE BRUTAL QUESTIONS WAS JUST YOUR WAY...
...OF TRYING TO GET THE REST OF US ON BOARD, RIGHT?
BUT, LIKE, DO YOU SERIOUSLY THINK THE IDEA OF ABANDONING LYRULE-CHAN AND ALL THE PEEPS OF THIS WORLD...
...JUST SO WE COULD SKEDADDLE ON HOME CROSSED OUR MINDS FOR EVEN A SECOND?
...GOOD.

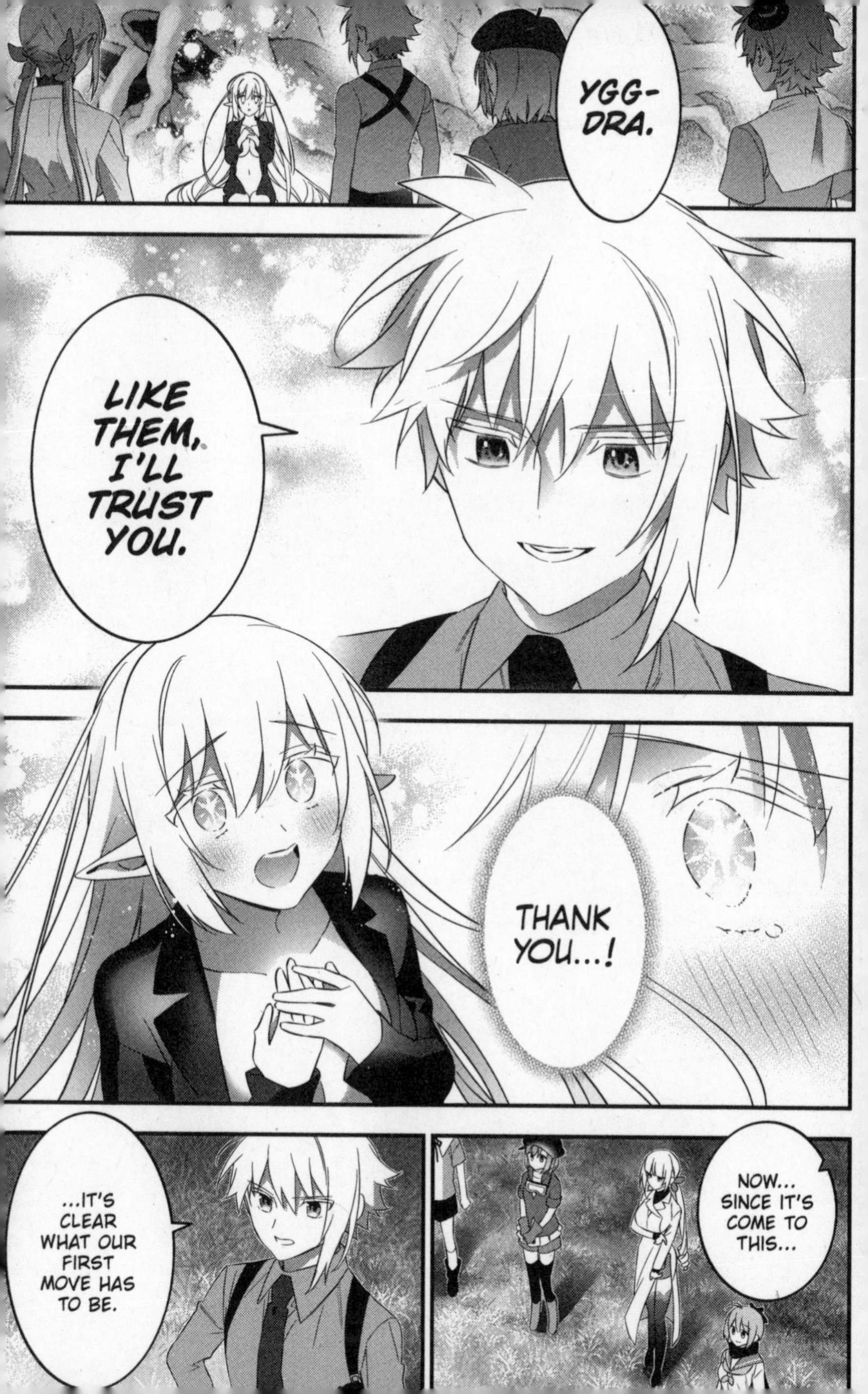
YGG-DRA.
LIKE THEM, I'LL TRUST YOU.
THANK YOU...!
NOW... SINCE IT'S COME TO THIS...
...IT'S CLEAR WHAT OUR FIRST MOVE HAS TO BE.

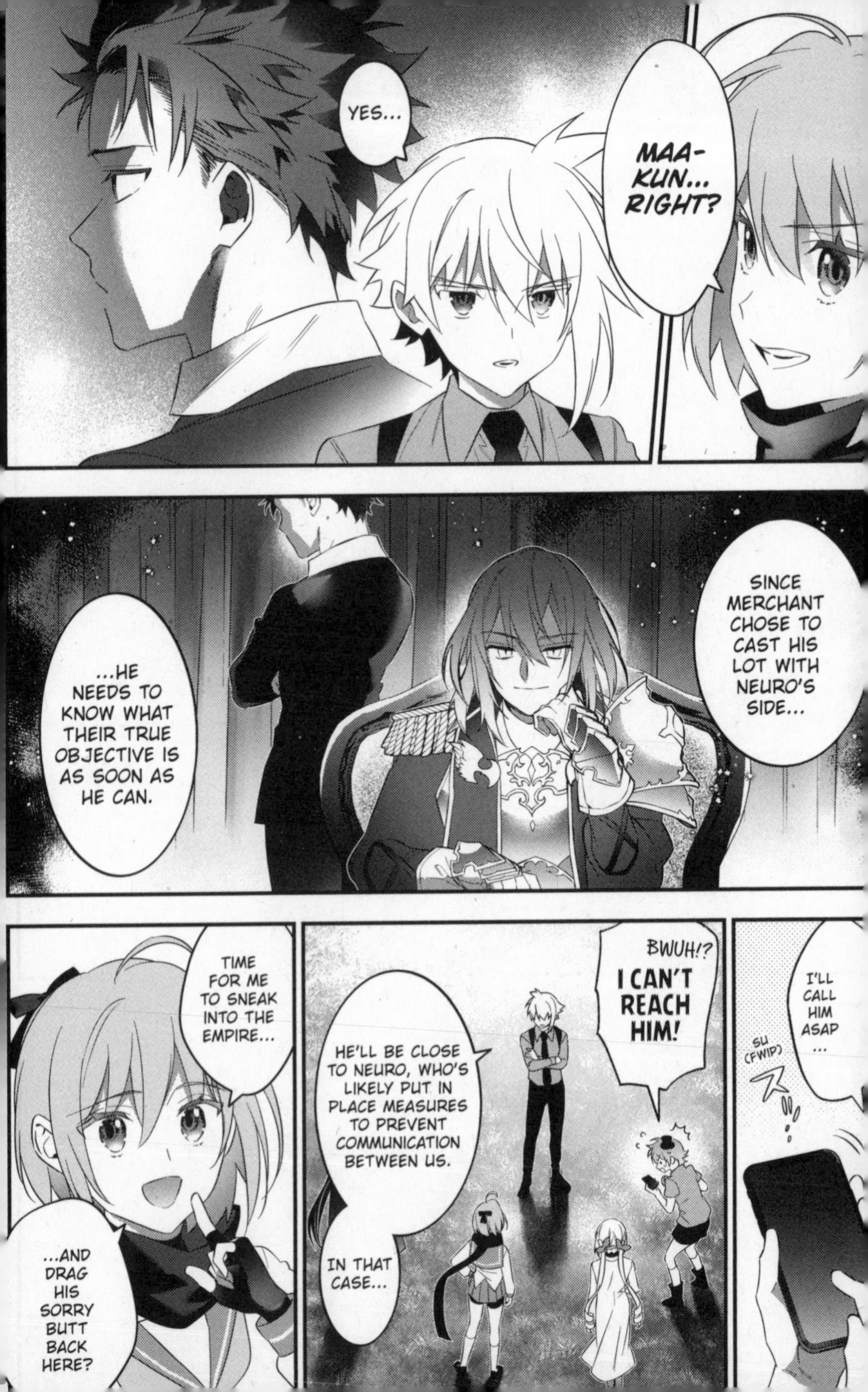
MAA-KUN... RIGHT?
YES...
SINCE MERCHANT CHOSE TO CAST HIS LOT WITH NEURO'S SIDE...
...HE NEEDS TO KNOW WHAT THEIR TRUE OBJECTIVE IS AS SOON AS HE CAN.
I'LL CALL HIM ASAP...
SU (FWIP)
BWUH!?
I CAN'T REACH HIM!
HE'LL BE CLOSE TO NEURO, WHO'S LIKELY PUT IN PLACE MEASURES TO PREVENT COMMUNICATION BETWEEN US.
IN THAT CASE...
TIME FOR ME TO SNEAK INTO THE EMPIRE...
...AND DRAG HIS SORRY BUTT BACK HERE?

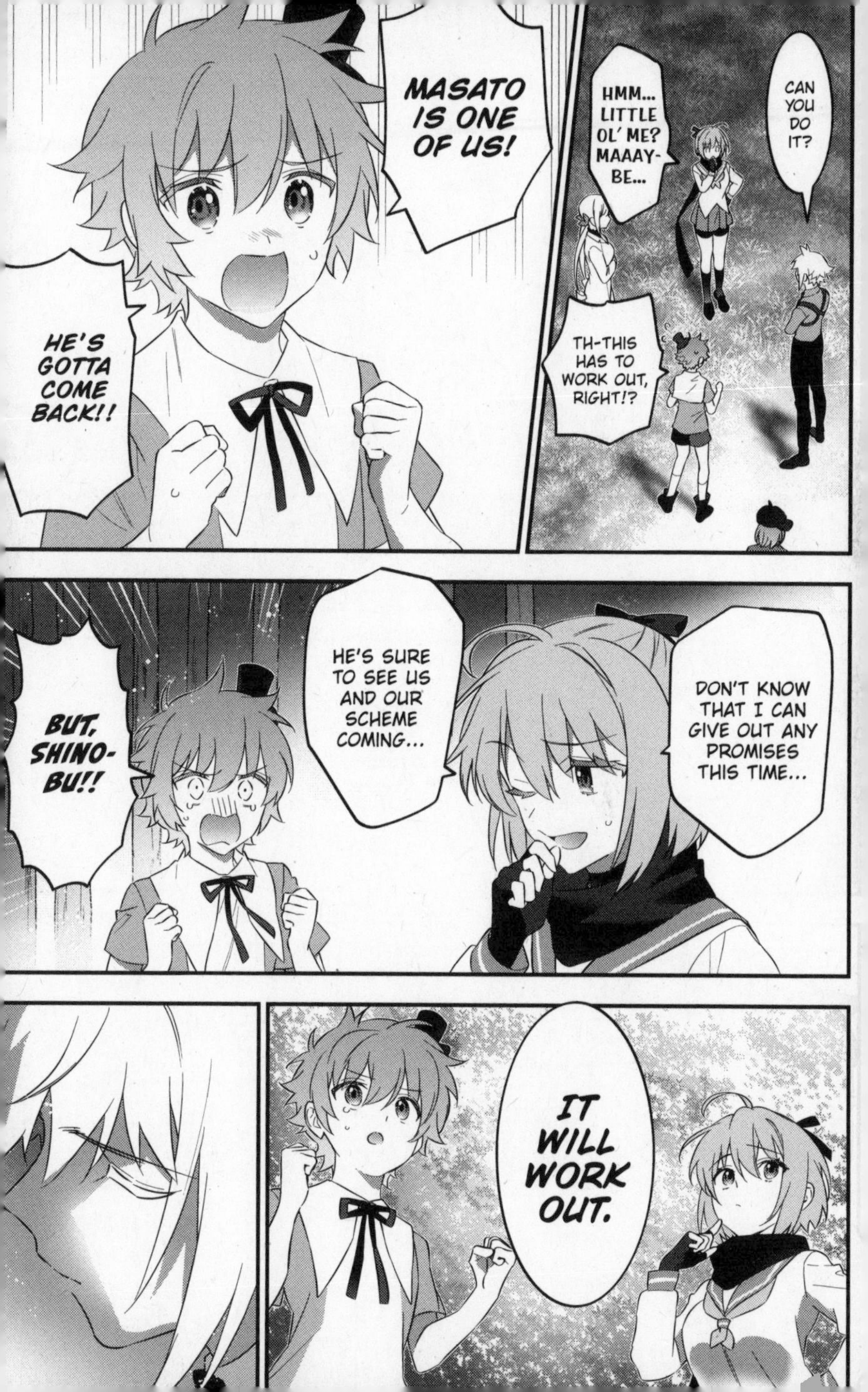
CAN YOU DO IT?
HMM... LITTLE OL' ME? MAAAY-BE...
TH-THIS HAS TO WORK OUT, RIGHT!?
MASATO IS ONE OF US!
HE'S GOTTA COME BACK!!
DON'T KNOW THAT I CAN GIVE OUT ANY PROMISES THIS TIME...
HE'S SURE TO SEE US AND OUR SCHEME COMING...
BUT, SHINOBU!!
IT WILL WORK OUT.

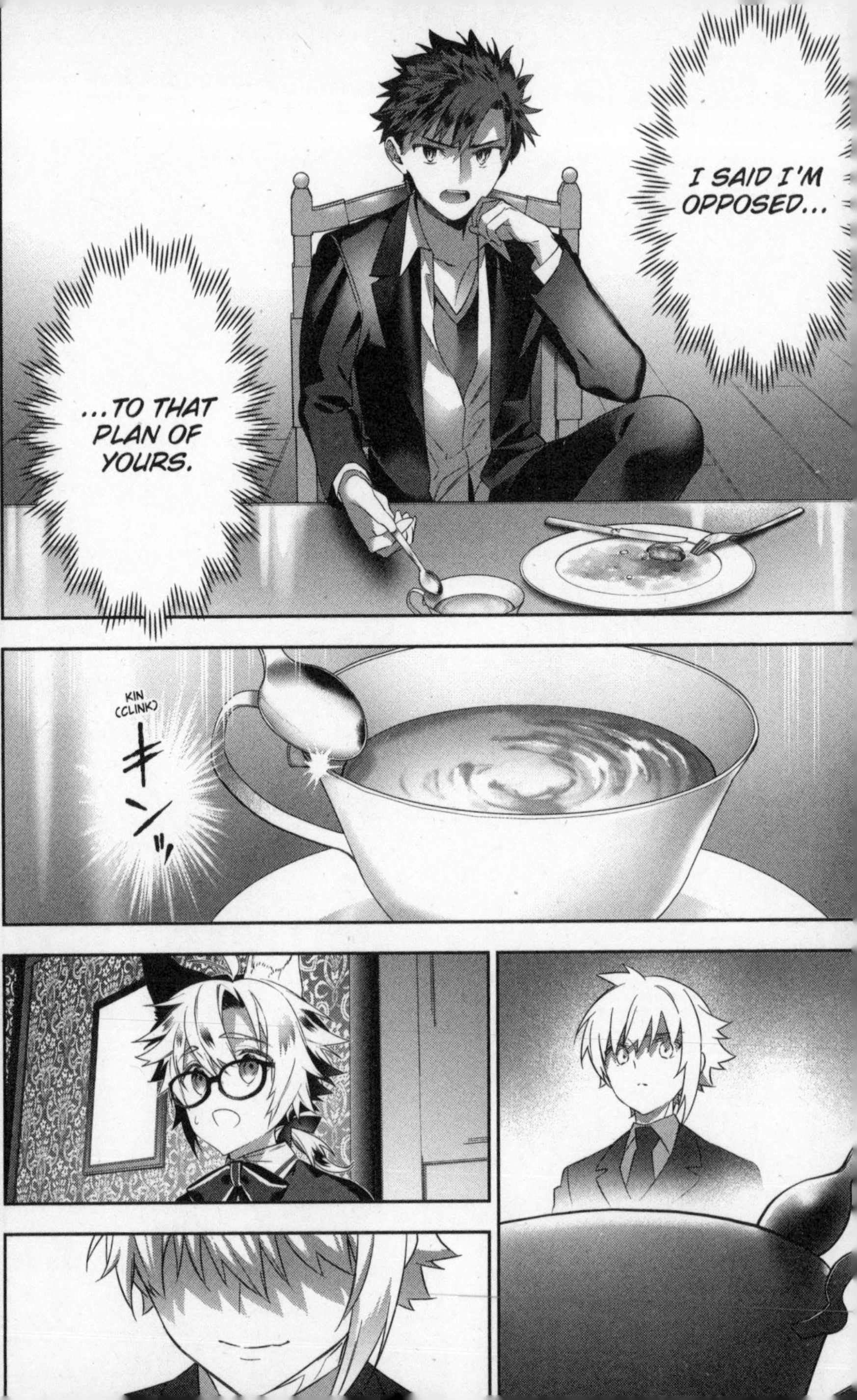
I SAID I'M OPPOSED...
...TO THAT PLAN OF YOURS.
KIN (CLINK)
キン

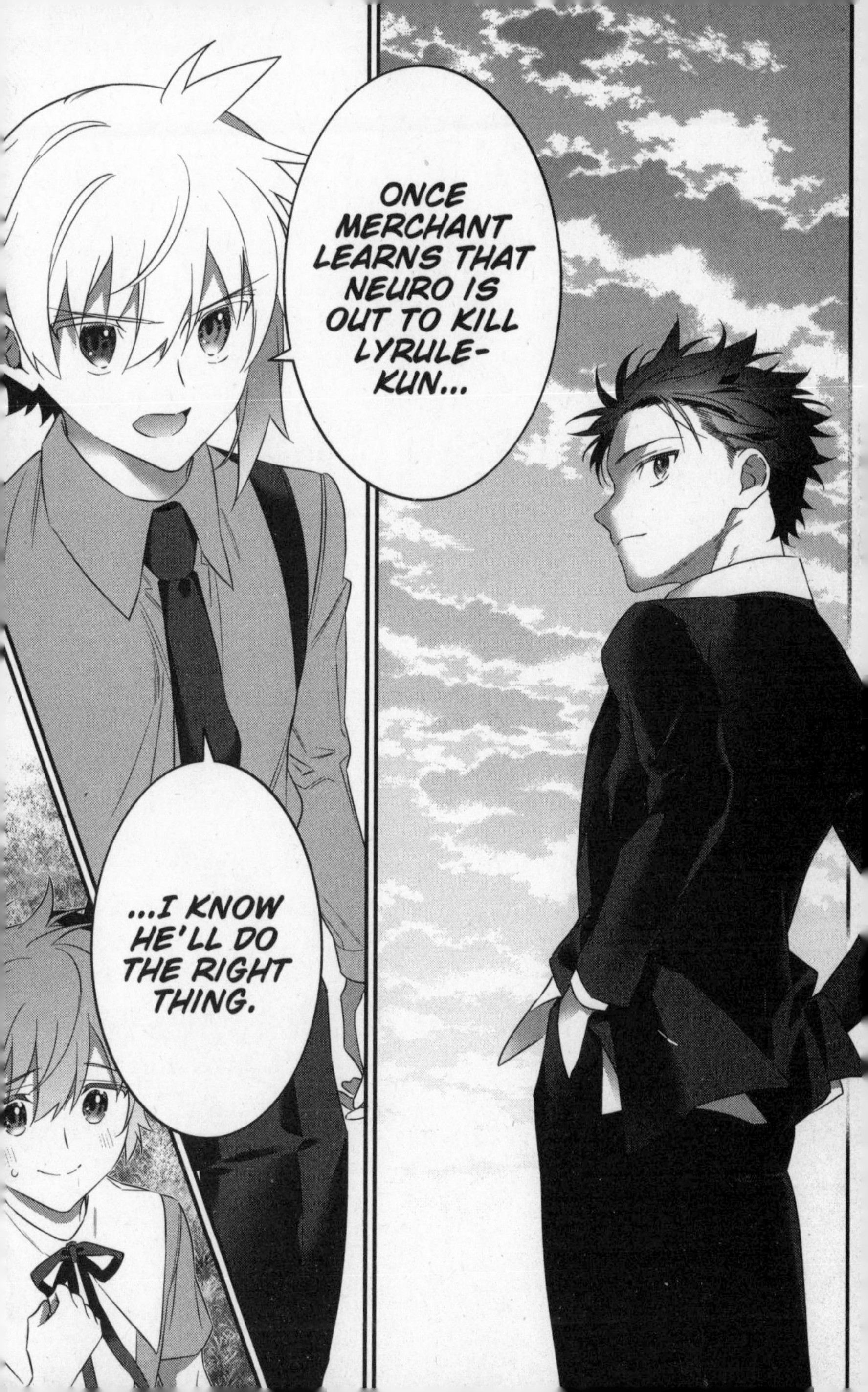
ONCE MERCHANT LEARNS THAT NEURO IS OUT TO KILL LYRULE-KUN...
...I KNOW HE'LL DO THE RIGHT THING.

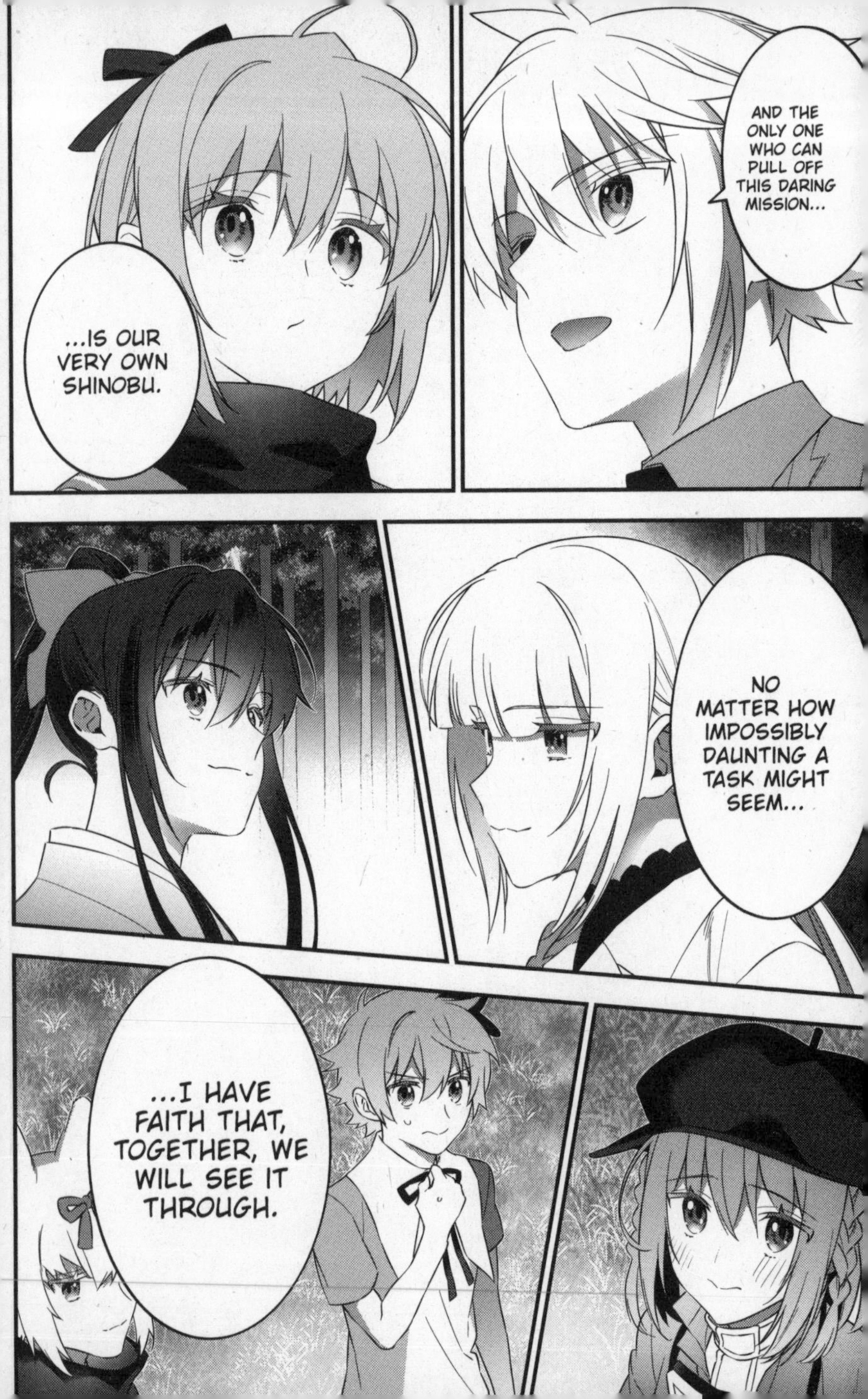
AND THE ONLY ONE WHO CAN PULL OFF THIS DARING MISSION...
...IS OUR VERY OWN SHINOBU.
NO MATTER HOW IMPOSSIBLY DAUNTING A TASK MIGHT SEEM...
...I HAVE FAITH THAT, TOGETHER, WE WILL SEE IT THROUGH.

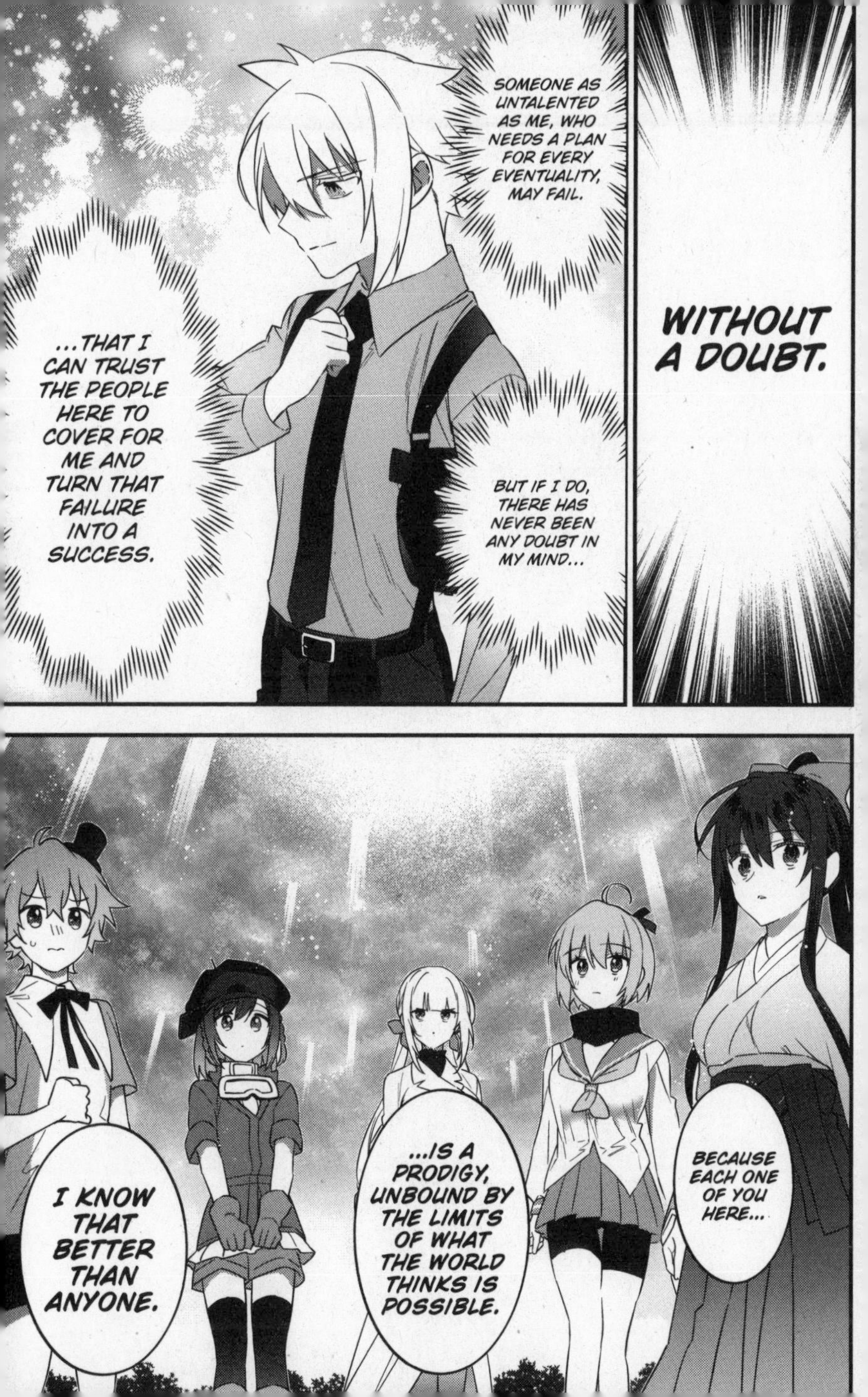
WITHOUT A DOUBT.
SOMEONE AS UNTALENTED AS ME, WHO NEEDS A PLAN FOR EVERY EVENTUALITY, MAY FAIL.
BUT IF I DO, THERE HAS NEVER BEEN ANY DOUBT IN MY MIND...
...THAT I CAN TRUST THE PEOPLE HERE TO COVER FOR ME AND TURN THAT FAILURE INTO A SUCCESS.
BECAUSE EACH ONE OF YOU HERE...
...IS A PRODIGY, UNBOUND BY THE LIMITS OF WHAT THE WORLD THINKS IS POSSIBLE.
I KNOW THAT BETTER THAN ANYONE.

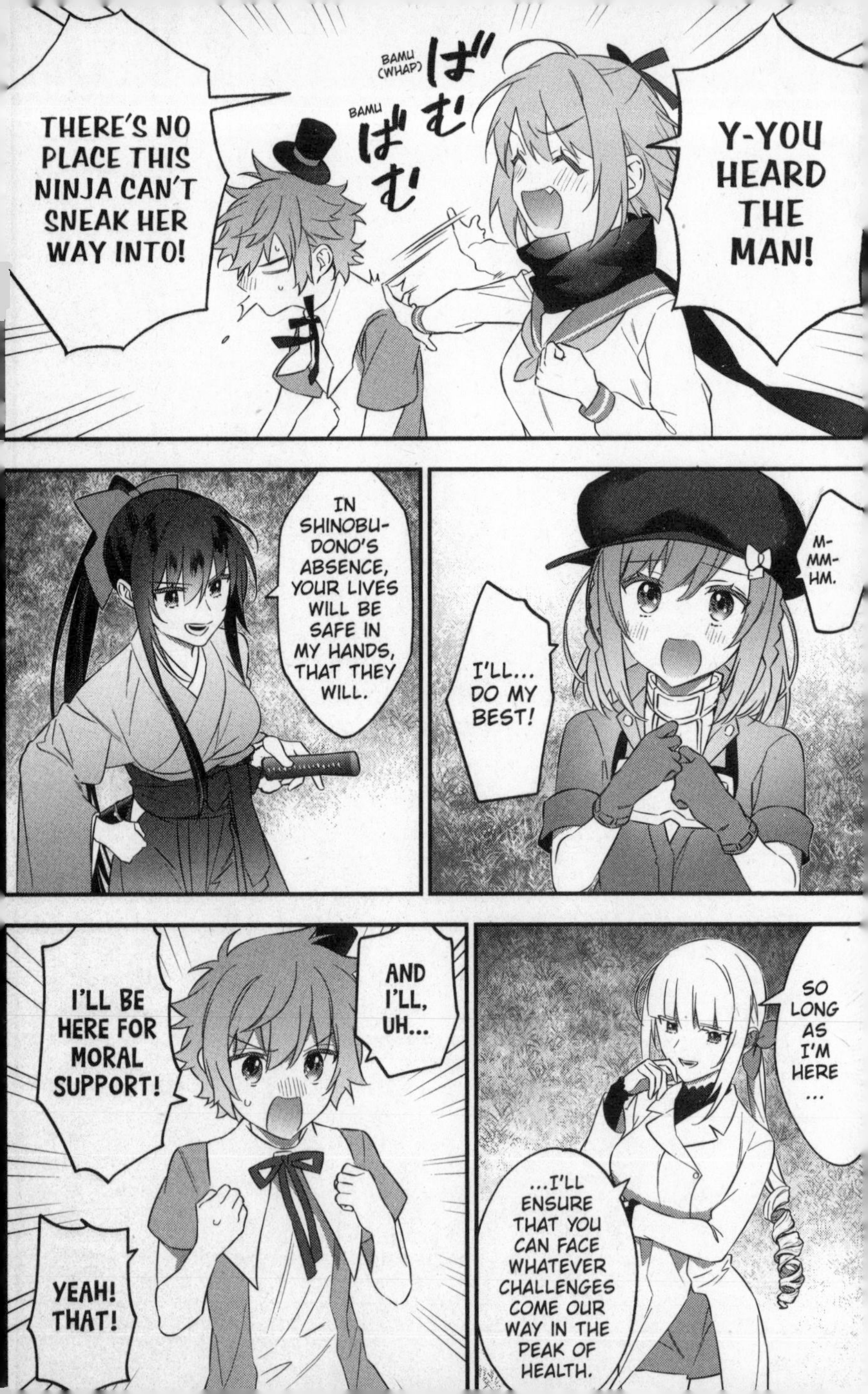
Y-YOU HEARD THE MAN!
BAMU (WHAP) ばむ
BAMU ばむ
THERE'S NO PLACE THIS NINJA CAN'T SNEAK HER WAY INTO!
M-MM-HM.
I'LL... DO MY BEST!
IN SHINOBU-DONO'S ABSENCE, YOUR LIVES WILL BE SAFE IN MY HANDS, THAT THEY WILL.
SO LONG AS I'M HERE...
...I'LL ENSURE THAT YOU CAN FACE WHATEVER CHALLENGES COME OUR WAY IN THE PEAK OF HEALTH.
AND I'LL, UH...
I'LL BE HERE FOR MORAL SUPPORT!
YEAH! THAT!

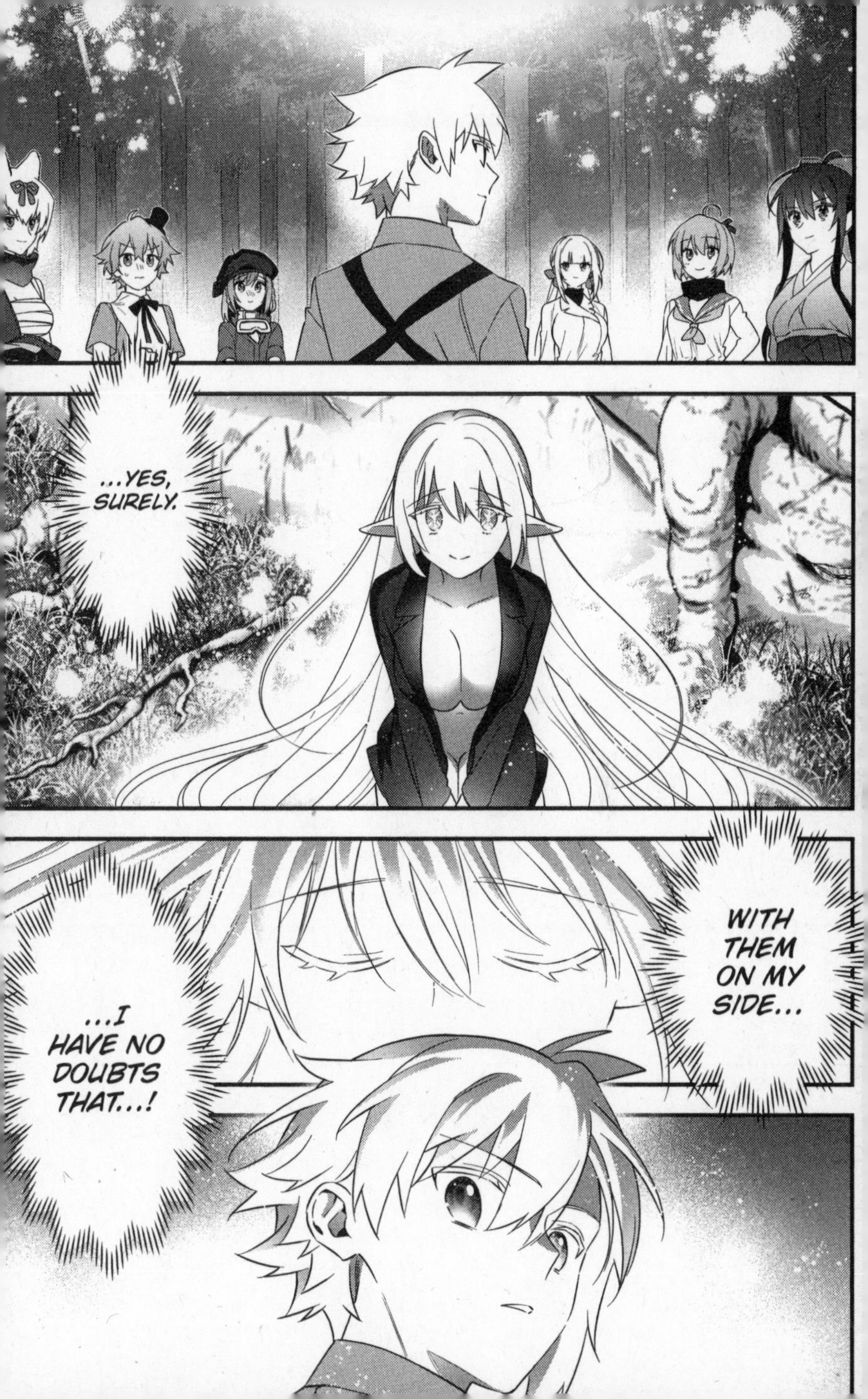
...YES, SURELY.
WITH THEM ON MY SIDE...
...I HAVE NO DOUBTS THAT...!

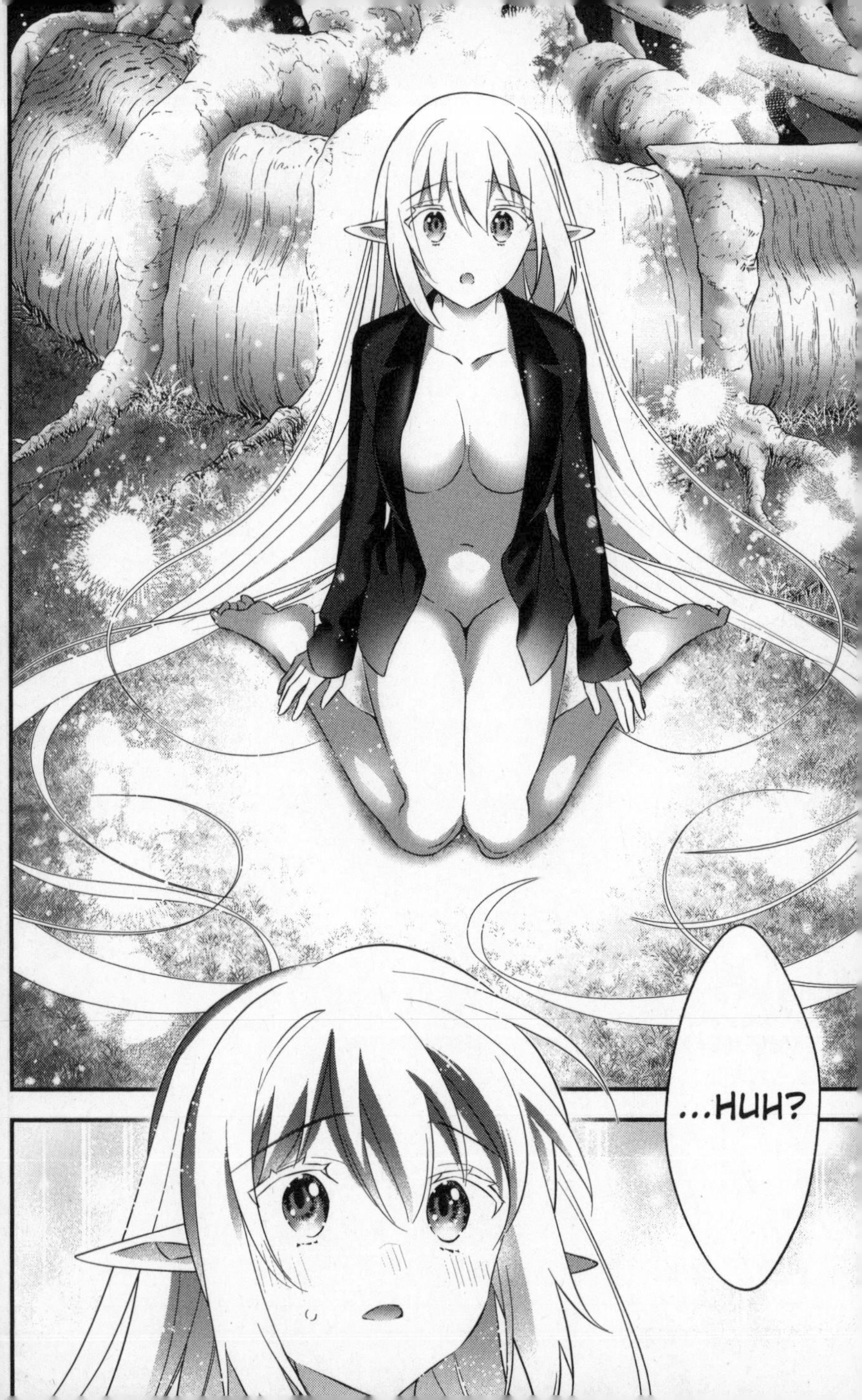
...HUH?

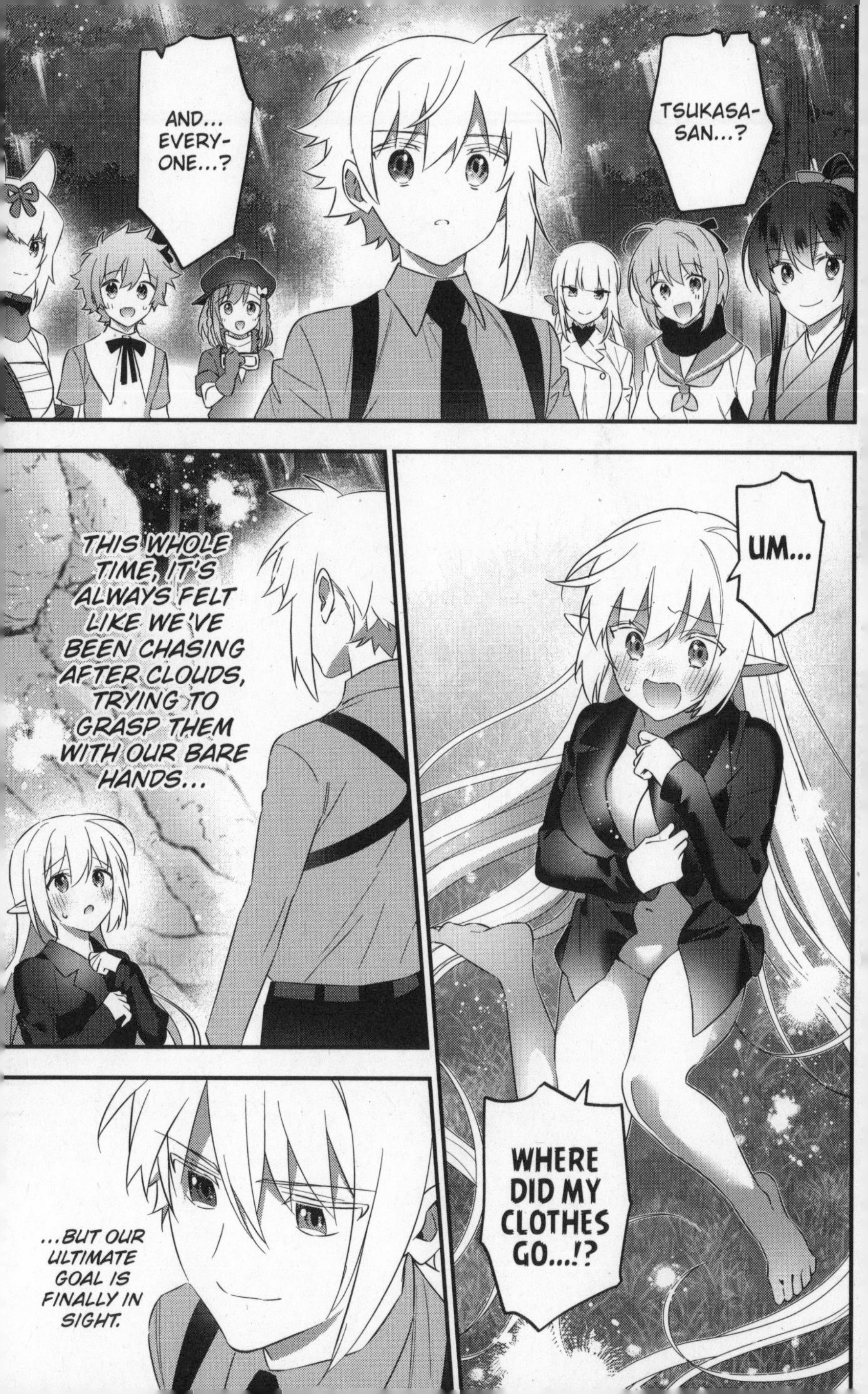
TSUKASA-SAN...?
AND... EVERYONE...?
UM...
WHERE DID MY CLOTHES GO...!?
THIS WHOLE TIME, IT'S ALWAYS FELT LIKE WE'VE BEEN CHASING AFTER CLOUDS, TRYING TO GRASP THEM WITH OUR BARE HANDS...
...BUT OUR ULTIMATE GOAL IS FINALLY IN SIGHT.

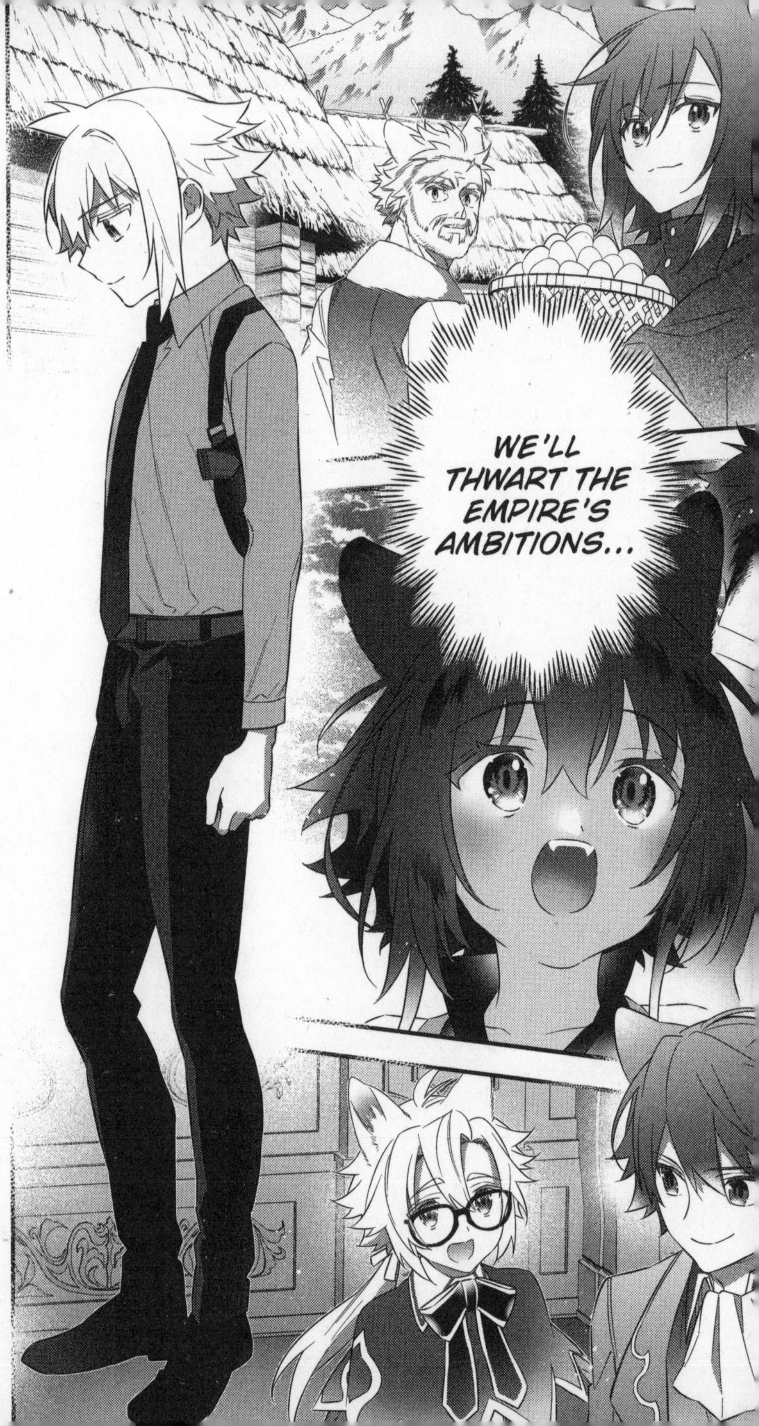
WE'LL THWART THE EMPIRE'S AMBITIONS...

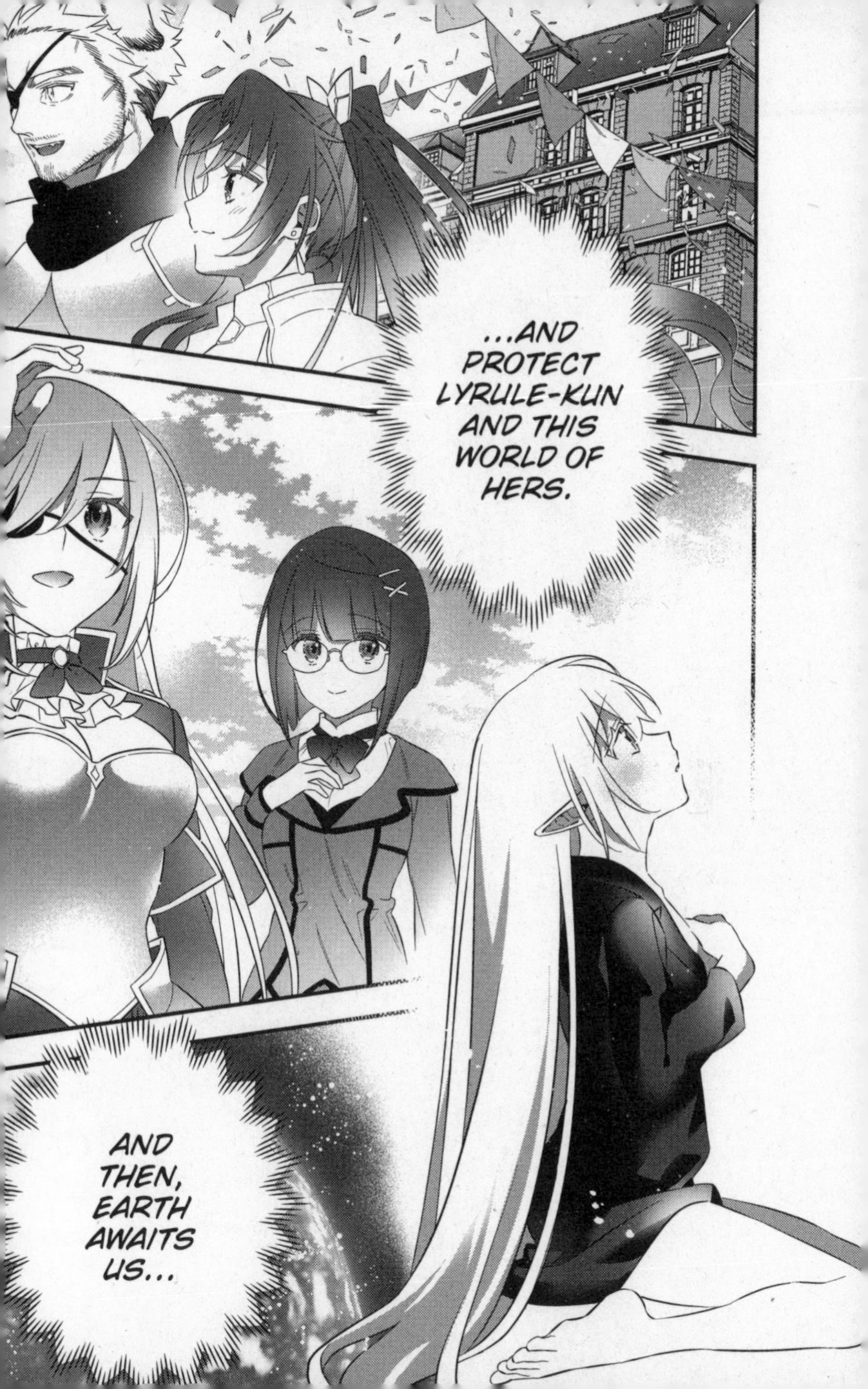
...AND PROTECT LYRULE-KUN AND THIS WORLD OF HERS.
AND THEN, EARTH AWAITS US...

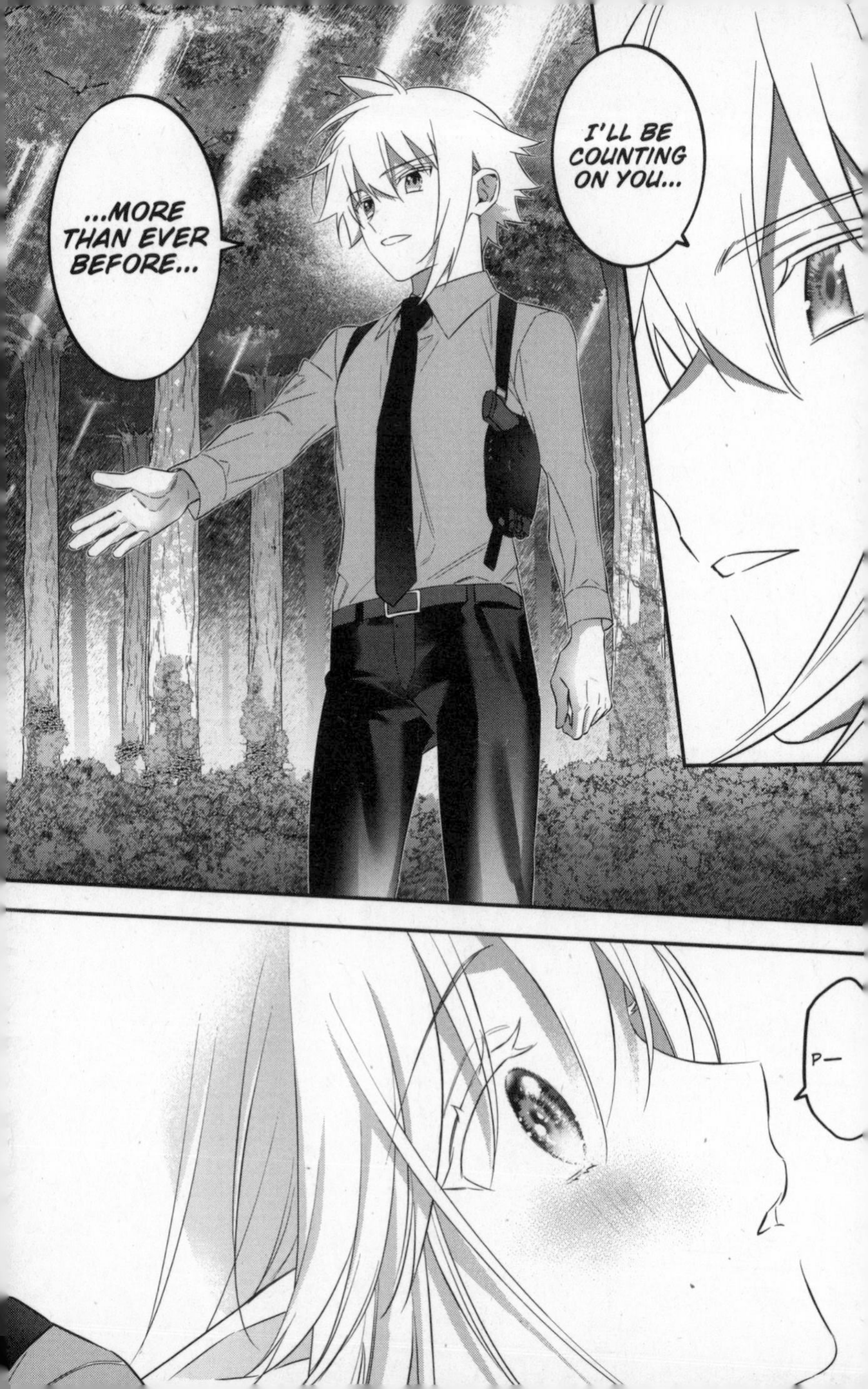
I'LL BE COUNTING ON YOU...
...MORE THAN EVER BEFORE...
P—

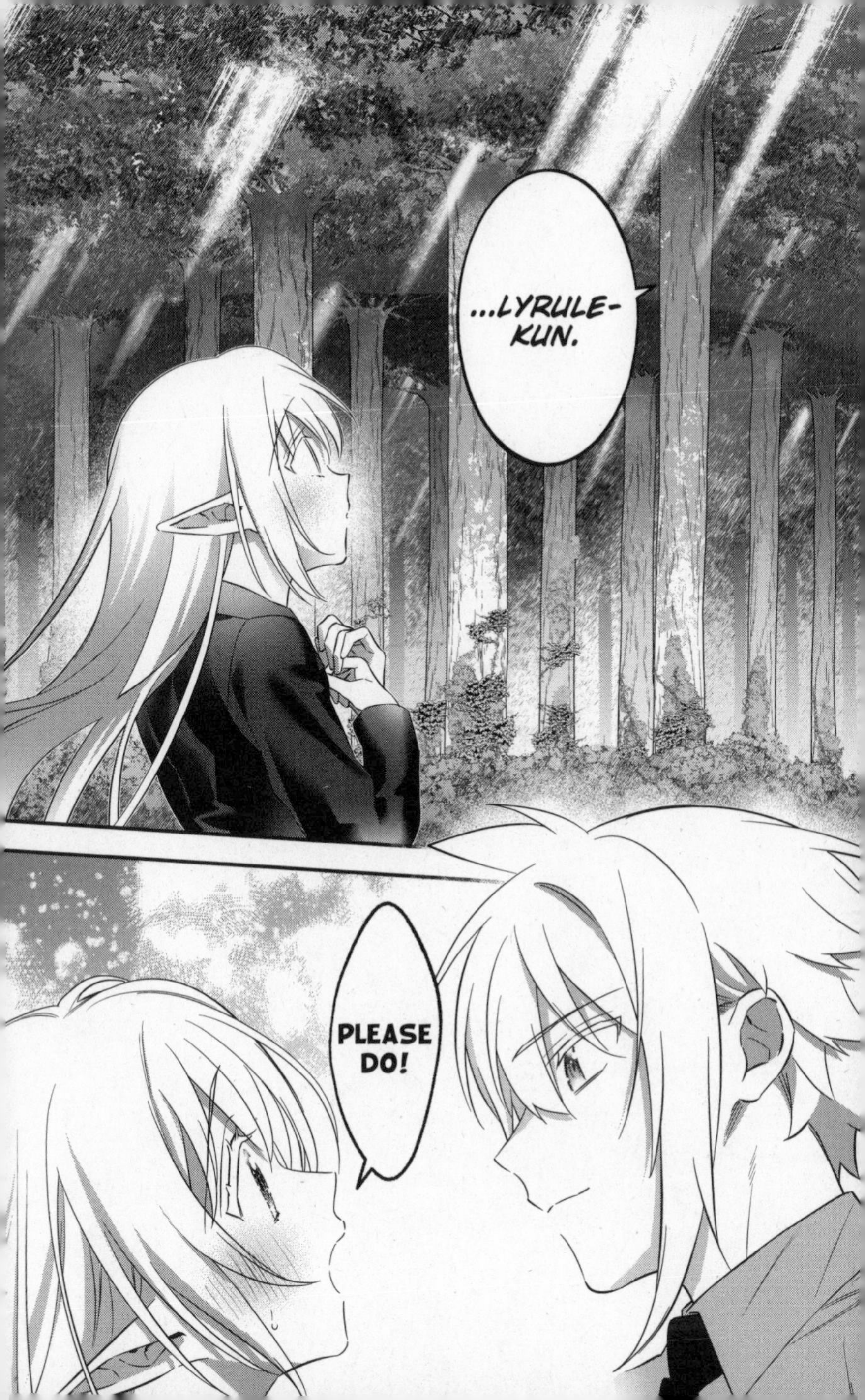
...LYRULE-KUN.
PLEASE DO!

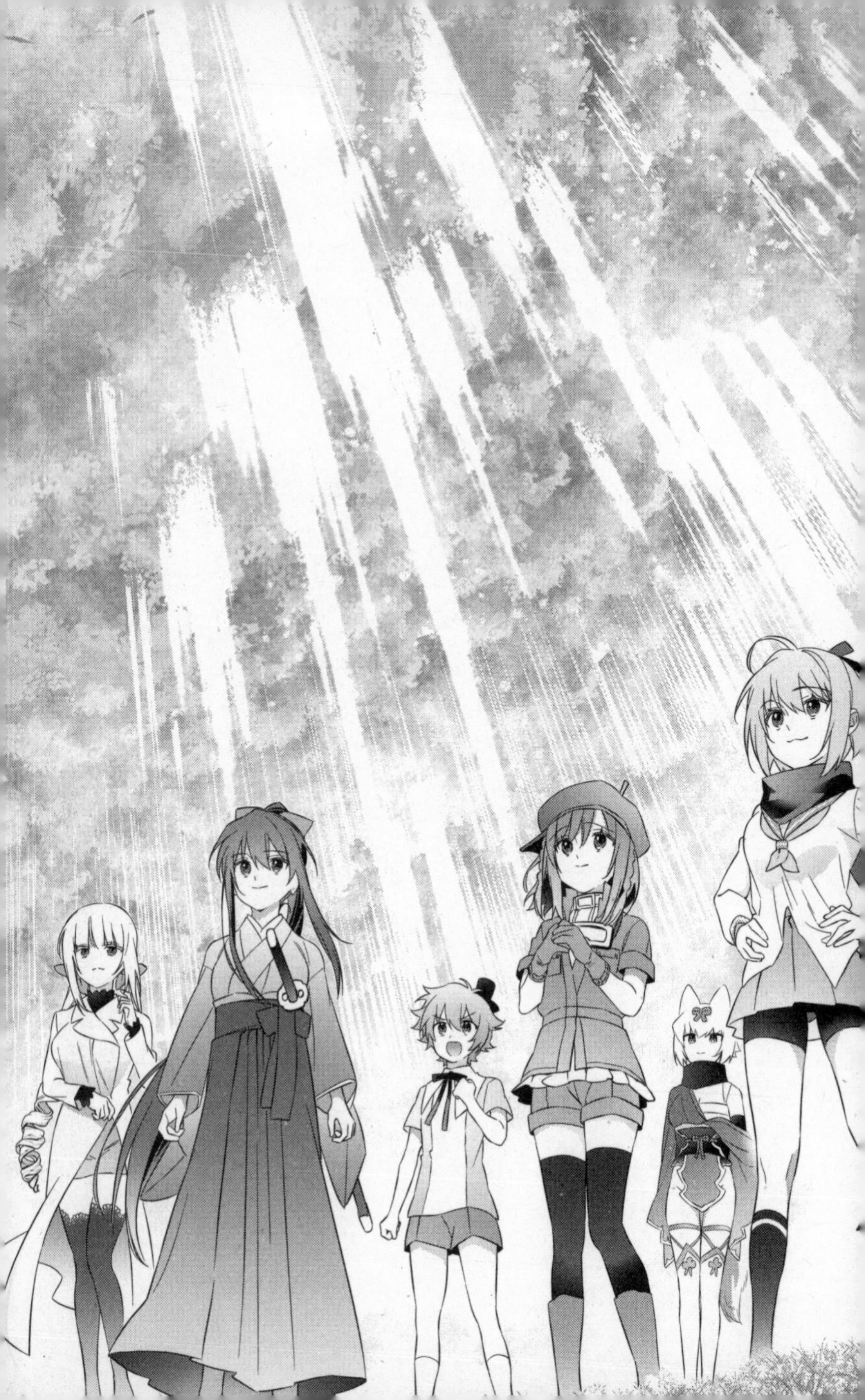

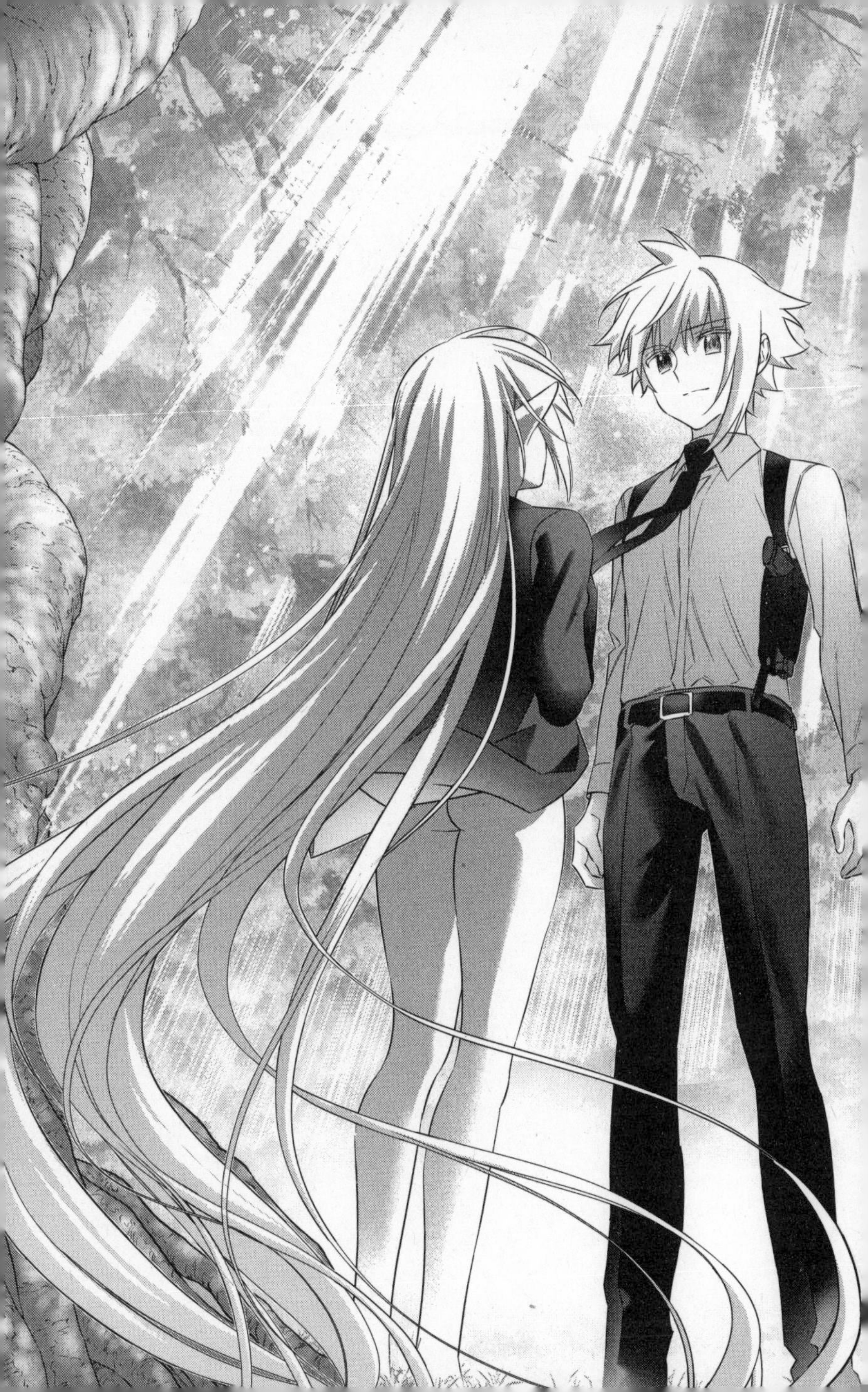

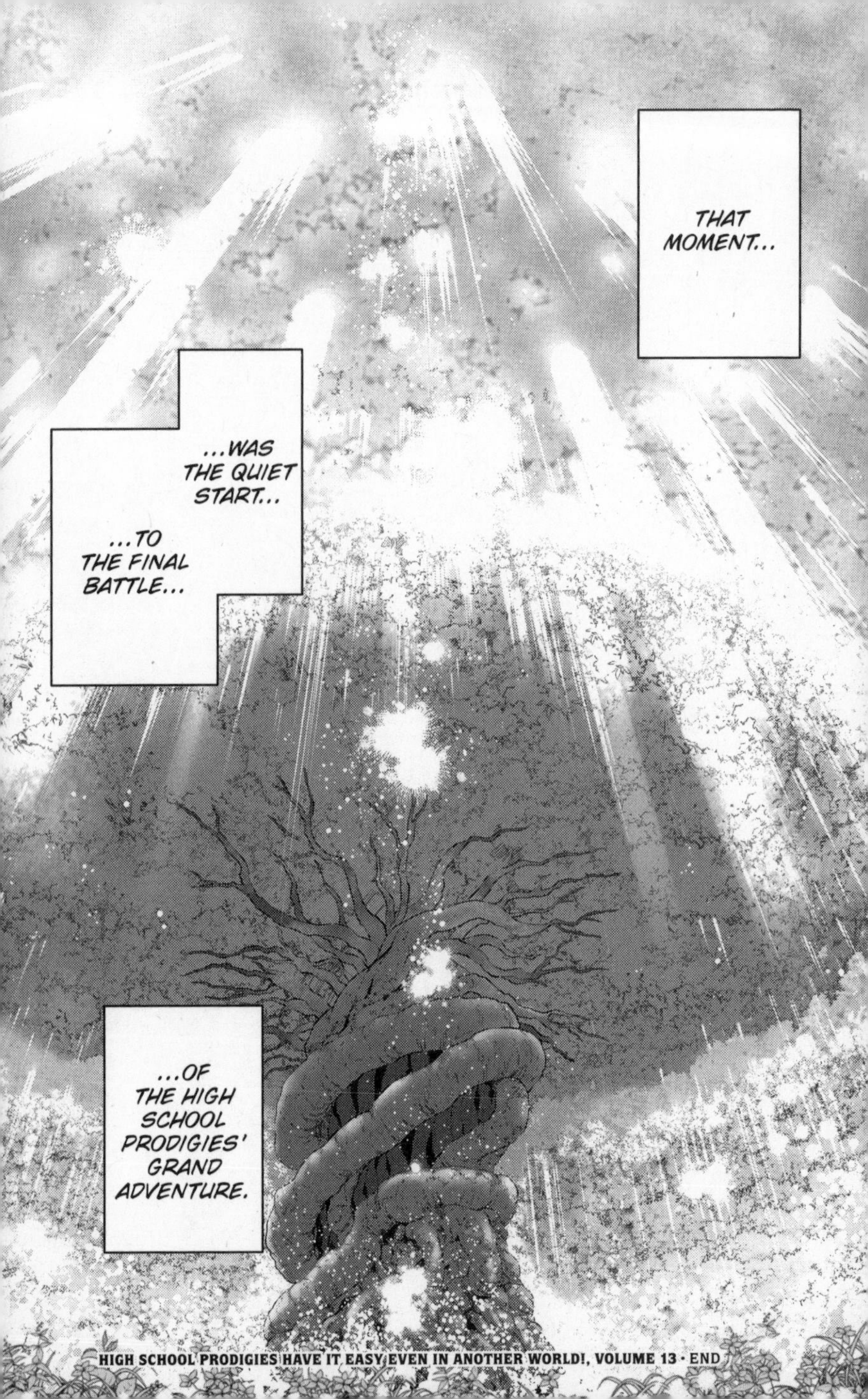
THAT MOMENT...
...WAS THE QUIET START...
...TO THE FINAL BATTLE...
...OF THE HIGH SCHOOL PRODIGIES' GRAND ADVENTURE.

HIGH SCHOOL PRODIGIES HAVE IT EASY EVEN IN ANOTHER WORLD!, VOLUME 13 • END

HIGH SCHOOL
PRODIGIES HAVE
IT EASY EVEN IN
ANOTHER
WORLD!

Illustration Gallery (7)

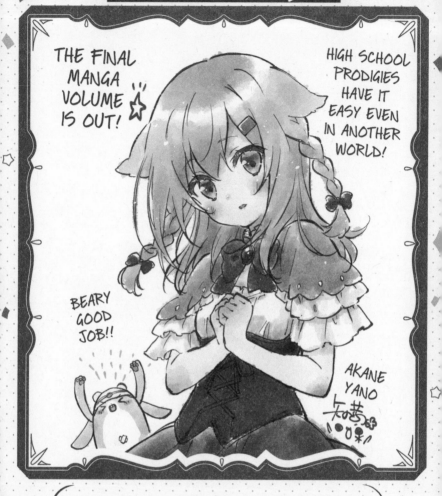

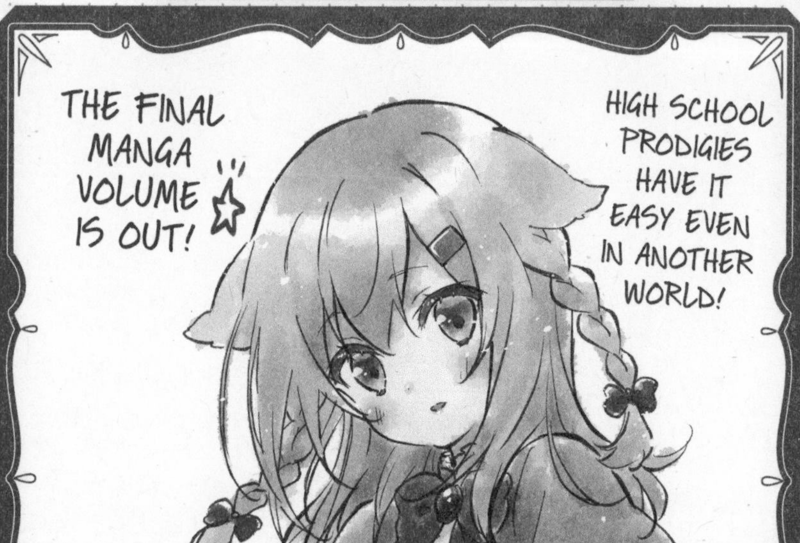
THE FINAL MANGA VOLUME IS OUT!
HIGH SCHOOL PRODIGIES HAVE IT EASY EVEN IN ANOTHER WORLD!
BEARY GOOD JOB!!
AKANE YANO

Akane Yano-sensei

An up-and-coming animator who's worked on a number of series and the Chief Animation Director and Character Designer for the *High School Prodigies* anime.

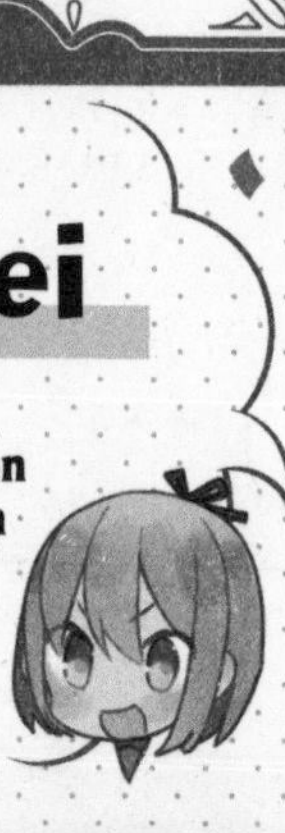

Turn to the back of the book
for an original short story by
Riku Misora, the author of
*High School Prodigies Have It
Easy Even in Another World!*

Illustration Gallery (8)

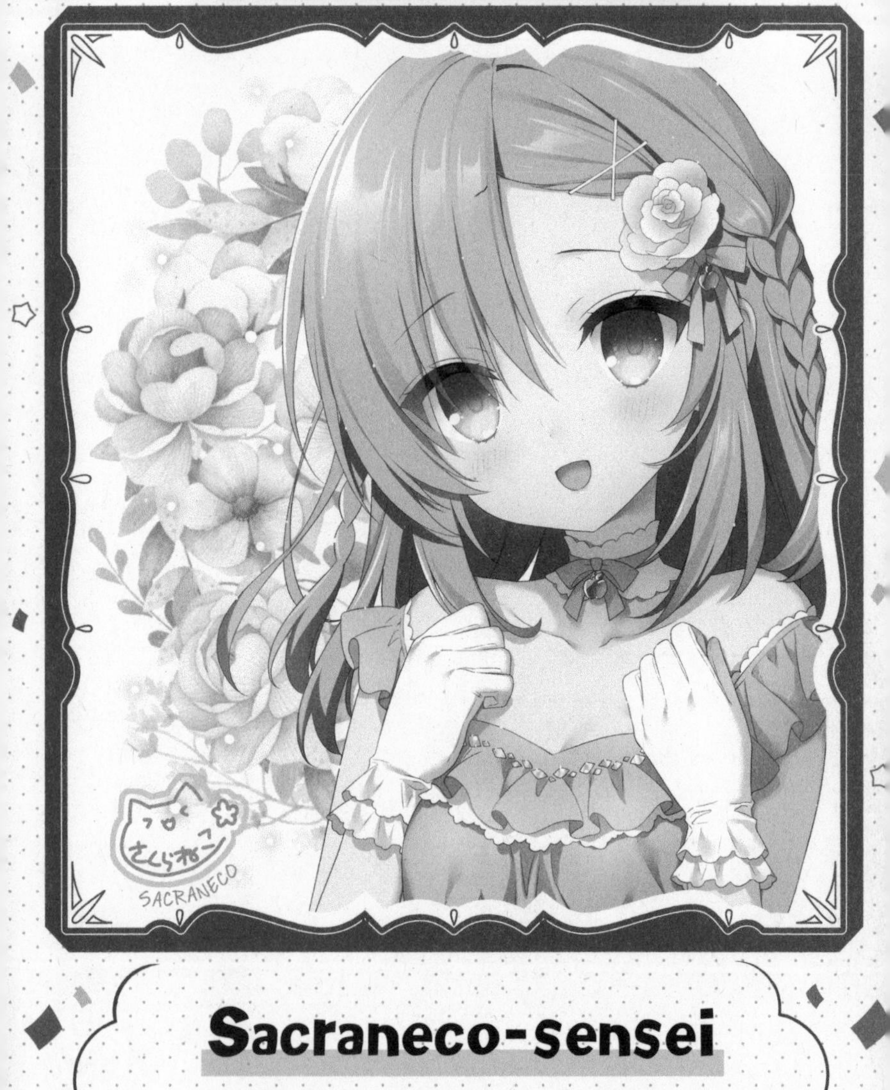
SACRANECO

Sacraneco-sensei

A flourishing illustrator who's done art and character design for a great number of series, including the original light novels of *High School Prodigies Have It Easy Even in Another World!*

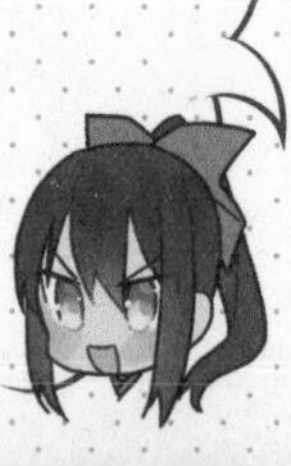

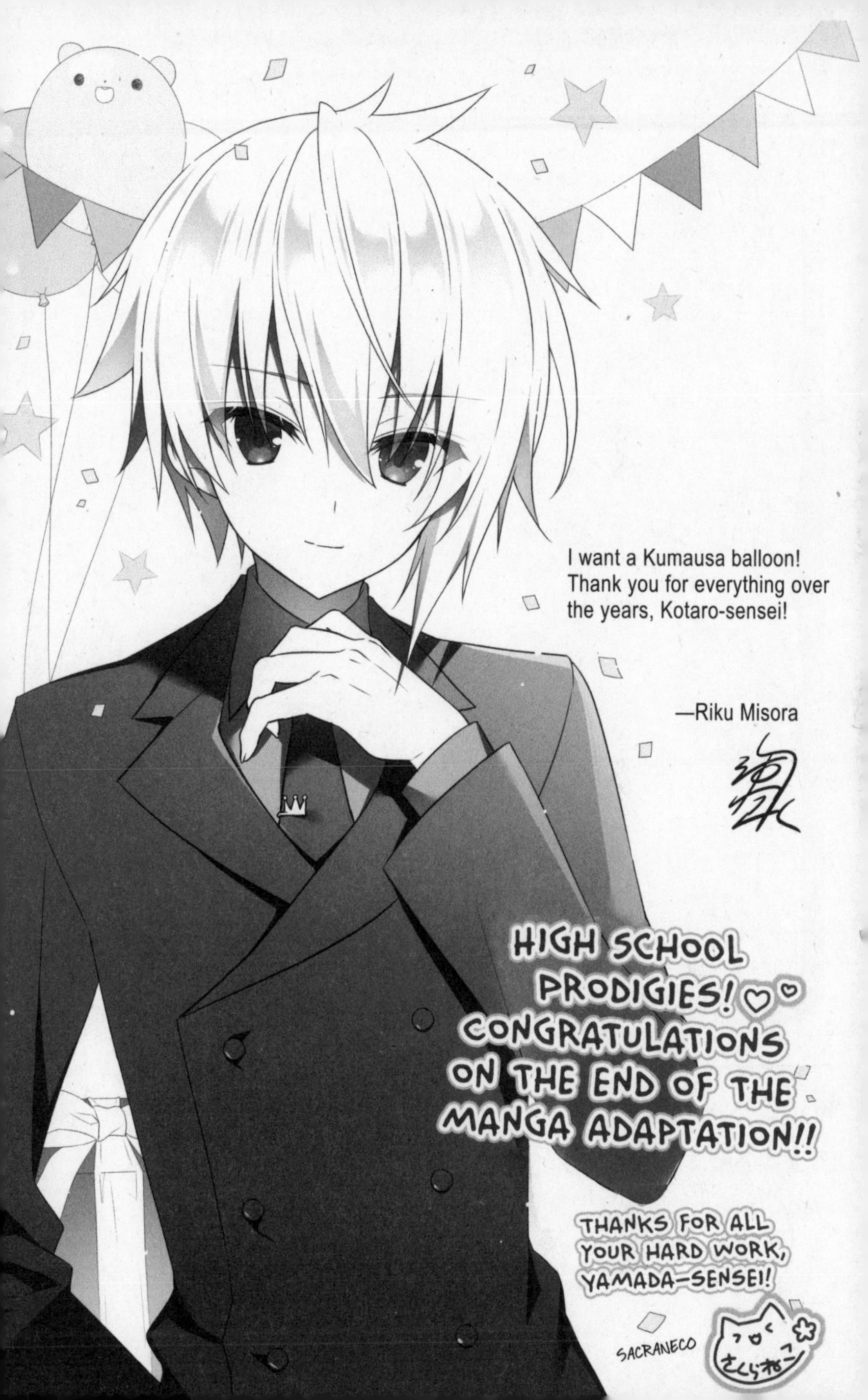
I want a Kumausa balloon!
Thank you for everything over the years, Kotaro-sensei!
—Riku Misora
HIGH SCHOOL PRODIGIES! ♡ CONGRATULATIONS ON THE END OF THE MANGA ADAPTATION!!
THANKS FOR ALL YOUR HARD WORK, YAMADA-SENSEI!
SACRANECO
さくらねこ

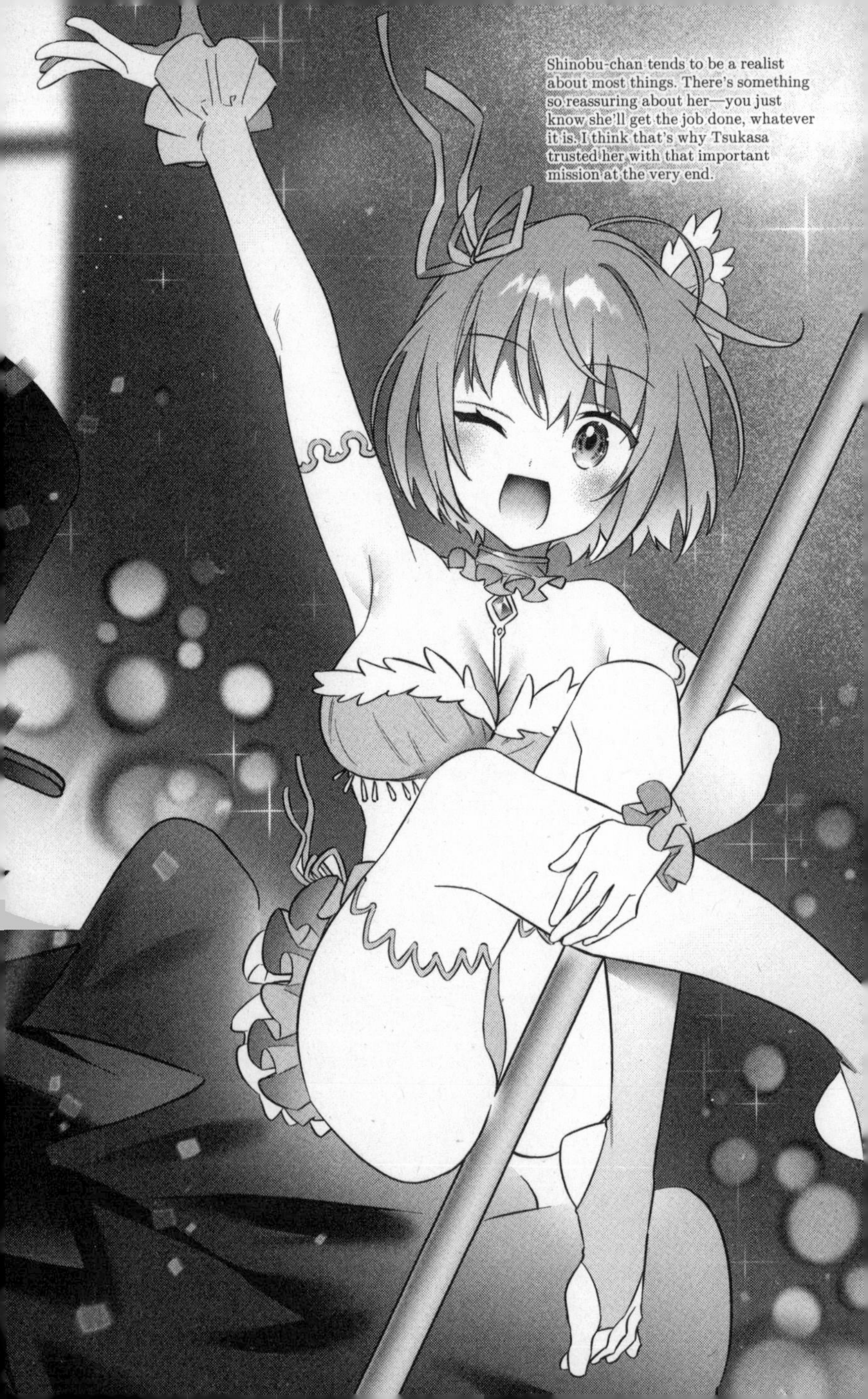
Shinobu-chan tends to be a realist about most things. There's something so reassuring about her—you just know she'll get the job done, whatever it is. I think that's why Tsukasa trusted her with that important mission at the very end.

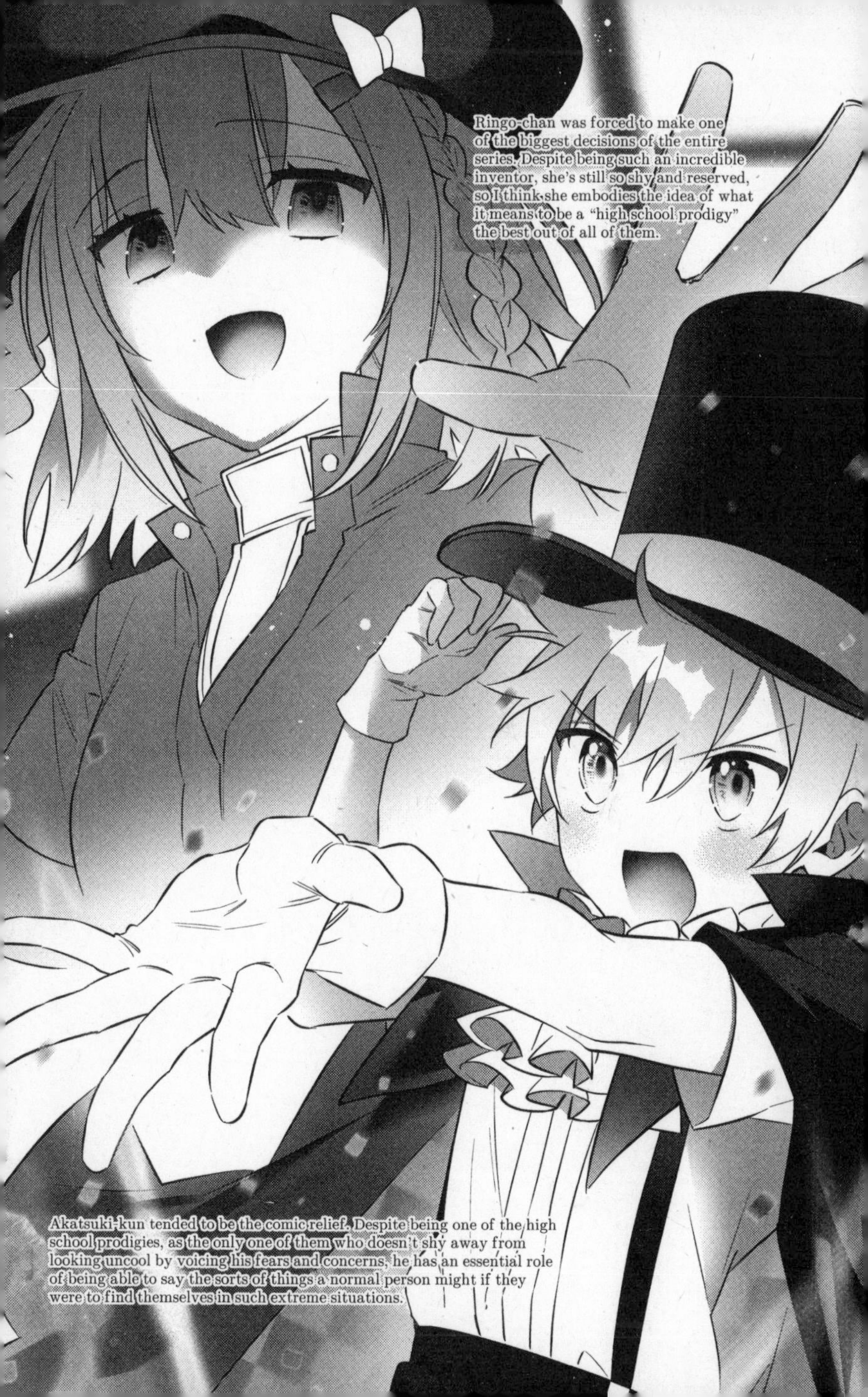
Ringo-chan was forced to make one of the biggest decisions of the entire series. Despite being such an incredible inventor, she's still so shy and reserved, so I think she embodies the idea of what it means to be a "high school prodigy" the best out of all of them.
Akatsuki-kun tended to be the comic relief. Despite being one of the high school prodigies, as the only one of them who doesn't shy away from looking uncool by voicing his fears and concerns, he has an essential role of being able to say the sorts of things a normal person might if they were to find themselves in such extreme situations.

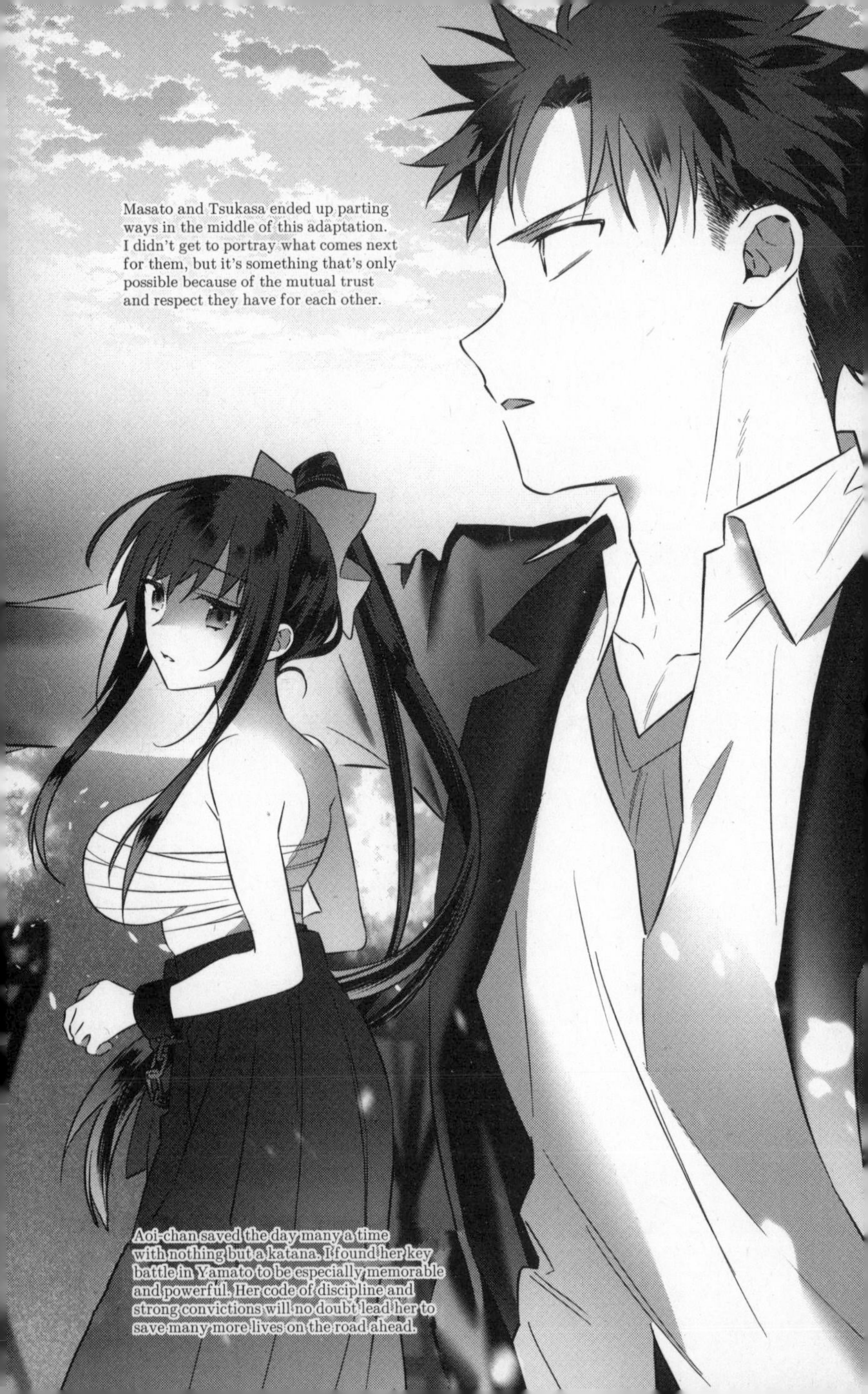
Masato and Tsukasa ended up parting ways in the middle of this adaptation. I didn't get to portray what comes next for them, but it's something that's only possible because of the mutual trust and respect they have for each other.
Aoi-chan saved the day many a time with nothing but a katana. I found her key battle in Yamato to be especially memorable and powerful. Her code of discipline and strong convictions will no doubt lead her to save many more lives on the road ahead.

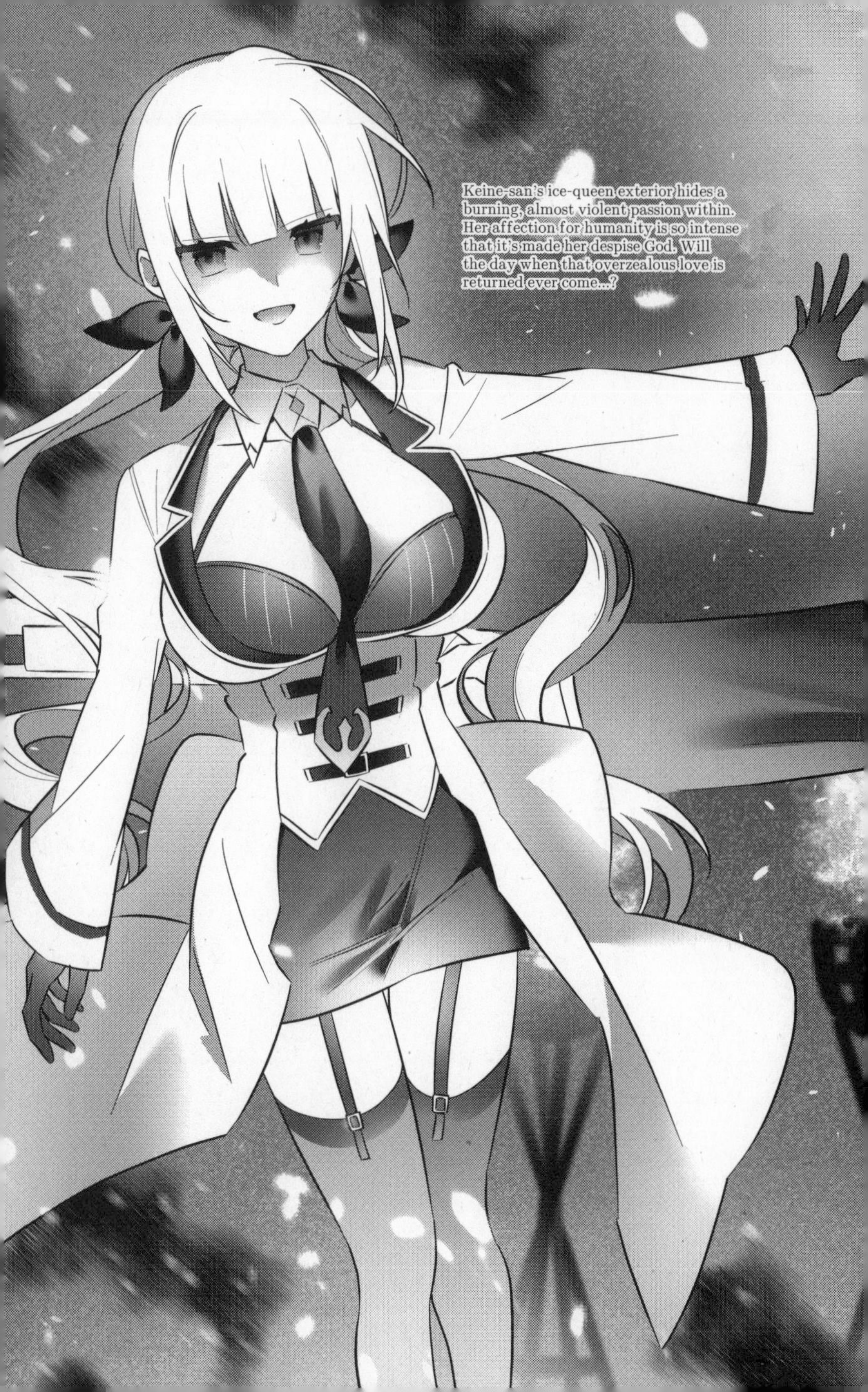
Keine-san's ice-queen exterior hides a burning, almost violent passion within. Her affection for humanity is so intense that it's made her despise God. Will the day when that overzealous love is returned ever come...?

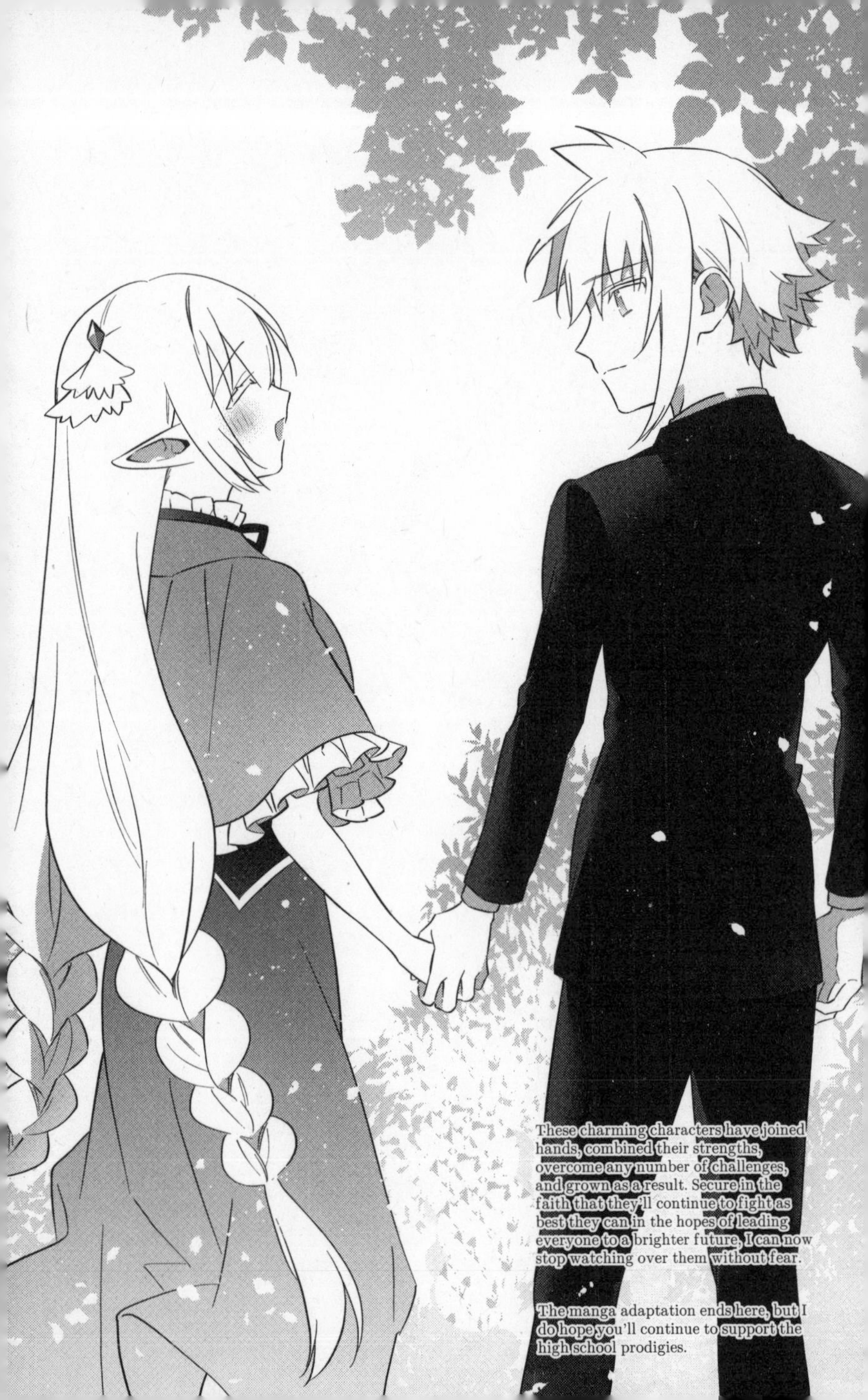
These charming characters have joined hands, combined their strengths, overcome any number of challenges, and grown as a result. Secure in the faith that they'll continue to fight as best they can in the hopes of leading everyone to a brighter future, I can now stop watching over them without fear.
The manga adaptation ends here, but I do hope you'll continue to support the high school prodigies.

HIGH SCHOOL PRODIGIES HAVE IT EASY EVEN IN ANOTHER WORLD!

Special Thanks

Original Story: Riku Misora-sensei
Character Design: Sacraneco-sensei
GA Bunko
YG Editor
My assistants

and everyone who read along all this time

The manga adaptation is over,
but it only made it up to the first half
of the eighth volume of the *High School
Prodigies* light novels, and the story
continues in those.

Thank you so much for accompanying me
on this five-year journey!

December 2021
Kotaro Yamada

Toilet-bound Hanako-Kun

At Kamome Academy, rumors abound about the school's Seven Mysteries, one of which is Hanako-san. Said to occupy the third stall of the third floor girls' bathroom in the old school building, Hanako-san grants any wish when summoned. Nene Yashiro, an occult-loving high school girl who dreams of romance, ventures into this haunted bathroom...but the Hanako-san she meets there is nothing like she imagined! Kamome Academy's Hanako-san...is a boy!

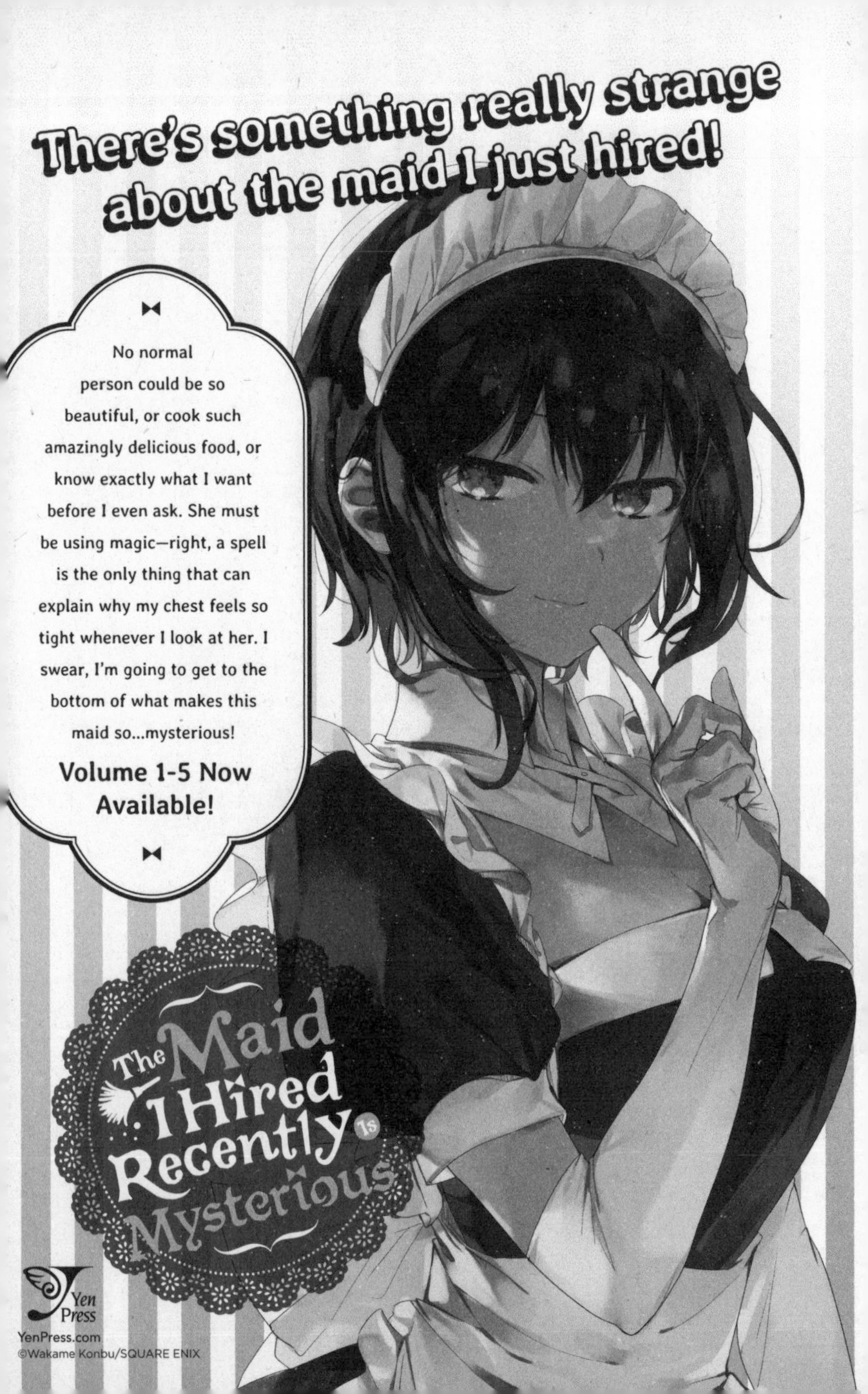
There's something really strange about the maid I just hired!
No normal person could be so beautiful, or cook such amazingly delicious food, or know exactly what I want before I even ask. She must be using magic—right, a spell is the only thing that can explain why my chest feels so tight whenever I look at her. I swear, I'm going to get to the bottom of what makes this maid so...mysterious!
Volume 1-5 Now Available!
The Maid I Hired Recently Is Mysterious
Yen Press
YenPress.com
©Wakame Konbu/SQUARE ENIX

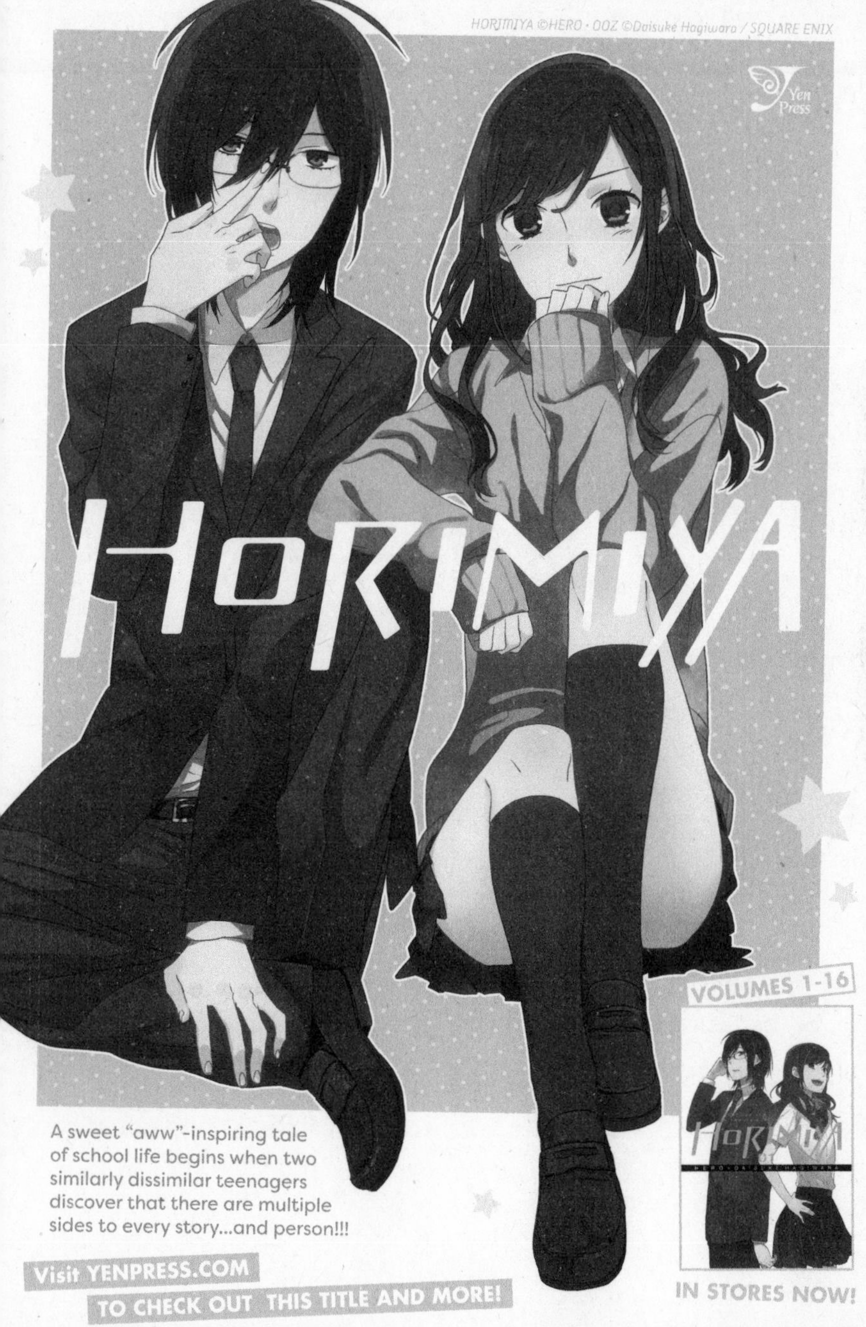

HORIMIYA ©HERO・OOZ ©Daisuke Hagiwara / SQUARE ENIX
Yen Press
HORIMIYA
VOLUMES 1-16
A sweet "aww"-inspiring tale of school life begins when two similarly dissimilar teenagers discover that there are multiple sides to every story...and person!!!
Visit YENPRESS.COM
TO CHECK OUT THIS TITLE AND MORE!
IN STORES NOW!

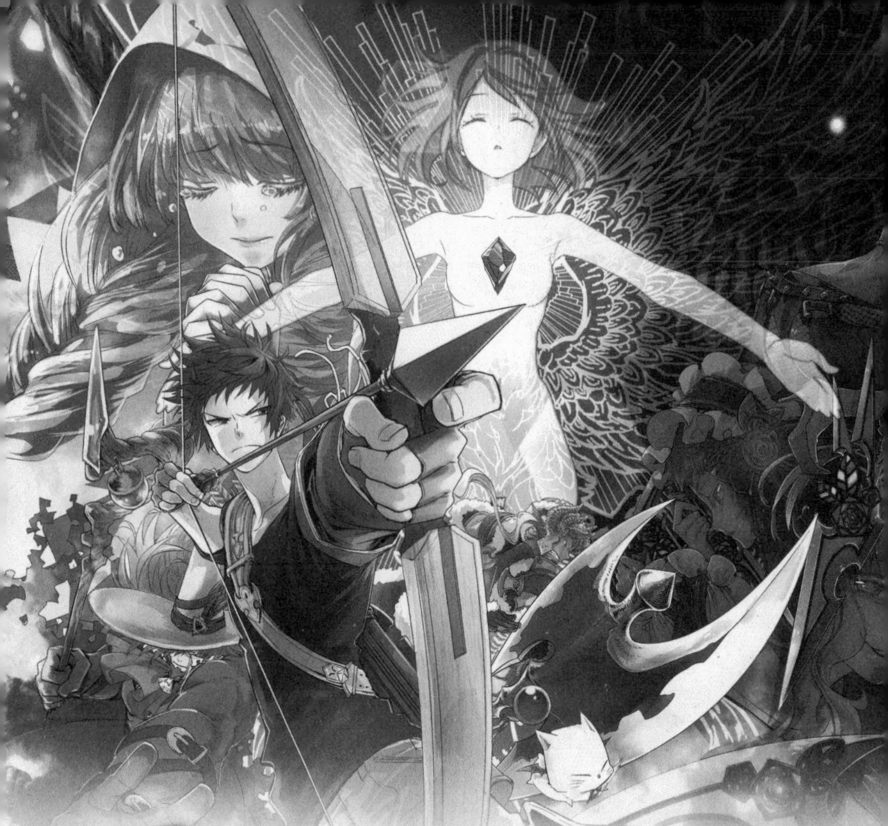

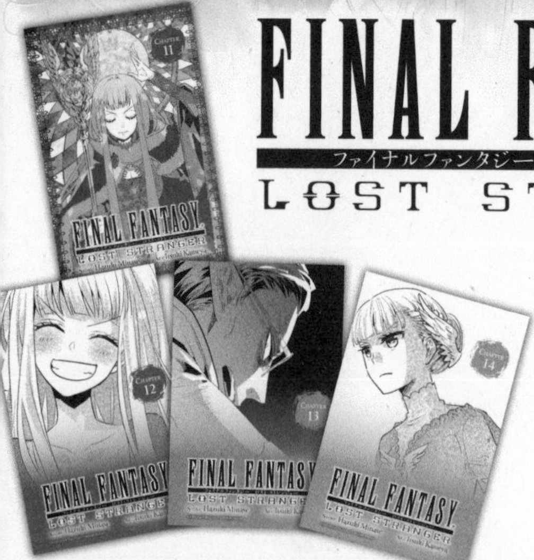
FINAL FANTASY
LOST STRANGER
Chapter 11
Chapter 12
Chapter 13
Chapter 14

HE DOES NOT LET ANYONE ROLL THE DICE.

A young Priestess joins her first adventuring party, but blind to the dangers, they almost immediately find themselves in trouble. It's Goblin Slayer who comes to their rescue—a man who has dedicated his life to the extermination of all goblins by any means necessary. A dangerous, dirty, and thankless job, but he does it better than anyone. And when rumors of his feats begin to circulate, there's no telling who might come calling next...

Light Novel
V. 1-15
Available
Now!

Check out the simul-pub manga chapters every month!

www.yenpress.com

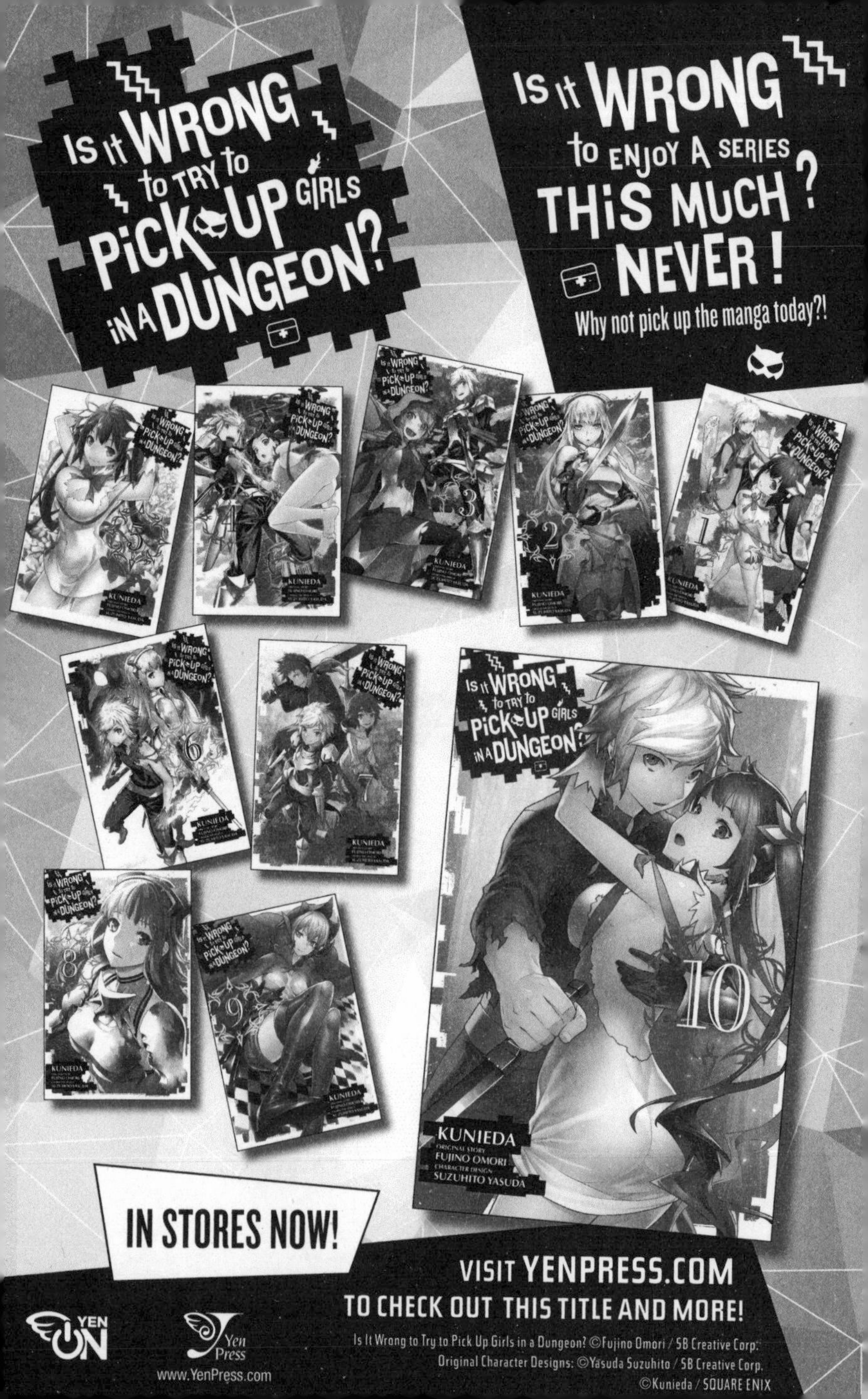
Is it WRONG to try to PICK UP GIRLS IN A DUNGEON?
Is it WRONG to enjoy a series THIS MUCH?
NEVER!
Why not pick up the manga today?!
Is it WRONG to try to PICK UP GIRLS IN A DUNGEON?
10
KUNIEDA
ORIGINAL STORY FUJINO OMORI
CHARACTER DESIGN SUZUHITO YASUDA
IN STORES NOW!
VISIT YENPRESS.COM
TO CHECK OUT THIS TITLE AND MORE!
Is It Wrong to Try to Pick Up Girls in a Dungeon? ©Fujino Omori / SB Creative Corp.
Original Character Designs: ©Yasuda Suzuhito / SB Creative Corp.
©Kunieda / SQUARE ENIX
YEN ON
Yen Press
www.YenPress.com

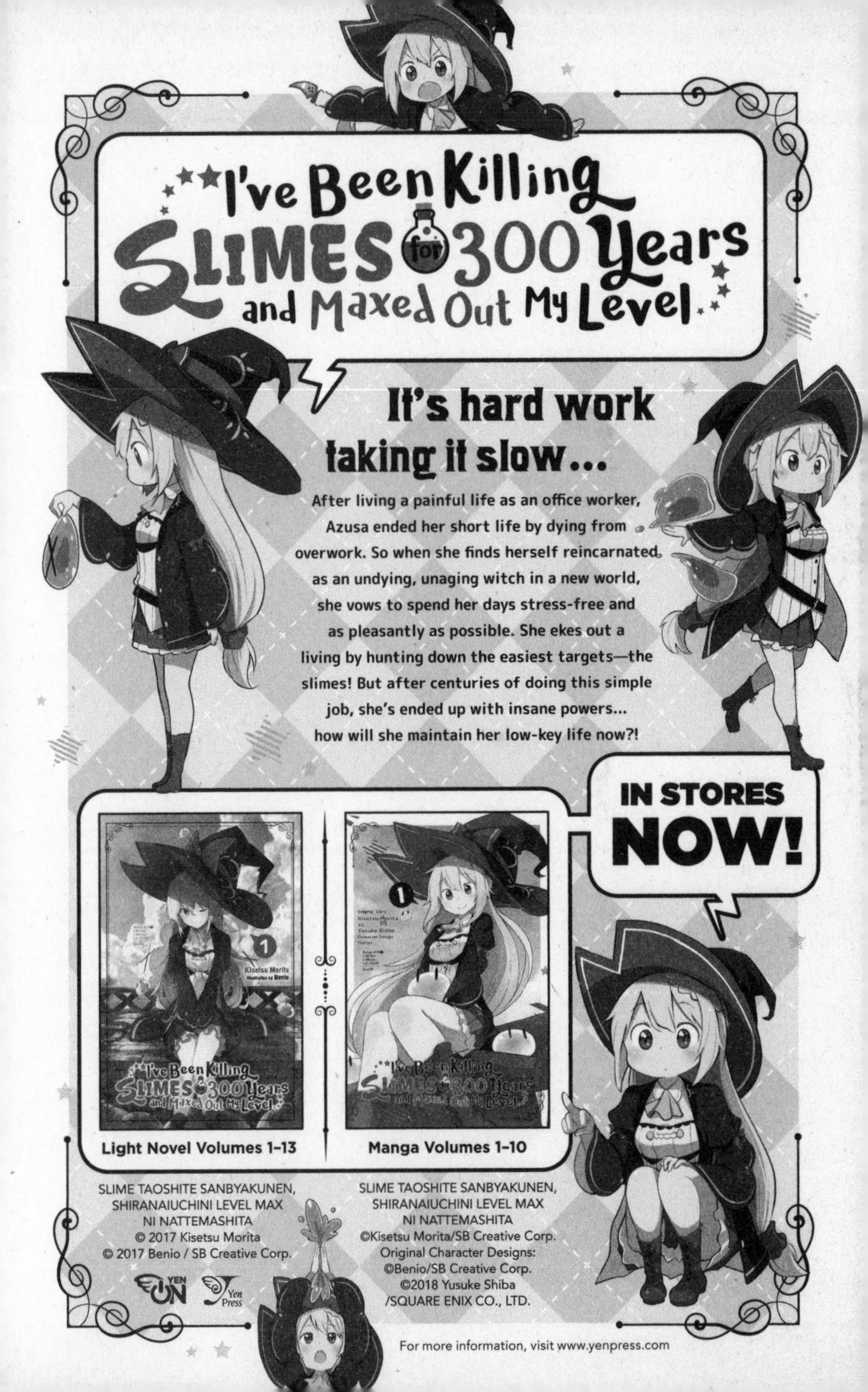
I've Been Killing SLIMES for 300 Years and Maxed Out My Level
It's hard work taking it slow...
After living a painful life as an office worker, Azusa ended her short life by dying from overwork. So when she finds herself reincarnated as an undying, unaging witch in a new world, she vows to spend her days stress-free and as pleasantly as possible. She ekes out a living by hunting down the easiest targets—the slimes! But after centuries of doing this simple job, she's ended up with insane powers... how will she maintain her low-key life now?!
IN STORES NOW!
Light Novel Volumes 1–13
Manga Volumes 1–10
SLIME TAOSHITE SANBYAKUNEN, SHIRANAIUCHINI LEVEL MAX NI NATTEMASHITA
© 2017 Kisetsu Morita
© 2017 Benio / SB Creative Corp.
SLIME TAOSHITE SANBYAKUNEN, SHIRANAIUCHINI LEVEL MAX NI NATTEMASHITA
©Kisetsu Morita/SB Creative Corp.
Original Character Designs: ©Benio/SB Creative Corp.
©2018 Yusuke Shiba /SQUARE ENIX CO., LTD.
For more information, visit www.yenpress.com

"Yes?"

"...Never mind. It's nothing."

Tsukasa swallowed the words that had leaped unbidden to his lips, his stomach constricting with terrible pain as they fell back into it.

I'm such an idiot, he thought.

He'd just gotten so affected by a dream that he nearly gave in to his weakness and said something he could never take back. He had almost tried to take advantage of her kindness, despite knowing full well how she would have responded if he had. Him, a person so devoted to his role as a public official that he'd been willing to consign his own father to death.

He had no right to do that.

So Tsukasa just pursed his lips, lacking the resolve to put something so selfish into words.

That resolve—that determination—wouldn't come to him until a bit farther down the line.

fin.

fixed on Tsukasa, until the moment the guard finished dragging him from the room.

"........."

As Tsukasa looked up and saw the blue glint of moonlight reflecting off the ceiling of the truck driving them back from the elven village, he realized that he'd been dreaming.

Shortly after, he noticed the feeling of a cloth against his cheek.

"Oh, I'm sorry. Did I wake you up?"

"...Lyrule..."

"You were sweating buckets in your sleep... Were you having a nightmare?"

"...Something to that effect, yeah."

After thanking Lyrule for her concern, Tsukasa rolled down the window of the truck heading down the road in the dead of night. Since the road wasn't as well maintained as asphalt would have been, the self-driving Kumausa AI wasn't taking them particularly fast, so the breeze wasn't too strong. In terms of how soothing it felt on his cheek, it was practically ideal.

I probably had that dream because of what Kaguya told me when we left the Yamato capital.

Back then, he hadn't been able to refute his father's words. Just as Mitsuhide said, Tsukasa had been lifted up by the fickle whims of the masses, and Tsukasa lacked the bravado to fully deny that he'd knowingly exploited those whims.

However...was that always going to be the case?

Was nobody ever going to be able to understand him?

Not his parents? His friends? *Her*?

"Lyrule... I..."

outside the realm of possibility."

"........."

"Nobody chose you, Tsukasa. Nobody *understands* you. Those morons *don't pay a second thought* to the things the politicians they elect actually do. You just happened to do a good job looking the part of a young leader, making big speeches about justice. And hey, you're a good-looking kid, too. But that's all you are to them—a piece of entertainment to be *used*, nothing more.

"You're a kid, but you're not an idiot, so you must have already known that. Hell, I bet you even deliberately sold the masses that image of you to get them all fired up. Are you really going to stand there and tell me you didn't make those calculations?! You can't, can you? I'm not the only one who took advantage of their stupidity. You did the same damn thing. The masses aren't the ones who killed me. It was you! You made the call to murder your own father! You're the one who destroyed our family!"

Mitsuhide was pressing his face so hard against the acrylic screen that his skin got caught in the holes, trickling blood down Tsukasa's side of the plastic. Even as the guard rushed over, yanking him away from the screen and pinning his arms behind his back—

"Take a good, hard look at things. They may be thanking you now, but it won't last. You're a child who doesn't know the difference between his ideals and reality, and sooner or later, they'll come to despise you for it. People don't walk the path of justice, not by nature—the straight and narrow is too cramped for anyone to want to follow you down it.

"You've lost me...! You'll lose your mother...! Each and every one of your friends! And when you do, I hope the regret eats you alive!!"

—Mitsuhide continued ranting, the burning hatred of his gaze care of Mom now, so you don't have to worry about her. I came here today and took up your time because that was the one last thing I had to tell you. Now, goodbye."

—he conveyed what his duty as the man's son asked him to, then rose from his seat. He turned his back on his father—on the political criminal he would probably never see again.

"Keh-keh-keh... Ha-ha-ha-ha!"

From behind him came the sound of a mocking cackle.

"You think the masses *chose* you? That they wanted to see justice carried out? Ha-ha-ha!"

Tsukasa turned back to see Mitsuhide pressing his face against the acrylic screen so hard his eyeballs were practically touching it, a more repugnant look than Tsukasa had ever seen on his face.

"Oh, that's priceless. As if those losers had the capacity for that. Just how many years do you think I and all the others like me spent exploiting those idiots? How many decades was I able to continue operating in the world of politics as I bled them dry? I never would have been able to pull it off if they had so much as half a brain between them!

"I twisted the law to tax them twice on the same income, incinerated countless official documents, and jacked the age they could take their pensions all the way up to eighty-five, when they'd already have one foot in the grave!

"The public had any number of chances to realize that I was never acting in their interests, but they chose not to think about it and just kept on putting their unconditional trust in us. Even monkeys are smart enough to remember and recognize the faces of people who've punched them, but the masses can't so much as manage that—that's just how incompetent they are. You seriously believe that those imbeciles are going to learn how to think all of a sudden and pick up on their past mistakes? That's fundamentally brought this on themselves! *Caveat emptor*! So why?! Why, why, why am I the only one who has to pay for it like this? Damn it, damn it all...! I was so close...so close to getting my hands on real, actual power, and to being able to move past being a politician in this dead-end nation..."

On the other side of the screen, Mitsuhide slumped onto the table and broke down in tears. He somehow seemed terribly far away to Tsukasa. Only now did he finally understand just how fundamentally unbridgeable the gap between his beliefs and his father's were.

"The people certainly have their share of blame for handing their sovereignty over to a man who thought it perfectly reasonable to use the authority of his office for personal gain. And that's precisely why they supported me when I ran on the promise of ousting you—as a way of owning up to their mistakes and putting the wrongs both they and you committed to rights. You accused me of betraying you, but you're not here because I exposed you. You're here because your own actions got you removed from office."

"........."

"You were an excellent father, and as a politician, you did a great job of gaining the people's trust... I only wish that you had valued your responsibilities as a public official above any of that."

Tsukasa had hoped that here, at the very end, his father would at least regret what he'd done—that he would behave like the man who had taught him that it was a politician's duty to do all that they could for the sake of their nation and its people. Seeing the way his father was acting, though, Tsukasa recognized that hope was in vain.

And so—

"Thank you for all you've done to raise me. I'll step up and take keep his mouth shut! I had no idea who you might end up spilling your guts to! But I guess the joke's on me—raising you like that somehow made it so that you never grew out of being a snot-nosed little blabbermouth!"

A spray of spittle accompanied this torrent of abuse, splattering against the acrylic screen.

"How could you sell me out to that bitch? Your own father! All you had to do, the one damn thing you had to do, was shut up, and I could've swept it all under the rug! What, did you resent me or something?! I fed you the finest food, got you a fantastic education, and put top-of-the line clothes on your back! Was I not a good father to you?! So why? Whyyy?! What more could you have possibly wanted from me, Tsukasa?!"

In his rage, Mitsuhide slammed his fist against the spit-flecked screen like he wanted to punch right through it to his son's face. The guard rushed over in a panic to try to drag him away, but Tsukasa gestured for him to stop.

This might well be the last chance he ever got to talk to his father.

"...It's true that as a father, you were a great man. But you committed unforgivable sins as a politician. You lied to the people, abused your position as a public official to line your own pockets...and worst of all, you broke the law."

"So what?! If you hadn't stabbed me in the back, nobody would have ever found out! Besides, what's so wrong about using your power to help yourself out? That's the only reason anyone becomes a damn politician in the first place! It's the way of the world for successful people to take from the weak, the incompetent, and the inferior! Especially when they were the ones who chose me! They gave me their votes! They gave me dominion over them, and that means I can do whatever I damn well please with them! They

He Who Walks the Straight and Narrow

Does hate truly fester *like that?*

When Tsukasa Mikogami saw his father enter the detention center's visitation room, he couldn't help but gulp.

"Even now, I still can't hide my shock."

His father, Mitsuhide, was the first to speak through the small holes of the acrylic screen that separated them.

"Betrayed like that by my own flesh and blood. No, even worse...by the very son I raised."

His eyes, which had dark bags under them, were glaring straight at Tsukasa, who couldn't even imagine the strict-yet-loving father in his memories ever wearing such a look on his face. Tsukasa's chest suddenly started aching, as if dealt a physical blow by the sheer magnitude of what he had lost.

Even so, he didn't avert his gaze. Looking his father straight in the eye, he said, "I didn't betray you, Dad. All I did was act like any good politician should. Ever since I was a kid, you taught me to—"

"You think I meant a word of those bullshit platitudes?!!" his father roared, practically bursting Tsukasa's eardrums. "Like hell I was going to tell the truth to a child who couldn't be trusted to

He Who Walks the Straight and Narrow

Riku Misora

High School Prodigies Have It Easy Even in Another World! 13

STORY BY **Riku Misora**   ART BY **Kotaro Yamada**

CHARACTER DESIGN BY **Sacraneco**

Translation: Caleb D. Cook, Nathaniel Thrasher
Lettering: Brandon Bovia

CHOUJIN KOUKOUSEI TACHI WA ISEKAI DEMO YOYU DE IKINUKU YOUDESU! vol. 13
©Riku Misora/SB Creative Corp.
Original Character Designs:©Sacraneco/SB Creative Corp.
©2021 Kotaro Yamada/SQUARE ENIX CO., LTD.
First published in Japan in 2021 by SQUARE ENIX CO., LTD.
English translation rights arranged with SQUARE ENIX CO., LTD.
and Yen Press, LLC through Tuttle Mori Agency, Inc.

English translation © 2023 by SQUARE ENIX CO., LTD.

Yen Press
150 West 30th Street, 19th Floor
New York, NY 10001

Visit us at yenpress.com

facebook.com/yenpress
twitter.com/yenpress

yenpress.tumblr.com
instagram.com/yenpress

First Yen Press Edition: July 2023
Edited by Yen Press Editorial: Riley Pearsall
Designed by Yen Press Design: Liz Parlett

Yen Press is an imprint of Yen Press, LLC.
The Yen Press name and logo are trademarks of Yen Press, LLC.

The publisher is not responsible for websites (or their content) that are not owned by the publisher.

Library of Congress Control Number: 2018948324

ISBNs: 978-1-9753-4810-6 (paperback)
978-1-9753-4811-3 (ebook)

10 9 8 7 6 5 4 3 2 1

LSC-C

Printed in the United States of America